Reforming Pensions

Reforming Pensions

Principles and Policy Choices

NICHOLAS BARR AND PETER DIAMOND

OXFORD
UNIVERSITY PRESS
2008

OXFORD
UNIVERSITY PRESS

Oxford University Press, Inc., publishes works that further
Oxford University's objective of excellence
in research, scholarship, and education.

Oxford   New York
Auckland   Bangkok   Bogotá   Buenos Aires   Cape Town   Chennai
Dar es Salaam   Delhi   Hong Kong   Istanbul   Karachi   Kolkata
Kuala Lumpur   Madrid   Melbourne   Mexico City   Mumbai   Nairobi
São Paulo   Shanghai   Singapore   Taipei   Tokyo   Toronto

Published by Oxford University Press, Inc.
198 Madison Avenue, New York, New York, 10016
www.oup.com

Oxford is a registered trademark of Oxford University Press

Library of Congress Cataloging-in-Publication Data
Barr, N. A.
Reforming pensions : principles and principles and policy choices / Nicholas Barr and
Peter Diamond.
p. cm.
Includes bibliographical references and index.
ISBN 978-0-19-531130-3
1. Pensions. 2. Pension trusts. 3. Pensions—Chile. 4. Pensions—China. I. Diamond, Peter A. II. Title.
HD7091.B253 2009
331.25′220951—dc22   2008015253

9 8 7 6 5 4 3 2 1

Printed in the United States of America
on acid-free paper

For Gill and Kate

Foreword

A key test of a decent society is the living standards of its older people, particularly the poorer among them. This includes their ability to participate in their community and thus their relative income and access to health care and other services. The financing of their consumption in old age depends on the accumulation of past resources, by themselves and by the state, and its reflection in overall current income flows. Any sensible set of policies must take into account both the effects on such accumulation and the uncertainties surrounding life expectations, abilities, and disabilities. Thus policy analysis must examine issues of efficiency, distribution within and across generations and over individual lifetimes, as well as substantial uncertainties in individual circumstances.

Any approach to the formulation of policies toward pensions that tries to oversimplify by focusing on just one element, such as efficiency, risks grave policy errors, which can have a profound effect on the welfare of many individuals. It is a special strength of this book that it refuses to oversimplify in this way, while at the same time offering clear and analytically sound principles for the formulation of policy. It shows not only where these principles lead but also the mistakes that can be made when simplistic or formulaic policies are followed.

Policy toward pensions, and particularly policy reform, must depend on the broad economic, social, and demographic situation in a country, on the starting point for pension and related policies, and on where the economy and society are likely to go. Although many of the examples in the book draw on experience in the United Kingdom and the United States, reflecting the experience of the authors, there is considerable discussion of other developed and developing countries, notably Chile and China, and the analytical principles they set out so clearly and rigorously can and should guide the formation of pension policy across a very broad range of country circumstances, tailoring, of course, to those circumstances.

It is not possible to summarize the richness of Barr and Diamond's analysis in a few sentences or paragraphs, but one or two examples may be helpful. First, the authors stress that it is not correct to design pension policy as if the sole purpose were consumption smoothing. That would involve only an efficiency perspective on market failure. Even if efficiency were to be in some sense achieved, the potential would remain for substantial (first-order) distributional gains from introducing an element of transfers into the policy, with only a small (second-order) loss in efficiency.

A second, and related, example is that a system that attempts to focus only on efficiency issues in relation to intertemporal allocation will lose an opportunity to provide insurance against adverse outcomes during working life and in old age. This insurance element is a key and worthy purpose of most pension schemes and cannot straightforwardly be allocated to another arm of policy in a world where markets for risk operate, for theoretical and practical reasons, in a very imperfect way.

Barr and Diamond go beyond these basic conceptual starting points and analytical perspectives and show explicitly how policy choices should be analyzed. For example, in the context of changing demography and increased life expectancy, they examine the choice among higher contribution rates, lower monthly benefits, later retirement, and policies, such as increased saving, designed to increase output. Further, they consider carefully the problems of administration, which loom large in schemes covering very large numbers of people over a long period. They not only show how analysis should be done, but also identify very instructive examples of serious mistakes that can arise and have arisen in practice by failure to apply a clear and comprehensive framework. This includes a number of important cases from the World Bank (see, for example, Box 10.1).

This is a most important book, which should be compulsory reading for all those involved in making, discussing, and studying policies on pensions. The subject matter is of great significance in a world whose demography and economic and social structures are changing so rapidly. We are extremely fortunate to have before us such a clear comprehensive and thoughtful analysis of the issues. Barr and Diamond, as outstanding theorists, have thought these issues through very carefully; they have also been very closely involved with the practicalities of administration and reform. Theirs is a splendid piece of work.

Nicholas Stern

Preface

This book is the result of two pieces of luck. The first came about when we were asked to participate in a group invited to advise the government of China on pension reform; the group presented its core recommendations, discussed in Chapter 15, to Premier Wen Jiabao in November 2004. The second was the opportunity that one of us had to participate in reforms of the pension system in Chile, including discussions with the Presidential Advisory Council in May 2006.

Although those experiences are reflected throughout, the book is also an attempt to step back from those activities and from the continuing and at times heated debate about pension reform. It sets out the relevant economic theory and international experience, its central aim being to arm readers with the analytics to enable them to form their own views about pensions policy. Thus the book's intent is educational; it is neither a polemic nor a training manual. In some ways the book should be set alongside Diamond (2003), which places the analysis of pensions in an optimal taxation context, and Barr (2004a), which sets pensions within the broader context of the welfare state.

The chapters in Part I set out the analytics that should shape discussion of pension reform. There is minimal use of algebra and diagrams, and the results are always explained verbally, so that any technical material can be skipped by readers prepared to take the conclusions on trust; the glossary and Box 1.1 explain some technical terms and disentangle a few differences of usage across countries. At the price of some repetition, the book is written so that the policy chapters in Part II can be read on their own; we have also provided frequent cross-references to relevant discussion in earlier chapters. The core of the book is summarized in Chapters 1, 10, 11, and 16.

In the academic world, the book will be of interest to economists because of its roots in economic theory, and to colleagues in departments of social policy because of its subject matter. The book should also be of interest in such related areas as political economy and public policy, and to colleagues studying the postcommunist transition and economic development. The book is written to be relevant to readers in a wide range of countries, developed, former communist, and developing; to officials in ministries of finance and of social security; and to readers in international organizations such as the International Monetary Fund, the World Bank, and the International Labour Organisation.

Our first—and considerable—debt is to the other members of the group that advised the government of China: Mukul Asher, Edwin Lim, and James Mirrlees. We are also grateful to colleagues who advised us during that process—Axel Börsch-Supan, Stanley Fischer, Nicholas Stern, and Salvador Valdés-Prieto—and to colleagues in China who provided us with background papers and other assistance, including Yonghong Cheng, Bihong Huang, Shi Ming Jiang, Shaoguang Li, Wei Zhang, and Bingwen Zheng.

The chapters on Chile owe a great debt to Ana Wheelock, who provided tireless advice on factual matters and contributed ideas. We are also grateful for helpful comments from Mario Marcel, Andrea Repetto, and Salvador Valdés-Prieto.

András Simonovits and two anonymous referees read the entire book in draft and provided cogent and helpful comments. A special issue of the *Oxford Review of Economic Policy* in the spring of 2006 (volume 22, number 1) gave us the opportunity to refine some of the analytical arguments: we are grateful to colleagues at an editorial seminar in Oxford in November 2005 for comments and guidance, including Christopher Allsopp, Christopher Bliss, Andrew Glyn, Dieter Helm, David Hendry, Stephen Nickell, and Margaret Stevens.

Many other people helped, by commenting on draft chapters, by providing information, and by asking pertinent questions. They included Mukul Asher, Martin Neil Baily, Fabio Bertranou, Lans Bovenberg, Axel Börsch-Supan, Agnieszka Chlon-Dominczak, Elaine Fultz, Gunnvald Grønvik, Robert Hancké, Bill Hsaio, Maureen Lewis, Frances Lund, Truman Packard, Debora Price, Susan St John, Annika Sundén, Lawrence H. Thompson, Peter Whiteford, and Adrian Wood. Aaron Grech and Johannes Spinnewijn read the entire text for coherence and readability and gave very helpful comments. Catarina Reis, Johannes Spinnewijn, and especially Maisy Wong provided valuable research assistance, supported by the National Science Foundation under grants SES-0239380 and SES-0648741.

We owe a particular debt to Michael Treadway for his customary skill, care, efficiency, and enthusiasm in editing the book, greatly improving its readability.

None of those mentioned should be implicated in the result, which is very much our joint responsibility: through discussions and primarily e-mail, exploiting our different time zones and complementary experiences and perspectives, the text has gone through repeated revisions to the point where virtually every sentence bears the marks of both of our pens.

Finally, and most important, our thanks to our wives, Gill and Kate, for their unfailing support and for their continuing forbearance over our forays to various countries and over truncated weekends.

Nicholas Barr
London, England
Peter Diamond
Cambridge, Massachusetts

Contents

Reforming Pensions

1

▷

The Backdrop

1.1 THE CONTEXT

The "aging crisis"—an amalgam of "pensions crisis" and "health care crisis"—is not a sudden surprise, nor wholly bad news, nor insoluble. The problem, projected large increases in spending on pensions and medical care, is largely the result of long-term trends that are good news: longer lives, lower birth rates, earlier retirement, and more and better medical care. Why does ongoing good news amount to a crisis? The answer lies less in the underlying economic and demographic realities than in the political difficulty of adapting pension and health care systems to those realities.

This book brings together the analytics of pensions with discussion of some country experiences, to explain how to design pensions so as to limit the negative side effects of what in reality is a valuable opportunity: comfortable retirements for millions more people. Our goal is to equip readers to understand and evaluate the debates about pension reform now taking place in many countries. We do not discuss the organization or finance of health care.

The starting point is a series of long-run and well-known trends.

Declining mortality. People are living longer in most countries, often considerably longer, and are expected to live even longer in the future. Figure 1.1 shows a very long run trend improvement in mortality—a trend that, as Figure 1.2 shows, is projected to continue. But to call this an "aging problem" is a grotesque misnomer—it is neither a "problem" nor entirely a phenomenon of the elderly. Much of the improved life expectancy at birth has come through large declines in child mortality. Although wonderful, this decline has little direct connection with pensions, which focus on people's earning and retirement years. Remaining life expectancy at the ages when most people start work, such as 16, 18, or 21, has also grown steadily; the fraction of those starting work who survive to an age where they can collect a pension has increased considerably; and, among those reaching pensionable age, life expectancy in retirement has also grown

3

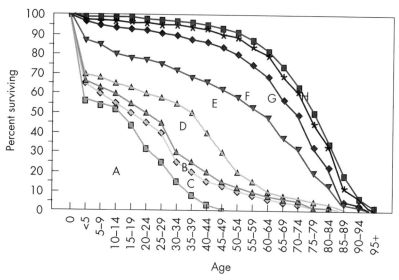

FIGURE 1.1.

Survival curves from the Stone Age to the present. A, Stone Age; B and C, Greece and Rome; D, England, 1800; E, United States, 1900; F, United States, 1941; G, United States, 1961; H, United States, 1998. *Source:* Foundation for Infinite Survival, Inc., Berkeley, California, historical slide no. 6, www.fis.org/public/slide06.html, based on Dublin, Lotka, and Spiegelman (1949, p. 42).

considerably, as Figure 1.3 illustrates. (Sadly, these improvements have been reversed in the countries worst ravaged by HIV/AIDS.) Among men currently retiring in the United Kingdom, for example, many more have lived to retirement age than their grandfathers did, their average age of retirement is 64 rather than 67, and they can expect to live on average for twenty years in retirement rather than eleven. These trends are not a catastrophe, but great good news. Longer healthy lives are in many ways the great triumph of the nineteenth and twentieth centuries, and looking ahead, there is every expectation of continuing improvements in mortality and morbidity.

Declining fertility. Alongside declining mortality, a second long-term trend, illustrated in Figure 1.4, is a decline in the number of children that the average woman has during her lifetime. On the whole, declining fertility is also arguably good news to the extent that, as infant mortality declines, people are choosing to have smaller families. It means that people are implicitly concentrating on the quality of life rather than the quantity. There are also potential advantages through reduced environmental pressures from slower-growing populations. The transition to smaller families is most marked in the developed world but is occurring in many developing countries as well.

These trends toward longer life and lower fertility together result in a steady change in the population age pyramid, illustrated by Figure 1.5 for China, India, and the United States for the 100 years after 1950. The result has been trend growth in most countries in the old-age dependency ratio—the number of older people relative to the number of people of working age—illustrated in Figure 1.6 for China, India, and the

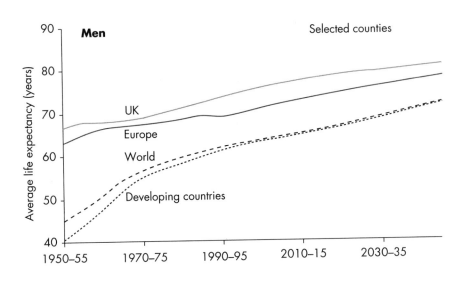

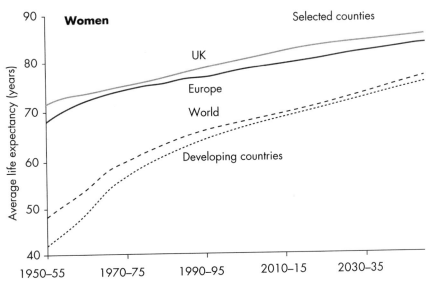

FIGURE 1.2.
Life expectancy at birth for men and women, various countries, 1950–55 to 2030–55.
Source: United Nations Population Division.

United States. With many pension systems relying on payroll tax revenue to finance current benefits, this trend is part of the reason many countries have faced and continue to face rising pension spending relative to GDP.

Declining labor force participation of older men. Figures 1.1 through 1.6 show how the number of older people has increased, in both absolute and relative terms. A separate question is how the number of pensioners has increased. Here another long-term trend is relevant, namely, a decline in the labor force participation of older

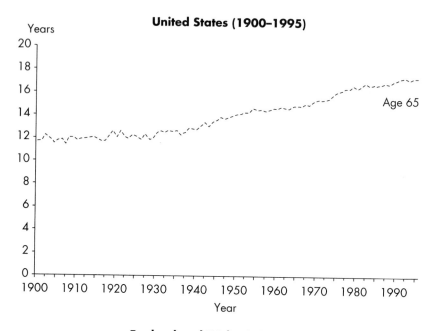

United States (1900–1995)

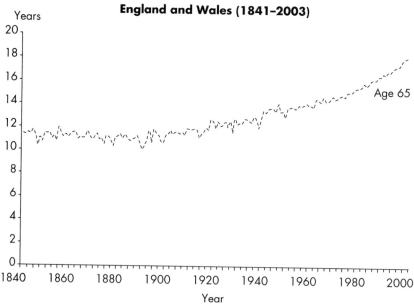

England and Wales (1841–2003)

FIGURE 1.3.
Life expectancy at age 65, United States, England and Wales, and Sweden. Period life expectancies using age-specific mortality rates for a given period, with no allowance for any later actual or projected changes in mortality. Life expectancies are calculated using the total (not just the civilian) population and thus include mortality due to war. *Sources:* Berkeley Mortality Database, demog.berkeley.edu/~bmd, and Human Mortality Database, www.mortality.org/. *(cont'd.)*

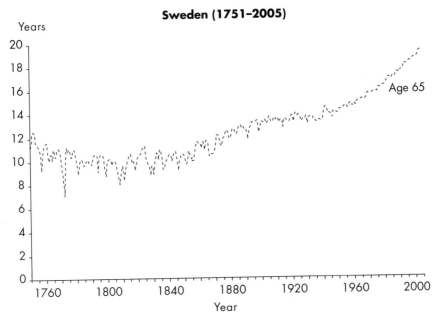

FIGURE 1.3. *(cont'd.)*

male workers, shown in Figure 1.7 for Britain, France, Germany, and the United States. Just as the workday has shortened in many countries, and the workweek and the work year, so has the working lifetime. Indeed, male labor force participation rates have declined at all ages in many countries, as Figure 1.8 shows for the United States. To the extent that this withdrawal from work is a voluntary response to sensible incentives, it is further good news that reflects the enormous growth in earnings that has accompanied (and contributed to) increasing life expectancies. And it has been helped by improved access to savings instruments for ordinary savers. Older people are also healthier than they used to be, and in many countries elderly poverty has declined over the long term.

The pattern of women's labor force participation has often differed from men's. Increasingly, women have become more active in the labor market and have often pursued longer careers. This pattern among working-age women, too, has implications for retirement, along with the general effects of increasing earnings and wealth and growing pension systems. We return to this issue below.

The result: Rising pension costs. Obviously, as people live longer, it becomes more expensive to provide a monthly pension of given size from a given age. The issue is compounded when people start work later and retire earlier, and compounded further when fertility rates fall. This increase in costs can be seen in rising ratios of pension spending to total output. In 2001 average pension spending in the (mostly developed) countries of the Organization for Economic Cooperation and Development (OECD) was 7.4 percent of GDP. But spending in some rapidly aging countries was already significantly higher: 10.4 percent in France, 10.8 percent in Germany, and 12.6 percent in Greece. If pension formulas remain unchanged, projected trends in longevity, fertility, and economic growth suggest that pension spending relative to GDP will increase

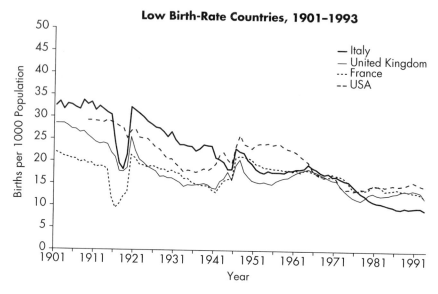

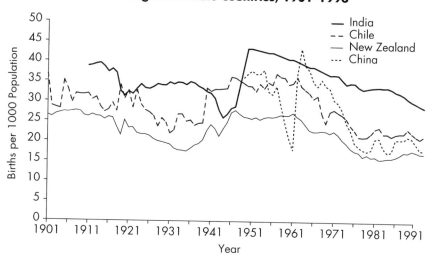

FIGURE 1.4.

Crude birth rates for selected low and high birth-rate countries, 1901–93. For India, rates before 1949 are for British India; rates between 1949 and 1969 are at five-year intervals, with rates within each five-year period interpolated using a second-order moving average; all other years for India are annual rates. *Sources:* Mitchell (1998*a*, 1998*b*, 1998*c*) for all countries except India between 1949 and 1969, data for which are from the United Nations Population Database.

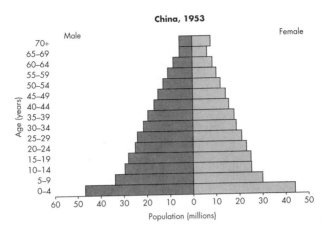

China, 1953

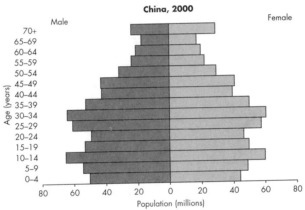

China, 2000

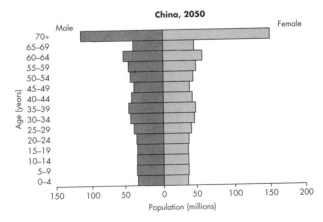

China, 2050

FIGURE 1.5.
Age pyramids, China, India, and the United States, 1950, 2000, and projected 2050.
Sources: Mitchell (1998*a*, 1998*b*); U.S. Census Bureau, International Data Base.
All data for India exclude Burma. Pakistan was separate by 1951. Goa is included
from 1961 and Sikkim from 1971.

(cont'd.)

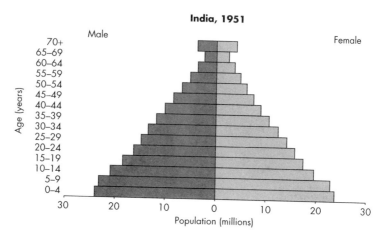

India, 1951

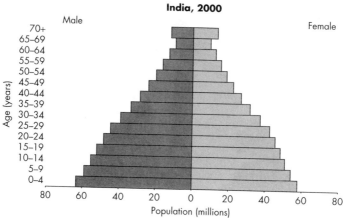

India, 2000

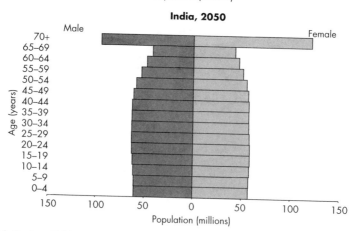

India, 2050

FIGURE 1.5. *(cont'd.)*

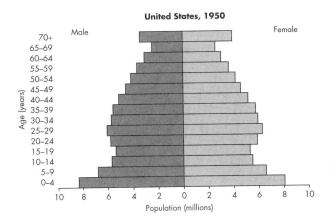

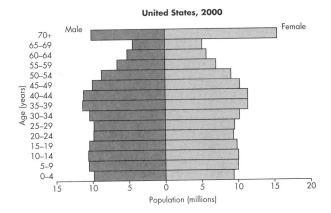

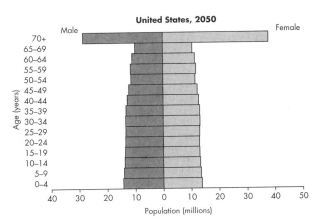

FIGURE 1.5. *(cont'd.)*

substantially: in Greece, for example, spending is projected to double to nearly 25 percent of GDP in 2050 if no action is taken (Figure 1.9).[1] These projected expenditure trends, although important, should not obscure the fact that problems of pension finance are, in part, a side effect of longer lives and, moreover, a side effect that can be contained.

Increasing rights for women. A fourth long-term trend, increasing political and economic rights for women, is separate from any influence on the cost of pension systems, but a considerable and continuing influence on the way pensions are designed. In particular, this trend has led to gender-neutral rules for pensions in many countries and, along with the increase in female labor force participation, to greater consideration of how the design of pension systems affects two-earner couples.

Table 1.1 shows one measure of the spread of women's political rights, namely, the extension of voting rights to women. The first quarter of the twentieth century saw a flurry of activity, with steady progress thereafter. In many countries, however, the date when women were first able to vote is not the date of full suffrage, which includes the right to stand for election.[2]

No single variable similarly encapsulates the trend toward more equal economic rights, and so the following examples only indicate the trend. Sweden was in many respects a leader: In 1884 the Married Women's Property Act was passed. In 1921 majority at age 21 was extended to married women, equalizing it with that of men, along with other rights, including equal division of property upon divorce. In 1939 it became illegal for employers to dismiss women for marriage or pregnancy.

In the United Kingdom, historically, a woman's property was absorbed by her husband upon marriage. The Married Women's Property Act 1882 gave married women the same rights as unmarried women to buy, sell, and own property. Although this was an important step toward equality, a major gap remained: "only in 1935 . . . did Parliament secure a married woman's right to assume personal liability for her contracts" (Shanley 1986, p. 74). Until the mid-1970s a woman could not normally obtain a mortgage without the countersignature of her father, husband, or similarly related man, and until 1990 a married woman's income was normally taxed in the hands of her husband.

In the United States the law relating to women and property was primarily a matter for states rather than the federal government. As a former British colony, the United States started from a point similar to that in the United Kingdom. The 1848 Married Women's Property Act in New York, amended to include more rights in 1860, played a key role by giving women the right to hold property. Ironically, although the Social Security Act was gender neutral from 1961 onward, control of property in some states was not.[3]

In France, women were given extensive property rights in 1907, with further extension to the rights of married women in 1938 (see Herchenroder 1938).

---

1. For wide-ranging projections of spending on pensions, health care, long-term care, and other services in the EU25 until 2050, see Economic Policy Committee of the European Union (2006).

2. Curiously, women in the United States were able to stand for election in 1788 but not to vote until 1920.

3. In Florida, for example, until the 1970s a woman had to petition the state for legal recognition that she was competent to control her property—a frequent occurrence for widows who had to be declared competent to manage their inheritance.

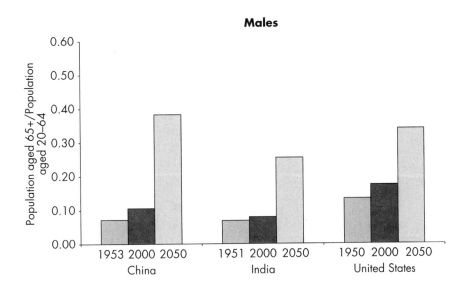

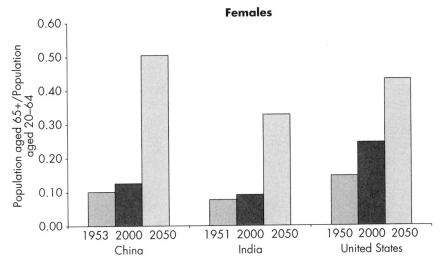

FIGURE 1.6.
Old-age dependency ratios, China, India, and the United States, 1950, 2000, and projected 2050. Ratio of population aged 65 and over to the total working-age population. *Sources:* Mitchell (1998*a*); U.S. Census Bureau, International Data Base.

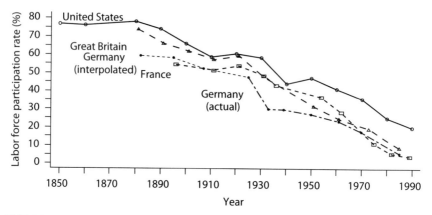

FIGURE 1.7.
Labor force participation rates of men aged 65 and over, Britain, France, Germany, and United States, 1850–1990. *Source:* Costa (1998, p. 12).

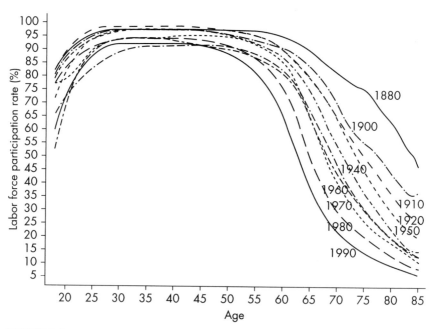

FIGURE 1.8.
Labor force participation rates of men aged 18–85 by age, United States, 1880–1990. *Source:* Costa (1998, p. 12).

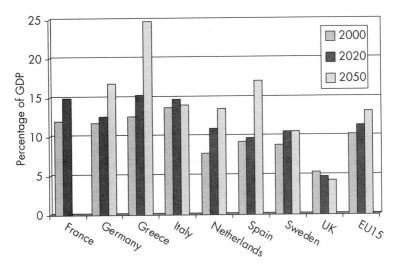

FIGURE 1.9.
Public pension spending as share of GDP, EU15, 2000–50. The EU15 are Austria, Belgium, Denmark, Finland, France, Germany, Greece, Ireland, Italy, Luxembourg, the Netherlands, Portugal, Spain, Sweden, and the United Kingdom. *Source:* Economy Policy Committee of the European Union (2001).

TABLE 1.1
Year when women were first able to vote, selected countries[a]

YEAR	COUNTRIES
1893	New Zealand
1902	Australia
1906	Finland
1913	Norway
1915	Denmark, Iceland
1918	Austria, Canada, Germany, Ireland, Poland, United Kingdom
1919	Belgium, Hungary, Netherlands, Sweden
1920	United States
1930	South Africa[b]
1931	Chile, Portugal, Spain
1944	France
1945	Japan
1946	Italy
1947	Argentina, Mexico, Singapore
1971	Switzerland

Source: Inter-Parliamentary Union, "Women in Politics," www.ipu.org/wmn-e/suffrage.htm.
[a]These dates do not necessarily represent the date of full suffrage: in some countries women faced additional restrictions, such as a later age of voting rights than men, and the right to vote did not always include the right to stand for election.
[b]For whites; the right to vote was extended to blacks of both sexes only in 1994.

Although the gender neutrality of rules has become standard in developed countries, concern remains about the different workings of gender-neutral rules on men and women, since, on average, women have lower annual earnings and shorter careers.

Postwar trends. The long-term trends outlined above are the main drivers of change in the demographics of pensions. Superimposed on these trends are a number of more recent phenomena. First is the growth since World War II of pension systems in terms of both benefits and coverage, which has contributed to the much larger share of GDP devoted to pensions, making the effects of population aging more important than when systems were small. In 2007 pension benefits in mandatory systems in the OECD countries averaged 59 percent of a worker's previous earnings (more precisely, the replacement rate for a worker with average earnings, averaged over all the OECD countries, was 59 percent). For such workers, benefits were lowest in the United Kingdom, Ireland, and Japan, averaging 32.6 percent, and tended to be highest in Southern Europe (Greece, Italy, Portugal, Spain, and Turkey), averaging 74.3 percent.[4] The average replacement rate for lower earners (those earning less than half the average) was 73 percent (all figures from OECD 2007, p. 33).

A second element in the postwar story is the speed of population aging coming from the population bulge representing the baby-boom generation. This factor aggravates the problem of pension finance, but the problem would exist even in its absence. The age pyramids for 2050 in Figure 1.5 are not strikingly different for the United States, which experienced a baby boom (Figure 1.10), than for India, which did not, and for China, whose one-child policy has led to rapid population aging. Thus the analysis in this book is not limited to countries that experienced a baby boom.

A third element, already mentioned, has been the strong trend growth in labor force participation by women, which partly derives from and further reinforces women's expanding economic rights.[5] In addition, the trend has partly offset declining participation by older men and is thus important for the finances of pensions.

Table 1.2 shows female employment rates in 1960, 1980, and 2000, and men's in 2000, for a range of OECD countries. The average participation rate for females rose from 36.5 percent in 1960 to 58.6 percent in 2000, still well below the male participation rate of 75.2 percent in 2000. There is considerable cross-country diversity around the average. In terms of rate of change, the increase was smallest in Finland (where participation was already high in 1960), France, and Italy, and largest in Norway and Sweden. In terms of level, female participation was lowest in 2000 in Greece, Italy, and Spain, at about 40 percent, and highest in Denmark, Norway, and Sweden, all over 70 percent; in Sweden the female participation rate was only slightly lower than men's.

Other countries have different patterns. Women's labor force participation was very high under communism and declined in some former communist countries after 1990. Other countries had, and continue to have, low rates of participation, particularly of married women. Thus not all countries have seen significant growth in participation.

---

4. In Greece the replacement rate for a worker with average earnings was 95.7 percent of previous earnings.

5. For discussion of the links between economic growth and changes in family formation, dissolution, and reproduction, see Lesthaeghe (1983).

FIGURE 1.10.
Crude birth rate, United States, 1909–93. *Source:* Mitchell (1998*b*).

TABLE 1.2
Female employment rates, 1960-2000, selected OECD countries: percent of all persons aged 15–64 years

| | FEMALES | | | MALES, 2000 | FEMALES IN 2000 AS |
COUNTRY	1960	1980	2000		% OF MALES IN 2000
Austria	n.a.[a]	52.4	59.3	78.1	75.9
Belgium	29.6	35.0	51.1	69.8	73.2
Canada	n.a.	52.3	65.1	75.2	86.6
Denmark	42.7	66.2	71.2	80.4	88.6
Finland	54.9	65.0	64.3	69.7	92.3
France	42.9	50.0	53.1	68.1	78.0
Germany	35.0	34.8	58.1	73.5	79.0
Greece	n.a.	30.7	40.4	70.2	57.5
Ireland	n.a.	32.2	52.2	74.0	70.5
Italy	28.1	33.2	39.7	68.5	58.0
Netherlands	n.a.	35.7	62.1	81.1	76.6
Norway	26.1	58.4	73.4	88.1	83.3
Portugal	n.a.	47.1	60.1	75.9	79.2
Spain	21.0	28.4	40.3	70.3	57.3
Sweden	38.1	67.6	72.1	76.2	94.6
United Kingdom	43.1	54.5	65.2	79.3	82.2
United States	39.5	53.9	68.0	80.4	84.6
Average	36.5	46.9	58.6	75.2	77.5

Source: Garibaldi et al. (2005, Table 2.1).
[a]Not available.

17

The international context. These trends play out against a backdrop of changes in the international economic environment. Since 1970, international trade has become increasingly open. A rising fraction of trade is electronic (software, music and video downloads, and the like), and although the size of the phenomenon should not be exaggerated, the result is to make national boundaries more porous. In addition, restrictions on capital mobility have been considerably reduced in many countries. International labor mobility has also increased since 1980 (see Jaumotte and Tytell 2007), including increased opportunity for movement within the European Union. Through all its dimensions—trade, finance, and labor mobility—globalization reduces, but does not eliminate, the ability of a country to act independently in designing its institutions; it also enhances the benefits of international coordination.

That said, the role of labor mobility should not be exaggerated. Immigration has many effects on an economy and society. It is beyond our remit to consider immigration policy, but we note that although immigration can ease somewhat the problems of an aging population, plausible levels of politically acceptable immigration are not sufficient to reverse the concerns discussed in this book. Grant et al. (2004), in a study for the European Commission, concluded that

> immigration does not offer a feasible solution to the problem of population ageing. The sheer numbers of immigrants required to offset population ageing in the EU ... would be unacceptable in Europe's current socio-political climate. . . . Thus the debate is more appropriately on whether immigration may be effectively used to *slow* as opposed to *prevent* population ageing. (Grant et al. 2004, p. xiv, emphasis in original)

1.2 POLICY RESPONSES

Policymakers have responded to these trends in various ways. As far as public pensions are concerned, they have

- Reduced benefits, either by changing the parameters of existing systems, as in the United Kingdom and the United States, or as part of a process of systemwide change, as in Sweden;
- Increased contributions (many countries), either by raising the percentage rate of contribution or by widening the range of income on which contributions are payable;
- Raised the age for full benefits (a few countries, including Norway and the United States), announced a future increase (the United Kingdom), or discussed doing so (many countries);
- Shared risks differently, by moving from a defined-benefit formula (see definitions in Box 1.1), to a notional defined-contribution arrangement (as in Sweden), or by indexing pensions less generously to changes in wages and prices (as in Finland);
- Put in place policies, such as incentives to increase saving, intended to increase national output and decrease the impact of benefit reductions on retirees;
- Adopted a mix of these policies; or
- Buried their heads in the sand, hoping to get by with minor adjustments, leaving painful strategic reform to the next government.

▶ Box 1.1 Terminology

The glossary defines many of the terms we use in this book, but a number require immediate discussion, not least where terms are used by different writers with different meanings.

Actuarial benefits. If a person's pension is fully actuarial, the expected present value of all of his or her future monthly pension benefits is equal to his or her pension accumulation at the time the pension starts. For a given accumulation, the size of the pension therefore depends on the person's remaining life expectancy and the rate of return on assets available to the provider of the annuity over the person's remaining expected life span. Similarly, actuarial adjustment of benefits for a delayed or an early start in benefits means that monthly benefits are raised or lowered, respectively, to maintain equality in present value, reflecting both of the above factors. A pension system that follows this approach in broad outline, but without precise use of projected life expectancy and market interest rates, is referred to as quasi-actuarial.

Compliance. Noncompliance arises where a person does not make contributions that are legally required.

Coverage. Coverage can be incomplete because of noncompliance or because a person is currently working at a job that is not covered by the pension system and does not make voluntary contributions (if that option is available). The most commonly used measure of coverage is the share of the economically active population contributing to the pension system at any time.

Defined-benefit pensions. In this arrangement, explained more fully in Chapter 3, a person's pension benefit is based on his or her wage history and commonly also upon length of service, and does not depend on the amount of assets accumulated in the person's name. Thus, a pure defined-benefit plan adjusts funds to meet anticipated obligations, and so the risk of varying rates of return to pension assets falls on the sponsor, that is, the employer or the government.

Defined-contribution pensions. In this case, explained more fully in Chapter 3, a person's pension benefit is determined only by the amount of assets accumulated toward his or her pension. Thus, a pure defined-contribution plan adjusts obligations to match available funds, and so the individual faces the risk that the portfolio might perform poorly.

Funded pensions. As explained more fully in Chapter 3, funded pensions are paid from an accumulated fund built up over a period of years out of contributions by or on behalf of its members.

Notional defined-contribution (NDC) pensions. As explained in Chapter 3, NDC pensions are financed on a pay-as-you-go basis through social insurance contributions, but a person's pension bears a quasi-actuarial relationship to his or her lifetime pension contributions. Pension benefits may be adjusted for the cohort's life expectancy, and credits may be offered for periods spent caring for children.

Pay-as-you-go (PAYG) pensions. As explained in Chapter 3, PAYG pensions are paid out of current revenue (usually by the state, from tax revenue) rather than out of an accumulated fund.

Replacement rate. The replacement rate is the ratio of the monthly income a pensioner receives to the income he or she received while working (both net of taxes and transfers). Thus defined, the replacement rate is a measure of the effectiveness of consumption smoothing. The term can also mean the ratio of the average pension to the average wage, in which case it is a measure of the pension system's ability to relieve elderly poverty.

Retirees and pensioners. For some purposes it is necessary to distinguish two separate events: stopping work, and receiving a pension. We use the term "retiree" for someone who has stopped work, and "pensioner" for someone who is receiving pension benefits. A retiree will usually also be a pensioner, although

(continues next page)

(continued from previous page)

not necessarily: for example, a person may choose to retire early and live off his or her savings until reaching pensionable age. Similarly, a pensioner may have retired, or he or she may be receiving a pension while continuing to work.

Social security. We avoid the term because it is used with different meanings. In the United States, social security refers to government retirement and disability benefits only, in the United Kingdom to all cash benefits provided by the government, and in mainland Europe to all cash benefits and health care. Instead of "social security" we use the term "pension system."

State pension system. The term "state" has different meanings. It can refer to a national government (for example, the federal government in the United States) or to subnational government (state governments in the United States). We therefore avoid the term where possible. Where used, the term "state" describes a national government and refers to a general system, not just one for government employees.

Public pension system. We use this term to refer to a government-run pension system (also called a state pension system) that is open to all workers.

Voluntary pensions. Pensions can be voluntary in two different ways. They can be voluntary for an individual worker, or a firm may voluntarily introduce an employer plan, membership of which may be compulsory for its workers. ◀

Policymakers have also been increasingly concerned with private pensions. Some countries have encouraged funded private pensions (the United Kingdom), and others have mandated them (Chile and, more recently, some of the former communist countries). And regulation and insurance of private pensions have been strengthened.

The question of when building up a pension fund (as opposed to paying for pensions out of current contributions and taxes) contributes to good policy outcomes, and when it does not, has been and continues to be the subject of a heated debate in which we are both protagonists;[6] The World Bank's "multipillar model" (World Bank 1994; Holzmann and Hinz 2005; see Glossary) explicitly advocated funded pensions. Given the Bank's importance in pension policy, subsequent chapters evaluate this view, and Box 10.1 and section 11.3 summarize our critique and that of a recent evaluation by the World Bank (2006*a*) of its own work.

The private sector has also responded to the various trends. Longer life spans increase the cost of providing a pension of given size, and increasing regulation, for example to protect workers' accumulated pension entitlements, has added further to the cost of employer schemes. These factors were brought to a head in many developed countries by stock market turbulence in the years after 2000. Many employers responded by reducing benefits, and many moved from defined-benefit to defined-contribution arrangements for newly hired workers, and in some cases also for future contributions by existing workers.

---

6. See Barr (2000), Diamond (2004), Diamond and Orszag (2005*a*, 2005*b*), and, for contrasting views, Feldstein (2005) and Holzmann and Hinz (2005). For an attempt to summarize the core of the dispute, see Barr and Rutkowski (2005).

1.3   ORGANIZATION OF THE BOOK

To assist the broader debate, the chapters in Part I set out the analytics of pensions that are central for considering pension reform. Although we are open about expressing our own views, the main purpose of this part, and of the book, is to lay out the analytical process by which we reach our conclusions, to enable readers to form their own views. Chapter 2 discusses the central purposes of pension systems, and Chapter 3 different types of pension arrangements. The next five chapters are the book's analytical core. They look at the basic economics of pensions (Chapter 4), labor markets (Chapter 5), finance and funding (Chapter 6), redistribution and risk sharing (Chapter 7), and gender and family issues (Chapter 8). These chapters establish the main conclusions that we derive from economic theory. Chapters 5 and 6, although they mostly avoid mathematics, are conceptually more difficult than the rest of the book. However, the conclusions of these and the other theoretical chapters are referred to where relevant in the later policy discussion, so they can be skipped (or skimmed) by readers for whom the details of the derivations are not essential.

The theoretical arguments have three centers of gravity:

- Pension systems have multiple objectives, including consumption smoothing, insurance, poverty relief, and redistribution, which cannot all be fully achieved at the same time. Thus policy has to optimize—not minimize or maximize—across a range of objectives. To illustrate, an exclusive focus on consumption smoothing (that is, redistribution to oneself over the life cycle) would suggest a system in which benefits bear a fairly exact relationship to a worker's accumulated contributions; but such a system would fail to relieve old-age poverty for low-paid workers and would not offer insurance against adverse labor market outcomes. Thus policy has to seek the best balance among consumption smoothing, poverty relief, and insurance, a balance that will depend in each society on the weights given to those and other objectives.

- The analysis is couched in what economists call "second-best" terms, that is, assuming a world with imperfect information, incomplete markets, and distorting taxation. For example, the goal of minimizing (as opposed to optimizing) labor market distortions is misplaced, not least because a pension system that provides poverty relief inescapably creates distortions; thus minimizing distortions would imply little or no poverty relief—the cure would be worse than the disease. Depending on their design, pension systems can have substantial effects on behavior, including labor supply, saving, and the division of resources within a household. But these effects are not always and everywhere adverse, and even where they are, the system can still be welfare improving if the benefits of improved old-age security outweigh the costs of the adverse incentives. In short, policy has to seek the best balance among poverty relief, insurance, and containing distortions, which again will depend on the weights given to these different objectives.

- Many people (particularly noneconomists) think that economics is only or mainly about efficiency. That view is, of course, mistaken: economics is, and always has been, about equity as well as efficiency—indeed, one of the major thrusts of the optimal taxation literature (Diamond and Mirrlees 1971a, 1971b) has been to integrate the two. Thus readers should not be surprised at the extent of discussion, both in the theoretical chapters and in the later policy discussion, of the distributional effects of different pension arrangements. This material is included not only for completeness but also because it reflects our value judgment that distributional effects are important.

Some omissions should be noted. Our focus is on retirement benefits, with little discussion, despite its importance, of disability insurance (on which see Reno et al. 2005). Nor, as already mentioned, do we analyze the provision of health care. We do not address the pension systems or reforms, actual or desirable, of all countries, or even all the major countries. Although we discuss the experiences of different countries to illustrate our theoretical discussion, this is not a comparative volume. The examples have a heavy center of gravity in the United States and the United Kingdom, since those are the countries we know best, but are chosen to illustrate points of general relevance. We rely on existing theoretical analyses. Where gaps in the literature arise, therefore, our analysis is less firmly grounded (such instances being clearly labeled). This is particularly an issue in Chapter 7, which deals with uncertainties, and in Chapter 8 on gender and family.

Chapters 3 through 8 address the question of good pension design. But good design is not enough. It is necessary also to implement that design, and that poses the question of what pension designs are feasible in different countries. Chapter 9 discusses implementation, including the financial and technical requirements—both for pension providers and for consumers—of different types of pension arrangements, with explicit discussion of what is necessary to run funded individual accounts. Chapter 10 brings together the strategic conclusions from the discussion in Part I, including lessons from economic analysis and discussion of a range of analytical errors.

The chapters in Part II apply the analysis in the earlier chapters to policy. Chapter 11 gives an overview of pension systems over time and across countries, discusses some common policy errors, and illustrates the wide array of pension arrangements in different countries. Chapters 12 and 13 discuss pension arrangements in Chile including major reform in 2008. Chapter 14 describes and assesses pension arrangements in China over the course of that country's economic reforms. Chapter 15 sets out a series of directions for reform in China, drawing on the earlier work of a panel on which we served (Asher et al. 2005). Chapter 16 sets out a series of questions about policy design and summarizes the key messages of the book.

Readers in a hurry should look at Chapters 10, 11, and 16.

Part I

Principles

2

▷

Core Purposes of Pension Systems

The quality of life has multiple dimensions. Economic security includes access to labor market opportunities and to an effective pension system. Personal autonomy has clear connections with physical independence, which in turn has connections with housing and with access to medical care and personal care. A third element, social inclusion, embraces family and social life and access to information. These issues matter at all ages but become more widely problematic as people age.

While acknowledging the broader aspects of old-age security, this book is about its economic aspects. To that end, this chapter considers two groups of primary objectives of pension systems. Pension systems should

- Provide insurance against low income and wealth in old age and offer a mechanism for consumption smoothing across one's lifetime (what might be thought of as the "piggybank" function of pensions), and should
- Relieve poverty and redistribute income and wealth (what might be called the "Robin Hood" function).

Addressing these objectives involves interactions, since saving for old age and insuring against the risk of outliving one's assets also help to relieve poverty and affect the distributions of income and wealth. In addressing these objectives it is necessary also to consider the costs of achieving them. As a useful shorthand:

- The primary objective of pensions is economic security in old age, achieved through consumption smoothing, insurance, poverty relief, and redistribution.
- The primary objective of pension design is to optimize old-age security, including the cost of providing it.

Employing those objectives makes it possible to assess a pension system in terms of three questions:

- How well does it achieve these objectives for individual workers? Does the system provide a pension that is adequate, relative both to the poverty line and to the

25

retiree's previous earnings? These dual measures of adequacy are based on actual, ex post outcomes; a related question is how well the system provides insurance against potential adverse financial outcomes.

- For how many does it achieve those objectives? That is, to what extent does the system cover the elderly population? In developed countries pension coverage is very high; in developing countries it is generally limited to urban workers in the formal sector.

- At what cost does it achieve them? In particular, is the system financially sustainable now and given likely foreseeable trends? Is the size of the system appropriate in the light of other needs, the role of voluntary pensions, and impacts on labor market equilibrium that reduce economic efficiency?

2.1 OBJECTIVES

In answering the questions set out above, two distinctions are useful: between primary and secondary objectives, and between the objectives of individuals and of government. In this section we discuss the primary objectives with respect to pensions of individuals (section 2.1.1) and governments (section 2.1.2), and then (in section 2.1.3) some secondary objectives.

2.1.1 Individual objectives

From an individual viewpoint, income security in old age requires two sets of instruments: a mechanism for smoothing consumption, and a means of insurance. For the lifetime poor, income security additionally includes transfers provided to them in old age.

Consumption smoothing. People seek to maximize their well-being not at a single point in time, but over time. Students sit in class not because they cannot think of anything more exciting to do, but because they hope that what they learn will contribute to their future earning capacity, job satisfaction, and enjoyment of leisure. Athletes do not train out of sheer enjoyment of the training process, but because of the resulting boost to their performance. People try to lose weight not because they enjoy dieting, but because they recognize the potential health benefits.

Saving raises identical issues. Someone who saves does so not because the consumption he gives up today has no value, but because he places a higher value on the resulting extra consumption in the future. A teenager who saves for an airline ticket is making a judgment that she will get more enjoyment from the trip than from spending the money now; someone who takes out a student loan is making a judgment that the returns (monetary and nonmonetary) to a college degree will exceed the cost of the loan.[1] Similarly, most people hope to live long enough to be able to retire, that is, to reach a period in their lives when they stop working but can continue to consume. They save to that end, in effect redistributing income from their younger to their older selves.

Thus a central purpose of pensions—consumption smoothing—is to enable a person to transfer consumption from her productive middle years to her retired years, allowing her to choose a better time path of consumption over her working and retired life. The core of the argument, discussed more formally in Box 2.1, is that a rational person optimizing over her lifetime is likely to borrow when young (say, to buy a house) and to save during her prime

---

1. On the economic analytics of student loans, see Barr (2004*b*).

earning years to finance consumption in retirement; she does so because she values the flow of housing services more highly than the extra consumption she could otherwise have financed with the loan repayments, and values consumption in old age more highly than the extra consumption she could otherwise have had earlier. The optimum for each person depends on the total wealth with which she starts, on her preferences between present and future consumption, and on the rates of interest at which she can save and borrow.

▶ **Box 2.1 Consumption smoothing: Choosing between present and future consumption**

The Fisher model depicted in the figure illustrates the options available to an individual over time under certain simplifying assumptions. The horizontal axis shows a person's potential consumption in period 1 (younger years) and the vertical axis that in period 2 (older years). With an initial endowment shown by point a, he can consume C_1 units in period 1 and C_2 units in period 2. However, he can increase his options by saving or borrowing. For example, he could save $C_1 - C_1'$ units of consumption in period 1 in exchange for $C_2' - C_2$ units in period 2, thus moving to point e.

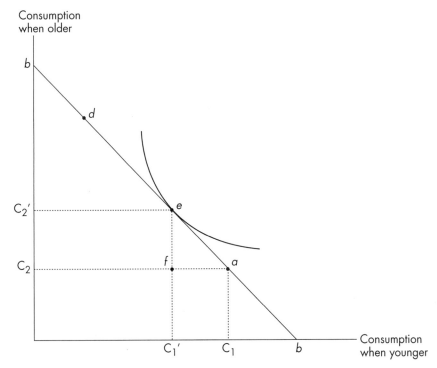

Choice between consumption at younger and older ages.

To illustrate the terms of the trade-off between the two periods, if the interest rate is zero, a person can save 1 unit in period 1 and consume an extra unit in period 2. If his initial endowment, shown by a, comprises 7 units in period 1 and 3 units in period 2, he could, by borrowing 3 units, consume 10 units in period 1 and 0 in period 2 or, by saving 7 units, consume 0 in period 1 and 10 units in period 2, or any combination in between.

(continues next page)

(continued from previous page)

Thus his consumption opportunities are shown by a budget constraint with a slope of –1. If instead the interest rate were 10 percent, the budget constraint would become steeper: for each unit he saves in period 1, he could consume 1.1 units in period 2. By saving he can therefore move from *a* to *e* in the figure. Thus the budget constraint *b-b* goes through the initial endowment point, *a*, with its slope determined by the interest rate. The interest rate thus establishes the relative price of present and future consumption and hence the amount of consumption that must be given up during working life in order to enjoy a unit of consumption after retirement.

For a person with an initial endowment of C_1 in period 1 and C_2 in period 2, and a lifetime budget constraint shown by *b-b*, the consumption pattern that maximizes lifetime utility is shown by point *e*, which the person attains by saving $C_1 - C_1'$ when younger, making possible consumption of C_2' when older. Similarly, if the initial endowment were *d*, on the same budget constraint, the person could move to *e* by borrowing in period 1.

Of course, the choices and the analysis become more interesting when there are multiple assets to use for savings, and when the simple assumption of rational choice over time is relaxed (see the discussion in Box 4.2 and Box 9.6). ◀

Insurance. In a world of certainty, individuals would save just enough during their working life to finance their retirement, so as to move from point a to point e in the figure in Box 2.1. However, people do not live in a world of certainty, not least because they do not know how long they are going to live. Thus a pension based on individual saving, as in the figure, confronts the individual with a choice: either risk outliving his or her retirement savings, or consume very little throughout old age to prevent that from happening. But although any one person does not know how long he or she is going to live, the average life expectancy of a group of people is much more predictable. Thus, in principle, a group of friends or neighbors could agree to pool their pension savings, with each person drawing a pension based on the total amount he or she has contributed to the pool and his or her actual life span. Going beyond the group, such pooling can be organized through an insurance company, thus involving many more people in absorbing the risk that the aggregate life expectancy is somewhat different from what was anticipated.

This is the essence of annuities, whereby an individual exchanges his or her pension accumulation at retirement for guaranteed monthly payments for the rest of his or her life, however long it may be. Annuities allow people to insure against the risk of outliving their pension savings; in the pure case of an actuarial annuity, an individual with the average life expectancy receives a pension stream whose expected present value is exactly equal to his or her contribution to the pool; the only redistribution is ex post, from people who live less than their life expectancy to those who live longer.[2] Pension systems can also insure against disability, and they can protect young children should a working parent die before retirement, and a spouse who outlives a worker.

How does insurance work and why does it matter? In essence, the price of insurance depends on two factors: the degree of risk and the size of the potential loss.

2. When individuals with different life expectancies are joined in a single pool with a single price, there is also redistribution ex ante from those with short life expectancy to those with long life expectancy.

Automobile insurance is expensive for a driver who is young or who lives in a high-crime area (both factors leading to a higher probability of loss) or for someone who drives a Rolls-Royce or a Ferrari (because the potential loss is large). A middle-aged person with a good driving record, driving a small, five-year old Ford in a rural area, pays a much lower premium. This, broadly, is the way in which private insurance operates, as set out more formally in Box 2.2.

To understand why insurance is important, suppose that life expectancy at age 65 is ten years, and compare two states of the world: in state A, insurance exists, so that it is possible to buy an actuarial annuity; in state B, there is no insurance. In A, a person who wants a pension of $25,000 a year can provide for one (assuming for simplicity a zero interest rate) by saving $250,000 over his working life, which he exchanges for an annuity upon retirement; that is, the cost of the insurance is based on the *average* duration of retirement. In B, where insurance is not available, a person has to save for the *maximum* duration of retirement; if she judges this to be forty years (in the developed world, a person aged 60 is increasingly likely to live to 100), she would have to save 40 × $25,000, or $1 million, to be sure of having $25,000 in each year of retirement.[3] The welfare gains where it is possible to switch from a savings model (that is, self-insurance), requiring substantial precautionary saving, to a pooled insurance model are clear and striking; although the contrast is less sharp, they remain strongly present with a positive interest rate. In this way insurance in the form of an annuity increases individual welfare by reducing the need for people to accumulate very large savings to avoid destitution should they live longer than their life expectancy.

▶ Box 2.2 The operation of actuarial insurance

Idealized actuarial insurance has an easy intuition. Suppose that 100 people are flying to a soccer tournament in Brazil, that each person has a suitcase whose contents are worth $1,000, and that on average 2 percent of suitcases get lost in transit. Thus each person faces a potential loss, L, of $1,000, with a probability, π, of 2 percent. In these circumstances it would be possible for an insurer to collect 0.02 × $1,000 = $20 from each of the 100 people, or $2,000 in total; when they arrive in Brazil, the insurer would find which two people had lost their suitcase and pay each $1,000 in compensation. The mechanism works only on average—a significant issue with as small a group as 100 sports fans—but is of less and less significance as a group gets larger. For example, the insurer suffers a $1,000 loss if three suitcases are lost and makes a $1,000 profit if only one is; as the size of the insured group increases, the percentage difference between the expected and the actual outcome will tend to narrow. In practice, insurance companies also have administrative costs and selling costs and may also face difficulties in estimating probabilities.

More formally, the actuarial premium for the *i*th individual, p_i, is defined as

$$p_i = (1 + \alpha)\pi_i L,$$

where $\pi_i L$ is the individual's expected loss and α is the insurance company's charge to cover administrative costs (for example, sending an expert to assess the damage) and competitive profit. In other words, p is the price at which the insurance will be supplied in an idealized competitive market. ◀

---

3. If insurance is not available, the retiree might choose a declining rather than a constant consumption path, reflecting the lower probability of being alive to consume in later years. Although this alters the size of the gain from access to insurance, the overall conclusion remains unchanged.

Are voluntary arrangements sufficient? In the simplest of all worlds, illustrated by Box 2.1, a person would provide for his or her pension through voluntary saving during working years so as to achieve an optimal time path of consumption (that is, a move to point e), and by buying an annuity to protect against the longevity risk. Were matters so simple in practice, pensions could be left to the voluntary decision of each individual worker, and to private insurance, with no need for government involvement beyond enforcing agreements—and no need for this book.

There are two strategic sets of reasons why this approach, on its own, is insufficient. First, as discussed shortly, it ignores additional public policy objectives such as poverty relief and redistribution. Second, the simple model assumes that insurance markets work perfectly. In fact, there are multiple reasons why they do not work perfectly, including a lack of perfect information, the absence of some possible market opportunities, and other distortions. Another reason is that individuals do not always do a good job of making and executing decisions about saving and insurance in the face of continuing pressure to spend more now, and with often limited understanding of the nature and value of insurance and of investment opportunities. The assumptions of idealized markets are useful for formulating a simple theory as a start to understanding the issues, but bad guides to policy design. As discussed more fully in Box 4.2 and Box 9.6:

- Imperfect information and understanding are widespread. People are often badly informed, particularly about complex pension products. Moreover, there are serious concerns about the ability of individuals to make the most of the market opportunities that are available to them, not least because not everyone has a time horizon that gives appropriate weight to future consumption. There is considerable evidence that if pension arrangements were left to people's voluntary decisions, many would not save enough: as older people they would regret their earlier choice not to have saved more. Similarly, on a voluntary basis people make little use of annuity markets, which, in turn, makes annuities more expensive. And many people do not do a good job of selecting long-term investments.

- Markets are often incomplete; that is, not every product that people would benefit from buying (in this case specific kinds of annuities or other insurance products needed to optimize over the life cycle) is available. The market for privately indexed contracts is thin, and the market for annuities is affected by difficulties in measuring the longevity risk.

- There are other distortions, including those caused by taxation: governments need tax revenue in order to function.

Given these and other problems, both economic and political arguments support government intervention, for example compulsory participation in a pension system, to prevent destitution in old age. More broadly, public policy may seek to reduce systemic uncertainty and increase social stability—a particularly important objective during times of rapid change, such as the reforms of the 1990s in Central and Eastern Europe or the current wave of reforms in China. Protecting people against uncertainty is important. If risk-averse people cannot buy insurance, they may build up large precautionary savings (as in China); as just discussed, their welfare can be improved if they could buy insurance.

Alongside the risk of outliving one's savings, which annuities can cover, there are also risks to future earnings during working life. The latter risks can be insured in part through unemployment insurance and disability insurance, but they also have consequences for retirement, which pension systems can at least partly address.

In sum, the assumption of a simple, first-best world of idealized, perfectly functioning markets ignores a range of real-world market failures and thus assumes away the very problems that government intervention is designed to address. In contrast, second-best analysis, based on models that incorporate some degree of realistic imperfections, seeks the optimal policy given the presence of such imperfections. These topics are taken up in detail in subsequent chapters.

2.1.2 Public policy objectives

In the face of these market imperfections, government intervention in a variety of forms can improve the efficiency of consumption smoothing and insurance, thus helping (and, where necessary, forcing) individuals to make better use of the resources they command. In addition, as already noted, public policy has further objectives, notably poverty relief and redistribution.

Poverty relief. In pursuit of this objective, pension systems target resources to people who are poor on a lifetime basis, and thus unable to save enough to support themselves in old age. In some respects the design of poverty relief is simpler for older people: potential labor earnings are less a consideration for people beyond retirement age, and therefore outright transfers to the elderly are less likely to weaken incentives to work. (Of course, such transfers may also influence labor supply and savings among the younger population looking forward to retirement, and this has to be taken into account.) With less concern about possible impacts on the labor market, it is potentially advantageous to have separate rules for the elderly. Such programs can target all the elderly or can concentrate on those who have contributed to the pension system. Many countries have both types of program.

Redistribution. Pension systems can redistribute income on a lifetime basis, and this may complement the role of progressive taxes based on income year by year. Lifetime redistribution can be achieved by paying pensions to low earners that are a higher percentage of their previous earnings (that is, a higher replacement rate) than higher earners receive, thus subsidizing the consumption smoothing of people who are less well off (but not necessarily in poverty). Since lifelong earnings are highly uncertain from the perspective of any one individual, such a system can also provide some insurance against the consequences for retirement of low earnings during an extended portion of one's career. There can also be redistribution toward families: for example, a married couple might receive a larger pension than a single person even though both households paid the same contributions.

Pension systems can also redistribute across generations. For example, a government may reduce the contribution rate or increase the benefits of the present generation, as was the case for retirees in the United States in the late 1940s and 1950s, who had lived through the Great Depression and World War II and had limited time working in the postwar economic boom. Such a move requires future generations to pay higher contributions or have lower pensions, thus redistributing from those later generations to the earlier elderly generation.

2.1.3   Other objectives

Alongside the primary objectives of consumption smoothing, insurance, poverty relief, and redistribution, policy may have secondary objectives that are not direct purposes of the pension system itself but are related. One is economic development broadly, and economic growth specifically. Even well-designed pensions create some adverse labor market incentives, and badly designed ones can have a large impact. Excessive public pension spending may contribute to high tax rates, putting economic growth at risk, and may excessively decrease national saving. The goal of pensions, after all, is to increase consumption by the elderly, but since their increased consumption comes out of current national income, it necessarily means less consumption and less saving somewhere in the economy, which means less investment (or more foreign borrowing), which may mean less national income in the future than otherwise. The real issue is how much less saving and investment is appropriate.

Conversely, pension arrangements can assist the operation of labor markets and may encourage saving, which may contribute to economic growth. And in some circumstances pension plans can improve the efficiency of the capital market. There is debate about the relative weights to be accorded to old-age security and to these secondary objectives. The former carries more weight with the Ministry of Social Security, the latter with the Ministry of Finance. In reality both are important—the ministries are both right—and links between the two ministries should be strengthened in most countries for this reason.

2.1.4   Recognizing costs

It is always important to recognize that providing resources—in this case consumption for retirees—has costs. Not only are the resources themselves costly, but costs also arise from the rules that determine how benefits are provided and how revenue is collected in order to pay for those benefits. Thus a key concern is to avoid implementing a system that costs more than is necessary to accomplish its objectives, and to balance the level of achievement of those objectives with the costs of achieving them.

2.2   ANALYTICAL ERRORS

To repeat, the primary objective of pensions is economic security in old age through consumption smoothing, insurance, poverty relief, and redistribution. Good analysis needs to consider the full range of these objectives, the relative weight attached to each, and the costs of achieving them. Errors arise where analysis omits any or all of these aspects.

It is generally mistaken to consider one objective in isolation, since, of necessity, that implies little consideration for the other objectives. It is wrong, for example, to focus too heavily on consumption smoothing while largely ignoring poverty relief, as the following World Bank self-critique recognizes: "the Bank acted too quickly to support multi-pillar reforms in other countries without examining options for complementary safety-net programs to protect informal sector workers from poverty in old age" (World Bank 2006a, p. 19). It is equally wrong to focus too heavily on economic growth: fostering growth is not a primary purpose of pensions, and in any case, as discussed in section 6.3, the links between pensions and growth are not simple.

A second error is to accept claimed objectives uncritically. It is argued that funding of pensions can increase saving rates. But increasing saving is good policy only where saving rates are too low, which they are in many countries, but not in countries such as China and South Korea, which have very high saving rates.

A third type of error is to blur the distinction between objectives (for example, old-age security) and constraints (for example, fiscal cost); the same World Bank self-critique notes: "The Bank's preoccupation with fiscal sustainability tended to obscure the broader goal of pension policy, that is, to reduce poverty and improve retirement income adequacy *within a fiscal constraint*" (World Bank 2006*a*, p. xxv, emphasis in original). The point is not one about value judgments—the relative weights that should be accorded to the various objectives—but rather an analytical point: that all the objectives are relevant. A related error is to blur the distinction between objectives and instruments. In the World Bank's original formulation a multipillar pension system comprised three pillars: a publicly managed, PAYG system; a system of mandatory, privately funded, usually defined-contribution plans; and a system of voluntary, privately funded plans. By focusing on instruments (for example, mandatory participation in a defined-benefit plan) this formulation bases pension design on a predetermined choice of instruments rather than as the outcome of a process of optimization. The categorization in this book talks about "parts" or "tiers" rather than "pillars," to make it clear that there are many ways of organizing the system as a whole. Although the "pillar" vocabulary has evolved to recognize more pillars and multiple ways of fulfilling the role assigned originally to each pillar, its use still has the risk of narrowing thinking about pension structure and possibly misjudging individual pillars by not paying adequate attention to the full context.

How should pensions be organized to achieve these various objectives? Policy design should reflect the weights a society wants to attach to the different objectives and the key constraints (discussed in Chapter 9), and should then consider instruments (outlined in the next chapter) for achieving the chosen objectives in ways that respect the constraints.

3

▷

Basic Features of Pension Systems

Policy design should consider a range of instruments—outlined in this chapter—for achieving a society's chosen objectives in ways that respect the constraints it faces (discussed in chapter 9). One of our central arguments is that there are many possible structures that can combine to address all the objectives. China, for example, has a three-part pension system, with mandatory basic pensions, mandatory individual accounts, and voluntary supplemental pensions. In suitable combination, this system can address all the objectives described in Chapter 2. Chile has introduced a noncontributory pension alongside its existing system of mandatory individual accounts and voluntary supplemental pensions. Other countries have different combinations of these and other pension institutions, examples of which are described in Chapter 11.

This chapter introduces some of the main features of pension systems and explores their differences, including differences in the way pensions are financed (section 3.1), in the relationship between contributions and benefits (section 3.2), and in how both are adjusted as the economic and demographic environment changes (section 3.3).[1] Some features are generally found only in public pension systems; others are common to both public and employer-based systems. Section 3.4 introduces a recent development, notional defined-contribution pensions, which combine some of the traditional features in a novel way. Section 3.5 briefly delineates the main areas of controversy with respect to the choices among these features.

3.1 FUNDED AND PAY-AS-YOU-GO SYSTEMS

In a fully funded system, which may be public, individual, or employer based, pensions are paid out of a fund built over a period of years from contributions by or on behalf of its participants, and the fund is sufficient to pay accrued benefit liabilities in full as they come due. In contrast, in a pure pay-as-you-go (PAYG) system, usually run by government, pensions are paid entirely out of current revenue sources. In practice no

1. For more on the different types of pensions, see Lindbeck and Persson (2003).

system is wholly PAYG and few are wholly funded: all well-run PAYG systems have a reserve of at least a few months' outflows; and pension guarantees for funded plans are, in effect, a PAYG element in the system; depending on their structure, tax advantages may also introduce a PAYG element into a funded plan.

Fully funded pensions. Fully funded pensions are based on savings. Contributions are invested in financial (or possibly physical) assets, the return on which is credited to the plan's participants, either individually or collectively. When a participant retires, the pension fund will be holding all of his or her past contributions, together with the interest and dividends earned on them. This accumulation is available to finance the participant's consumption in retirement, either in the form of an annuity or by drawing down the accumulation in some other way. Funding is thus a method of accumulating assets, which are exchanged for goods and services at some future date. The full matching of funds and future obligations can in principle be preserved in either of two ways: by adjusting obligations to match available funds (a defined-contribution plan) or by adjusting funds to meet anticipated obligations (a defined-benefit plan), as discussed further in section 3.2.

Deviations from full funding are common, for example when governments use general revenue to top up pension benefits that are regarded as too small. The future cost of such increases is paid on a PAYG basis. Another example arises in defined-benefit systems, for example when the employer sponsoring the system adjusts for fluctuations in the fund's asset values only with a lag.

Fully funded systems have two major implications. First, such a system in principle always has sufficient reserves to pay all outstanding financial liabilities. Second, if the plan makes no redistribution across generations, a generation is constrained by its own past saving, and a representative individual gets out of the plan no more and no less than he or she has put in, including returns on assets acquired with the savings.[2]

PAYG pensions. PAYG pensions are contractarian in nature,[3] based on the fact that a government does not have to accumulate savings in anticipation of future pension claims, but can instead tax the working population to pay the pensions of covered retirees.[4] (Because, as previously noted, PAYG pensions are usually run by the government, this discussion assumes a government-run system.[5]) Most public pension systems are primarily PAYG; if there is funding, it typically covers only part of anticipated payments.

---

2. In reality matters are more complex: real rates of return, and thus future asset values, are a random variable (see, for example, Burtless 2002); analogously, future liabilities are a random variable, particularly if life expectancy is uncertain. Thus analysis in terms of simple present values is useful conceptually, but for policy purposes a more complete analysis needs to take account of stochastic factors. In addition, a fully funded system could shift balances from higher earners to lower earners, thus redistributing while preserving full funding.

3. By contractarian we mean a social contract, not a binding legal contract.

4. Although it is common to tax only earnings to finance pensions, many countries use a wider tax base in financing their public pension. For example, the Netherlands finances its universal pension through a tax on income rather than earnings, Sweden uses general revenue to pay pension contributions for those caring for young children, and Germany and Italy have used general revenue to finance pension budget deficits.

5. PAYG systems have also been run by corporations, however. Just as a public PAYG system is dependent on the presence of a future tax base, so a corporate PAYG plan is dependent on the presence of future corporate earnings to pay pensions. Because of the risk of nonpayment, such plans have been found unsatisfactory and are banned in many countries.

PAYG systems can be looked at from the perspective of the individual contributor or from an aggregate, macroeconomic perspective. In the first case, a worker's claim to a pension is based on legislation stating that if the worker pays contributions now, he or she will be given a pension in the future. Although the terms of the legislation are fairly precise, and frequently referred to as "promises," that does not mean that the tax and benefit rules can never be amended. Rather, it is assumed (and hoped) that the political process will be reasonably respectful of legitimate expectations and will not raise taxes or reduce benefits without good reason.[6] From an aggregate viewpoint, each year the government is simply taxing one group of individuals and transferring the resulting revenue to another. PAYG plans, from this perspective, thus differ little from explicit income transfer programs, although the determinants of who pays and who receives, and therefore the resulting incentive structure, can be very different. In particular, income transfer programs generally consider the current earnings and family position of potential recipients to determine eligibility and the amount of the transfer. In contrast, pension benefits look back to much, or possibly all, of a person's earnings history.

A major implication of a PAYG system is that it relaxes the constraint that the benefits received by any generation must be matched by its own contributions.[7] The real role of PAYG has two aspects: to redistribute resources across generations, particularly toward retirees and older workers when a system starts or expands, and to redistribute and share risks across generations, as discussed more fully in Chapter 7.

3.2   THE RELATIONSHIP BETWEEN CONTRIBUTIONS AND BENEFITS

Whether a pension system is funded or PAYG, a separate question is how benefits are related to a worker's previous contributions. Again there are two polar extremes: Benefits can be strictly determined by past contributions and the returns on those contributions, in which case benefits can exceed or fall short of initial expectations; this is called a pure defined-contribution plan. Or benefits can be determined on other criteria and guaranteed to be paid no matter what the eventual return on contributions: this is the definition of a pure defined-benefit plan.

Defined-contribution plans. In a fully funded defined-contribution plan, also called funded individual accounts, each participant pays into an account a fixed fraction of his or her earnings. (Defined-contribution plans that actually accumulate contributions are

6. The nature of the "promise" can be complex: with incomplete specification of all possible future circumstances, whether the promise is kept depends on future actions by the government. The worker may or may not be aware of this contingency or of the nature of the future process that the promise will follow. Fully funded plans are also subject to possible legislative change that can affect the taxation of assets, returns on assets, and payment of benefits.

7. Samuelson (1958) showed that, with a PAYG system, it is possible in principle for every generation to receive more in pension benefits than it paid in contributions, provided that the rate of growth of total real earnings exceeds the interest rate adjusted for inflation; this can happen when there is sufficient technological progress, and/or steady population growth and excessive capital accumulation (see Aaron 1966). That is, it is possible for a country to be on a track to have so much capital indefinitely that lowering investment (increasing consumption) is possible without harming the ability to sustain consumption in the future. Since this does not appear to be empirically relevant over the longer term, we ignore its possibility.

by definition funded; notional defined-contribution plans collect but do not accumulate contributions; these plans are discussed in section 3.4.) These contributions are used to purchase assets, which accumulate in the account along with the returns earned by those assets. When the participant retires and the pension starts, the assets in the account are used to finance his or her retirement in one of several ways, typically as an annuity, a regular periodic drawdown, or a lump-sum transfer.

In a pure defined-contribution plan with no tax advantages and no transfers to or from accounts, a person's consumption in retirement, given life expectancy and the rate of interest, is in principle determined by the size of his or her lifetime pension accumulation. This arrangement preserves the individual character of the person's lifetime budget constraint—there is no redistribution within or across generations.

The pure case can be modified to redistribute among covered workers (for example, through redistribution across accounts) or to covered workers from other sources outside the pension system. For example, deposits into workers' accounts may be made from general revenue (as in Mexico's public pension system), or the government may establish a tax-financed guaranteed minimum pension (as in Chile before the reform discussed in Chapter 13), or tax-financed contributions may be made on behalf of nonworkers caring for their children (as in Sweden). The pricing of annuities (for example, unisex pricing versus separate pricing for men and women) also affects the relationship between an individual's contributions and expected benefits.

In a fully actuarial system, the relationship between contributions and benefits is preserved as workers make different choices about the age at which to start their pensions. For those who start receiving benefits later, assets have more time to accumulate, and the expected number of years of annuitized benefits decreases; the monthly benefit is increased accordingly. For those who start receiving benefits earlier, assets have less time to accumulate, the expected number of years of annuitized benefits increases, and the monthly benefit is decreased accordingly.

Defined-benefit plans. In a defined-benefit plan, pension benefits are based not on the worker's accumulation, but on some combination of the worker's wage history and length of service and the plan's benefit rules, particularly its accrual rate. A key design feature is the way wages enter the benefit formula. In a final-salary plan, benefits are based on wages in the worker's final year or final few years. At the other extreme, the pension can be based on the worker's wages over his or her entire career (as in Sweden's public pension system) or most of it (the U.S. Social Security system considers a worker's highest-paid thirty-five years). Where benefits depend on earnings over a long period, the wages entering the benefit formula are indexed to economy-wide wages, either explicitly (as in Germany) or implicitly (as in Sweden), although this was less common in the past (or possibly, as in Finland, indexed to a mix of prices and wages). In either case a key determinant of a person's annuity is, in effect, his or her past wages indexed until retirement age.[8] If the plan is financed through worker contributions, the contribution is generally set as a fraction of the worker's wage (typically with

8. In the United States wages are explicitly indexed to wages, but only up to age 60, with no indexing beyond that point. This limit on indexing has been criticized, for example by Diamond and Orszag (2005a).

limits on the portion of the wage that is taxed); the role of the plan's sponsor is to ensure that the fraction is set large enough so that financing balances expenditure.

Defined-benefit plans have rules about how the level of benefits changes when a worker delays claiming a pension. Such adjustments may or may not be actuarially balanced. Although adjustments in the public pensions of some countries are approximately actuarial (for example, in the United States for ages from 62 until the "normal" retirement age), most systems offer smaller-than-actuarial increases in benefit, and often increasingly so at older ages.[9]

3.3 ADJUSTING CONTRIBUTIONS AND BENEFITS OVER TIME

The need for adjustment. Future earnings, future rates of return, future life expectancies, and future growth of the labor force are all uncertain. Thus any system must adapt to unexpected developments. A pure defined-contribution system adjusts benefits to maintain balance,[10] whereas a pure defined-benefit system adjusts future contribution rates or injects funds from outside the system. In practice, systems regularly adjust both contributions and benefits (and, in public systems, government transfers) to preserve financial balance. Moreover, since legislation will occur in the future, the design of a public system can influence future political outcomes. Employer plans are also subject to future changes.

Thus the relation between contributions and benefits needs to be considered not only at a point in time, for example for a given cohort of workers or pensioners, but also over time, for example in response to rising longevity, falling fertility, or a baby boom. In part our discussion of risks immediately below is a discussion of the relative treatment of different generations. So, too, is our discussion of funding in Chapter 6. Choosing methods of adjustment poses a range of questions:

- Should some adjustment be built into legislation, so that it is automatic, or should it be managed fully through periodic legislative changes?
- Should adjustment take place through changes in contributions, changes in benefits, or a mix?
- What relative weights should be given to the various social purposes of pensions, and how should the achievement of those purposes be weighed against the costs of achieving them?

We discuss this topic in more detail in section 5.4.

Who bears the risk? Since they rely on different forms of adjustment, different systems share risks differently among workers, employers, pensioners, and taxpayers, and between current and future generations.

A pure defined-contribution plan leaves the individual facing the wide range of risks, discussed in section 4.2.3, associated with variable returns to pension savings and variable future earnings. These risks are absorbed by changes in the individual's

---

9. Mortality rates rise with age; thus, to be actuarial, the percentage benefit increase should also rise with age.

10. However, after the purchase of annuities from an insurance company, the insurance company bears the risk, subject to its solvency.

monthly pension benefit. The pure case can be modified to allow the sharing of risks more broadly: annuities shift the risks associated with individual longevity away from the individual pensioner, typically through an insurance company; governments can offer various sorts of guarantee, including a minimum pension, or other types of transfer.

Defined-benefit systems can be run by employers or by the government. In a pure employer-based defined-benefit plan, the risk of varying returns to pension assets falls on the employer, and hence on some combination of the company's workers (through effects on wages), its shareholders and taxpayers (through effects on profits), its customers (through effects on prices), and its past or future workers (if the company uses surpluses from some periods to boost benefits or reduce worker contributions in others). Deviations from a pure arrangement can include government guarantees or transfers, for example through a government pension regulatory agency, and risks can be shared with beneficiaries through adjustment of benefits. In a pure public defined-benefit system, the risk of adverse outcomes falls on current and future contributors; if a trust fund has been built up, past contributors have provided resources for absorbing risk; if funds are taken from general revenue, some of the risk falls on current taxpayers or, through government borrowing, on future taxpayers. Thus, in contrast with a fully funded defined-contribution system, defined-benefit systems can share risks across generations. In practice, governments at times change benefits as well as contributions in the face of imbalances; thus beneficiaries share in the risk as well.

A key difference between the two approaches is in how widely risks are shared. Defined-benefit systems generally spread risks more widely than defined-contribution systems: risks on the revenue side do not fall only on the worker; risk can be addressed both through changes in contributions and through changes in benefits; and, importantly, risks can be shared across generations. Box 5.3 sets out a broader comparison of defined-contribution and defined-benefit arrangements; risk sharing is discussed more fully in section 7.3.

3.4 NOTIONAL DEFINED-CONTRIBUTION PENSIONS

The idea. A recent innovation internationally, notional defined-contribution (NDC) plans parallel traditional defined-contribution plans in the sense that a pension entitlement is accumulated, but differ from a funded system in two important respects: the interest rate is set by government rules (NDC plans are public programs), not market returns; and the accumulation is only notional, in that the system is not fully funded and may be entirely PAYG.[11] In such a system:

- Each worker contributes a prescribed percentage of his or her earnings each period, which is credited to a notional individual account; that is, the government "pretends" that financial assets are added to the account dollar for dollar with contributions. In fact, some or all of the contributions are used to pay benefits to current retirees as in a PAYG system.

- The cumulative contents of the notional account are credited with a notional interest rate, calculated according to a formula specified in legislation to protect the long-term sustainability of the system.

11. For fuller discussions of NDC systems, see Palmer (2005) and, on the example of the NDC system in Sweden, Sundén (2006).

- At retirement the value of the worker's notional accumulation is converted into an annuity in a way that mimics actuarial principles: benefits over the worker's expected remaining lifetime (given mortality rates based on the worker's birth cohort and age) are set equal in present value to the worker's notional accumulation, using the notional interest rate as the discount rate. The method of determining the mortality rates used for this calculation is also set by the government and generally differs from the way an insurance company would operate.
- The account balance is called "notional" because it is for recordkeeping only; the plan does not own matching funds invested in the financial market.[12]

The definition of the notional interest rate is an important design feature. It can be related to the rate of growth of average wages, w, or to the rate of growth of the wage bill, wL, where L is the number of workers. In a system that uses wL as the notional interest rate, pensions adjust more to adverse macroeconomic and demographic shocks, thus helping to protect the solvency of the system. A system that uses w as the notional interest rate protects replacement rates relative to a worker's previous earnings, and hence the relative living standards of pensioners, but may require periodic adjustment to maintain financial balance.

It is important to be clear that NDC pensions, whatever their other advantages, do not per se solve the demographic problem. In Sweden the effect of introducing NDC pensions was to reduce pension benefits: "replacement rates are likely to be lower in the new system compared to the old" (Sundén 2006, p. 144). What NDC pensions do is to bring in a system in which it is less likely that expenditure exceeds income; the resulting level of benefits may or may not be compatible with effective poverty relief or adequate replacement rates. As with defined-contribution pensions, there are multiple ways of incorporating a redistributive element, for example by providing a minimum pension guarantee or by subsidizing the pension contributions of people who are out of the labor force because they are caring for young children or are unemployed.

NDC, defined-contribution, and defined-benefit systems: How different are they? On the face of it, NDC plans, where benefits depend on a history of contributions, are very different from standard defined-benefit arrangements, where benefits depend on a history of earnings. The reality is more subtle.[13] Suppose a person's earnings in a particular year are 70 percent of average earnings that year; call that variable x. Call the average value of x over n years $\bar{x}$, which is thus a measure of the person's earnings each year indexed by the rate of wage growth. $\bar{x}$ can be the earnings base on which pension benefits in a defined-benefit plan are determined. If n relates only to earnings in the last year before retirement, the plan is a final-salary plan. In contrast, if n spans an entire working life, it is a defined-benefit plan in which pensions are based on lifetime earnings compounded each year by the rate of wage growth. This is the approach in France and Germany, which use point systems that achieve this pattern. In a funded defined-contribution plan, annual contributions are compounded by the return on assets (for short, the interest rate), again over a person's working life. If the interest rate and the rate of wage

---

12. Preserving the abbreviation, NDC pensions have also been referred to as nonfinancial defined-contribution pensions.

13. For a fuller discussion, see Diamond (2002, pp. 55–57).

growth are similar and the contribution rate does not change, the difference between mature defined-contribution and defined-benefit systems is minor; the difference is even smaller between a lifetime defined-benefit plan and an NDC plan with an accrual rate equal to wage growth.[14]

In the limit, assume a defined-benefit plan with the following three features: it bases benefits on a person's entire working life, its accrual rate is age-related (contributions in early years have a heavier weight, analogous to compound interest in a defined-contribution plan), and it offers an annuity rate that is announced only at the time that a person retires. In that case defined-benefit and NDC arrangements converge.[15] The conclusion to be drawn is that the differences among types of plan depend very much on the detailed design of each.

3.5 CONTROVERSIES

There is much agreement among pension analysts about many of the features of a good system, and particularly about what sort of features a well-designed system does *not* have. But there are also controversies.

What role for funding and for mandatory individual funded accounts? Among the many controversies, two related ones stand out, both of which are analyzed in Chapter 6.

- Should pensions be PAYG or funded?[16] and
- What role should be given to mandatory funded individual accounts?

Chile (discussed in detail in Chapters 12 and 13) has become a famous exemplar in the debates both about funding and about mandatory funded accounts. In 1981 Chile moved from a public system of traditional PAYG pensions to one of individual funded accounts. This strategy, in essence a form of privatization, underpinned the World Bank's advocacy of the "multipillar model" (World Bank 1994) with a significant mandatory funded individual account component. The demonstration effect of Chile and the advocacy of the World Bank were powerful, leading many countries, notably in Latin America and in Central and Eastern Europe, to adopt mandatory individual accounts as a small or a large part of their systems, and others are debating their introduction.[17]

In assessing this debate, it helps to be clear about what is controversial. At its simplest, the World Bank multipillar model has three elements (also called, with some mixing of metaphors, "tiers"): the first is a public PAYG plan, either a contributory or a universal system,[18] or a means-tested backup to the other parts of the system;

---

14. NDC plans, however, unlike defined-benefit plans in general, adjust benefits on the basis of the life expectancy of the cohort. Some defined-benefit plans, for example in Finland and Germany, do include adjustments for demography.

15. On the similarity between the German defined-benefit plan and an NDC plan, see Börsch-Supan and Wilke (2006).

16. For contrasting views on the relative merits of PAYG and funded systems, see the references in Chapter 1, footnote 6.

17. For trenchant assessments of the multipillar model in Latin America, see Arenas de Mesa and Mesa-Lago (2006), Gill, Packard, and Yermo (2005) and World Bank (2006a, 2006b); see also the discussion in Box 10.1 and section 11.3.

18. A universal pension system is one that pays benefits at retirement age regardless of the beneficiary's work history. In that sense, the system introduced in Chile in 2008 is universal.

the second is mandatory participation in a privately managed, funded defined-contribution plan, usually run on a fairly strictly actuarial basis; the third comprises voluntary contributions to funded plans. Although the level and design of the first-tier public pension is a matter for discussion, its desirability is not; likewise nobody seriously questions the desirability of suitably regulated voluntary private pensions—the third tier. The point of acute controversy concerns the middle tier: whether a pension reform should introduce mandatory participation in a system of private individual accounts, or introduce mandatory participation in a funded defined-benefit plan, or mandate participation in a public PAYG plan aimed at more than poverty relief, or leave such arrangements voluntary (that is, have no middle tier). Although the degree of funding as opposed to PAYG and the use of individual accounts are separate issues, in practice they are linked in the debate, and the controversy focuses largely on the desirability or otherwise of the second tier – a question that recurs throughout this book.

The debate has different dimensions. There are

- Debates about what is the correct underlying economic model, for example how to model individual saving behavior;
- Debates about empirical magnitudes, for example about labor supply elasticities and about life expectancy in 2050;
- Debates about institutional capacity: Does the country in question have the capacity to collect and record contributions for a complex public system? Does government have the capacity to regulate financial markets? Does the private sector have the capacity to manage funds and administer individual accounts cost-effectively? Does the insurance industry have the capacity to provide annuities on good terms? Does the government have the capacity to regulate insurance companies? Will a government agency invest better or worse than many individual investors?
- Debates about the political economy of reform, for example whether citizens regard their future pension as more soundly based on a promise by government to use future revenue to pay pensions, or on themselves as owners and private financial intermediaries as managers of capital on which to draw to finance their consumption in retirement;
- Debates about government behavior, particularly the impact of pension design on the rest of the government budget; and
- Debates about ideology, notably about the role of government.

A public PAYG system arguably has considerable advantages, including the capacity to use social insurance to address uncertainty in ways that a strictly actuarial system cannot, and the ability to redistribute within a generation and across generations. On the other hand, it can be argued that the ability of government to set unsustainable rules and to change the terms of its pension promises is one of the great dangers of public pensions. A second debate, discussed shortly, concerns the relative weights given to different objectives.

Discussion of different pension regimes has at times become confused, because some writers blur the different elements of the debate. It is an error, for example, to carry a political economy argument for reform across different countries without testing its applicability in each country. An even more egregious error is to blur the distinction between an efficiency argument and an ideological one.

Policy may be flawed also because it is based on one element of the debate, ignoring others. A sound theoretical construct may fail if the necessary institutional capacity is absent, or if, for ideological reasons, political support for the reform is inadequate. These issues arise repeatedly in the following chapters.

What weights should be given to the different objectives of pensions? A second debate, often implicit, is about the relative weights to be given to the objectives of consumption smoothing, insurance, poverty relief, and redistribution. Some writers argue that an additional objective is to promote economic growth. Pension design can favor generous poverty relief and significant redistribution to low earners, or it can give greater weight to consumption smoothing, accordingly favoring benefits that are more strongly actuarial.

A specific question in the debates is whether pensions should be defined-contribution or defined-benefit; the issue is discussed in more detail in Box 5.3. As already noted, a pure funded defined-contribution arrangement does little to address poverty relief and, the important longevity risk apart, offers no insurance (for example, against uncertain lifetime income prospects); such pensions thus give heavy weight to the consumption smoothing objective.

NDC pensions are a PAYG analogue of funded defined-contribution plans. The NDC construct is relevant to the debate about weights, in that a pure NDC system concentrates on consumption smoothing, although, not being fully funded, it necessarily involves intergenerational redistribution. Thus NDC pensions are also relevant to the debate about PAYG versus funding: if a country wishes to have an element in its pension system that offers fairly pure consumption smoothing, there are circumstances where an NDC system might be more appropriate than a funded defined-contribution system. One such case, China, is discussed in Chapter 15.

4

▷

The Basic Economics of Pensions

Pension systems have the primary objectives discussed in Chapter 2. But pension systems do not exist in isolation; they have important effects on the economy, notably on labor and capital markets. The design of pensions should take account of those effects—the subject of Chapters 4–8.

It is not possible to have a mandatory system of pensions without distorting the labor market. Analysis has to recognize the trade-off between narrow efficiency in labor markets, on the one hand, and achieving the goals of the pension system, on the other. Thus the real issue is to balance the efficiency goal with other goals such as poverty relief, not to pretend that there is a way to accomplish all those goals without distortions. Meanwhile, although the vocabulary of a trade-off between labor market efficiency and other goals is useful, it is worth remembering that, with incomplete markets and imperfect decision making, certain government interventions can improve labor market efficiency (broadly defined) while simultaneously advancing other goals. What is needed, therefore, is second-best analysis (see glossary), which considers the multiple impacts of the entire program for retirement income. Not all of these issues are of immediate importance in those developing countries where public pension coverage is currently small and employment in the public sector regulated. But even there it is important to set up a pension system that adapts easily to the desirable long-term evolution of the labor market. These topics are discussed in Chapter 5.

A mandatory pension system also affects national saving. An important issue, therefore, in countries where saving is low, is the extent to which the system is funded in a way that increases national saving, and so increases future output (or at least avoids decreasing saving too much). Chapter 6 presents a framework for thinking about the extent of funding, recognizing that different degrees of funding, from none to full, may be the right choice, depending on the country's saving needs.

Although private insurance markets, along with capital markets, are important institutions for sharing risks, a public pension system offers valuable ways of risk sharing that are not available to the private market; a public system can also overcome some significant limitations of private insurance markets. And a mandatory pension system affects the income distribution within and across generations in ways that vary with different pension designs. Chapter 7 discusses redistribution and risk sharing. And all these effects can affect men and women differently, as discussed in Chapter 8.

It assists analysis to have in mind three propositions, all of which arise repeatedly in the following chapters:

- National output matters.
- Imperfect information and imperfect decision making are widespread.
- Both pension plans and individuals saving for retirement face large risks.

A fourth important point is that pension plans and individual saving arrangements all incur administrative costs, which can be high. It also assists analysis to have in mind a number of common analytical errors, including excessive focus on a single objective, treatment of one part of the pension system in isolation, improper use of first-best analysis, improper use of steady-state analysis, and failure to consider distributional effects; these are discussed in Box 10.1.

4.1 OUTPUT MATTERS

There are two (and only two) ways for individuals to seek economic security in old age.[1] One is to store current production for future use. But, housing excepted, this approach is inadequate for most consumption needs: it is expensive, it does not address uncertainty (for example, about how a person's tastes might change), and it cannot be applied to services deriving from human capital, notably medical services.

The alternative is for individuals to acquire a claim on future production.[2] There are two broad ways to do so. One is by accumulation: by regularly saving part of his wages, a worker can build up a stock of assets, which he can then sell in order to finance the purchase of goods and services produced by younger people during his retirement. The other is by obtaining a promise: a worker can have an arrangement—with her children, her employer, or the government—that she will be given goods and services produced by younger workers after her retirement. The two main ways of organizing pensions broadly parallel these two types of claim. Funded plans are based on accumulations of financial assets, and pay-as-you-go (PAYG) systems on promissory-type agreements. As discussed in Chapter 3, actual systems can be, and often are, only partly funded and hence a mix of these pure types.

The purpose of pensions is to allow people to continue to consume after they have stopped working. Ultimately, pensioners are interested not in money but in consumption—food, clothing, shelter, medical services, and the other things they need to live. Nearly all consumption is of goods and services produced, domestically or abroad, not long before they are consumed, and therefore by people who are working, not retired. Thus future output is central. The common feature of PAYG and funding is that both are financial mechanisms for organizing claims on that future output.

1. For a fuller discussion, see Barr (2000).
2. The government can also set up a noncontributory pension system that does not link future benefits to earlier contributions.

In macroeconomic terms, although there are differences between the two approaches, those differences should not be exaggerated. The centrality of output remains true in an open economy, as discussed in Box 4.1.

4.2   IMPERFECT CONSUMER INFORMATION AND DECISION MAKING ARE WIDESPREAD

On the microeconomic side, the advantages of consumer sovereignty are predicated on consumers being well informed and on the potential shortcomings of substituting

> ## ▶ Box 4.1 How much difference does an open economy make?
>
> Goods produced in one's home country can be exchanged for goods produced abroad. Goods produced abroad can also be purchased from returns on investments previously made abroad or by selling assets to foreigners. The latter is similar to increasing consumption out of given domestic output by reducing investment. Thus opportunities for trade enhance the availability of consumption in the future, without changing the basic story significantly.
>
> Similarly, savings accumulated to finance retirement can be used to purchase assets abroad as well as assets at home. In considering such investment, a retirement saver would look to see how the foreign asset might provide future consumption at home. Having more investment opportunities gives savers greater scope for diversifying risk. Thus, as with opportunities for foreign trade, opportunities for foreign investment give savers a wider set of options. And both trade and investment across borders affect wages as well.
>
> Of course, population aging affects both anticipated returns on assets and anticipated future wages. And in a global economy with expanded foreign trade and foreign investment, these effects arise more on a worldwide basis than just on a domestic basis. But aging is such a widespread phenomenon, including all of the OECD countries and many others (China being a notable example), that the overall picture is not altered much by this recognition. To illustrate, if British workers use some of their savings to buy shares in Australian firms, they can in retirement use the dividends and sell some of the shares for Australian money. The money can be used either to buy British currency with which to buy British goods, or to buy Australian goods to import to the United Kingdom. However, the success of the policy depends on future production by Australian workers—the policy would fail if they all were to retire; thus the age structure of the population in the destination of wealth holdings matters.
>
> In short, although international diversification is generally helpful, its impact for all but the smallest economies should not be exaggerated. Investors require a risk premium to be induced to invest in a risky asset. And the riskiness of investment in a country may look larger to investors outside the country than to those inside, particularly for a country with underdeveloped financial markets and uncertain politics. There is potential value in investors in two countries investing in each other's industries, in that it allows the risks in both countries to be spread more widely. But it may be expensive for a country to attract investors from abroad. And if a country's capital markets and financial institutions are not well developed, allowing foreigners to invest in one's economy can affect macroeconomic stability, and should be approached carefully.
>
> None of this is an argument against having an open economy: although expanded trade and investment may not be a major solution to population aging, they can raise rates of return and expand opportunities for the individual saver or pension plan. But taking advantage of these opportunities requires that individuals, plan sponsors, and policymakers are all well aware of the potential pitfalls. ◀

government decisions for individual ones. Pensions, however, are complex products, so it is highly questionable to base policy on the assumption that consumers are well informed about them. It is important in this context to distinguish between limited information (that is, lack of information) on the part of consumers, and limited capacity to process information. In the abstract, problems arising from imperfect information can be resolved by providing the necessary information, even though in practice not everyone will pay attention to it. However, where complexity results in imperfect information processing, as discussed in Box 4.2, information, even if provided, will not be very helpful. It is possible to buy both information and information processing in the form of professional advice, but this can be expensive and sometimes unsatisfactory: some "experts" have additional incentives beyond giving the best advice, nor is it clear how an underinformed consumer would distinguish between better and worse advisers, or even between honest professionals and charlatans. An additional set of arguments against naive reliance on consumer sovereignty, drawing on recent lessons from behavioral economics, is discussed in Box 9.6.

Some information problems can be reduced by public education. However, evidence suggests that it is difficult and expensive to provide information that succeeds in altering behavior; and where the problem is one of information processing, public education is likely to be the wrong instrument, since the level of education needed can

▶ Box 4.2 Deviations from first-best

Box 2.1 set out the simple theory of saving over time in a first-best world with a well-functioning market for savings. The underlying logic continues to apply in an economically richer environment (one with uncertain variable returns to savings) in the setting of a model where all markets needed for retirement savings exist and function well. In those circumstances, consumer choice and competitive markets maximize welfare. Pensions, however, face a number of serious deviations from such a theoretical world.

Imperfect information. Although complete markets can help people adapt to uncertainties about the future, they require people to understand the uncertainties they face and the options that markets offer in order to make good use of those options. In fact, individuals are imperfectly informed in several ways:

- Some individuals have a poor sense of the risks and uncertainties they face, for example about their longevity.
- Individuals are unlikely to be well informed about complex products such as defined-contribution pensions, which are based on an array of financial institutions and financial instruments. Many do not understand basic concepts in finance: Orszag and Stiglitz (2001, p. 37) quote the chairman of the U.S. Securities and Exchange Commission as stating that over 50 percent of Americans did not know the difference between a stock and a bond. The problem also has distributional implications, since the worst-informed people are disproportionately among the least well off; that is, information poverty and financial poverty are highly correlated.
- Defined-benefit plans are also complex products that participants may understand only incompletely. Complexity is a particular problem with corporate plans, where labor mobility and any financial problems the firm faces have implications for pensions that can be hard to see. Complexity may be less of a problem with a public system, although arrangements in some countries—the United

Kingdom being an example—are sufficiently complex to be very hard to understand. And public systems are likely to need to be adjusted to changing demographic and economic conditions and may also change with political circumstances, adding to their complexity.

- For some purposes it is useful to recognize that the problem may not be lack of information but what New (1999) calls an information processing problem. An information problem in a given market—say, the market for automobiles—can be resolved by providing the necessary information, in this case the characteristics of different models of automobile. Once informed, the individual can then make his or her own choices. With an information processing problem, in contrast, the problem is too complex for many agents to make rational choices even when they have the necessary information. For example, judging between two automobiles of differing fuel economy involves calculations and estimates, projecting both miles to be driven and future fuel prices, that some buyers might lack the sophistication (or the time) to make. Similar problems can arise in any market, particularly where the time horizon is long, where the good or service involves complex probabilities, or where information about the features of the product is inherently complex. All of these conditions characterize most pension products.

For these and other reasons, people can be myopic, giving a justification for compulsion. The problem is not trivial, and implies that the simple assumption of rational utility maximization may not hold in the market for pensions.

Incomplete markets. Even for a well-informed consumer with good information processing, actual markets may be limited in their ability to provide products tailored to his or her exact needs and wants. In the case of pensions, the markets for indexed contracts, for example, are thin. Asymmetric information in the insurance market makes perfect insurance impossible. When insurance is linked to employment, labor market decisions must be distorted if workers are to have insurance—another manifestation of an incomplete market. Indeed, a theorem holds that if there is asymmetric information, the *absence* of distorting incentives is a sign of nonoptimal provision of insurance. This can make it hard to judge whether the design of a particular insurance product is optimal for a particular worker. Insurance firms, meanwhile, must cope with potential consumers with different risks, and so different costs, should the firm sell insurance to them. This problem of adverse selection can be eased by making insurance mandatory. Generally, insurance products marketing is highly costly, leaving the possibility of government provision of a uniform product at much lower cost.

Progressive taxation is a further deviation from first-best. In comparing defined-contribution and defined-benefit plans, it is not possible to say that one approach dominates the other if labor market distortions are present:

> With a progressive annual income tax and age-earnings profiles that are generally increasing in real terms, the marginal income tax rate is rising with age, on average. Thus, a well-designed DB [defined benefit] system may well have better labor market outcomes since the overall tax burden, income tax plus net tax from social security, will vary less over the life-cycle. That is, income taxes are lower on the young and net social security taxes are higher. Therefore, without a detailed calculation, one cannot reach an efficiency conclusion. In any case the difference is likely to be much smaller than the difference between DB systems with long and short averaging periods. (Diamond 2002, p. 57)

All these deviations from first-best call into question the simple model of market choice and competition. The resulting problems with the exercise of consumer choice are taken up in section 9.3, particularly Box 9.6.

be beyond what is feasible.[3] Given the high potential cost of some mistaken choices, imperfect information creates an efficiency justification for stringent regulation to protect consumers in an area where they are not well enough informed to protect themselves.

Beyond imperfect acquisition and processing of information, there are issues of the quality of decision making as it affects both workers and their families. Workers may make decisions about saving or annuitization that are not time consistent (that is, decisions today based on today's preferences, which might be regretted tomorrow even if events turn out as expected), or their decisions may fail to pay sufficient attention to the future needs of other family members. These circumstances provide a justification for government intervention, as indeed has been recognized for centuries, for example through restrictions on the bequest of estates to protect widows.

These and other deviations from first-best (Box 4.2) can call into question the welfare gains from more choice and competition in some circumstances. Yet identification of shortcomings of private markets becomes an argument for intervention only when there is good reason to believe that the intervention will be sufficiently well executed. Pension systems have several characteristics that make them good candidates for mandates beyond the regulation of financial markets, and consumer markets generally.

First, government mandates generally involve more uniformity of outcomes than occurs with a market offering wide individual choice. Where needs and tastes differ considerably, this can be a serious shortcoming. However, in saving for retirement and annuitization there is considerable uniformity: what is needed—secure income in old age—is qualitatively the same for all. What remains of the problem can be minimized if government mandates only a foundation for retirement income: mandatory contributions can be set below what will meet the needs of many people, leaving voluntary private arrangements to fill the gap between the mandate and the ideal for each individual—a gap that some people, even if not all, will seek to fill.

Second, pension systems can have clear rules and so can readily be reviewed by people outside government. This strengthens the incentive for the government to do a good job. Thus shortcomings in individual decision making do not lead to the conclusion that voluntary pension arrangements should be banned, but rather that on their own they are unlikely to be sufficient, and that their regulation is an important part of striking a good balance between mandatory and voluntary.

4.3 PENSION SYSTEMS FACE LARGE RISKS THAT ARE HARD TO PREDICT

Pension plans face a series of risks:

- *Economic risk:* Unforeseen macroeconomic events (shocks) can affect output, prices, or both. Since both funding and PAYG are simply different ways of organizing

---

3. This should not be taken as a patronizing remark by two academic economists. Many people, including some of the most highly educated, would not be able to become well informed about the detailed operation of pensions, and, even if they could, many would not regard the acquisition of the necessary knowledge and skills as welfare enhancing compared with relying on others. Parallel arguments apply to medical care.

claims on future output, it should not be surprising that output shocks are likely to affect any pension arrangement.

- *Demographic risk:* Shocks to fertility, mortality, or other demographic variables also affect all pension arrangements (see section 6.3.3) by affecting market prices and quantities, and thus pension revenue and claims.
- *Political risk:* Political uncertainty affects all pension arrangements because all depend critically—albeit in different ways—on effective and stable government.

Although these sources of risks affect all pensions, whether funded or not, their effects are not identical. For example, fertility risks affect both funded defined-contribution and unfunded defined-benefit pensions, but the effects on each are different and, in the typical absence of automatic adjustments, may be more pressing for unfunded defined-benefit systems. Although the intention of social insurance is to spread risks more widely than the market can manage, this spreading may be done badly. The general expectation that an unfunded defined-benefit system with limited automatic adjustments will require more frequent legislative change can represent more political risk. Incorporating well-designed automatic adjustments can reduce the need for and extent of later legislated changes.

Alongside these common risks, the presence of funds to be organized and managed results in additional risks:

- *Management risk:* This can arise through incompetence or fraud, which imperfectly informed consumers generally cannot monitor effectively.
- *Investment risk:* Pension accumulations held in the stock market until retirement are vulnerable to market fluctuations. Pension accumulations held in nominal bonds are vulnerable, in addition, to unanticipated inflation.
- *Longevity risk:* Holding assets that are not in the form of an annuity leaves the individual facing the risk of outliving his or her assets.
- *Annuities market risk:* For a given pension accumulation, the value of an annuity depends on a person's remaining life expectancy and on the rate of return the insurance company can expect over those years, and thus involves both investment risk and longevity risk.

Private insurance markets can help individuals address some of the risks inherent in preparing for retirement. But there are limits to private insurance—from adverse selection, from selling costs, from the limited ability of consumers to make good decisions, and from incomplete markets for risk sharing, particularly across cohorts. With social insurance, as discussed in section 7.3, the institutional structure is explicitly intended to share risks more broadly.

4.4   COSTS OF ADMINISTRATION CAN SIGNIFICANTLY AFFECT PENSIONS

The previous arguments all apply even in a frictionless world. But analysis must also take into account the fact that any method of arranging for future consumption has administrative costs. These include the costs of keeping records and communicating with workers and the costs of transactions insofar as there are accumulations of assets or purchases of benefit streams. Different ways of organizing future consumption have very different costs and thus reduce that consumption to varying degrees. For example, the individual mutual fund market is far more expensive—has higher costs per dollar of assets—than the institutional mutual fund market. The topic is taken up in section 9.2, especially Box 9.4.

5

▷

Pensions and Labor markets

This chapter starts with an overview of the impacts of pension systems on the labor market (section 5.1), in particular the important role of labor mobility, and the balance between mandatory and voluntary pensions. The next two sections examine the implications of these impacts for pension design. Section 5.2 discusses pension design in the accruals phase, that is, how a person builds up an entitlement to pension benefits during working life, and section 5.3 considers how benefits are determined once a person starts to receive a pension. Both sections 5.2 and 5.3 assume a pension system in financial balance. Section 5.4 discusses how to adjust a pension system over time in the face of any imbalance.

5.1 THE PENSION SYSTEM AS A WHOLE

Taking a holistic view. The impact of a pension system on the labor market depends on the design of the system as a whole, not on any one part in isolation. This observation has two dimensions. First, when considering the impact of the system, one has to consider all of its parts simultaneously, along with all other explicit and implicit taxes on earnings. Analyzing a single part of the system while ignoring the rest can result in analytical errors. Second, the pension system is designed in recognition of multiple objectives, as detailed in Chapter 2. Normative analysis needs to consider these multiple objectives along with the impacts on the efficiency of the labor market of pursuing them. It gives a distorted picture to consider only efficiency as narrowly defined (deadweight losses and the like) while ignoring broader aspects of efficiency such as insurance and other objectives such as poverty relief and redistribution. For example, a basic, flat-rate pension helps with poverty relief and offers insurance to workers with low lifetime earnings, whereas individual accounts concentrate on consumption smoothing. Thus some combination of the two, along with some level of minimum income guarantee, can address all of these objectives. Labor market incentives—affecting both work effort during a career and the choice of when to retire—are influenced by the system as a whole, and its evaluation should include its consumption smoothing effects, its insurance effects, and its redistributive effects.

In developed countries, coverage of the pension system, whether through public provision or mandated private pensions, is close to universal. In less developed countries it is common for coverage to be less complete. In that case, alongside the considerations commonly addressed in the literature on developed countries, analysis must also consider movement of workers between covered and uncovered sectors and possible redistribution between covered and uncovered workers. Projection of the future of the system needs to consider the eventual extension of coverage, with its social effects and financial consequences (see Box 7.2).

The importance of labor mobility. Labor mobility is essential for an efficient labor market. Pension design should therefore pay particular attention to limiting impediments to labor supply generally, and to labor mobility in particular—topics that permeate the discussion in this chapter. To that end, pensions should be portable in the face of at least four types of movement by a worker: from one employer to another, from one geographical area to another, between the public and the private sector (including self-employment), and between uncovered (rural, informal) and covered (urban, formal) sectors.[1] Such portability is achieved most readily when the system has a uniform structure across the covered population, both across localities and across sectors.[2]

In developed economies some workers remain with a single employer for most of their career, perhaps having moved among employers early in their working life before settling into a long-term job. But this pattern is far from universal. In the United States, for example, only a quarter of 55- to 64-year-old men have been with the same employer for twenty years or more. The numbers are considerably higher in Europe, but even there it is not the overwhelming pattern. On a flow basis the movement of workers from job to job, and in and out of the labor force, is large. In the United States, 3.4 percent of workers leave their jobs each month. Many move directly to new jobs; others experience a spell of unemployment before finding new work; some, particularly those with small children, move out of and back into the labor force; some leave the labor force permanently. Meanwhile other workers are seeking work for the first time.

These large movements, which are general to developed economies, are important for the efficiency of the economy. New and growing firms need to find suitable workers. Firms in decline need to shed labor if they are to avoid bankruptcy. Workers need to move from jobs where their potential output is of little value to jobs where their productivity is higher. Movement can be initiated by the employer or by the worker. The incentives for workers to change jobs or stop working depend on a range of factors, including the design of unemployment benefits and any potential loss in eventual retirement benefits: the public pension, any mandatory second-tier pension, and any voluntary pension.[3] All the elements of the pension system are relevant to

---

1. Preservation of accrued pension claims is needed for workers who move from the covered to the uncovered sector, for later return to the covered sector or entitlement to an eventual pension. In addition, some uncovered workers might contribute to a voluntary defined-contribution plan.

2. However, as discussed in Chapter 15, in a country as large and diverse as China the system should accommodate regional variation.

3. The term "voluntary" is used with different meanings here (see the glossary). A voluntary individual pension will not limit mobility; in contrast, a plan run voluntarily by an employer, depending on its design, can be a major impediment to mobility, as illustrated in Box 5.2.

labor mobility, and so all should be designed to be compatible with labor flows from less productive to more productive uses. The efficiency of the incentives depends on all parts of the system working together.

In transition economies such as those in Central and Eastern Europe and China, the labor system is moving from a central planning model, where workers who succeeded in getting jobs with large state-owned enterprises could count on staying there for life, to a market model, which relies on labor mobility to sustain economic growth. Mobility concerns therefore loom especially large in pension design.

The balance between mandatory and voluntary pensions. An important element in any pension system is the extent to which contributions are mandatory. Voluntary pensions accommodate more choices for workers, including workers with

- Different preferences about the time path of saving for retirement and about the balance of living standards in old age compared with those while working
- Differences in the timing of key life events, for example, whether children are born earlier or later
- Different degrees of risk aversion
- Different working conditions, so that industries where people work in harsh conditions, or where working life is short for other reasons, can provide for earlier retirement
- Different regional and private initiatives.

The mix of voluntary and mandatory must strike a balance between, on the one hand, the inefficiencies that arise from a uniform mandate that takes incomplete account of such differences in preferences and constraints, and on the other, the gaps that arise if the mandatory system is small. Consideration of the appropriate size of the mandatory system focuses on the adequate provision of retirement income and on the system's impacts on the labor market, both of which will vary across workers.

To establish a theoretical benchmark, consider the saving behavior of an individual optimizing over the life cycle in a first-best world (see glossary) in which all pension and saving decisions are voluntary. Such an individual will have different saving rates at different times in his or her career, will invest in some combination of assets with their risk varying over time, and will purchase an annuity of some sort with at least part of his or her accumulation. Lifetime consumption—and hence saving—adjust over time as the individual's lifetime budget constraint changes in response to changes in current earnings, changes in anticipated future earnings, the realized and anticipated rates of return on assets, and the emergence of spending opportunities and needs. If, for example, the rate of return on assets increases, an individual who regards the increase as long term might respond by reducing his or her retirement saving out of earnings, since a higher return makes it possible to achieve a given replacement rate with less savings, or the individual might respond by retiring earlier.

In contrast, a mandatory system typically does not adjust the contribution rate to changes in earnings (apart from minimum and maximum levels of covered earnings) or in the return on assets, which can vary from person to person. Nor does it typically adjust for age, although financial needs generally vary with age as younger workers finance the purchase of a home and the rearing of children. Instead there is a relatively uniform saving

▶ Box 5.1 The incidence of pension contributions

In strictly economic terms, it is inappropriate in a market economy to attach too much importance to whether pension contributions are paid by the worker or the employer. Mandatory contributions imposed on employers generally have the effect of reducing the wages they offer workers: the employer passes on the cost of the contribution in the form of a lower wage. Thus the worker ultimately bears the burden whether the worker or the employer pays.

There are two exceptions. First, a change in the contribution rate may shift some of the burden to the employer in the short run, because it takes time for wages to adjust. Second, if there is a mandatory minimum wage, the employer may not be able to lower the wage enough to pass all of the contribution costs on to a minimum wage worker.

Analyzing contributions in political economy terms can give a different result. Shared contributions may be perceived as being fairer and so might be politically more durable. ◀

rule that does not respond even to predictable changes in the liquidity needs of all workers over the life cycle, much less to individually experienced changes in earnings, asset returns, and spending needs.[4] Some countries therefore keep their mandatory saving rate low, to allow room for individual adjustment through additional voluntary contributions.

On the other hand, a mandatory component prevents the worst errors of inadequate saving and annuitization (see Box 9.6) and guards against free riding by people who fail to save, intending to rely on the guaranteed minimum benefit. Thus there are real gains from a contribution rate for a mandatory system that is significant but not too high—that leaves room for additional voluntary arrangements by individuals or employers. However, not all developed countries do a good job of selecting that balance. Contribution rates vary considerably, and a high contribution rate may indicate a larger-than-optimal mandatory element. And as Box 5.1 explains, what matters is the total contribution rate, more than its division between worker and employer.

5.2 BENEFIT DESIGN DURING WORKING LIFE

Two issues are particularly relevant to the labor market effects of pensions during the accruals phase. One is the treatment of earnings in different years in determining the pension benefit (section 5.2.1); here a particular concern is with plans that base the amount of benefit on the worker's final salary. The other is the extent to which a strictly actuarial relationship between contributions and benefits is or is not advantageous (section 5.2.2).

5.2.1 The treatment of earnings in different years

The way earnings in different years affect a person's pension benefit can have a powerful influence on his or her labor market behavior. Two related questions stand out: Should the benefit depend on a person's entire contributions record or only on a subset of years? And what should be the relative weights given to contributions in different years?

---

4. An exception is Switzerland, which has different contribution rates above and below age 35; some countries exempt low levels of earnings from the payroll tax or offset the payroll taxes of low earners with refundable income tax credits.

In a defined-contribution plan, pension benefits are based on a worker's contributions over an entire career. Thus each year counts, and the effect of each year's contribution depends on (1) its size (likely to be smaller early in a career), (2) the year in which it was made (given positive real returns, the benefit will be higher the earlier the contribution), and (3) the rate of return on accumulating assets.

At the other extreme, in a final-salary defined-benefit plan, benefits are generally based on the number of years of service and on salary in the final year or final few years of work. Thus again each year counts, since years of service matter, but the final year, or last few years, have a heavy weight, since those are the only earnings that enter the benefit formula. Thus, although the prospect of a pension provides an incentive for employment in all years (up to a possible cap on the number of years that count), the incentive to seek additional earnings is stronger in the final year or years and considerably weaker earlier.

As a third example, an NDC pension bases benefits on contributions in all years, with the weights on different years depending on the notional rate of return. Between the extremes of a final-salary plan and an NDC plan, benefits can depend on an intermediate number of years. A number of countries (such as Sweden and Finland) used to use a limited number of years but have now moved to considering all years. Countries that have traditionally looked at earnings over most of a career have generally retained this aspect of benefit determination. For example, the U.S. Social Security system bases benefits on the best thirty-five earnings years, with earnings in years through age 60 indexed by the economy-wide average wage. On the one hand, this approach can reduce the impact on benefits, and so the work incentive, in years that will not count, or are unlikely to count, in the best thirty-five. On the other hand, it provides insurance against having some years of low earnings in the course of a long career, whether due to bad luck or to choice (such as a return to college or time spent caring for young children).

Analysts agree that a well-designed plan should base benefits on a fairly long period of contributions. Within that consensus it is not clear whether the period should include a person's entire career (as in Sweden) or somewhat less (as in the United States and the United Kingdom). In important respects the choice is determined by the weights given to the different objectives of pension systems. Systems that include an entire career give relatively greater weight to consumption smoothing; including less than a full career allows a worker to exclude years with low or no earnings, thus giving relatively greater weight to insurance and redistribution. We will argue that either of these approaches makes sense, and will explain why pension systems—whether employer-based or public—should not place heavy reliance on final wages in determining a person's pension.

Employer plans. Around the world, employers use pensions to attract and retain workers. Historically, many plans paid benefits at a standard retirement age that depended on length of service and the worker's wage toward the end of his or her career. Such a structure makes it easy for workers to see the advantages of staying with that employer until retirement, and thus serves an important role in labor retention. On the other hand, such arrangements can reduce labor mobility, may create other labor market distortions, and raise equity issues.

A young worker enrolled in such a plan will recognize that the current year of work adds to her length of service, but that her current earnings will not affect the size of her future pension. This weakens the incentive to work extra hours or to take on a harder job at higher pay. There are, of course, countervailing incentives: such a worker might recognize that hard work and accomplishment improve her chances for promotion, and so for a higher wage and hence a larger pension later on.

In contrast, a worker enrolled in the same plan but toward the end of his career might be over-eager to work extra hours, especially if overtime pay enters the benefit calculation (pensions usually depend on base pay rather than total earnings, precisely to limit the excessive use of overtime). An extreme version of this problem arose in Boston, where the public mass transit system bases pensions on the earnings of workers at the end of their career. As a result, older workers do a great deal of the overtime in the system—and have the opportunity because those with seniority have first access to available overtime. This has caused accidents when older workers, putting in too many hours, fell asleep at the controls. A similar problem arises in many large organizations when middle managers give promotions to favored employees toward the end of their careers simply to raise their pension entitlement. This practice endangers no lives but does cheat the company's owners or stockholders (or the taxpayer, if the organization is a government agency). The shorter the period of earnings used in determining benefits, the stronger the incentive for such manipulative collaboration. Thus the issue is one of balance: too short a period creates excessive incentives against work effort earlier in a career, and the opposite later; too long a period penalizes workers (typically lower earners) with patchy earnings records.

Alongside these distortions earlier and later in a career, a second problem with final-salary defined-benefit plans is their effect in locking a worker into employment with that organization. That may well be in the employer's interest, and indeed, historically it was one of the main purposes of that benefit design. In a modern economy, however, the resulting impediments to labor mobility, illustrated in Box 5.2, may have substantial efficiency costs. Moreover, such a design tends to reduce the benefits of workers who choose to move, perhaps for noneconomic reasons, or who are forced to move as a firm downsizes. Again, the issue is one of balance: although major

▶ **Box 5.2 How final-salary defined-benefit plans impede labor mobility**

Final-salary plans can inhibit voluntary labor mobility and can harm workers who have no choice but to change jobs, as the following example shows. Consider a pension plan with an annual accrual rate of 1/80th of final salary per year of service, paid at a standard retirement age. A worker who remains in this plan for twenty years, during which his pay rises from 100 to 200, accumulates a pension entitlement of $(20/80) \times 200 = 50$.

Suppose that, after twenty years, the worker faces a choice of staying in his job or moving to a new job with an identical pension plan, but no transfer of rights from the current plan. Assume that, if he stays, his salary over the next twenty years will rise from 200 to 400, so that his pension entitlement will be $(40/80) \times 400 = 200$. If instead he moves to the new job and gets a similar increase in pay, his pension entitlement in the new job will be $(20/80) \times 400 = 100$.

Now compare the two outcomes. If the worker stays in job A, he retires on a pension of 200; if he moves in mid-career, his final pension is 150: 50 from his twenty years in the first job plus 100 from his twenty years in the second job. In other words, simply moving from one job to another would cost this worker one-quarter of his pension. ◀

impediments are detrimental, mobility does have costs (to employers) as well as benefits. Mobility should be optimized, not maximized.[5]

A third issue relates to the distribution of pension incomes, which favors workers whose earnings rise more rapidly, particularly toward the end of a career. Since highly paid workers tend to have more rapidly rising earnings, a final-salary system tends to favor them more than a system that bases pensions on a longer period of earnings, a tendency that can be heightened by manipulation such as pay increases or promotions at the end of a career. These features can be regarded as unfair. A similar distributional issue arises, but to a much smaller degree, in the choice between price indexing and wage indexing of earnings records (discussed further below), since the two methods weight different years differently. For all these reasons, it is generally more efficient and more equitable if a worker's pension depends on most or all of his or her earnings history.

Alongside the decision whether to base benefits on earnings during most, all, or only some of a worker's career is the more general question of whether pensions should be defined benefit or defined contribution, discussed in more detail in Box 5.3. There has been a trend toward the latter in recent years in a number of countries, including the United States and the United Kingdom. In assessing such a move, a key issue is the treatment of current employees' expectations with respect not only to rights that have already accrued, but also to future accruals.

▶ Box 5.3 Comparing private defined-benefit and defined-contribution plans

Employer pension systems in the United States and the United Kingdom have been moving from defined-benefit to defined-contribution plans. Some analysts criticize this move for placing all of the risk of variable asset returns on workers. Other analysts applaud the change as a way of ending the shortcomings of typical employer defined-benefit plans. What are the relative advantages and drawbacks of each type of plan?

Cash balance plans. To highlight some of the differences, we start with a pension arrangement called a cash balance plan, which is a legally defined institution in the United States. In such a plan, the employer credits a worker's retirement account with a fixed fraction of earnings in each year of work; in addition, a fixed rate of interest, say, 5 percent, is added to the balance each year. On reaching retirement or leaving the firm, the worker may take the balance as a lump sum or use it to buy an annuity, with pricing sometimes organized by the employer. The plan is supposed to be fully funded.

A cash balance plan thus resembles a defined-contribution plan holding only nominal bonds that pay 5 percent.* One difference is that, as in a defined-benefit-plan, the employer has committed to providing benefits according to this rule, but is not required actually to hold 5 percent nominal bonds. Thus the employer has a choice. It can hold nominal bonds that mature when the worker reaches retirement age, thus fully hedging its accrued liability. Or it can invest in some other portfolio that it thinks offers a better combination of risk and return. Thus there can be a tension between the portfolio that hedges accrued legal liability and the portfolio that is most useful for the employer. The choice of a nonhedging portfolio can affect the worker if the employer becomes

(continues next page)

---

5. The cost to the employer if an experienced worker leaves is part of the basis of Arthur Okun's (1981) "invisible handshake"; hence employer pension plans are to some extent designed to retain experienced workers. A parallel literature discusses optimizing international capital mobility.

(continued from previous page)

sufficiently weak financially that it cannot cover a fall in the portfolio's value. If there is a national or other system that guarantees at least some pension benefits, the risk in portfolio return is shifted to others. But because this guarantee may not cover the entire pension entitlement, evaluating the actual risk the worker bears is complex. If the firm pays an insurance company to take on the accrued liability, the risk on the worker will depend on the soundness of the insurance company and what guarantees it has.

If an employer is not perfectly hedging its accrued liability, workers and the providers of guarantees have reason to be concerned about the degree of funding. If the employer is holding some stocks and their value drops, the plan may be underfunded, affecting the workers or the pension guarantor if the employer cannot replace the missing assets. And forcing the employer to make up the shortfall quickly may be difficult, since drops in the stock market tend to coincide with times of reduced profitability. One possible outcome (discussed in more detail in Box 9.3) is that the employer instead terminates the plan. If the size of any guarantee is capped, it might not cover the worker's balance in full.

With this arrangement, the worker's accumulated balance is the sum of each year's fixed fraction of earnings, compounded at 5 percent a year.** During a worker's working life, the financial market risk in principle falls on the employer, as in a defined-benefit plan, but, for a given accumulation, the worker's benefit at retirement depends on annuity pricing at that time, if the worker annuitizes. Thus the worker bears the annuity pricing risk unless the firm offers a monthly benefit whose formula does not vary with the price of annuities.

Defined-benefit plans. Using this cash balance plan as a benchmark, we can consider alternative ways of organizing defined-benefit plans. One is to set the implicit annuity price in advance, so that the employer bears the annuity pricing risk. Another is not to offer workers the option of taking the balance as a lump sum or some other form of drawdown, but instead require them to take monthly benefits, perhaps also requiring that benefits take the form of a joint-life option. As a third possibility, the weighting on different years might differ from compounding at 5 percent. The percentage rate might be higher for older workers, implying different rates of accrual; such "backloading" encourages workers to stay with the firm. Another variant is to count years of service but consider only a few earnings years. Thus a traditional formula differs in the way different years affect the benefit, but still relates benefits to the worker's history of earnings and in principle leaves the risk associated with the assets backing the pension on the employer. The different weights on different years are important in determining how the benefit accrues as the worker ages, and thus the impact on a worker of leaving the firm, voluntarily or involuntarily. As with a cash balance plan, the firm does not require the worker to make contributions, but instead incorporates the worker's earnings in the formula without any action by the worker. Whatever the structure of the plan, the worker bears some risk unless the firm commits to perfect hedging of its obligations, if that is possible.

Defined-contribution plans. A defined-contribution plan differs from a cash balance plan in several ways. First, a worker must typically make voluntary contributions in order to build up an account, with the employer often matching those contributions up to some limit. Second, workers may contribute more than the limit that is matched, so that the plan represents an opportunity to accumulate retirement savings (tax favored in most countries) other than through some individual arrangement, which may or may not be available and may have higher charges or other limitations. Third, the worker normally has a choice of assets, not just a single nominal bond. Fourth, the employer may not organize annuity options on a group basis. Since the worker owns the assets, whereas in a defined-benefit plan the assets belong to—and benefits are an obligation of—the firm, the risk borne by the worker is more readily apparent.

Thus the defined-contribution plan gives the worker more investment options but typically requires him or her to make contributions in order to receive a match, and to make certain investment decisions. And, in common with many cash balance plans, the plan may not help the worker find a good annuity.

In sum. The appeal of the defined-benefit plan (from the worker's perspective) is that investment risk falls on the employer, so long as the employer is able to meet its obligations. Where that is not the case, the worker or the taxpayer, or both, may bear some risk. And the specifics of the formula have implications for workers who leave the firm at different times and after different periods of employment. An appeal of a defined-contribution plan is that, through the choice of a portfolio, the worker has some control over the risks he or she bears, and over the expected returns. The worker need not worry about whether the employer's plan is adequately funded, or about its ability to bear the portfolio risk, or about the rules of any guarantee. Adjustments for earlier or later retirement are strictly actuarial, whereas those under a defined-benefit plan may be, but typically are not. (Of course, an employer can offer a retirement bonus or a continuation bonus to change retirement incentives with a defined-contribution plan.)

Generally, firms retain the option of changing the rules of their pension plans, while preserving the obligation of accrued liabilities. A change in rules may change a worker's anticipated future accrual of benefits. This raises an issue of fairness that legislatures may be called on to address—a particular issue when the change is from a defined-benefit plan to a defined-contribution plan.

Whatever the other arguments, a public defined-benefit plan offers one strong potential benefit that the other types do not, as discussed more fully in section 7.3. As a well-known consequence of basic economic theory, a defined-benefit plan is better able than a defined-contribution plan to spread risks across cohorts. Market systems can spread risks only among market participants. Defined-benefit systems can share risks with future workers and retirees who are not current participants. As discussed in Box 7.3, the value of such risk sharing, if done well, can be large, but the opportunity to do so is limited for employers, who must attract workers in the future if they are to continue to operate. ◀

---

*If the interest rate is not 5 percent throughout a worker's career, the firm is responsible for the difference between 5 percent and the market rate. This does not prevent hedging, since the firm can hold more or fewer bonds as needed to cover the 5 percent accumulation.

**So, if the worker earns w_t in year t, started work in year s, and retires in year T, the benefit at retirement is $B = \sum_{t=s}^{T} w_t (1.05)^{T-t}/P$, where P is the price of an annuity, so that a balance B is worth B/P in monthly benefits.

Currently, employers are liable for accrued pension liabilities, that is, the pension benefits that a worker would be entitled to receive if the pension plan were terminated today or if the worker quit or were dismissed. After accepting a job, a worker receives pay and the accrual of pension rights. In addition, the worker has expectations about future employment with the organization and, if still employed, future pay and future pension accruals. Both pay and accruals tend to rise with age and experience. It is not only current pay but also these expectations about future opportunities that attract workers to an employer. In that sense, some employer pensions are part of an implicit contract, one that does not have the backing of the legal system or any guarantee, but is inherently dependent on the financial success of the employer and on the employer's policies. Some workers may not understand the risks they are taking in the face of this distinction between explicit and implicit contracts. It is common to have regulations setting the maximum period until a pension becomes vested, that is, how long the worker must be on the payroll before the pension represents a legal liability of the employer. However, the fact that something is a legal liability does not ensure that it will be paid: the employer may be unable to pay, hence the concern that pensions deliver what was reasonably expected. Indeed, in the early days of pensions, the entire pension was part of the implicit contract, and a worker might discover just before retirement age that the pension would not be paid.

Thus it is appropriate to consider the effects on current workers from changes in pension plans, including changes from defined benefit to defined contribution. Avoiding this complexity, in the analysis that follows, we consider the comparison between defined-contribution and defined-benefit arrangements only in the context of newly hired workers.

Public plans. Public final-salary plans create the same problems as employer final-salary plans. In addition, they are based on actual earnings, not base pay, and lack some of the oversight that can limit some of the adverse effects in employer plans.[6] Young workers will perceive no link between their current earnings and the size of their eventual pension once they have earned the minimum needed for the year to count as a year of service for the purposes of benefit calculation. At the same time, young workers are influenced by the reduction in their net wage from the taxes they or their employers pay to finance the pension system. This distortion creates inefficiency: it may reduce the incentive to work longer hours or to take a harder job, and it strengthens the incentive to seek work in the informal sector for at least part of the year.

Conversely, older workers have an incentive to inflate their earnings. As the case of the Boston mass transit system illustrates, excessively strong incentives to labor supply are inefficient, just as excessively weak incentives are inefficient. And older workers can often collude with their employers to boost late-career pay at the expense of early pay so as to get a larger public pension. A related issue, already noted, is that, in a system that bases benefits mainly on late-career earnings, workers with earnings that rise rapidly do better than those whose earnings rise more slowly or decline, the beneficiaries typically being higher-paid workers. This leads to equity concerns and to incentives to manipulate the system similar to those facing older workers. Within a single organization, such manipulation can be lessened by the other controls the employer has over its workers. In a public system, however, the government lacks similar controls over the entire economy. Thus it is important that a public system base pension benefits on most or all of a worker's earnings history, provided the pension administration has the necessary administrative capacity. In the absence of adequate records, changing a pension system from one based on earnings over a short period to one based on earnings over a longer period may require the use of approximations. Any such change will inevitably upset some expectations while moving to a fairer and more efficient system.

As mentioned above, employer defined-benefit plans that look at earnings over only part of a worker's career often relate the benefit to base earnings, not total earnings. Such a rule removes some of the inefficiency in the incentives arising from the focus on only a few years. Public systems do not normally gather information on

6. This was less of an issue under central planning, where pay rates did not play the same role in labor allocation as under capitalism.

base earnings, however, and would find it difficult to do so. This difference is another reason it is important that public systems do not rely on earnings over a relatively short portion of a worker's career.

A separate feature commonly found in mandatory systems is an upper limit on the earnings that are subject to contributions and used in calculating benefits. Similarly, countries offering tax advantages for retirement saving often cap the amount of an individual's saving that qualifies. In a system without explicit redistribution, with benefits strictly proportional to earnings, an upper limit on mandated contributions is appropriate, because when the benefit is sufficiently high, the social concern about adequate replacement rates no longer applies: these recipients will have sufficient consumption from their pension and are likely to have additional retirement funds as well. Without this social concern, the mandate loses its role in promoting old-age security. In a progressive system like that in the United States, there is a separate concern about the pattern of redistribution arising from the contributions of higher earners.[7] In setting a redistributive pattern, policymakers have considered together the choice of the ceiling on contributions and the degree of progressivity of the benefit formula. Given the lack of social concern about the retirement incomes of very high earners, some analysts have proposed retaining a ceiling on the earnings used to calculate benefits, while applying a lower contribution rate on earnings above the ceiling. Diamond and Orszag (2005a), for example, propose for the U.S. Social Security system a 3 percent tax on earnings above the maximum used for calculating benefits, alongside the existing 12.4 percent tax rate on earnings below the ceiling that are counted toward benefits.

5.2.2 How important are actuarial benefits?

It is frequently implied that a strictly actuarial relationship between contributions and benefits is optimal. For example, recent World Bank analysis argues for "the need for the closest possible link between contributions and benefits . . . to minimize distortions in the labor market" (Holzmann and Hinz 2005, p. 35). It is claimed that actuarial benefits confront each individual with an efficient choice between consumption when younger and consumption when older, thus minimizing distortions to labor supply, improving compliance with contribution rules, and encouraging later retirement. Each of those claims requires scrutiny.

Labor market distortions. The argument that actuarial benefits will minimize labor market distortions makes a series of errors:

- Actuarial benefits will generally not minimize distortions given the presence of other distortions, as noted in Box 4.2.
- Actuarial benefits will not address objectives additional to consumption smoothing, such as poverty relief, and the alternative policies (such as taxation) necessary to achieve those other objectives inescapably involve labor market distortions of their own.

---

7. In a system that is not fully funded, later generations pay the cost of the higher benefits given to earlier generations. A cap on the system affects the sharing of those costs.

▶ Box 5.4 Pension design and the decision about when to retire

Pension rules have a major impact on decisions about when to retire. In particular, badly designed rules can encourage people to retire earlier than is efficient; in the limit, such incentives can have an effect similar to that of a mandatory retirement age.

Empirical studies that support this conclusion include a collaborative project analyzing pensions and retirement in eleven countries (Gruber and Wise 1999, 2004). The authors calculated for each year the implicit tax on earnings by workers eligible to retire (the decrease in expected lifetime income as a consequence of the pension rules should the worker continue earning for another year). The variable they call the "tax force" then adds up these implicit taxes from the age at which a male worker becomes eligible to claim a retirement benefit up to age 70. In a crude, aggregate way, this variable measures the extent to which the design of the pension system contains a financial incentive to do less work.

To see how this measure of retirement incentives related to actual retirement decisions, the study used a simple aggregate measure of labor supply. For each age between 55 and 65, the authors calculated the fraction of the male population not in the labor force and added up these fractions over these ages. They called the resulting variable "unused productive capacity." The first figure shows their regression of unused productive capacity on the logarithm of the tax force. A strong correlation is evident (the R^2 is about 0.8), and

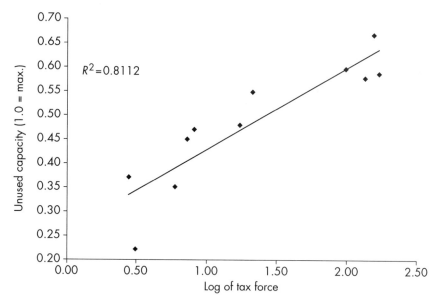

Unused labor force capacity and the implicit tax on earnings due to pension rules. Unused capacity is among workers aged 55–65. Each observation represents a single OECD country; the countries represented are Belgium, Canada, France, Germany, Italy, Japan, the Netherlands, Spain, Sweden, the United Kingdom, and the United States. The "tax force" variable measures the implicit tax on earnings from working an additional year between the age of earliest eligibility for retirement with a pension and age 70. See text for details. *Source:* Gruber and Wise (1999).

the coefficient on the tax force variable was sizable and statistically significant: at the mean, the coefficient (which can be interpreted as the elasticity of unused capacity with respect to the tax force) was 0.36. Moreover, time-series evidence and analyses using data on individuals suggest that at least a large part of the correlation reflects the impact of the implicit tax as an incentive to early retirement.

In contrast, the same tax force variable had no impact on male unemployment rates in the same countries (as measured by a decade-long average unemployment rate), as the second figure shows. The conclusion is the same whether the regression is interpreted in either of two ways: as showing directly that large implicit taxes to encourage early retirement do not lower unemployment rates; or as an instrumental variables regression demonstrating that early retirement does not reduce unemployment (Diamond 2006a). The research indicates that discouraging work through high implicit tax rates creates large inefficiencies that do not accomplish social goals, and therefore should be avoided.

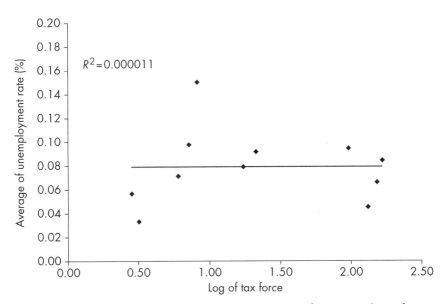

Male unemployment and the implicit tax on earnings due to pension rules, 1991–2000. *Source:* Diamond (2006a). Each observation represents a single country. See Figure 5.1 and text for details.

- The desirability of insurance against adverse labor market outcomes, particularly toward the end of a career, calls for deviations from actuarial benefits to provide better insurance protection. That is, in the presence of asymmetric information, optimal insurance inevitably distorts choices. The information asymmetry comes from the fact that low labor market participation may be either voluntary (preference for more leisure) or involuntary (low pay or no work available), and only the worker knows which is the case.

These arguments suggest two conclusions: first, actuarial benefits do not minimize labor market distortions; and second, minimizing labor market distortions is not the right objective in any case. Again, policy should not consider labor market efficiency in isolation, but instead balance it against the multiple other objectives of pension systems.

Coverage and compliance. Pension systems can have low coverage for either of two reasons: because many workers participate in the uncovered sector, or because workers or employers in the covered sector fail to comply with their legal obligations. The incentives for compliance in the covered sector depend on the perceived payoff from making additional contributions, on the cost of those contributions, and on the strength of enforcement. Actuarial benefits eliminate very weak links (and very strong ones) between benefits and contributions in any one year, thus strengthening the incentive to work in the covered sector and to comply with pension rules. That incentive, however, is absent for workers who are guaranteed a minimum income, either as part of the pension system or in a separate program. And improved compliance depends on individuals being well informed and able to afford contributions out of current earnings or through borrowing. In reality, people may be badly informed about the relationship between contributions today and pensions tomorrow; or they may be myopic, with too great a preference for consumption today over consumption tomorrow; or constraints on their current earnings and borrowing capacity may lead them to choose current over future consumption.[8] For all these reasons it is no surprise that the change in Chile in 1981 from a diverse set of defined-benefit plans to a defined-contribution system did not have a noticeable impact on coverage.

Once more, however, the issue is one of balance. A person might be entitled only to a small pension either because of adverse labor market experiences or because he or she evaded contributions in the expectation of receiving a guaranteed minimum pension. The first is an exogenous risk for which insurance is appropriate; the second, free riding, is a form of moral hazard. Pension design has to address both exogenous and endogenous outcomes (unemployment benefits face a similar problem). Thus the relation between contributions and benefits is important, but a strictly actuarial relationship is suboptimal.

Later retirement. Actuarial benefits, it is also argued, encourage appropriate decisions about later retirement by offering a larger pension when retirement is deferred. Once more, this is true only for workers who are well informed and not liquidity constrained. And once more this argument avoids the extreme disincentives that can arise if there is little or no increase in benefits for delaying receipt of a pension, the importance of which is illustrated in Box 5.4. In assessing this argument, it is important to distinguish between (1) how benefits are determined at the earliest age of pension eligibility, and (2) how benefits are adjusted for later retirement. The argument that actuarial benefits encourage later retirement, to the extent it applies, holds only for the second. Although it does affect earlier labor supply, granting a larger

8. In some developed countries a significant number of people on low incomes have more or less permanent credit card debt, at interest rates of around 20 percent. In those circumstances it makes no sense to save in a pension plan, which is unlikely to offer an annual rate of return anywhere close to 20 percent. Any saving should go to paying off their credit card debt.

pension when a person is first eligible for retirement benefits (with actuarial adjustment for later retirement) can be redistributive, providing insurance and poverty relief. Even the adjustment after the earliest eligibility age should not be exactly actuarial, however, in order to provide insurance and redistribution relative to working beyond this age.

Conclusions. In all three respects—minimizing distortions, improving compliance, and encouraging later retirement—the simple argument that actuarial pensions are optimal holds only in a first-best world. Formulating the issue as an optimal taxation problem in the presence of market imperfections would make it clear that, in a second-best world, an arrangement that is strictly actuarial is generally suboptimal. This does not mean that the relationship between contributions and benefits is unimportant. Indeed, good policy design should seek to avoid obvious and major distortions in the relationship, not least because of potential moral hazard.

It is also worth remembering that a strictly actuarial system by itself provides no poverty relief; and if one part of the system does provide poverty relief, there is no particular virtue in having another part that is strictly actuarial. It is the impact of the entire system that matters for the efficient provision of poverty relief, consumption smoothing, and insurance.

5.3   BENEFIT DESIGN IN RETIREMENT

This section considers the design of benefits during retirement in a pension system that is broadly in balance. (Adjusting for system imbalances is discussed in section 5.4.) An array of possible design features apply at the point of retirement, which can have markedly different effects on labor markets. We begin by getting out of the way a claim that is frequently made but usually false, namely, that earlier provision of retirement benefits can ease unemployment. We then discuss the choice of the age at which a worker is first entitled to benefits (section 5.3.2), the adjustment of benefits for earlier or later retirement (5.3.3), and methods of indexing pension payments (5.3.4). Section 5.3.5 discusses the terms on which a person should be able to receive a pension while continuing to work.

5.3.1   The dog that did not bark: early retirement and unemployment

If the number of jobs in an economy were fixed, inducing an older worker to retire would free up a job for some other worker to fill, in which case early retirement could ease unemployment. But the number of jobs in an economy is not fixed, and the broad historical evidence suggests that early retirement does not reduce unemployment: over many decades, developed countries have seen a large decrease in the average retirement age, with no parallel decline in unemployment rates.

It is wrong for several reasons to think in terms of a fixed number of jobs. First, as additional workers enter the labor force, they exert downward pressure on wages and make it easier for employers to find suitable workers, encouraging job creation. Thus the number of jobs is variable and influenced by the number of workers. Second, taking a pension early does not necessarily remove workers from the labor force, since some workers continue to work elsewhere while receiving a pension from a previous employer. Third, in a developing economy (China being a good example) urban unemployment

▶ **Box 5.5 Mandatory retirement is neither necessary nor desirable**

Since forcing people to leave the labor force has no sustained benefit for workers seeking jobs (see section 5.3.1), there is no reason to have a mandatory retirement age on a nationwide basis. Older workers differ greatly in their health, interest in work, ability to work, and job opportunities. Employers differ greatly in their potential use of and need for older workers. Flexibility in ending employment relationships is an important part of the efficient long-run use of labor.

With some exceptions, the United States has outlawed mandatory retirement rules at the level of the firm, and the European Union is following suit. But it is not necessary to go that far to recognize the importance of allowing employers and workers to choose retirement ages on their own. It is sufficient to avoid mandatory retirement on a national basis, as both the United States and the European Union have done. Mandatory retirement fails to recognize that it is good, both for the workers and for the economy, for some people to continue to work to very advanced ages. ◀

is often influenced heavily by migration to the cities from rural areas. Such migration may overwhelm any attempt to reduce urban unemployment by encouraging early retirement.

Thus it is mistaken to change the pension system to encourage early retirement (Box 5.4) or to lower a mandated retirement age, if there is one (Box 5.5)—both longer-term solutions—as palliative responses to cyclical unemployment, which is a short-term issue.[9] Better to focus on unemployment benefits and on incentives for long-run economic growth than to distort the labor market in the vain hope that retirement will have a large impact on unemployment. Similarly, disability benefits should be awarded on the basis of actual disability, not as a response to unemployment.

5.3.2   What should be the earliest age for pension eligibility?

At what age should a person first become eligible to receive a pension? Practice varies widely across countries.[10] Our analysis starts from the following facts:

- There are necessary connections among the adequacy of monthly pension benefits, their cost, and the average retirement age. The average retirement age, in turn, is strongly influenced by the earliest age at which workers are eligible to receive a pension. If the costs of the system are regarded as excessive, policy-makers can reduce them by increasing the earliest eligibility age while holding monthly benefits constant, or by reducing monthly benefits without increasing the earliest eligibility age.

- However, if increases in benefits bear a roughly actuarial relationship to the age of retirement, an increase in the earliest eligibility age with no change in benefit levels will have little or no impact on long-run costs, although it will help the system's short-run finances.

---

9. Structural unemployment may raise different issues. Additionally, labor markets may take time to adjust to an increased supply of older workers; see Spiezia (2002).

10. See Turner (2007) for a survey.

- People are living longer. This is great good news, but it implies that if people continue to retire at the same age as before, the cost of providing a given monthly pension will rise.
- Leisure is a superior good. Over the long term, as countries have grown richer, it is not surprising that, on average, people have chosen to consume more leisure through a shorter working day, a shorter working week, longer holidays, and earlier retirement. Thus the average age at which a working population will choose to retire depends in part on average income per capita. The historical evidence among male workers in developed countries is consistent with this conclusion: a large increase in life expectancy has been accompanied by a large decrease in the average retirement age. Over the last twenty years, however, some countries have seen an end to the trend toward earlier retirement.

The concept of retirement is multidimensional: its dimensions can include stopping work, receiving a pension, regarding oneself as retired, that is, a state of mind (Banks and Smith 2006), or a mix. When thinking about "the retirement age" in a pension system, two variables are particularly important. Employer plans often give a single retirement age a central role, perhaps with a smaller or larger pension for earlier or later retirement. We refer to the age that plays this central role as the *age for full benefits*. For a public system it may be more useful to think in terms of the earliest age at which a worker may start benefits—what we called above the *earliest eligibility age*—and the increase in pension benefit granted to someone who delays the start of benefits beyond that age. The earliest eligibility age differs across countries and can be a signal about a social norm. In some, the earliest eligibility age and the age for full benefits are the same (in the United Kingdom, both are 65 for men); in others they differ (the U.S. Social Security system has an earliest eligibility age of 62, but an age for full benefits that was 65 and is gradually being raised to 67).

Determining an optimal earliest eligibility age is difficult. Determining how it should increase over time is more difficult. As discussed below, a change in earliest eligibility age hurts some workers and helps others. The optimum should balance the help and the hurt. Over time the point of balance will shift, but the drivers of that shift are not simply related to life expectancy. For example, optimal retirement will tend to occur at earlier ages as real income rises. On the other hand, health, and with it the ability to continue working, are expected to improve along with increased life expectancy, but the link is not a tight one. A theoretical treatment of these countervailing trends has yet to be developed, and the observational difficulties of judging when people are making mistakes on a decision with such large intertemporal and stochastic implications are great.

In those circumstances, what factors should guide the choice of earliest eligibility age? An increase does not help pension finance if benefits rise actuarially in line with the increase in the age at which they start. Increasing the earliest age at which the pension starts improves system finances only if benefits are reduced at each age below what they would have been under the old system.[11] In a system with roughly actuarial

---

11. This is very different from a change in the age for full benefits, an increase in which reduces benefits at any given retirement age.

adjustments, the choice of earliest eligibility age is important more for the adequacy of pensions than for the finance of the system.

Suppose that a country with an earliest eligibility age of 65 is considering increasing it to 66, without changing monthly benefits at 66 or after. Such a change has several effects:

- It hurts workers who should sensibly stop working at 65 but do not have enough savings to stop working unless their pension starts immediately.
- It helps workers who ought to wait until 66 but who would, given the choice, retire at 65 on an inadequate pension.
- It helps workers who retire at 65 and can afford to live on their savings until benefits start at 66, by providing higher benefits, assuming that they were under-annuitized before the change.[12]
- Similarly, if benefits are not conditioned on actual retirement, it helps workers who would have worked until 66 anyway, by providing higher benefits. It also helps those who might have consumed too much, given their cash flow, to save more for later spending.
- If benefits are paid only to workers who retire, it will not affect those who would have worked until 66 anyway.

In sum, an optimal earliest eligibility age strikes a balance between helping some workers and hurting others. To strike that balance, it should be set within the range of sensible retirement ages for different workers (just as the size of the contribution under a mandatory system should be set within the range of sensible saving rates). As an additional dimension, it is possible in some settings to have an earliest eligibility age but to allow workers to retire earlier if their pension accumulation provides them with a replacement rate above a government-determined threshold. Such an arrangement exists in Chile. Whatever the earliest eligibility age, the system should be designed to allow flexibility in retirement decisions.

5.3.3   Adjusting pensions for earlier and later retirement

Traditional employer plans had a formula for calculating a worker's benefit only at the age for full benefits. As described above, this formula is some function of years of service and the worker's earnings in the years relevant to the formula. However, some employers want some workers to continue beyond the age for full benefits, at least on a part-time basis, and in other cases it may be in the interests of both worker and employer for the worker to retire at a younger age.

Actuaries can estimate what reduction for earlier retirement allows the employer broadly to break even from offering an early retirement option. Actuarially fair adjustments, however, may or may not be in the employer's best interest. The employer might want to give workers more or less encouragement to retire early by setting benefits above or below the level that breaks even. Setting benefits for these alternative

---

12. Although a mandatory system could make too much use of annuities, voluntary overannuitization is not likely given retirees' needs for liquid funds and given the shortcomings of the workings of the private annuity market.

options represents an additional control variable for encouraging or discouraging retirement at different ages, separate from the rules that determine benefits at the age for full benefits. In addition, an employer can choose at which ages the early retirement option is available and may offer that opportunity only to a subset of its workers. And an employer might make early retirement available only at certain times, when the employer has less need to maintain employment.

If an employer wants to retain some workers beyond the age for full benefits, it can offer a higher pension benefit for delayed retirement. Alternatively, it can pay workers benefits, wholly or in part, while continuing to employ them—for example, as consultants—after they have formally retired. Employers recognize that they do not want all their workers to retire at exactly the same age, because of differences in jobs and in the abilities of different workers.

Similar issues arise in a public system. Whatever the rules for determining benefits at the earliest eligibility age or at some normal age, there are good reasons—for the economy, for society, and for the workers themselves—for different workers to retire at different ages. Some workers enjoy their work and want to continue working. Others no longer enjoy their work (if they ever did) and are eager to stop as soon as they can afford a decent retirement. A good pension system will not excessively discourage the first group from continuing to work at ages at which the second group will already have retired; a good system may also be concerned with distribution and insurance beyond the earliest age of eligibility, as opportunities differ across people.

The increase in benefits for delayed retirement should rise with age because remaining life expectancy decreases as mortality rates rise with age. In practice, however, increases for delayed retirement are too small in the public pension in many countries and often follow patterns that make no apparent sense.[13] Adjustments in the U.S. Social Security system have an erratic pattern and are at some ages (slightly) higher and at others much lower than the actuarially appropriate level, for no apparent reason, and Canada makes decreasing rather than increasing adjustments with age (Figure 5.1).

5.3.4   Indexing pension benefits to prices or wages

If benefits were based on nominal earnings, a worker's initial real benefit would bear an erratic relation to past earnings, depending on the pattern of past inflation rates. If benefits themselves were set in nominal terms, real benefits would decline over time and in an erratic pattern as inflation rates vary. This section considers proper and improper ways of indexing pensions, discussing in turn

- What indexation rules should apply to a worker's history of covered earnings (or contributions based on covered earnings) in determining the worker's initial benefit;
- What indexation rules should apply after initial benefits are determined; and
- Some problems that can arise from faulty rules.

---

13. We suspect that these patterns arise from administrators considering benefit levels rather than percentage increases in determining benefits.

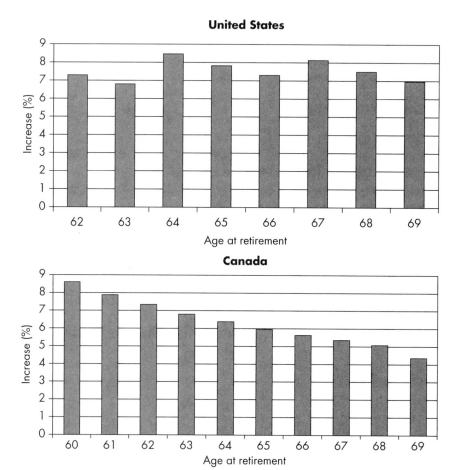

FIGURE 5.1.
Percentage increase in monthly public pension benefit from a one-year delay in start of benefits, United States and Canada.

Indexing a worker's history of earnings or contributions. A defined-benefit system relates benefits to a worker's history of earnings (or, in the case of NDC plans, contributions). Typically, as described above, an average is taken of earnings in some number of highest earning years or across all years. To avoid the ill effects of subjecting benefits to the vagaries of inflation, benefits can be indexed in one of two pure ways, or a mix:

- *Price indexation:* If a worker's past earnings are indexed to changes in prices (such a system is known as a real system), then initial real benefits are based on the worker's history of real earnings. Thus the initial pension depends on the worker's nominal earnings in each of a number of years, adjusted by the increase in the price level from each year up to the year when initial benefits are calculated.

- *Wage indexation:* In a wage-indexed system, initial real benefits are based on the history of a worker's earnings in each year relative to economy-wide average earnings in that year. Thus the initial pension depends on the worker's earnings and on average earnings in each year.[14]

• It is also possible to have a mix of price and wage indexation, provided that the mix is a proper weighted average of the price and wage indexes, as defined below.

The relationship between benefit levels and indexation method is not simple. For a given benefit formula, if real wage growth is positive, a worker's initial benefit will generally be higher with wage indexation than with price indexation. In practice, however, a country chooses an indexing method and a benefit formula together. Thus, even though past earnings upgraded by wage growth will typically be larger than past earnings upgraded by price growth, the pension need not be larger if the formula is different.[15] If two systems, one price indexed and one wage indexed, give equal benefits on average for a cohort, some workers will do better under one system and some under the other. Those with relatively higher earnings early in their career will do better with wage indexing, which gives more weight to earlier years, and those with lower earnings will do better with price indexing. Matters are yet more complex if the system of indexation is faulty, as discussed in Boxes 5.6 and 5.7.

▶ Box 5.6 Overindexing initial benefits for inflation: United States, 1972-77

Faulty indexation can affect both a person's initial pension and benefits in payment (see Box 5.8). The experience of the United States in the 1970s provides an example.

Before 1973, the U.S. Social Security system did not adjust benefits automatically in response to inflation. Instead Congress voted changes in the benefit formula periodically, reflecting concern about the extent to which prices had risen since the previous change. These changes applied both to benefits paid and to the formula for future initial benefits. Legislation in 1972 called for automatic adjustment for inflation, both of initial benefits and benefits in payment, roughly incorporating the practice that Congress had previously followed. As a result, the benefit formula used a worker's average nominal earnings while also increasing the benefit formula for inflation. So high inflation affected benefits in two ways: directly through changes in the benefit formula, and indirectly to the extent that higher inflation raised wages.

This overindexing was recognized at the time of the legislation, but it was thought that the progressivity in the benefit formula would be sufficient to offset the rising cost. Although the method would have kept costs in line with projections had inflation remained within a narrow band, actual inflation was rapid. As a result, the real value of benefits grew far more rapidly than Congress had intended, contributing to a financing crisis. The system remained overindexed until legislation enacted in 1977 introduced wage indexing of initial benefits while continuing price indexing of benefits in payment. ◀

14. There can also be differences in the benefit formula based on a worker's date of birth. One can have a mixed price-wage system by incorporating some price calculations as well as wage calculations. A system with this character was proposed by the commission appointed by U.S. President George W. Bush (U.S. President's Commission 2001) to consider reforms of the Social Security system.

15. This point is readily made in a linear system: $A \sum_{a=21}^{65} w_a (1+\pi)^{65-a} = B \sum_{a=21}^{65} w_a (1+g)^{65-a}$

where π is the rate of inflation and g the rate of real earnings growth. Of course, changing real earnings growth would change the relative sizes of the two systems.

▶ **Box 5.7 Methods of indexing initial benefits for inflation**

A simplified example where workers work for two periods illustrates how price indexing or wage indexing can make real benefits independent of the inflation rate, and how the method legislated in the United States in 1972 did not. Assume that in the first period every worker earns w, and that in the second period every worker earns $w(1 + g) \times (1 + h)$, where g is the growth rate of real earnings and h is the inflation rate. Assume that the pension benefit is a constant fraction c of average lifetime earnings, evaluated in second-period units.

With price indexing, first-period earnings are worth $w(1 + h)$ in second-period dollars. Thus lifetime average earnings are $w\{[1 + h + (1 + g)(1 + h)]/2\} = w(1 + g/2)(1 + h)$. In inflation-adjusted terms (in first-period dollars), the benefit is $cw(1 + g/2)(1 + h)/(1 + h) = cw(1 + g/2)$. Thus inflation-adjusted benefits are independent of the inflation rate.

With wage indexing, first-period earnings are worth $w(1 + g)(1 + h)$ in second-period dollars. Thus lifetime average earnings are $w(1 + g)(1 + h)$. In inflation-adjusted terms (in first-period dollars), the benefit is $cw(1 + g)(1 + h)/(1 + h) = cw(1 + g)$. Thus inflation-adjusted benefits are independent of the inflation rate.

With the indexing method used in the 1972 U.S. legislation, first-period earnings are used in nominal terms in the calculation. Thus lifetime average nominal earnings are $w[1 + (1 + g)(1 + h)]/2$. If nominal benefits were proportional to this measure, inflation-adjusted benefits would be $cw\{[1 + (1 + g)(1 + h)]/2\}/(1 + h)$. Since this expression is decreasing in the inflation rate, h, inflation-adjusted benefits would be lower, the higher the inflation rate. This is a result of using first-period earnings in nominal terms. In the U.S. legislation, the benefit formula was also multiplied by the inflation rate. Thus, in inflation-adjusted terms (in first-period dollars), the benefit was $cw[1 + (1 + g)(1 + h)]/2$. Thus the higher the inflation rate, the higher the inflation-adjusted benefit. When inflation is sufficiently high, this allows benefits to grow faster than wages, which drive the tax base. ◀

If the benefit formula is stable across cohorts, and if the rate of wage growth varies over time, wage indexation will tend to result in the same replacement rate (relative to final pay) across cohorts, whereas price indexation will produce varying replacement rates. But a full analysis would need to take account of possibly shifting relative wages of cohorts that overlap in the labor market (and so in the determination of average wages), which would be far more complicated.

Indexing pensions after retirement. In some developed countries, benefits after retirement are indexed to inflation rates, in some to the change in average wage rates, and in some to a proper weighted average of the two ("proper" meaning that the weights sum to one). For example, in Finland benefits increase at 80 percent of the growth of prices and 20 percent of the growth of wages. Another approach is illustrated by Sweden, where benefits are indexed to wage growth minus 1.6 percentage points. The choice of an index involves two related issues: the average expected rate of increase in benefits over a retiree's remaining life, and the risk characteristics of different methods of adjustment. (The discussion here does not consider adjusting benefits for changes in life expectancy, a topic discussed in section 5.4.1 below.)

For a given initial pension, the more rapidly benefits grow, the more expensive the system; the less rapidly they grow, the further retirees fall behind average living standards over time. Thus price indexation places greater emphasis on containing costs and preserving purchasing power, and wage indexation greater emphasis on the relative adequacy of benefits. Policy needs to strike a balance between these two concerns, while recognizing their different distributional impacts.

Another way to think about the growth of benefits is to recognize that, at a given long-run cost, there is a trade-off between the initial benefit and the rate of growth of benefits thereafter: the more rapidly benefits grow, the lower the initial replacement rate must be to hold cost constant. This is how initial benefits are determined in a system that sets initial benefits on an actuarial (or quasi-actuarial) basis, for example in funded defined-contribution systems that purchase annuities from insurance companies, and in the NDC system in Sweden.

Since workers differ in life expectancy, different combinations of initial benefit levels and growth rates of benefit with the same aggregate long-run cost will affect different workers differently. Those with shorter expected lives will prefer higher initial benefits with slower subsequent growth. Both men and women with higher earnings tend to live longer than others of the same sex; thus the choice of growth rate of benefits has important ex ante distributional effects. Since on average women live longer than men, there is also an issue of gender equity. Moreover, a system with a lower initial pension and more rapid indexing may encourage later retirement, insofar as workers, particularly those with few other resources, may pay particular attention to initial benefits. Such a focus (perhaps influenced by media coverage that looks primarily at initial benefits) may make a sensible choice politically more difficult. That is, choosing a lower initial benefit and more rapid growth thereafter may be portrayed as a benefit cut even if the overall long-run cost of the system is unchanged.

With conventional modeling of individual preferences, the desired growth in consumption (and thus benefits) over time depends on how consumption at different times is valued relative to the increased consumption available from delay. This is usually specified in terms of the difference between a utility discount rate and the rate of return for delayed consumption. A constant real consumption path is optimal when these two rates are equal, and this provides potential support for the common practice of price indexing. However, conventional modeling ignores the changes in people's tastes and constraints as they age—changes that are reflected in observed patterns of expenditure. We know of no evidence on how this consideration should affect the time pattern of benefits. Conventional modeling also ignores issues of relative consumption— that is, of retirees relative to that of workers. Since wages tend to rise faster than prices, a given real benefit over time declines relative to average wages.[16]

A relevant question is whether aging is associated with increased poverty; the answer will depend in part on whether poverty is measured in absolute or relative terms. There is an association between aging and poverty in the United States, for example, although it is due primarily to the increasing number of widows as a cohort ages, rather than to a pure aging effect, family structure held constant. In the absence of other sources of antipoverty insurance, an increase in pension benefits over time may be useful, for example to finance long-term care.[17]

16. As discussed in Chapter 11, from the late 1980s the U.K. basic state pension was indexed to prices and thus fell increasingly behind average earnings. The more widespread poverty among pensioners that resulted was one impetus for the creation of the U.K. Pensions Commission (2004a, 2004b, 2005).

17. On the financing of long-term care see Barr (2001a, Chapter 5).

Wages tend not only to rise faster than prices but also to fluctuate more than prices. Thus the choice of method of indexation also has a risk dimension. Consider two systems with the same initial benefit, one that is price indexed and one (similar to Sweden's) that is indexed to the change in wages minus a constant set equal to the anticipated growth rate of real wages. The two systems have the same expected cost but different degrees of risk. Choosing a wage index minus a constant involves the real possibility that the chosen constant will not track average real wage growth over a period of a decade or even more, meant to keep retirees in roughly the same position, and may stray far from it. Historically, some countries have seen extended periods with quite different real wage growth, as Figure 5.2 shows for the United States. Thus the use of real wages minus a constant involves more risk than a weighted average of price and wage changes with the same expected cost.

That additional risk matters. It is good to share risks widely, but those who are more risk averse should bear less of the risk. Employed workers have a greater capacity to bear risk than retirees: they can adjust both their earnings and their consumption, and because their remaining life expectancies are longer, they can more easily smooth consumption following an unexpected income shock, by making smaller adjustments over more years. These considerations suggest that if benefits adjust by less than wages, this should be done through a mix of price and wage indexation rather than relying on wages less a constant.

Potential problems. What is clear is that the real value of a person's pension benefit should not vary erratically with the level of inflation, all the more because inflation rates can vary significantly across years, even consecutive years. If pensions are fully indexed for price inflation but no more, their real purchasing power is preserved, but retirees will over time fall increasingly behind general living standards, assuming wage growth exceeds inflation. If instead pensions are indexed to nominal wage growth,

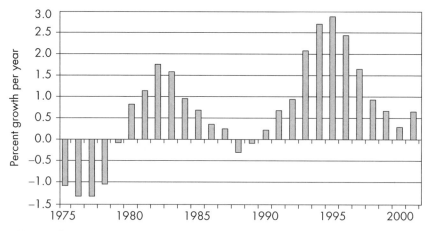

FIGURE 5.2.
Real wage growth in the United States, 1974–2002. Data are five-year rolling averages of annual wage data (www.ssa.gov/OACT/COLA/AWI.html) deflated by the consumer price index for urban wage earners and clerical workers (CPI-W; www.ssa.gov/OACT/STATS/cpiw.html). *Source:* Authors' calculations using data from the Social Security Administration.

> **Box 5.8 Overindexing benefits in payment for inflation:
> United Kingdom, 1975–80**

Faulty indexation can affect both a person's initial pension (Box 5.6) and benefits in payment. Under 1975 legislation, the U.K. basic state pension was indexed to the higher of wage growth or inflation, but with each year's decision made strictly on its own. Thus, if wages doubled in year 1 with no change in prices, and prices doubled in year 2 with no change in wages, real wages afterward would not have changed, but the pension would have doubled in year 1 (in line with wages) and again in year 2 (in line with prices). This created an unintended upward bias, which was significant given the high rates of wage and price change in the later 1970s. ◀

they will be adjusted for inflation insofar as wages keep up with inflation, and will preserve the position of retirees relative to workers; but since over time wage growth generally exceeds inflation, the system will be more expensive for a given level of initial benefits. In this case there is some risk sharing between workers and retirees over the impact of inflation on wages, at least in the long run. Either of these rules, or a proper weighted average, is reasonable, given different objectives. What is not reasonable is to use improper weights when indexing for inflation, that is, weights that do not add up to one. Boxes 5.6 and 5.8 give two illustrations of faulty indexation, and, as discussed in section 14.2.2, the same problem arises in China. Also of concern is the use of a cap on the extent to which benefits adjust to inflation. Although this may assist the finances of the system, a cap undercuts the social purpose of indexing.

Proper indexing avoids this sort of erratic response to inflation. Depending on concerns about the initial level of benefits, the relationship between benefits and average wages, variation in life expectancy, and the financing available for pensions, different countries can reasonably make different choices.

5.3.5 Pensions and continuing work

Should a person be able to receive a pension while continuing to work? Typically, retirement from an employer is a condition for the start of a pension from that employer. But that does not necessarily mean the end to all work. Many workers retire from one employer, collect a pension from that employer, and then work elsewhere. In addition, some employers allow workers who have retired from full-time work to continue part time while receiving some or all of their pension.[18] As discussed earlier in the chapter, such flexibility is appropriate.

Public systems can also choose how continued work affects the receipt of benefits from the system. They can decide that benefits may start at a given age only if a worker has stopped working more or less totally (in that case the pension is said to be subject to a retirement test), or that benefits may start whether the worker stops work or not. Or the system can set an age-varying rule: within a certain range of ages, benefits are paid only if work stops, after which benefits are paid unconditionally. In addition, a worker who is eligible for a pension might be allowed to defer benefits in order to receive higher benefits once they do start. If priced correctly (that is, with a suitable

---

18. Since 2006, U.K. legislation has allowed a worker to receive an employer pension while continuing to work for the same employer.

increase in benefits for delay), this increase in opportunities can come at little or no financial cost to the system. There is little concern that workers will harm themselves by delaying the start of benefits in order to receive higher benefits later.

Consider a system that has an earliest eligibility age at which benefits start for everyone. A variant is to add a requirement, at least for some ages, that benefits are paid only if the person is not working. Another is to pay benefits as long as the person's earnings do not exceed some low threshold, to facilitate part-time work and work by those with very low incomes.

A retirement test has different effects on different people. For those who continue to work, it raises their monthly benefit once they do retire; this is advantageous to the extent that consumption would otherwise have fallen too far after the end of work. Higher benefits at a later age also have important redistributive effects across workers with different life expectancies. On the other hand, a retirement test discourages work by people who place a low value on higher benefits later, including those with a shorter life expectancy. A combination of a retirement test and increases in benefits that are less than actuarial may also provide some insurance against low earnings toward the end of a career. The implicit tax on later working years in this case helps to finance higher benefits for those retiring earliest, which amounts to insurance for people with lower earnings opportunities later in their careers. To serve this role, the increase in benefit should not be much below the level that is actuarial; that is, the implicit tax should not be too high, and in particular not so high that it loses rather than gains revenue. In addition, to the extent that those who retire as soon as they are eligible are lower earners, and those who defer retirement are higher earners, and if pension benefits are not adjusted fully actuarially for later retirement, the insurance effect is complemented by a redistributive effect. In that case the distortion to labor supply from a retirement test may be more than offset by improved insurance and redistributive gains.[19]

The effects of rules governing the payment of benefits while working will change with age. A retirement test may make sense at or around the earliest eligibility age, but not at all later ages,[20] suggesting that eligibility rules should vary systematically with age. In countries with limited administrative capacity to enforce such rules, however, this would not be a prime candidate for using that limited capacity.

These arguments notwithstanding, it is bad design to have both a retirement test and a large implicit tax on those who postpone retirement, through zero or inadequate increases in benefits for a delayed start. Such an arrangement functions similarly to a mandatory retirement age, with the result that too many people retire as soon as they are eligible for benefits. Unfortunately, as discussed in Box 5.4, this structure has historically been far too common. Either benefits should start at some age without a retirement test, or benefits should increase noticeably for a delayed start. As discussed in Box 5.9, given diversity in life expectancies and the differing extent to which people might delay retirement, the latter approach is not as simple as it appears, and this has

19. In the United States, lifetime earnings and remaining life expectancy are both lower among those retiring at 62 (the earliest eligibility age) than at higher ages.

20. In the United States, for example, benefits are subject to an earnings test between age 62 and the age for full benefits, which is in the process of changing from 65 to 67. There is no earnings test after the age for full benefits.

▶ **Box 5.9 Actuarial balance and incentives with varying life expectancies**

Remaining life expectancy at (and after) the earliest eligibility age varies in the population. To be revenue neutral, actuarial adjustment for delayed benefits should reflect the average life expectancy of those who delay, not of the entire population. Further complicating the issue, that average should be weighted by the amounts of benefits that individuals delay. This implies a difficult calculation to arrive at a system that is both revenue neutral and actuarially fair for the workers who take advantage of the option to delay. If an equilibrium that achieves both can be found, the additional choice for workers from allowing a delay is a gain. If it is actuarial on average, of course, that means it is better financially for some and worse for others. But because of the value of the additional insurance, some workers may choose to delay even if it lowers the expected value of their benefits, just as people buy fire insurance even though it lowers the expected value of their wealth.

Two issues arise when considering the incentive effects of the option to delay. If a person can receive a pension without stopping work, the option to delay is an incentive to arrange for a larger pension, without directly encouraging or discouraging labor force participation, although liquidity constraints and the appeal of a larger future benefit may result in increased work. If benefits must start when work stops, then someone who prefers larger benefits must continue to work in order to get the larger benefit. In this case the option to delay permits those with adequate liquidity to stop work and to delay benefits, and so may result in decreased work. Insofar as workers are making good decisions about when to stop work, increased options are good. There may not be a behavioral concern about the timing of stopping work for workers who have sufficient foresight to delay the start of benefits. In considering the consequences of continued work on the actuarial balance of the system, one must incorporate the impact of additional work, through more taxes and higher benefits later, as well as the impact through the rules relating benefits to the age at which they start.

If the increase in benefits from delay is less than actuarial, the effect is to discourage some who would otherwise choose to delay (an efficiency cost). But at the same time it permits redistribution from those who delay and receive less-than-actuarial compensation to those who do not. As discussed earlier, since those delaying are likely to be better off than those not, such a deviation from actuarially fair pricing can provide both insurance and redistribution. ◀

implications both for actuarial balance and for incentives to labor force participation. That is, a level of adjustment that is actuarially fair on average will be an implicit tax for some and an implicit subsidy for others.

The central conclusion of section 5.3 concerns two elements of the relationship between a person's pension benefit and the age at which that benefit is first received:

- The pension should be larger for a worker who is older when benefits begin, so as to preserve incentives to work until a suitable age.
- Either benefits should start at a given age without requiring an end to work, or they should increase significantly for a delayed start.

5.4 ADJUSTING PENSION SYSTEMS OVER TIME

How should a pension system be adjusted to reflect differences across cohorts, considering, for example, that people born later are likely to have higher earnings and longer lives?

Specifically, how should the relationship between contributions and benefits vary, and how should the earliest eligibility age and the adjustments for early and late retirement vary? We discuss adjustments in respect of greater life expectancy, adjustments for a changing labor force (notably the effects of declining fertility), and adjustment for changing social risks.

5.4.1 Adjusting for longer life expectancy

Although mortality rates are likely to continue to decline, there is debate about the speed of change. History suggests that, even if current projections are on average accurate over long periods, significant deviations should be expected from time to time. In 1981 the U.K. Government Actuary projected that male life expectancy at 65 in 2004 would be 14.8 years; in reality it turned out to be 19 years, a 28 percent error. Thus the Second Report of the U.K. Pensions Commission (2005, p. 90) notes that

> around the 2003-based [Government Actuary's Department] principal projection of life expectancy for a man aged 65 in 2050 of 21.7 there was a wide and asymmetric range of uncertainty stretching at least from 20.0 to 29.0, but with small probabilities of still wider divergence. ... It is therefore essential that both state pension policy and occupational pension provision, in both the public and private sectors, is designed to be robust not just in the face of increasing life expectancy but of major uncertainty about how fast that increase will proceed.

Thus projected mortality improvements face a widening funnel of doubt about future outcomes. If current legislation sets future adjustment factors, they will generally not match actual mortality rates. It is, of course, always possible to change the adjustment factors. But legislating change may be difficult and may include an asymmetric transition: slow if larger benefit decreases are needed, but rapid if smaller benefit decreases are sufficient and can be financed. Thus there is considerable advantage in designing a system that, at least up to a point, responds automatically as uncertain outcomes eventuate. For example, in its NDC system, Sweden includes automatic indexing for benefits at the earliest eligibility age and for the increase in benefits for delayed retirement, but has not included automatic adjustment of the earliest eligibility age itself.

A further issue is that mortality improvements in the United States (and presumably elsewhere) have not occurred at the same rate across the earnings spectrum. Those with higher lifetime earnings have enjoyed more rapid improvements in mortality, and this is true of both men and women (Diamond and Orszag 2005a, pp. 67–69; Pappas et al. 1993). This issue is particularly important when considering the earliest eligibility age and is a further complication in trying to predict the future. Changes in the distribution of mortality are of limited importance for their effect on the costs of a pension system, but of considerable importance for the distribution of sensible retirement ages, and so for the choice of earliest eligibility age.

In a defined-contribution system an increase in life expectancy has no effect on the finances of the system, since benefits at any given age are lowered to meet the level that can be financed. If people continue to retire at the same age as those in earlier cohorts with lower life expectancy, replacement rates will necessarily be lower. Individuals can offset this effect by working proportionally longer. But historically they have not done so: retirement ages have generally decreased until recently, and recent growth of labor force participation has not been rapid enough to represent a fully offsetting trend. Since many workers may not respond to longer life expectancy by working longer on their own accord, an increase in the earliest entitlement age may help to protect some workers from retiring too soon.

With a defined-benefit system that is roughly actuarial, increased life expectancy has an adverse effect on pension finances if there is no adjustment for life expectancy. This adverse impact is not helped by longer average careers if adjustment of benefits is roughly actuarial. Indeed, adjustments to benefits can become too large as life expectancy rises. Thus a defined-benefit system needs to adjust the benefit formula.

A process of automatic adjustment that relies heavily on projected mortality rates could easily become politicized. Thus a system may function better if it adjusts benefits on the basis of realized mortality information. In Sweden this is done by using historic mortality data in calculating pensions, with no adjustment for anticipated improvements in mortality after a cohort has retired. Another approach is through year-by-year adjustments based on year-by-year changes in mortality.

When aligning a system over time to changing life expectancies, several separate (and fully separable) instruments are available. It is possible to

- Reduce the average monthly benefit at the earliest eligibility age to reflect the increased cost of providing given benefits as life expectancy increases. This can be done automatically and is so done in defined-contribution systems that rely on market provision of annuities.

- Increase the earliest eligibility age over time, either automatically or through periodic review, thus reducing the average duration of benefits, while removing the offsetting increase in the monthly benefit for a delayed start. This combines the first option with an increase in earliest eligibility age.

- Adjust the increase in benefits for later retirement, since the value of an increase in benefits is larger, the greater is remaining life expectancy after the increase, because the period over which benefits are paid is longer. Thus the increase in the benefit for delaying retirement by one year might be reduced as life expectancy increases.[21]

However, it is not necessary, nor does it seem optimal in all circumstances, to place all adjustment on the side of benefits. An additional option is to increase contributions. The increase can be indexed to the cost of increased life expectancy.

The first and third options are the choice of policymakers in Sweden and are inherent in a standard, fully funded, defined-contribution system, such as Chile's. The first option was also one of the proposals for the U.S. Social Security system put forward by the commission appointed by President Bush. The second option is being pursued for the basic state pension in the United Kingdom. A different approach would combine the first option with an increase in contributions, the balance of the two

---

21. A typical plan adds a fixed percentage to benefits for each year by which the start of benefits is delayed. This results in a declining percentage increase. A constant percentage increase would result from multiplying the benefit by a fixed percentage increase, rather than adding a fixed percentage. However, mortality rates increase with age, and so the percentage addition to benefits should rise if the aim is to provide actuarial adjustment.

depending on the existing contribution level and available resources. This has been proposed for the United States, where contribution and replacement rates are low by international standards, by Diamond and Orszag (2005*a*, 2005*b*). In general, it is likely to be good policy to make use of a range of these instruments.

As discussed in section 5.3.2, adjusting the earliest eligibility age raises complex issues, because the factors determining how many workers gain and how many lose from such a change vary not only with increases in average life expectancy and the average level of earnings, but also with individual circumstances and decisions. A simple rule making the earliest eligibility age proportional to life expectancy has advantages in terms of transparency but may be suboptimal in theoretical terms: people are living longer, adding to the cost of pensions, but that effect is partially offset by the fact that people are better off than in the past and so can afford to spend more on retirement; and, as noted, improvements in life expectancy can be very different across income classes. Thus periodic adjustment of the earliest eligibility age—perhaps based on recommendations from a nonpartisan commission—may be better than automatic adjustment. Or a given change in life expectancy may be presumed to call for an adjustment, while still requiring legislation to enact it.

Once a government has decided to adjust pension benefit and eligibility rules regularly, the decision should be implemented on the basis of the principles set out in Box 5.10.

▶ Box 5.10 Principles for adjusting pensionable age

If benefits and eligibility are to be adjusted for mortality changes, automatic adjustment should be based on three principles.

- The rules should relate to date of birth, not to the date of retirement; otherwise there will be a wave of retirements just before any reduction in the generosity of benefits goes into effect. Such an incentive to retire is inefficient.
- Changes should be made annually, to avoid large changes in benefit levels across nearby cohorts. Large changes are inequitable and politically difficult, since benefits could differ significantly between people born in successive years, sometimes only days apart. The combination of large changes and rules determined by date of retirement would exacerbate the inefficient incentive to early retirement.
- As far as is sensible, rules for changing benefits should be explicit. The case for explicit rules for adjusting benefit levels as life expectancy changes is clear, since the cost of benefits depends primarily on life expectancy. Automatic adjustment with explicit rules leads to greater predictability and decreased political pressure. Automatic adjustments may function better if based on actual mortality outcomes rather than projections. Nevertheless, as with the indexation of income tax brackets, there always remains the option of legislation to change whatever the automatic rules produce.

The case for an explicit rule automatically adjusting the earliest eligibility age is weaker than the case for periodic reevaluation, since the normative analysis of the choice depends on much more than just life expectancy.

The legislated increase in women's pensionable age in the United Kingdom, announced in 1991, illustrates all three of the above principles. The key date is April 6, 1950. For women born before that date, the state pensionable age will continue to be 60. The pensionable age for a woman born on May 6, 1950 (one month after the key date) will be 60 years and one month, for a woman born on June 6, 1950, 60 years and two months, and so on. For women born on or after April 6, 1955, the pensionable age will be 65. ◀

5.4.2   Adjusting for a changing labor force

Apart from the postwar baby-boom period in some countries, there has been a long-term declining trend in fertility rates in much of the world. For some of that time, declining child mortality more than offset the decline in fertility, leading to rapid growth of the population of working age. But in many countries child mortality rates are now sufficiently low that the scope for further decline is limited, and consequently growth of the labor force is slowing, a trend that we anticipate will continue.

Such a slowdown affects the economy in general and pension systems in particular. (We focus on the slowdown, since there does not seem to be any particular significance in whether the trend actually crosses over from positive growth to negative.) If that were the only change, it would be expected to lead over time to higher wages and lower rates of return on assets. In practice, however, the impact of slower labor force growth on the age-earnings profile or on the growth of wages across cohorts is not simple. Some analysts have hypothesized that with an older labor force will come slower technical progress, and particularly less of what is called learning-by-doing. In addition, for the next few decades those effects may be more than offset by the effects of globalization. Meanwhile empirical studies have found little reliable connection between demography and rates of return. Nevertheless, one can consider how an economy should react to a fall in interest rates. We begin by considering a fully funded defined-contribution system, before going on to analyze a less than fully funded defined-benefit system.

With a fully funded defined-contribution system, if interest rates fall while everything else remains the same, more savings will be needed to finance a given level of retirement benefits starting at a given age. Although there could be a legislated increase in mandated saving rates, there will be no financial pressure for such a change, apart from a possible increase in the cost of providing a minimum pension. The same conclusion holds for the earliest eligibility age. In the absence of an increase in the mandate, some people would save more, others not, and some people would work longer, others not. By its nature, a fully funded defined-contribution system does not redistribute across cohorts and might continue that pattern. The underlying insight is that a fall in the interest rate makes workers less well off, since lower interest rates make retirement consumption more expensive relative to earlier earnings.

With a partially funded defined-benefit system, in the absence of automatic adjustments, a decline in interest rates creates a financial problem for the system. Thus some response is necessary, either to lower benefit levels, raise contribution rates, raise ages of eligibility, or some combination of these. Since a less than fully funded system got that way by redistributing across cohorts, the legislative package should address the redistribution inherent in the change in policy. With lower interest rates, the loss of consumption in the future is less for a given increase in consumption today. Other things equal, this lessens the value of funding. This topic is discussed in more detail in section 7.2.

5.4.3   Adjusting for changing social risks

As stressed throughout this book, pension systems have multiple objectives that extend beyond consumption smoothing. For example, Chile, which has a fully funded defined-contribution system, also provides poverty relief, historically through a minimum pension guarantee and from July 2008 through a noncontributory basic pension; there are also legislated constraints on the speed with which a family may draw down its pension accumulation, and life and disability insurance are available to help protect families. In the United States, as discussed in section 8.3, Social Security provides supplementary benefits for spouses, surviving spouses, and divorced former spouses. Interestingly, in Sweden the separate parts of the pension system have different rules for spouses: the funded system allows individuals to purchase joint-life annuities with their accumulations, whereas the NDC system does not. Many countries have benefits for surviving spouses, with a wide variety of rules covering eligibility and benefit levels.

The circumstances that led to such rules change over time, as do social attitudes. Rates of marriage, divorce, and remarriage have changed. Attitudes toward cohabitation and toward same-sex marriages have changed. Male and female life expectancies have diverged and may diverge further (or become more similar) in the future. The level of a minimum guarantee thought to be socially appropriate may shift relative to average earnings. It is natural to think that changing circumstances and attitudes call for changes in the details of pension systems. But we have seen no proposals calling for automatic responses to measurable changes of this kind, nor have we any to propose. Thus we simply note that it may be useful to review the design of pension systems relative to social objectives from time to time—and that such a review may be easier politically when combined with adjustments needed to accommodate, or made possible by, changes in the financial position of the system. In the United States, for example, reforms made necessary by financial shortfalls—and, in earlier years, reforms made possible by financial surpluses—have both been recognized as times to address certain social issues. Thus, for example, the commission appointed by President Bush called for greater financial protection for some vulnerable groups but also for broad benefit cuts to address the projected financial shortfall. Our focus here has been to point out the value of reviewing the details of pension systems that relate to social objectives, not to discuss such objectives directly; we discuss some of the issues related to male-female differences in Chapter 8.

6

▷

Finance and Funding

Pension benefits are paid from receipts from contributions and (in the case of public pensions) taxes, and from the returns on assets and sometimes their sale. We use the term "financing" to refer to this current cash flow used to pay benefits, whatever its source, and "funding" to indicate financial assets held by the pension system, whether in a central trust fund or in individual accounts. Financing is said to be from dedicated revenue if it comes from taxes or contributions that, by law, are for the pension system or from the returns on assets belonging to the pension system. Financing can also come from outside the system, in the case of public pensions from general government revenue.

This chapter discusses the pros and cons of relying on dedicated revenue (section 6.1); how to measure the financial position of pensions, including the difference between implicit and explicit debt (section 6.2); the relationships among funding, national saving, and economic growth (section 6.3); and the proper methodology for comparing the returns from PAYG and funded systems (section 6.4), the last topic being a natural bridge to the discussion of risk sharing in Chapter 7. Finance and funding are controversial topics, afflicted by recurring faulty analysis and overstated conclusions. As this chapter unfolds, we take opportunities to identify and correct the most important examples.

6.1 DEDICATED REVENUE

Some countries finance public pensions entirely from dedicated revenue (for example, the United States), others wholly from general taxation (Australia and New Zealand), and others from a mix (Chile, Germany, Italy, and Sweden). The most common source of dedicated revenue (also commonly called earmarked revenue) is a payroll tax, the proceeds of which are used to pay current benefits, to purchase assets for a trust fund, or to buy assets to be held in individual accounts. There are many variations. For example, the Netherlands has an earmarked tax in the form of an addition to the income tax paid by people under age 65 for a pension benefit based on length of residency, not on a record of contributions. In the United States part of the dedicated revenue of the Social Security system comes from the taxation of Social Security pension benefits.

6.1.1 Arguments for dedicated sources

Arguments in favor of dedicated revenue include greater worker security, a longer planning horizon, and possibly greater political sustainability.

Worker security. Short of returning to work, people who have already retired have little or no ability to increase their income, and so are less able to bear risk than workers, who can adjust their earnings and consumption to save more for their eventual retirement. However, workers rely on the expectation of retirement benefits and should therefore be protected from large shocks to those expectations at short notice. Thus pension benefits should be broadly predictable, and changes to the rules of the system made infrequently, with considerable lead time and with the effects spread widely over cohorts. The more the financing of pensions is kept separate from the rest of the government budget, the less likely are benefits to be adjusted too frequently or unduly influenced by short-run fiscal matters unrelated to pension finances.

A longer horizon for financial planning and political balancing. Mixing the financing of pensions with other annual expenditures makes benefits vulnerable to the fluctuating needs of the rest of the budget (as has occurred in Germany and Italy). But pension payments are long-run liabilities and relatively predictable. It is therefore sound fiscal planning and good political practice to separate decisions about contributions and pension levels from short-term budgeting.[1] A system that relies on dedicated revenue (including a buffer of past accumulated surpluses in the form of a trust fund) largely achieves this distance, although pensioners are still affected by policies that affect everyone, such as changes in the income tax. Pensioners are also affected by the way in which benefits are indexed (see section 5.3.4), which, again, should not be subjected to large sudden changes.

Although pensions should be protected from short-run fiscal volatility, there needs to be a reliable process of political balancing over the long term between the level of pension benefits and available financing. A defined-benefit system financed from a dedicated revenue source will not balance revenue and expenditure exactly year by year. It will therefore be necessary to keep track of surplus revenue, since that revenue was raised for pensions and should be used for pensions. Long-term political balancing also requires credible long-term projections based on accurate accounting, both for financial planning and to improve public discussion of and understanding about options for reform. In a system that relies on dedicated revenue, there is likely to be greater public understanding of the budgetary link between total benefits and total contributions. Clear and accurate disclosure about the link, together with good projections, will enhance that understanding and raise public confidence in the future receipt of pensions, which may in turn reduce worker resistance to a realistic level of contributions.

---

1. This may not always be possible, however. For example, under Norway's constitution, budget legislation may not cover revenue or spending beyond the end of the following year, so pensions are necessarily part of the annual budget process. Since Norway has large oil reserves and a long history of consensual politics, pensions have not suffered under this arrangement, so Norway may be the exception that proves the rule.

Credible projections also constrain the tendency to legislate benefits much higher than can be financed with current contribution rates. A country that lets its projection of long-term costs and revenue become politicized is missing an important opportunity to foster public understanding of the true trade-offs, and needs to develop institutions that can provide reliable, independent projections.

Political economy. Arguments of political economy may stand on their own or reinforce the previous points:

- Contributory pensions make the notion of social insurance explicit. People might feel better about paying "contributions" than about paying "taxes" because they regard contributions as more obviously and directly connected with the corresponding benefits. They might also feel stigmatized by the receipt of benefits financed from taxation, but consider benefits paid from their own previous contributions as self-financed (whatever the extent to which this is true).

- People might regard benefits financed from dedicated contributions as safer than benefits financed from general taxation. And they may well be right that the politics of benefit changes are influenced by the method of financing.

- They might also think that a mix of worker and employer contributions is more equitable. Although Box 5.1 suggests that in economic terms this view is misplaced, it may be widely and deeply held and hence have a political reality.

For such reasons, a contributory system may create a more robust political settlement.

6.1.2   Arguments for some use of general revenue

A pure defined-contribution system will provide inadequate benefits for many workers, including those with fragmented careers, careers divided between covered and uncovered work, or low lifetime earnings. The same holds for a strictly proportional defined-benefit system without any explicit redistribution. If a pension system is to provide effective poverty relief, these pure cases need to be modified. The adequacy of benefits for workers with a limited contributions record can be increased either within the mandatory pension system (for example, through a minimum pension or a progressive benefit formula) or outside it (for example, through social assistance). If it is done within the system, the increased benefits can be financed either from inside the system (using part of the dedicated revenue) or from outside (from general revenue). Different countries have chosen widely from among these options, making it clear that there is no single optimal solution. As discussed in Chapter 7, the method of financing has important distributional effects within and across generations. Choices about the source of financing are a natural part of the political process and will have different implications in different political environments.

6.1.3   Conclusion

The main argument for financing part of benefits from general revenue is that this approach supports the adequacy of benefits. The main argument against is that it renders benefits vulnerable to short-term budgetary exigencies. A further argument against depends on the coverage of the system: use of tax financing may be regressive if taxes are collected from the population broadly but benefits limited mainly to urban, middle-class workers in the formal sector. The main argument for dedicated revenue is the potential for insulation from short-term fiscal trends, which enhances the security of covered workers, and the potentially greater robustness of the political settlement. Thus a mix of dedicated and general revenue, used for explicitly different parts of the system, may be a good design.

Coexisting with arrangements to improve adequacy within the pension system are antipoverty programs for the general population or the elderly. These are typically financed from general revenue, often include an income test (see Glossary), and may also include an assets test.

6.2 IMPLICIT AND EXPLICIT DEBT

"Implicit pension debt" has become part of the vocabulary of international dialogue on pensions—unfortunately without a standard definition, making it a source of much confusion. The core argument is that the pension promises of government have a future cost, which is not explicitly counted in budget projections in the same way as some other future costs, specifically debt service. There is good reason to be concerned about the long-run sustainability of government expenditure generally, and particular reason to be concerned about pension systems, which often have explicit long-term rules and serve a significant social purpose that makes changing those rules undesirable. However, there are key questions about how the long-term financial position of a pension system should be measured, and how each measure should be interpreted. We discuss these aspects in turn.

6.2.1 Measuring the financial position of pensions

Projections of future annual flows of contributions, benefits, changes in trust fund assets, and asset returns are important for showing whether a pension system is sustainable. Stochastic projections that recognize uncertainty about economic and demographic variables contain further information. Figure 6.1 shows projections for the cumulative balance of the trust fund of the U.S. Social Security system, which is expected to peak at around $2.5 trillion between 2010 and 2015 and then decline, finally turning negative around 2040. Figure 6.2 is a stochastic version of the same data, showing a range of possible outcomes. Thus the peak ratio of net trust fund assets to annual outflow has a high estimate of 500 percent (that is, sufficient to pay about five years of benefits) and a low estimate of about 350 percent.

Although detailed annual projections are helpful for analysts, summary measures of the financial position are needed for communication with the public and for the political process. There are multiple measures of the position of a pension system financed fully from dedicated revenue. (A system that also makes use of general revenue introduces further complications.) We first consider alternative approaches to measurement and then some of their uses.

Alternative approaches to measurement

Three methods are commonly used: the open group method, the closed group method, and the shutdown calculation. The calculations can be done either year by year, to show the overall financial position of the system, or cohort by cohort (Box 7.2), to show the distributional effects across cohorts.

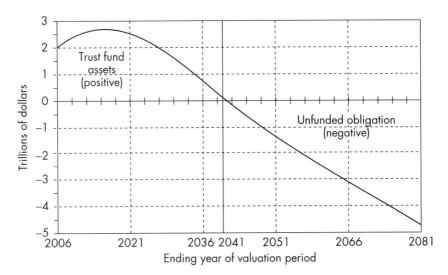

FIGURE 6.1.
Projected balance of the U.S. Social Security Trust Fund. Projections are present values as of January 1, 2007. *Source:* U.S. Social Security Administration (2007*a*, Figure II.D4).

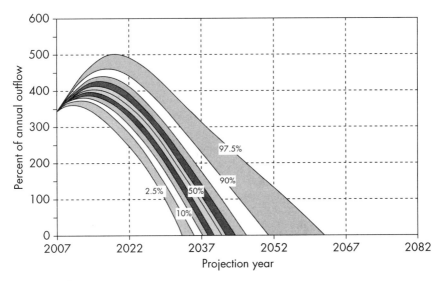

FIGURE 6.2.
Stochastic projections of the U.S. Social Security Trust Fund balance. *Source:* U.S. Social Security Administration (2007*a*, Figure VI.E1). Shading indicates forecasts with associated uncertainty bands.

Whichever measure is used, there are three natural units of measure of pension spending: the absolute measure (in national currency units), percent of payroll (or taxable payroll), and percent of GDP. The absolute measure is not a good way to communicate the position of a plan: it is hard for the public or the political process to distinguish among very large numbers. The other two measures are appropriate for considering the financing of the system itself and its role in the economy, respectively. Even if a system is sustainably financed from dedicated revenue, one might conclude that it is too large or too small. Consideration of size needs to reflect the needs of retirees relative to their own past earnings and to the position of younger cohorts still in the workforce, and to take account of the alternative uses of the resources being raised to finance pensions.

The open group method. This method includes all current and future workers and is the relevant measure when assessing the finances of a continuing system. Calculations can consider the indefinite future or can be limited to a given horizon, such as seventy-five years, reflecting the extreme uncertainty of projections far into the future.

The choice of time horizon is important. Traditionally in the United States, a seventy-five-year horizon has been used. This is long enough to allow considerable time for adjustment if the finances are found to be out of balance. Recently, however, some analysts have argued for an infinite horizon (see the discussion in section 11.2.3). One of the arguments for doing so is that, with a seventy-five-year horizon, imbalances in annual flows beyond the horizon mean that calculations only a few years later, using the same horizon, will find imbalances even if the current picture shows balance. On the other hand, using an infinite horizon is controversial, since projections beyond seventy-five years are little more than guesswork. A useful compromise is to preserve the seventy-five-year horizon but add the condition that the projected finances not be deteriorating at the end of the horizon.

The closed group method. This measure assesses the finances of a system that is closed (or assumed for purposes of analysis to be closed) to new entrants. Thus the calculation includes all past and present workers but excludes future workers. The approach considers all workers now aged (say) 16 and over and calculates the financial position of net cash flows associated only with these people, including the current trust fund but without a terminal trust fund. This is the relevant measure for an existing system when considering a new system for all new entrants to the workforce. It is also a way of measuring the net cost being left to future cohorts not yet in the labor force.

The closed group method can also be applied to all retirees plus a subset of current workers close to retirement age, for example those over 55. If reform proposals incorporate the principle of not changing the system for anyone close to retirement, this measure represents the net cost of existing arrangements that must be incorporated into any reformed system (or financed from outside) and hence is a constraint on reform for all younger cohorts. This measure is also termed the "legacy obligation," since it reflects the financial history of the system as well as the cost of continuing the system for those nearing retirement.

The shutdown calculation. This approach assesses the finances of a system that is to be terminated in the near future and replaced with new pension arrangements for everyone. Thus it measures the balance necessary to honor commitments to current retirees and commitments accumulated to date by current workers, without considering future contributions by current and future workers. The resulting balance thus includes the cost of benefits for retirees already receiving benefits and the accrued benefits of current workers once they do retire. This approach can be useful in a reform process, since it is a measure of the obligations of the old system that need to be covered, if the old system is to keep its accrued promises. This is relevant if mid-career workers are changing to a different system. However, measurement is not easy: in a nonlinear system (for example, one that redistributes toward workers with a worse lifetime earnings record), there is some ambiguity as to how those with incomplete working lives should be treated.

Net and gross implicit debt

Net implicit debt. When using the open group method and a chosen horizon, a useful concept is actuarial balance, defined as the present discounted value (PDV) of annual net cash flows up to the horizon, plus the value of the current trust fund, minus the present discounted value of any planned trust fund at the end of the horizon, usually set equal to a level appropriate for a precautionary balance (for example, one year's outflow).[2] Expressed as a percentage of the PDV of the covered earnings of workers, this concept shows the immediate increase (or decrease) in the contribution rate that would produce balance over the horizon. This concept is a good indicator of the financial sustainability of the existing pension system and a measure of what it would take to adjust the system for balance in terms of taxable payroll.

Using the closed group method, the calculation of actuarial balance yields a measure of the cost left for the future if the current system is continued for the closed group, with a different system for later cohorts. And using the shutdown method yields a measure of the cost of recognizing accrued obligations when switching to a different system for everyone.

Gross implicit debt. Again using the open group method and a chosen horizon, gross implicit debt is the PDV of annual pension payments alone (that is, ignoring inflows) if the existing system continues. By itself, as discussed in section 6.2.2, this measure is not a useful concept. Expressed as a percentage of the PDV of the total earnings of covered workers, however, the measure shows the contribution rate that would produce balance, allowing a check on whether the projected pension payments are viable. This definition results in the largest estimate of implicit pension debt in any given circumstances.

6.2.2   Errors in interpretation

Reporting implicit pension debt rightly emphasizes the fact that pensions have a future cost. But overemphasis impedes good analysis. The proposition that it is harmless, or possibly even beneficial, to replace implicit with explicit debt in public reporting makes a series of analytical errors.

---

2. When the condition is added that the projected finances not be deteriorating at the end of the horizon, this measure is called sustainable actuarial balance.

Focusing exclusively on liabilities. It is a crude error to look only at gross implicit debt, as in the following:

> implicit pension debt [is] the present value of the pensions that are owed to current pensioners and to workers. . . . This debt is inherent in pay-as-you-go systems. . . . But assets are not accumulated to cover this debt; instead, the obligation is covered by implicit government IOUs. In many countries, the implicit debt exceeds the country's conventional explicit debt . . . and in some cases exceeds 200 percent of GDP. (James 1998, p. 278)

The PDV of pension promises for the next, say, seventy-five years is a large number that will sound alarming to the layperson but is misleading, first, because it considers only one side of the financial ledger, liabilities (that is, future pension payments), while ignoring the assets side (future revenue). Here the most notable asset is the government's ability to collect taxes, particularly future taxes that have already been legislated. A more useful approach is to compare total pension outflows with the expected yield of a "sensible" tax or contribution rate, that is, one whose size, when considered alongside the taxes necessary to finance other government spending, does not cause excessive labor market distortions. Suppose that the current contribution rate is 20 percent and there is a consensus that it should not be increased. If projected pension spending requires a 22.5 percent tax rate, it would normally be right to argue that the system is not sustainable and should be adjusted. But the variable that should worry policymakers is not the entire 22.5 percent contribution rate (the simple measure of implicit pension debt above), but the 2.5-percentage-point excess above the plausible limit of 20 percent. In short, looking at total future pension liabilities but not at assets overstates, often considerably, the true magnitude of implicit pension debt.

An equally egregious error is to project a small annual deficit over a long time horizon, cumulate those deficits, and report the sum in dollars rather than as a percentage of payroll or GDP. This approach generates a large and, to nonexperts, alarming number. It takes no cognizance of the range of measures available to close the deficit; often only a small increase in contributions or reduction in benefits will suffice. This error illustrates the importance of relating costs to measures of the economy.

A third error in emphasizing costs is to ignore the improved well-being from the payment of benefits. Pension benefits are not money poured down the drain: they contribute to all the objectives—consumption smoothing, poverty relief, and the like—discussed in detail in section 2.1.

Treating implicit and explicit debt as equivalent. The concept of implicit debt is useful because it reminds people that explicit debt is not the only claim being made on future generations. However, the common practice of measuring implicit debt for social insurance programs but not for other government expenditures is incomplete; the implicit pension debt needs to be placed in the context of the entire projected financial position of the government. In addition, the concept has led some analysts to treat implicit debt as fully (or nearly fully) equivalent to explicit debt, as in this example:

> The true net economic costs of moving from an unfunded pay-as-you-go system to a fully funded system are zero. That is to say, the total funded and unfunded debt of a country does not change by moving from an unfunded system to a funded one. (Rodríguez 1999, p. 11)

In particular, some analysts have argued that governments should issue new government bonds equal to the amount of implicit debt and place these bonds in newly created individual accounts, viewing such a step as creating accounts at no cost. Such an action, however, would have real economic effects.

Government can lower implicit debt as part of a pension reform, and many governments have done so, by cutting benefits, increasing taxes, or both. Explicit debt can likewise be reduced by spending cuts and tax increases. But turning implicit debt into explicit assets with property rights and placing them in individual accounts removes the option of reducing the debt by reducing benefits without altering anything else in the economy. Similarly, restricting pension contributions to deposits into individual accounts forgoes the option of using those contributions to finance the pension system generally, for example to pay off the legacy debt. Once explicit debt has been issued in place of the implicit debt, that debt is subject to the same rules as other explicit debt. Lowering the value of explicit debt by actions such as repudiation or increased inflation would have widespread harmful effects on the economy.

Moreover, unless issued as consols (government bonds that pay interest in perpetuity and never mature), the market for which is unclear, explicit debt needs to be rolled over repeatedly, exposing government finances to additional bond market risk. And uncertainty about future conditions in bond markets is far more important when there is considerably more debt outstanding—which is exactly what would happen if implicit debt were converted into explicit debt. If, as is likely, markets perceive explicit debt as different from implicit debt, they will respond with some reluctance to the large and rapid increase in the supply of bonds that such a conversion would entail, a likely outcome being an increase in the interest rates at which the government borrows. Finally, a further difference is that pension benefits are typically indexed for inflation, whereas most explicit debt is in nominal terms. In short, implicit and explicit debt are not equivalent.

Arguing that implicit debt should be minimized. Paying off implicit pension debt in full is often suboptimal. It is mistaken to argue that a country should pay off all its explicit national debt in all circumstances; what is critical is that the ratio of debt to GDP does not rise to the point where it induces large increases in interest rates, or becomes unsustainable, or has adverse effects on the economy that outweigh any benefits from borrowing. For exactly the same reasons, a country need not pay off its implicit debt; what is critical is that the contribution rate needed in the future does not rise so high that it undercuts participation in the pension system to the point where the system becomes unsustainable.

The point is fundamental. Consumption smoothing is an objective of pensions precisely because, as Figure 2.1 illustrates, it can be welfare improving for people to borrow at certain times of their lives and save at others. People in their peak earning years can redistribute from their younger to their older selves by saving, or from their older to their younger selves by borrowing, for example for college or to buy a home. But whereas an individual might be required by lenders to have zero net debt by the end of his or her lifetime, such a requirement does not apply for an entity with an infinite life span and is not necessarily the right goal. Just as a corporation that is a going concern might want to set up its capital structure with a permanent mix of equity and debt, so can government justify issuing and rolling over a reasonable amount of debt in perpetuity, say, to finance investment in infrastructure. In short, the existence of some debt can be welfare enhancing; hence the proper objective is to optimize its quantity, not to minimize it. Thus, as discussed in section 6.3.2, giving some assets to a pension trust fund to reduce implicit debt may be a sensible part of policy, but allocating enough assets to bring the implicit debt down to zero is not a necessary condition for good policy.

The critical element in decisions about the time paths of both explicit debt and implicit pension debt is the evaluation of intergenerational redistributions that will result from the chosen paths. This is discussed in more detail in Chapter 7.

Ignoring the intergenerational redistributive effects of paying off implicit pension debt in full. Suppose that a country reduces its implicit debt by increasing pension contributions in order to finance more of the PAYG pensions of people already retired; such a move reduces the consumption of the current generation of workers while increasing that of retirees. Similarly, suppose workers are moved from an existing PAYG system to a system of fully funded individual accounts, and at the same time are required to contribute to pensions for existing retirees; again the change reduces the consumption of current workers, and if the reform lowers PAYG pensions, it also reduces the consumption of current retirees. All these changes benefit future generations of workers, who will make lower PAYG contributions; they thus redistribute from today's generations to future generations. As discussed more fully in section 7.2, different forms of finance have different intergenerational effects. Such redistribution may or may not be good policy, but in arguing for lower implicit pension debt, it is an error to ignore these intergenerational redistributive effects.

6.2.3 Conclusion

In sum, the simple argument for reducing implicit pension debt makes a series of errors: it considers only liabilities and ignores assets; it focuses on financing arrangements, ignoring the fact that what matters is real resources; it fails to recognize important differences in the economic effects of implicit and explicit debt; it erroneously implies that paying off implicit debt in full is optimal; and it ignores the intergenerational distributional effects of a change in the balance between implicit and explicit debt.

None of this is to deny that implicit debt can be a useful concept. The cost of pensions matters considerably. Excessive pension spending can reduce investment and cause major distortions that interfere with economic growth. Thus it is important to project future pension costs, but also important to interpret such projections correctly. Analysts should place the costs in proper perspective and consider whether the proposed financing of those costs is plausible. All this requires careful actuarial work, careful projections of cost and of future output, and careful interpretation of the results, including the distribution of burdens within and across generations.

6.3 FUNDING, NATIONAL SAVING, AND GROWTH

Three sets of strategic arguments are frequently made for funded pensions:

- Funding increases economic growth by increasing national saving (section 6.3.1) or by helping to develop capital markets (section 6.3.2).

- Funding assists adjustment to demographic change (section 6.3.3).
- People regard their property rights as more secure when based on the ownership of assets (section 6.3.4).

The first two points are macroeconomic arguments, the third a political economy argument. All three illustrate some of the errors and overstatements mentioned at the start of the chapter. A fourth argument is often overlooked:

- Funding redistributes burdens across generations.

This fundamentally important point is discussed in Chapter 7.

6.3.1   Funding and national saving

As discussed in section 4.2.1, pensions are about consumption. Thus national output is central, and so is macroeconomic balance, that is, how output is shared between different uses: the consumption of different people and the investment that provides future output. The degree to which contributions are used to accumulate assets for the pension system can affect national saving and thus the rate of growth.

Effects on saving. An increase in national saving today requires a decline in someone's consumption today: raising contribution rates now will lower the consumption of today's workers; cutting benefits now will lower the consumption of today's pensioners. Increased funding of pensions can bring about just such an increase in saving, and thus, other things equal, raises the burden on current generations in order to lower the burden on future generations, in the same way as a budgetary decision to increase taxes or cut public spending so as to reduce public debt.

But other things are not necessarily equal. Thus, depending on how it is done, and depending on the behavioral response, increased funding of pensions may lead to a large increase in national saving, or a small increase, or have zero net effect, or even decrease national saving. Hence it is important to distinguish between funding that actually does increase saving (sometimes referred to as broad funding) and funding that increases the assets of the pension system without increasing total saving, for example, by issuing government bonds and placing them in individual accounts (narrow funding). If workers' accounts hold newly issued government bonds, saving by workers thereby increases, but this saving is offset by an equal increase in government borrowing, with no net effect on national saving. Critical to this analysis is whether the bonds are newly issued, rather than purchased from the public with funds raised through higher taxes or lower government spending. There is often a failure to distinguish between the implications of different types of assets and the implications of different ways of acquiring those assets. It is the latter that matters for the impact on national saving, as Box 6.1 explains.

There are two questions: does funding increase saving, and if so, is the result welfare enhancing? The answer to the first will depend on the reaction of private savers and of the rest of the government budget.

Consider private savers first. In a new system, if workers are obliged to make contributions to funded accounts, in effect saving more, they are likely to respond in part by reducing their consumption and in part by reducing their other, voluntary saving.

▶ Box 6.1 Government bonds and national saving

Consider the following quotation:

> Note that domestic government bonds do not provide a demographic reserve since they are claims on future tax payers just as pay-as-you-go pension claims are claims on future contribution payers. In fact, financing a pension system through domestic government bonds is macroeconomically equivalent to a pay-as-you-go system (Diamond 1965; Pestieau and Possen 2000). Using foreign government bonds effectively internationalizes the pay-as-you-go system by securitizing claims on taxes paid by future foreign citizens. (Börsch-Supan 2005, p. 30, writing about Finland)

The statement is correct that a swap of Finnish government bonds held by the pension system for U.S. government bonds held by its pension system would alter the risk-sharing characteristics of both pension systems. But the statement is potentially misleading in failing to distinguish between *holding* government bonds and *issuing* government bonds.

Consider a PAYG system with no assets, financed by a payroll tax. If the government issues new bonds and gives them to the pension system, that shifts future liabilities from payroll taxpayers to general revenue taxpayers, which will involve some shifting of liabilities among members of the same cohorts even if the timing of payments does not change. Issuing bonds in this way does not directly alter national saving, although the different responses of different taxpayers may result in different levels of national saving (Diamond 2006c). Following such a move with a swap of government bonds for, say, corporate bonds or bonds of another country still does not directly alter national saving.

In contrast, increasing taxes and using the additional revenue to purchase existing government bonds from the public to transfer to the pension system does directly increase national saving, although the full effect depends on private responses to the tax and transfer. Thus the impact on national saving depends not on the type of asset being held but on how the asset is acquired—through increased debt or through increased taxes or reduced government spending.

Similarly, moving assets (whether government bonds or other assets) from a trust fund to individual accounts does not directly alter national saving. In contrast, raising taxes to purchase assets for individual accounts does directly increase national saving, although the overall impact also depends on the response of private savers and the rest of the government budget. ◀

If they reduce voluntary saving dollar for dollar with the increase in mandatory saving, there is no net change in saving. However, not all workers will do this, and some cannot. For example, workers who would not have saved at all voluntarily, and who have limited ability to borrow, cannot reduce their voluntary saving in the face of the new contribution mandate, so their total saving will increase.

Within an existing system, increasing the contribution rate has an effect similar to starting a new system: it raises saving. In contrast, redirecting contributions from an existing central trust fund to individual accounts has no direct impact on national saving and may have little or no impact on worker consumption. Since their taxes are the same as before, the prime consideration from the workers' perspective is whether they alter their saving outside the pension system because they perceive a different system for providing benefits. For example, workers in this situation may choose to save less, because individual accounts bear a stronger parallel to voluntary saving. A central issue is how the government adjusts the old system for the loss of contributions that are redirected to individual accounts. If the government makes no changes beyond issuing new debt to cover benefits under the old system, and if shifting contributions from a central fund to individual accounts leads workers to save less, the overall impact can be negative. Effectively, in this case the increase in narrow funding comes from issuing additional government debt.

Part of the difficulty in evaluating worker responses to changes in pension design is that workers are not well informed about the rules of pension systems (see section 9.3). Although this observation is well supported, there is little evidence of what people's perceptions are or of how those perceptions affect private saving. Aligning perceptions more closely with reality may follow from increasing emphasis on transparency and the provision of information. Countries like Sweden and Norway, and increasingly also the United States, emphasize annual individual communication with workers, informing them of their contributions record and forecasting the pension benefits they can expect on the basis of plausible assumptions.

Alongside these private responses, it is necessary also to consider government responses. Putting additional contributions into individual accounts may lead the government to spend more, since it can easily borrow from the accounts (indeed, legislation may require funds to hold significant amounts of government debt). In this case there may be little increase in national saving, as the increased government borrowing and spending to a greater or lesser extent offset the increased saving by workers. When revenue is shifted from a trust fund to individual accounts, any small decline in saving by workers (for example, if they save less because they regard assets in individual accounts as safer than in a trust fund) may be accompanied by a decrease in government spending elsewhere, since it may affect reported deficit measures. But the reporting effect may be subject to manipulation (see Box 6.2).

In sum, although considerable evidence exists on individual saving responses to pension design, it is much harder to reach a solid conclusion about the response of the rest of the government budget—that response, moreover, is likely to vary with the ability of the government to undertake additional borrowing.

If funding does raise national saving, is the outcome beneficial? In other words, is an increase in saving the right objective? The correct way to pose the issue is to ask whether it makes sense for the economy as a whole to raise contributions or reduce benefits now in order to have lower contributions or higher benefits in the future. As already discussed, increased funding through lower benefits or higher contributions necessarily redistributes across generations. Thus there can be no universal answer about whether funding raises welfare. Each country must consider the question in the context of its own circumstances and priorities, including its current saving rate and anticipated growth in earnings. If the saving rate is already high and growth rapid, as in China today, it may make little sense to adopt a policy to increase saving even further. But in a country with low saving and slow growth, there may be a strong case for increasing contributions, reducing pension benefits, or cutting other parts of the government budget explicitly to increase saving.

Finally, and a more general point, the discussion of growth in the pensions literature concentrates on the links through increased saving and capital accumulation to increased output. The literature on growth and development recognizes the importance of a number of additional factors, including human capital accumulation, entrepreneurship, and innovation. For all three, imperfections in the capital market are important

▶ Box 6.2 Do funded individual accounts increase reported deficits?

Financing the old system. In moving toward funded accounts, a key question is how to finance the ongoing obligations of the old system. In a PAYG system the contributions of today's workers pay the pensions of today's retirees. But if the system changes to a funded basis, the contributions of today's workers must instead go into a fund. If the government wishes today's pensioners to continue to receive benefits, then the move to funding has an inescapable cash-flow cost. The government can pay today's pensions either by increasing the contributions paid by today's workers, or by increasing the taxes on today's workers and pensioners, or by borrowing, in which case the costs fall on future generations of workers and pensioners. As the experience of Chile shows (Chapter 12), those cash-flow costs can continue for a long time.

Effect on reported deficits. Under plausible government budget accounting, transferring contributions from a trust fund to individual accounts increases the reported government deficit. Under international rules on public accounting, if contributions that were previously counted as government revenue (since they went into the trust fund), are no longer counted as revenue (since they now go into individual accounts), the deficit increases; similarly, if the transfer is treated as an expenditure, the deficit increases.

Some governments, for example those of Hungary, Poland, and Sweden, argued when they made the move to funding that they were reducing implicit pension debt, and that such a reduction should be treated as an offset against explicit debt in the public accounts. Thus they included contributions to individual accounts as part of government revenue when reporting the fiscal deficit. Eurostat disallowed this procedure, ruling that the measure should instead be phased out, falling from 100 percent of contributions to individual accounts to 80 percent in 2006, and subsequently by 20 percent each year until eliminated.

Under the methodology used by the Congressional Budget Office to measure the U.S. budget deficit, a transfer of contributions from the Social Security trust fund to purchase assets (other than government debt) held in individual accounts would be measured as additional government expenditure, thereby increasing the reported deficit. In the debate over President George W. Bush's proposal to introduce such accounts, it was proposed to legislate a change in the Congressional Budget Office methodology so that purchases of assets would not be included in public spending. This would have the same impact on the deficit as counting the deposits as revenue, as above. Most countries do not have the same freedom as the United States to set aside international rules on public accounting (on which see International Monetary Fund 2001; parallel issues arise in deciding whether to classify student loans as part of public debt or as private borrowing; see Barr 2001a, Chapter 14). ◀

and enlarge the potential role of other government policies. How and how much pensions policy should reflect its impact on such issues is worth exploring. For a general treatment of growth, see Helpman (2004).

Analytical errors. Discussion of funding is prone to errors. One of these is to accept objectives uncritically. As just discussed, although increased saving may be beneficial in many countries, it is still necessary for each country to ask whether it is the right objective. Reformers, however, may overlook the point:

> Eight countries enacting funded reforms had savings rates in excess of 20 percent of GDP at the time of their reform. . . . Low-income countries with negative savings rates also may prefer a PAYG pension system. (World Bank 2006a, p. 27)

Second, analysis often starts by comparing alternative steady-state outcomes under different degrees of funding, and follows with a comment that there is a transition cost to reaching a steady state with a higher level of funding. As discussed in section 6.4, this approach is misleading. It gives little insight into the trade-off between the benefits of having a larger fund and the cost of building one. Indeed the term "transition cost" itself suggests something small, yet a transition period may extend over decades. It is more informative to analyze funding as described above (and discussed more fully in section 7.2), by considering the implications of increasing funding today in order to have some combination of lower taxes or higher benefits in the future. This way of posing the issue does not focus on funding per se but on the tax, benefit, and debt decisions that should underpin the analysis.

A separate, widely made, but incorrect argument for funded accounts holds that a funded system is better if the rate of interest (that is, the return on pension funds) exceeds the rate of growth of wages (that is, the return to a PAYG system). In fact, a complete analysis (section 6.4) shows that there is no gain for everyone from funding per se, but rather an intergenerational redistribution. That is, comparing the rate of return on assets with the rate of growth of taxable earnings involves basically the same incomplete analysis of comparing steady states without considering the adjustment to the new steady state.

Another suspect argument is that "a multipillar structure [that is, one that includes funded individual accounts] allows for tactical sequencing, strategic bundling, packaging, and compensation and thus is useful for overcoming resistance to reform" (Holzmann and Hinz 2005, p. 42). The argument, in essence, is that including funding in the reform package makes it politically easier to introduce reforms that increase efficiency in the public PAYG system. However, those efficiency gains are available without funding, by better design of a PAYG system, so this is misattribution, unless it really is the case that the efficiency gains are not available politically without such bundling. In politics bundling does matter, but it may not be necessary for reform, and indeed it may make reform more difficult (see Börsch-Supan and Wilke 2006 on the German case). In any case, political arguments are separate from economic arguments and should be clearly labeled as such.

Finally, some analysis implies that funding necessarily requires individual defined-contribution accounts, with worker choice over portfolios offered by private providers. That argument erroneously conflates three separate concepts: funding, defined contributions, and worker choice. If policymakers want more funding, there are many ways to bring it about—funding is possible in a defined-benefit system and consistent with centralized choice of investments by a trust fund. For example, Sweden has funded a diversified central portfolio within a defined-benefit system for many years, and similar arrangements have been started in Canada and Switzerland. A related example is the Norwegian Government Petroleum Fund (Norway Central Bank 2006). Malaysia and Singapore have central provident funds within defined-contribution systems. Thus the choice of a level of funding and of portfolio diversification is economically unrelated to the choice between defined-benefit and defined-contribution systems, or between individual and more broadly based accumulations. We return in Chapter 9 to the central topic of portfolio choice.

6.3.2 Funding and capital market development

Alongside any effects on saving, funding can assist economic growth if it helps to improve the efficiency with which that saving is channeled into investment. The argument for efficiency gains rests on greater development of domestic capital markets and of their regulation.

The argument, however, is not simple. It implicitly assumes that pension funds are largely invested in the domestic capital markets. In considering whether such a policy is appropriate, it is necessary to separate arguments about strengthening old-age security from arguments about promoting growth. If the objective is to increase old-age security, restricting investment to the domestic market will be suboptimal, since some international diversification will generally benefit the participating workers by spreading risk. This is particularly the case in a small country, where the domestic market offers more limited opportunities to diversify across industries and firms. On the other hand, if the objective is to promote growth, the optimal policy depends on the terms on which a country can attract capital inflows to balance, at least in part, the outgoing portfolio investment of pension funds. This is not a major problem for developed countries, so that the gains from international diversification are clear. Developing countries, however, face two potential problems: a country risk premium may be necessary to induce capital inflows, and, to the extent that such inflows take place, the country may become more vulnerable to capital flight by foreign investors. Thus there is a tension: it may be in the short-term interest of participants to hold internationally diversified assets; but from the perspective of the economy as a whole, premature diversion of pension savings to other countries can increase the cost of capital domestically, slowing economic growth.

Even when the analysis is restricted to domestic investment, the argument that funding strengthens the domestic capital markets fails in two polar cases. In developed countries financial markets are already highly developed, so that additional deepening through mandatory pension saving is unlikely to bring about substantial further improvements. True, if such funding increases the number of investors making good use of the capital markets, risks may be spread more widely, and so more efficiently. But in the United States the concern is precisely that a mandate that brings large numbers of new, inexperienced investors into the markets through individual accounts could call forth regulatory changes that might lower capital market efficiency. At the other end of the spectrum, in countries with very limited institutional capacity, the existing financial infrastructure is too weak to risk the pensions of large numbers of workers by mandating funded individual accounts.

Between the two polar cases is a range of country capacities where the potential to improve capital markets exists, but so does the risk that, without enough improvement, workers will not get good returns on their contributions, or government will have to bear the cost of bailing out the pension system. The risk is easy to comprehend. Inadequate markets can yield low returns. They also have much higher costs than better developed ones, a point of particular relevance to small accounts. And the presence of significant capital flowing into markets may result in opportunities for embezzlement that are not available with PAYG. Adequate capital markets require significant government regulation; they do not function well by themselves. It also helps to have a large capital market, which generally means one based in a large economy. As discussed below, ineffective capital markets not only hurt pensioners but may also imply a worse allocation of investment than would occur with less formal ways of allocating saving to investment.

The possibility of gain is also easy to comprehend, since better-functioning capital markets increase economic efficiency and so economic growth. What is critical for realizing that gain is a sustained effort to improve the regulation of markets and the functioning of the economy generally. Committing the funds of workers may help to improve regulation by adding to the political support for improved regulation, which capital market institutions generally resist, and so enhance the ability to legislate and implement a better regulatory regime. Indeed, individual accounts in Chile (and the use of bonds as backing for individual annuities) resulted in stronger government regulation, the emergence of a corporate bond market, and a stock market with a much larger capitalization (more shares selling for higher prices) relative to the economy. However, since pension funds are largely buy-and-hold investors, the growth in the value of the stock market has not been accompanied by similar growth in the volume of transactions. Thus the market has not grown in liquidity in step with its growth in value.

An alternative approach is to encourage voluntary pensions as a stimulus to capital market development, particularly where the economy is large enough that voluntary savings can reap economies of scale. This has two advantages: it increases political pressure for well-regulated capital markets; and the risk of poor market outcomes, possibly due to corruption, falls on a group better able to bear it, namely, the corporations themselves and workers in large corporations, who tend to be better off than the average covered worker.

To explore the efficiency issue in more detail, consider four channels through which savings are allocated to investment:

- Market transactions: purchases of newly issued bonds and stocks (as opposed to trading of existing ones)
- Intermediation: deposits in banks and other financial intermediaries, which are then lent to investors
- Direct pairwise loans: loans from friends and families to people starting small businesses, trade credit, and seller-provided credit more generally
- Financing of one's own direct investment in a business.

In a country where market structure is weak and the banking system functions poorly, progress is not likely to come through either of the first two channels. Yet funded individual accounts, financed by taking more money from workers, reduce flows through the other two channels, leaving no places for pension funds to allocate savings that offer any evidence of functioning better in the short run.

A second set of arguments, picked up in section 7.2.2, about the role of pension funds in improving the efficiency of capital markets centers on transferring shares of newly privatized state-owned enterprises to the public pension trust fund (as in some of the former communist countries in Central and Eastern Europe). This approach, it is argued, will improve corporate governance, a key ingredient in economic efficiency and growth in market economies.³ In developed countries, centralized pension funds (such as defined-benefit or provident funds) can result in additional players in corporate governance, which can influence outcomes for better or worse.⁴ But good governance also needs good legislation, effective oversight by the regulatory authorities, and effective oversight and exercise of voting rights by shareholders, all of which require scarce skills and significant institutional capacity.

6.3.3 Funding and demographic change

Although the point was shown to be flawed many years ago (Barr 1979), the argument that funding necessarily assists pension finance significantly in the face of demographic change still reappears:

> The PSA [personal savings accounts] system solves the typical problem of pay-as-you-go systems with respect to labor demographics: in an aging population the number of workers per retiree decreases. Under the PSA system, the working population does not pay for the retired population. Thus, in contrast with the pay-as-you-go system, the potential for inter-generational conflict and eventual bankruptcy is avoided. The problem that many countries face—unfunded pension liabilities—does not exist under the PSA system. (Piñera 1995, p. 160)

The argument needs to be considered separately in the context of a decline in both fertility and elderly mortality. Suppose that a large workforce is followed a generation later by a smaller workforce. In a pure PAYG system the revenue from a given public pension contribution rate will fall, putting upward pressure on the contribution rate, or downward pressure on benefits, or both. This problem is well understood and not controversial.

It is argued that funding can ease the problem: each member of the large workforce in the first generation builds up pension savings; the defined-contribution pension available for a representative worker is then exactly what can be covered by those savings. This argument, in essence that in the quotation above, is correct in terms of *finance* but may fail to provide workers with the *consumption* they expect in old age. With PAYG, the shortfall comes through a decline in contributions. With funding, the mechanism is less direct but has the same cause: unless a decline in the number of workers somehow has no effect on output, output will fall relative to what it would have been with a workforce of constant size; and if output falls, consumption or investment, or both, must fall. Several outcomes, or a combination, are possible:

- Pensioners do not get the consumption they expected, because of higher prices or lower rates of return on their pension savings, as explained in Box 6.3
- Workers have lower consumption than they would choose because of mandatory increases in pension saving

---

3. See the symposium on corporate governance in the *Oxford Review of Economics Policy*, vol. 21, no. 2, Summer 2005.

4. The California Public Employees' Retirement System (CalPERS), for example, with over $150 billion in assets, takes an active shareholder interest; more generally, see Börsch-Supan and Winter (2001).

▶ **Box 6.3 How falling output affects holders of individual accounts**

Falling output creates problems for individual accounts, independent of whether the account holds cash-like assets or equities. Continuing the example of a large generation of workers followed by a smaller one, suppose that pensioners of the large generation seek purchasing power over future production during their retirement by building up bank accounts. Their desired consumption (the amount that they wish to spend out of accumulated savings in retirement) may exceed what the smaller generation of workers wants to save, given fiscal and monetary policies. This can lead to excess demand in the goods market, causing price inflation, thus reducing the purchasing power of nominal annuities. Anticipation of the possibility of such an outcome will generally affect the interest rates used to attract bank deposits. Hence the impact of demography, which is visible to savers and investors, gets spread over a long time.

Suppose, instead, that workers seek purchasing power over future production by accumulating non-nominal assets such as equities. In that case, as retirees they must finance their consumption by selling their financial assets. But because the next generation is smaller, there will be relatively less aggregate demand, hence less need for productive assets, leading to excess supply in asset markets, leading in turn to lower asset prices than if generations were of equal size. (To see this, suppose that every couple has one child; thus each couple of the next generation will inherit two apartments and, other things equal, apartment values will fall.)* This will reduce the value of pension accumulations and hence of the resulting annuity. In practice, asset prices would show slower growth (or even decline) much earlier, as investors anticipate the effect of asset sales by larger cohorts of retirees.

Under either outcome, retirees may not get the real pension they expected. ◀

_____

* We are indebted to András Simonovits for this example.

- Investment falls, crowded out by the increase in the combined consumption of workers and pensioners, putting future growth at risk.

As noted earlier, PAYG and funding are both mechanisms for organizing claims on future output; since demographic change affects that output, it causes problems for pension systems however they are organized. Consideration of output is one way to see that funding does not circumvent the consequences of population aging. Another way is to follow the accounting for funds to be used to finance consumption in retirement. A slowdown in the growth of the labor force (or an absolute decline) will tend to lower the return to capital, hence the return to investment, and hence the accumulation of funding when it comes time for retirees begin to spend that accumulation.

An even closer parallel between funded and PAYG systems arises if the birth rate is stable but the life expectancy of retirees increases. If the average retirement age is unchanged, the effect is to increase the number of retirees per worker. With a pure PAYG system, this increase requires a higher contribution rate or lower monthly benefits to maintain system balance. With funded accounts and no change in interest rates, the sustainable level of monthly benefits is lower if the average lifetime is longer. The effect is further compounded if interest rates fall, as they are likely to in response to a rising capital-labor ratio, as retirees spread their consumption over more years. Thus, with PAYG, preserving financial balance requires lowering benefits. With funded accounts, lower benefits follow automatically as market forces raise the price of annuities.

The underlying economic problem is similar in both cases, but not identical, since the rate of return on assets, which determines the necessary fall in benefits from annuity pricing, may not match the implicit return under PAYG.

In short, what matters is not financial accumulation but output. If output increases, it becomes easier to meet the claims both of workers and retirees, whether those claims are organized through PAYG or through funding. The solution to population aging lies not in funding per se but, once more, in output growth. This argument remains true in an open economy for the reasons set out in Box 4.1.

6.3.4 Funding and property rights

In a country with a public defined-benefit system, the legislature generally has the authority to change the benefit formula. Thus protection for current and future beneficiaries comes from the properties—good or ill—of the political process, although the desire to be reelected and to avoid street demonstrations generally limits the extent to which politicians will make large, sudden downward changes in pension benefits and accruals. Similarly, even in countries where property rights are respected, the presence of assets in individual accounts does not eliminate the government's ability to lower the value of current or future pensions. This can happen in multiple ways. In one approach the government treats assets in individual accounts similarly to assets elsewhere: it can lower the value of nominal assets such as government bonds through unexpected inflation; or it can raise taxes on corporate profits, depressing stock values; or it can raise taxes on incomes, including pensions, or on consumption spending, thus reducing the value of benefits to current and future retirees; or, if the country taxes asset returns within individual accounts (as was formerly done in Australia), it can raise that tax. More generally, the special tax treatment of pension accumulations can be changed. It is not uncommon for advocates of individual accounts to point out the political risk in defined-benefit systems and make no mention of possible political risks with individual accounts.

In the United States the taxation of Social Security benefits has been changed twice: in 1983 when up to 50 percent of benefits became taxable for some retirees, and again in 1993, when this was raised to 85 percent for some of these already-taxed retirees. Another example is the reduction of the tax privileges of U.K. pension funds in 1997. The tax rates and the income levels at which taxation starts are both variables that may properly be changed by legislation and not a violation of property rights.

Thus the value of anticipated benefits can be changed by legislation, both in a national defined-benefit system and in a system where assets are held in individual accounts. Should this be regarded as a problem? Is the ability to change future benefits simply a source of risk to workers and retirees, or is it an opportunity to do a better job of sharing the risks inherent in pension systems—an opportunity that may be used well or badly? As discussed in section 7.3, whatever the other arguments for or against them, defined-benefit arrangements, unlike defined-contribution arrangements, have the ability to spread risks across cohorts. As discussed in Box 7.3, the value of such risk sharing, if done well, can be considerable.

In sum, the role of property rights in protecting the expectations of workers and retirees is not as simple as some analysts would make it appear.

6.3.5 Conclusions

The relationship between funding and growth is neither simple nor automatic.

Funding does not necessarily increase saving. The relationship between increases in national saving and increases in pension funding is complex. How much national saving will increase or decrease depends on the extent to which the increase in mandatory pension saving is offset by any reduction in voluntary private saving and in saving by government elsewhere in the budget. And narrow funding can have little effect on saving. Thus saving may or may not increase.

Increased saving does not necessarily increase output. The simplest argument, usually portrayed in a neoclassical model with a simple capital aggregate, is that a move to funding increases saving, which increases investment, which in turn increases output by the marginal product of capital. These links hold in many circumstances, but not always or necessarily, and the mechanisms are not simple. Apart from the possibility of the familiar short-run Keynesian impact of decreased aggregate demand on output, increased saving can affect asset prices as well as capital quantities:

- The link between an increase in saving and increased investment is complex. Increased saving may increase investment, and thus output, but it may also simply drive up the prices of assets in limited supply, such as urban land.[5] Other increases can raise equity prices. Separately, in an economy with an open capital market, an increase in domestic saving, although relevant for national wealth, may have little or no effect on domestic investment.

- Funding may improve the allocation of saving to investment, or it may not, in which case it may not increase output by very much. Inefficiencies in capital allocation may make the marginal product of investment low, as in the countries of Central and Eastern Europe and the Soviet Union under communism, all of which had rates of investment that were exceptionally high by Western standards, yet growth stagnated and in some countries turned negative.

In any case, as discussed in section 6.4, returns on financial assets include an adjustment for bearing risk. Thus it is wrong to use financial returns as a measure of the return to society without incorporating an adjustment for risk, and hence wrong to identify the expected return on stocks as the gain from increased funding.

Increased funding may not be optimal for other reasons. The fact that an increase in funding may increase output does not mean that the policy is necessarily welfare improving. Funding may promote growth, but also, and inescapably, it redistributes burdens. Depending on rates of return to increased investment and the growth rate of the economy, redistribution to later generations may or may not be worthwhile, as discussed in section 7.2.

Whether a move to funding will have beneficial effects depends on country-specific features:

- Is saving in the country lower than optimal? Will funding increase saving? Will it improve the efficiency of domestic capital markets?

---

5. In the 1970s a British trade union famously invested part of its pension fund in valuable paintings. This did nothing directly to expand the capital stock.

- What are the intergenerational distributional effects? Increased investment through increased funding implies lower consumption in the present. Thus funding that increases growth is worthwhile only if the current consumption forgone is less valuable than the expected increase in future consumption.

Funding may not be feasible. A country may lack the institutions necessary to operate a funded system. For example, it may lack the skills necessary for administering pension accounts or allocating pension funds, or it may lack the capacity to regulate financial markets, as discussed in Chapter 9. Even if such skills exist, they may be scarce, and deploying them to run pension funds may not be their most efficient use.

In sum, the argument is neither that funding is unsound policy nor that it cannot help ease the effects of population aging, but rather that its helpfulness is contingent on funding having beneficial effects on growth and intergenerational equity, which in turn depend on a range of country-specific factors. Funding may be important for boosting economic growth, but the case has to be made in each country, not just assumed or asserted.

6.4 COMPARING THE RETURNS TO PAYG AND FUNDING

Some analysts argue for funded over PAYG systems by comparing the long-run rate of return on assets in which a funded system might invest with the rate of growth of the economy (or of wages), which is the long-run return in a PAYG system:

> In contrast to the 2.6-percent equilibrium return on Social Security contributions, the real pretax return on nonfinancial corporate capital averaged 9.3 percent over the same . . . period. . . . [As a result], forcing individuals to use the unfunded system dramatically increases their cost of buying retirement income. (Feldstein 1996, p. 3)

A similar claim is made in the following World Bank analysis: "Since the financial rate of return is generally expected to be higher than the rate of economic growth, NDC requires a higher level of contributions to achieve the same payout as a [fully funded] scheme, *and for this reason an NDC scheme is second best in economic terms*" (Holzmann and Palmer 2006, p. 4, emphasis added)

Since long-run rates of financial return do in fact exceed long-run rates of growth of the economy, the difference between the two is sometimes presented as a pure gain available to funded systems. But it is wrong to analyze policy by considering only the long run, ignoring the short-run costs and benefits associated with moving to a different long run. The argument is flawed because it does not compare like with like. A fuller analysis considers the costs of the transition from PAYG to funding (section 6.4.1), the relative risks of the two sets of arrangements (section 6.4.2), and their respective administrative costs (section 6.4.3).

6.4.1 Inappropriate comparison of steady states

If proper account is taken of the costs of transition from a PAYG to a fully funded system, the rates of return in the two arrangements are generally equivalent.[6]

6. The argument draws on Orszag (1999), a nontechnical summary of results originally established by Breyer (1989). For applications of the argument to the United States, see Geanakoplos, Mitchell, and Zeldes (1999), and Belan and Pestieau (1999). The argument leaves out the complications that occur when there is taxation of capital income.

To demonstrate the flaw in the argument that pensioners are better off in a funded system if the stock market return exceeds real economic (or wage) growth, consider a country with a PAYG system where policymakers are contemplating a move toward funding. When the PAYG system started, the initial generation received a pension even though it had not paid contributions. The benefits paid to that first generation are a sunk cost; a move toward funding will involve transition costs that, as explained below, are a necessary consequence of that gift to the first generation. A central question is on whom the transition costs should fall. Since they have to fall somewhere, the move to funding is not a pure gain; some people are helped by the move and some are harmed, an issue that is ignored by looking only at the long run, after the costs have been paid by earlier cohorts.

Case 1: Constant benefit rules, transition costs financed by public borrowing. In Table 6.1, each generation pays $1 in contributions when young and receives $1 in pension when old. In period 1 the $1 pension of older generation A is paid by the $1 contribution of younger generation B. In period 2, when generation B is old, its pension is paid by the contributions of young generation C, and so on. Now suppose that the real rate of return on assets is 10 percent. Under a PAYG system generations B, C, and so on each pay $1 in contributions in one period and receive $1 in pension in the next; the real rate of return is zero. In contrast, with individual accounts these generations save $1 in period 2 and get back $1.10 in period 3; the 10 percent real rate of return appears to be a pure gain over the PAYG system.

The flaw in the argument is that if, say, generation C's contribution goes to its own funded accounts, generation B's pension must be paid from some other source. If that source is government borrowing, generation C receives a pension of $1.10 but has to pay taxes to cover interest of 10 cents on the borrowing that financed generation B's pension. Thus the real return, adjusted for the additional taxes, is zero—the same as under PAYG. The lower return on the PAYG system is not the result of some inherent flaw but is precisely the cost of the initial gift to generation A. Formally (see Breyer 1989, Belan and Pestieau 1999), there is an equivalence between the two arrangements if the move to funding is considered not in isolation but alongside the cost of financing the change. Thus generation C is not made better off by a move to funding. As another study put it, "Falling money's worth in this model is *not* due to the aging of baby boomers, increased life expectancy, or massive administrative inefficiency, but rather to

TABLE 6.1
A simplified pay-as-you-go system

	GENERATION			
PERIOD	A	B	C	D
1	+$1	-$1		
2		+$1	-$1	
3			+$1	-$1
4				+$1

Source: Orszag (1999, p. 9).

the simple arithmetic of the pay-as-you-go system" (Geanakoplos, Mitchell, and Zeldes 1999, p. 86, emphasis in original).

The fact that one can explain the different returns to PAYG and funding in this way does not mean that the difference does not matter; if the gap is too large, it creates incentives for workers to evade contributions to the PAYG system, seeking to earn higher returns from other forms of pension saving. Section 7.2 discusses in more detail the mechanism of the redistribution between generations through the initial transfer to earlier cohorts, and policies to share costs across cohorts to avoid excessive differences in rates of return.

Case 2: Constant benefit rules, transition costs financed by taxation. Suppose that in period 2 generation C puts its contribution of $1 into an individual funded account, as before, but in this case the $1 pension of generation B is paid from additional taxes rather than by borrowing. The pension benefit that generation C receives is again $1.10. But generation C also pays $2 in taxes—$1 to pay generation A's pension and $1 for its own. Thus the overall rate of return is negative. (The negative rate of return was avoided in Case 1 because the taxes necessary to repay the government borrowing were spread across many cohorts, not just generation C.)

The analysis is similar if a budget surplus is available to pay the pension of generation B. That surplus might have been used to cut taxes for generation C, making the analysis the same as case 2. Or the surplus could have been used to reduce the national debt, making the analysis the same as in case 1. The surplus thus has an opportunity cost. The same result follows if the surplus is used to prefund the PAYG system, with the returns used to increase pensions.

Case 3: No benefits to the transition generation. Another way to finance the transition is to throw generation B out of the lifeboat by not paying their pension at all. Generations C and onward enjoy a 10 percent real return, but those gains are at the expense of generation B, on whom the entire cost of transition is concentrated. In this case, the cost of the gift to generation A is offset by the negative gift to generation B.

In sum. The fundamental point is that the first generation and subsequent generations face a zero-sum game. The cost of the gift to the first generation has to be paid. It can be paid entirely by the transition generation (generation B) by reneging on the PAYG promises made to them, or entirely by the generation of workers at the time of transition (generation C) by financing generation B's pension out of higher current taxes, or the cost can be spread over succeeding generations by financing the transition through borrowing. It is possible to alter the time path of the cost, but not to avoid the cost itself. Again, the only way out of the impasse is if the move toward funding somehow leads causally to higher rates of growth, an issue on which, as we saw in the previous section, controversy continues. Box 6.4 explains more fully why erroneous analysis in this context is serious.

6.4.2 Adjusting for differences in risk

The cost of financing the transition is only part of the comparison between PAYG and funding. A second element is risk. The expected return to any financial asset is not totally safe, and thus includes a risk premium, incorporating both market risks and political risks. Hence it is mistaken to compare the gross return on pension assets with the return on a PAYG system as though both were risk free: the real returns to PAYG

▶ **Box 6.4 Inappropriate use of steady-state analysis:
More than a trivial intellectual error**

The errors that result from inappropriate use of steady-state analysis are more profound
than is immediately apparent. Consider the following statement: "Some of the problems—
such as the inevitability of intergenerational transfers and low rates of return to later
cohorts—are inherent in pay-as-you-go systems" (World Bank 1994, p. 236). It is
correct that PAYG systems, through their gift to the first generation, reduce the rate of
return to later generations. However, the unqualified statement that this is a problem is
mistaken.

First, in referring to the gift to the first generation as a "problem," the statement
makes an implicit assumption about the distribution of income across generations,
a topic discussed more fully in Box 7.2.

Second, the argument leads to invalid claims for the Pareto superiority (see
Glossary) of some policies. The point is most obvious if policymakers are establishing
a pension system in a brand new country. As discussed in section 7.2, if they introduce
a PAYG system, the first generation of retirees receives a pension, but returns to
subsequent generations are lower; if they introduce funding, later generations benefit
from higher returns, but the first generation does not receive a pension. Thus it is
mistaken to present the gain to pensioners after the first generation as a Pareto
improvement, since it comes at the expense of the first generation. The same argument
applies in a country that already has a PAYG system: a decision to move toward
funding redistributes from the current generation to future generations. The claim that
a move to funding is a Pareto improvement is invalid.

Finally, the argument is wrong in that, as discussed in section 7.3, it is generally
optimal to have a PAYG element in a pension system, because the resulting possibility
of intergenerational risk sharing is welfare enhancing. As discussed in section 6.2.2,
the argument that paying off implicit pension debt is necessarily beneficial makes the
same error. ◀

and to funded plans should each be adjusted to account for risk. We discuss risk
adjustment in the next chapter.

6.4.3   Controlling for administrative costs

That the administrative costs of individual accounts are higher—often considerably
higher—than those of PAYG systems is well established (see Figure 9.1 and the
accompanying discussion). These costs should not be underestimated. As discussed in
section 9.2.3, under plausible assumptions, over a working life an annual administrative
charge of 1 percent reduces a worker's total accumulation by about 20 percent.

6.4.4   Conclusion

In assessing proposals for pension reform, it is important to be clear what question is
being asked. Feldstein (2005), for example, argues that the U.S. Social Security system
reduces national saving. A key question is what normative conclusion to draw from
this observation. U.S. Social Security is less than fully funded because benefits were
paid to earlier cohorts in excess of what their contributions would have financed
(see Box 7.2). The purpose of paying higher benefits was to raise the consumption of
those cohorts in retirement, and (short-run Keynesian issues aside) this inevitably
reduced national saving. Thus the decline in national saving was not an avoidable side

effect of poorly designed policy but a necessary consequence of the policy of increasing the consumption of earlier retirees. The observation about saving needs to be seen in that light, not isolated as an independent basis for making policy.

If one does not include the value to earlier generations of the consumption that resulted from lower investment, the analysis implicitly makes a steady-state comparison; that is, it compares the economic situation in the United States today with what it would have been in an alternative steady state with funded pensions. Thus the underlying question is: How does welfare in long-run steady state B differ from that in steady state A? Most of the analysis in this book is about a different question: What are the welfare effects of *moving* from position A to position B? Either question (and its related answer) is legitimate. What is not legitimate is to take the answer to one question and apply it to the other, nor is it a sound basis for policy analysis to consider only part of the consequences of a policy (in this case the long-run part).

Matters are more complicated than a simple comparison of rates of return:

- It is mistaken analysis only to compare steady states in a situation where policy involves a move from one steady state to another. A proper comparison of a move from PAYG toward funding should take proper account of the costs—both their total and their distribution—of that move. Sharing costs across cohorts is discussed in more detail in section 7.2.

- A proper comparison also takes account of differences in risk and of any difference in administrative costs.

- All three adjustments remain relevant to the choice of pension regime in a hypothetical new country, where the issue of transition costs is replaced by the issue of whether to give benefits to people who have already retired or are close to doing so.

Finally, Atkinson (1999, p. 8) points out that critics of the welfare state tend to consider its costs without taking account of its benefits:

The emphasis by economists on the negative economic effects of the welfare state can be attributed to the theoretical framework adopted . . . which remains rooted in a model of perfectly competitive and perfectly clearing markets. [This] theoretical framework incorporates none of the contingencies for which the welfare state exists. . . . The whole purpose of welfare state provision is missing from the theoretical model.

The point here is exactly the same: that the benefits from a move to funding should not be considered in isolation, but alongside the relevant costs.

7

▷

Redistribution and Risk Sharing

Pension systems have powerful redistributive effects, which may or may not be intended and may or may not be desirable. They can redistribute within a generation (section 7.1). Indeed, unless there is complete reliance on tax-financed minimum incomes for the elderly, virtually all pension systems include such redistribution as an explicit objective, notably to raise the retirement incomes of the elderly poor. Pension systems can also redistribute across generations (section 7.2). A system with less than full funding inescapably makes choices about redistribution across generations; so does a move toward funding that increases national saving. And pension arrangements affect men and women differently in important ways, as discussed in Chapter 8.

These major distributional effects by no means exhaust the list. Using general tax revenue to finance a system that covers only a small proportion of workers transfers income from the much larger population of taxpayers to the smaller group of covered workers. Some countries have separate benefit formulas for white- and blue-collar workers and can use transfers between the systems to redistribute from the lower-paid blue-collar workers to the higher-paid white-collar workers through more generous benefits relative to contributions for the latter. As discussed in section 5.2.1, many defined-benefit plans favor workers whose major pay raises come toward the end of their career, relative to those with earlier increases, a feature that tends to benefit higher earners over lower earners. And a pension system that provides annuities on uniform terms inevitably favors the longer lived over the shorter lived.

Alongside these possibilities for redistribution, all pension systems face risk. A central question for policymakers, discussed in section 7.3, is how these risks can be shared and how widely they should be shared—questions with implications for both efficiency and equity.

7.1 RAISING THE RETIREMENT INCOME OF PEOPLE WITH LOW PENSION BENEFITS

There are many ways in which a country can raise the retirement income of people who, for whatever reason, enter retirement with low pension benefits. Some countries offer a minimum income guarantee, such as means-tested social assistance for which all elderly people are eligible, whether covered by the pension system or not. The discussion here concentrates on the impact of the pension system itself on the income distribution, ignoring the complementary role of social assistance. In addition to poverty relief, public pension systems in some countries provide people on lower incomes, but who are not poor, with a pension that is a larger fraction of their previous earnings, so as to assist their consumption smoothing.

Approaches to redistribution. In recognizing these concerns, countries have adopted different approaches to income redistribution among the elderly. Some countries offer a guaranteed minimum pension for workers with a sufficiently long record in the pension system. Chile had offered such a guarantee to workers with at least twenty years of contributions (see Chapters 12 and 13). In the United States pensions are based on a progressive benefit formula, with a replacement rate that decreases smoothly with lifetime earnings.[1] Another redistributive approach is followed in Mexico, where a flat amount is added to individual accounts receiving earnings-related contributions. One difference between these approaches is that redistribution in the United States is financed within the pension system, whereas in Mexico the financing is from general revenue. The use of general revenue, as in Mexico, requires careful consideration of the incidence of the taxes providing that revenue relative to the incidence of receipt of the transfers. This is particularly an issue in countries where the coverage of the pension system is limited, with low earners more likely to be outside the system. Issues also arise for redistribution within the system. In the United States a concern is that the spouse benefit, as currently designed, tends to worsen the distributional characteristics of the system as a whole.

Some countries combine a flat-rate pension (which varies with years worked but not with the level of earnings) with a second system that is strictly earnings related.[2] Such an arrangement, however, generally leads to incomplete coverage of the elderly population. Thus the contributory principle can be modified in various ways:

- Benefits can be based on a shorter period than an entire career. The United States uses the highest thirty-five years of earnings when calculating benefits. Beginning in 2010, the United Kingdom will award a full basic pension at pensionable age on the basis of thirty years of contributions.[3]

- Credit toward the pension may be given for years without contributions, for example to reflect years devoted to child care or military service or to compensate for periods of unemployment. Such credits can be financed from general revenue or within the pension system. As a variant, the number of years required for a full

1. A central issue is whether these considerations apply to a worker or to a family, reflecting the earnings of both husband and wife, and reflecting the greater need for income replacement when supporting a family than when supporting a single individual.

2. Although "flat-rate pension" may seem a misnomer for a pension that varies with the number of years of contributions, it is given that name because benefits do not vary with earnings levels.

3. On the specific proposals, see U.K. Department for Work and Pensions (2006a) and U.K. Pensions Policy Institute (2006); for broader discussion of the contributory principle, see U.K. Pensions Policy Institute (2005).

basic pension can be reduced by a year for each year of such activity. Pension credits for care activities are discussed in section 8.3.2.

A different approach is to have a noncontributory flat-rate pension:

- Some countries award a pension on the basis of an income test or, as in Australia, an affluence test.[4]
- Some countries base benefits on years of residence (as in Finland and New Zealand) or of citizenship and residence (as in the Netherlands).[5] Such pensions can be financed either from dedicated or from general revenue.

The two elements—flat-rate and earnings-related—together produce a replacement rate that decreases with income. China has a variant of this approach, with a basic pension and individual accounts. So does Argentina.

In addition to these ways of improving benefits for individual workers, a pension system can protect not just the worker but also a spouse, through survivor benefits, which are a key part of how pensions affect income distribution among the elderly. Countries vary greatly in their use of survivor benefits and in how they are financed. Some systems also include protection for a spouse in the event of divorce, and some provide benefits differently for single and married individuals. These issues are discussed in Chapter 8.

Which approaches work best? In part these different approaches to raising the incomes of the elderly poor—a minimum guarantee, a progressive formula, or a combination of flat-rate and earnings-related pensions—reflect different objectives, different histories, and different political economies. In part they also reflect the different approaches to targeting set out in Box 7.1. Economic theory offers no simple basis for arguing that any of these approaches is unambiguously superior to the others. What is feasible will depend on a country's political economy and institutional capacity; what is optimal will depend on its relative weighting of objectives (such as poverty relief and consumption smoothing) and on the values of the parameters that determine the distortionary effects of implicit and explicit taxation, which may differ across countries.

It is not possible to change the income distribution without causing some distortions. A flat-rate benefit for all pensioners must be financed from some revenue source. Unlike a strictly earnings-related system, where higher taxable earnings lead to higher future benefits, the taxes that finance a flat-rate benefit are, by definition, not associated with an increase in benefits to the taxpayer.[6] Thus, with a flat-rate benefit financed by a payroll tax, the tax is fully distortionary. If instead a country offers a guaranteed

---

4. An income test is designed to screen out everyone except the least well off; an affluence test is designed to screen out only the best off. Thus an income-tested benefit is designed to be received only by the poor; an affluence-tested benefit goes to everyone except the rich.

5. These are sometimes called citizens' pensions. However, since they often depend on residency rather than citizenship, we refer to them in later chapters as noncontributory universal pensions.

6. If years of contributions of at least a minimum amount are counted as partly determining benefits, the analysis is a little different, since there is then an incentive to participate in the labor market, although no incentive for additional earnings once the minimum amount for credit has been reached.

▶ **Box 7.1 Targeting benefits: Income test or indicator targeting?**

Well-targeted poverty relief should aim to assist all the poor (sometimes referred to as horizontal efficiency) and only, or mainly, the poor (vertical efficiency). There are different ways of targeting benefits (see Barr 2004a, pp. 217-19). In the present context two are especially relevant: income testing and indicator (or proxy) targeting. Another option, not discussed here, is self-targeting, which awards benefits on the basis of an incentive structure (for example, subsidies for goods consumed mainly by poor people) that induces only the targeted population to claim the benefit.

Income testing seeks to identify poor people by their incomes. Its advantage is that, at its best, it can target benefits tightly. If the poverty line is, say, $100 per month, it is in principle possible to pay a benefit that brings the incomes of poor people up to $100, thus spending nothing on anyone whose income from any source is over $100.

Income testing, however, has significant disadvantages. If benefits are tightly targeted, as above, a person who receives an extra dollar from earnings or asset income loses a dollar in benefit. This creates a serious disincentive against work and saving. If benefits are less tightly targeted, either some people are not raised above the poverty line, or some benefits are paid to people above the poverty line, or both. In addition, income testing is typically based on family income, creating disincentives for family formation. Income testing is also administratively demanding, even in developed countries, and raises even more serious measurement problems in developing economies, where much income arises in the informal sector or through household production. Finally, in at least some countries, the receipt of income-tested poverty relief and, in particular, the operation of the income test itself, is regarded as stigmatizing.

Any use of income or asset testing to determine benefits weakens the incentive to save for old age. Indeed, one argument for mandatory retirement saving is that it limits the free riding that occurs when people choose not to save, given the larger transfers they will receive if they have few assets, and hence little income from assets.

Indicator targeting seeks to identify the poor not by their income but in terms of other indicators (the classic article is Akerlof 1978). The idea is best illustrated by example. Assume that only redheads are poor, that all redheads are poor, and that there is no hair-dyeing technology. In these circumstances it is theoretically possible completely to eliminate poverty, as defined by the poverty line, by paying a redhead benefit. Additionally, because benefits go only to the poor, expenditure is minimized, and because identification is easy, the administrative demands are small. Thus the ideal indicators are highly correlated with poverty, to ensure accurate targeting; beyond the control of the individual, to minimize disincentives; and easy to observe, to assist administration. In practice, commonly used indicators are the presence of children in the family and sufficiently old age.

The great advantage of indicator targeting is that it avoids some of the worst effects of income testing. Although it can discourage saving for retirement (since people anticipate future pension benefits), it does so in a nondistorting way in that it does not alter the amount of income generated by additional saving. But the approach is no panacea. First, as with all transfers, benefits are financed from distortionary taxes. In addition, measurable characteristics are in practice not perfectly correlated with poverty: some benefits will go to people who have the relevant characteristic but are not poor, and some who lack the relevant characteristic are in fact poor. Finally, the use of family structure to determine either eligibility or the benefit level again creates disincentives for family formation. Thus, in practice, a system based on indicator targeting needs to be supplemented by a system of income-tested benefits.

Some programs do exactly this, for example paying disability benefits only to poor people and earnings-related benefits only to people with children. The United States has two disability programs, one for covered workers that is not income tested and one for poor people that is.

In developing countries (see Coady, Grosh, and Hoddinot 2004) a pension awarded on the basis of age can be implemented without heavy administrative requirements; in particular, the approach avoids the need to keep a history of contributions. Such a pension will generally be well targeted and, if pensionable age is sufficiently high, may also be fiscally feasible. ◀

minimum pension of the same size, the benefit goes only to a retiree whose total pension is below the guarantee level, and hence to fewer retirees; thus the cost of the transfer, and hence the revenue necessary to finance it, are considerably reduced. However, the guaranteed minimum introduces a different distortion. For workers who anticipate receiving the guarantee, its presence removes the return to the payroll tax: additional work brings no increase in benefits. Thus the distortion is stronger for them than under a flat-rate benefit. In contrast, a flat-rate benefit does not take away the increased benefit from additional work under the earnings-related system. Thus a minimum guarantee, compared with a flat-rate benefit, produces less distortion associated with the need to raise revenue for the transfer, but more distortion for those who are eligible for the guarantee. The latter distortion can be reduced, at a cost of higher spending, by phasing out the guarantee more slowly. But the contrast remains between greater distortions generally and greater distortions on a subset of the population. In general it is not possible to say which of the approaches is relatively more efficient. The two approaches also differ in their distributional implications.

In addition to explicit redistribution according to income, groups with different life expectancies will benefit unequally from a system that collects contributions from those who are working and pays benefits for the lifetimes of retired workers. Two such patterns are widely recognized. Women on average live longer than men, so that, other things equal, a mandatory system with unisex tables redistributes from men to women in the aggregate relative to a system that uses separate tables for each sex. In addition, within each sex, people with higher incomes tend to live longer than those with lower incomes—a divergence that is growing in the United States and the United Kingdom. Thus a system that sets benefits proportional to earnings redistributes from low earners to high earners within each sex relative to one that uses separate tables for different earnings levels.[7] If policymakers wish at least partly to offset this redistribution (a position we favor), it is attractive either to have a progressive benefit formula or to redistribute through a minimum or flat-rate benefit or through a mechanism outside the pension system, such as a guaranteed minimum income.

7. Comparing mandatory annuitization with allocations without annuities also involves differential gains from the presence of annuitization, something that would typically benefit lower earners more (Brown 2001); see also Simonovits (2006).

7.2 REDISTRIBUTING COSTS AND BENEFITS ACROSS GENERATIONS

Besides redistributing within a generation, pension systems can also redistribute across generations, as discussed in section 7.2.1. Section 7.2.2 discusses how this can be achieved by using assets to finance part of pension costs.

7.2.1 Redistributing across generations

How redistributive effects across generations arise. A country introducing a public pension system can in principle choose whether it should be organized on a PAYG or a funded basis. Alongside the effects of the choice on labor markets, saving, and economic growth, discussed in Chapters 5 and 6, are the inevitable effects on the intergenerational distribution of resources. As illustrated in Table 6.1 and more fully in Box 7.2, a decision to introduce a PAYG system makes transfers to the early cohorts of pensioners, who receive larger pensions than their contributions could finance. The costs of that transfer fall on later generations. In contrast, a decision to introduce a fully funded system means that the early generations receive very small pensions. If a country already has a PAYG system, a decision to move toward funding that involves an increase in saving will redistribute from earlier to later generations.

> ### Box 7.2 Benefit determination in the early years of public programs in the United States and Canada

In defined-benefit systems it is common to relate benefits to a measure of average earnings over a full or nearly full career. The U.S. Social Security system bases benefits on the thirty-five years with the highest earnings, and Canada's public pension system looks at 85 percent of the years from age 18 until retirement. Given the distortions that arise from basing benefits on a short period of earnings (discussed in section 5.2.1), reliance on a long period is widely seen as the right approach for a defined-benefit system. This, however, raises the question of how to measure a person's average earnings when the system is immature (that is, has not existed for the full period over which earnings are counted). The United States and Canada solved this problem by using a short but growing averaging period as the system matured.

This approach contributed to a large redistribution to the early cohorts. People who retired when the system was young had paid payroll taxes for only a few years, yet received benefits on a similar basis as later workers who paid the payroll tax for a full career. In both the United States and Canada, this effect was compounded by starting with a low payroll tax rate, which was steadily increased over time by more than the benefit formulas. This combination contributed to a substantial unfunded obligation for future generations.

The first figure shows that the earliest cohorts in the United States received more than they paid in present discounted value—a positive transfer. Since the program as a whole was small in the early days, the transfer to each cohort was small, and the cumulative net cost grew slowly. However, as successive cohorts retired, the program covered more and more people, and so the cumulative transfer grew rapidly. Following reforms in 1983, cohorts are scheduled to pay back more than they receive, reducing the legacy cost that is passed onto the future. The early cohorts, who received a full benefit on the basis of limited contributions, received the highest return on their contributions, with the rate of return declining for later cohorts, as the second figure shows.

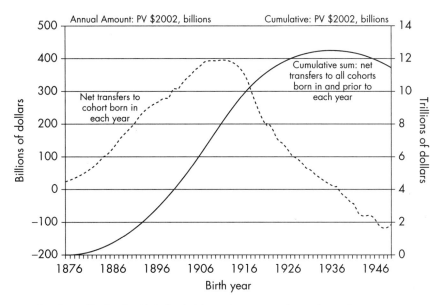

Pension benefits in the U.S. Social Security system by cohort. Data are present values in 2002 dollars. *Source:* Leimer (1994).

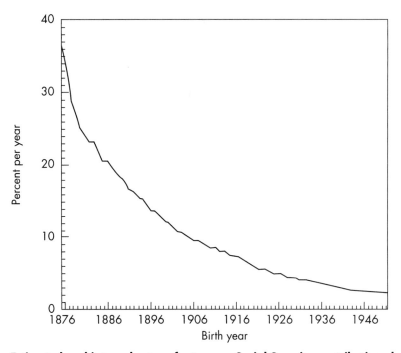

Estimated real internal rates of return on Social Security contributions by cohort. *Source:* Leimer (1994).

As discussed in section 6.2.2, the existence of an unfunded liability is not a problem per se but should be judged in terms of its costs, notably in terms of sustainability but also, and importantly, its benefits. It can be argued that the decision in the United States to grant full benefits to early cohorts represented a humane response to the suffering imposed by the world wars and the Great Depression: it reduced elderly poverty and reduced the cost of transfers to the poor elderly from other programs. Arguably the decision benefited today's workers as well: some, at least, are glad that their parents and grandparents were assisted, and for some the transfers removed the burden of supporting their parents in old age.

The underlying objective of such defined-benefit systems is to provide an appropriate replacement rate. But determining the level of benefits for early cohorts exclusively from this perspective leads to an unfortunate division of the transfer to the workers in the early cohorts: much of it went to high earners since, in an earnings-related system, the higher the earnings, the larger the transfer. This aspect of the transfers was bad policy. The implied income patterns do not do a good job of reflecting history, but instead reward the better off. A progressive system reduces this upward redistribution, but larger transfers to the better off remain.

The problem could have been avoided in several ways while still providing the early cohorts with effective poverty relief. A simple approach would have been to use a long earnings "history" in determining benefits from the start, but use legislatively chosen earnings (for example, average earnings) for the years before the system came into being. Another approach would have used a long earnings history but recorded zero earnings in the years before the system started, combined with a uniform flat-rate benefit whose value would decline year by year as the earnings-related system grew. In a country like China, with low initial coverage, the rules need to be drawn carefully as coverage expands. ◀

A fully funded defined-contribution pension with no tax advantages will not redistribute across generations. That, however, is itself a distributional choice. The central point is that a decision that a system should be funded rather than PAYG is also and necessarily a decision about the intergenerational distribution of income. Inescapably, some people are made better off and some worse off. As noted in Box 6.4, such redistributive effects rule out simple claims for the Pareto superiority (see Glossary) of different ways of paying for pensions.

What approaches work best? How should one think about the balance of costs and benefits between generations? Since consumption plus investment equals national income, a policy that raises national saving will necessarily lower consumption. Conversely, a policy to give higher benefits to some pensioners (such as the early cohorts in the U.S. system) is designed to raise their consumption and so decreases national saving, aggregate output held constant. Thus decreased saving is a necessary implication of higher pension benefits, not a surprise unlucky outcome.

If the additional resources generated by any increase in saving are used to raise future benefits or to reduce future contributions, the effect is to increase future consumption. To evaluate whether such redistribution across cohorts is worthwhile, one needs to consider not only the return on the additional capital, but also the extent to which consumption would have grown anyway in the absence of the policy to increase saving. One also needs to consider the distribution within each cohort of the decreases in consumption now and the increases in the future. As discussed in section 6.4, the analysis is incomplete if it evaluates a proposal to increase contributions or lower benefits in order to increase national saving simply by comparing the marginal product of capital with the implicit rate of return on taxes in a PAYG system; that comparison omits the intertemporal distributional effects and is thus not a basis for a normative conclusion.

More specifically, consider what happens if contributions are increased now and used to purchase assets so as to allow a lower contribution rate later. Workers today will pay a higher contribution rate and thus have lower consumption, and later workers will pay a lower contribution rate and have higher consumption. How should one evaluate this redistribution from today's workers to tomorrow's? There are three parts to the comparison:[8]

- What is the effect on the utilities of different cohorts? That is, how much will future workers value the increase in their consumption, and is it more or less socially valuable than the value current workers place on the corresponding decrease in their consumption? With diminishing marginal utility, the higher a person's consumption, the less an increase in it is worth. Thus, if earnings are growing rapidly, consumption moved into the future is less valuable to future cohorts, who will have higher incomes, than if earnings growth were slower. Similarly, a country with a high saving rate has low consumption relative to its earnings. If the saving rate is lower in the future, future consumption will be higher relative to earnings. Thus, for a given rate of earnings growth, if the saving rate is expected to decline, consumption moved into the future is less valuable to future cohorts than otherwise.

- What is the return on the additional saving? The greater a country's investment needs, the greater the marginal product of capital is likely to be, assuming adequate markets for allocating investment. But a country with a high saving rate is likely already to be investing in opportunities with the highest rates of return. Thus the return to yet higher rates of saving may not be very high.

- The pure public weighting of the utilities of different cohorts: it is common to discount across lifetime utilities of cohorts as well as, separately, discounting the utility of future consumption during a worker's life.[9]

Thus, increasing national saving by raising contributions or lowering benefits redistributes toward future cohorts. Also important is the issue of whose consumption goes up or down within the different cohorts. A program to tax the highest earners today to build a fund to be used to raise benefits across the board tomorrow is different from a program to raise taxes across the board today to build a fund to be used to raise benefits for the well off tomorrow.

---

8. The analysis here sets to one side the question of whether an increase in mandatory pension saving is or is not offset by a fall in voluntary saving or by increased government borrowing; see the discussion in section 6.3.1.

9. On the issue of discounting across cohorts in the context of global warming, see the Stern Review (U.K. Treasury 2006) and the comment by Nordhaus (2007).

7.2.2 Using assets to finance part of legacy costs

The issue. A pure PAYG system has no assets, because it gave larger benefits to the earliest cohorts than their contributions could have financed. To keep the system running, it needs to finance its past promises to current pensioners from current contributions. Beyond this basic fact, contributions may face additional pressures:

- The workforce may grow more slowly or even decline because of a fall in fertility, as is currently anticipated in many countries.

- In countries moving from PAYG toward funding, some or all of the existing contributions of current workers go into their individual accounts; thus unless contributions increase by enough to cover the increase in funding, the benefits of current pensioners must be financed at least in part from other sources, or be reduced.

- Workers in state-owned enterprises in centrally planned economies (notable examples being Central and Eastern Europe and China) received compensation through a combination of wages and pension benefits, both being a return for work. As a result of the move to a market economy, these enterprises became less able to pay the pensions they had promised, given accrued pension liabilities and the need to be competitive.

The obvious question is how to finance PAYG pensions in those circumstances. There are two broad approaches:

- Finance from inside the pension system: In this case benefits are financed by the future workforce covered by the pension system—both currently covered workers and workers from outside (for example, from rural areas) who are being added to it.

- Finance from outside the pension system: One way to implement this approach is through transfers to the system in the form of assets or claims on future annual revenue flows.

The following discussion sets out the pros and cons of different sources of transfers of assets from outside the pension system and considers how large a quantity of assets it makes sense to transfer in seeking a sensible balance between inside and outside financing.

Transfer of bonds. One approach is to use future general revenue to cover financial shortfalls, shifting burdens from future workers to future taxpayers without altering the intertemporal pattern. Where initial coverage of the pension system is low (as in China) and growing slowly, the distribution of the legacy burden on covered workers is quite concentrated. Section 6.1 sets out the pros and cons of financing pensions from dedicated sources of revenue. Although dedicated sources can increase the political commitment to provide benefits in the future, it remains possible to use future general revenue to finance pensions by giving long-term government bonds to the pension trust fund. This approach, too, can result in stronger commitment compared with legislating future transfers out of general revenue (particularly if such legislation takes effect only in the future), with the government paying interest on the bonds, which helps to finance benefits. A potential shortcoming of conventional bonds is the sensitivity of their value to the rate of inflation. Thus it is better for government to use inflation-indexed bonds for this purpose. Policymakers can cover whatever fraction of the legacy obligation they choose in this way; the fraction chosen should be that which brings about policymakers' preferred distribution of costs.

Obligations not covered by the transfer of assets will affect future workers. The rate of return on taxes paid by workers depends on the extent to which they are financing the shortfall between assets and liabilities coming from previous cohorts of workers. Some decrease in the rate of return for newly covered workers is not a large problem—after all, they gain significant advantages from public pension coverage, including low-cost annuitization and less risk than on direct individual investments in financial assets. But if the gap between the return on PAYG contributions and the return on financial assets is too large, the incentive to stay outside the system, legally or illegally, becomes stronger, compromising the efficiency of the labor market. (The contribution rate itself also affects the efficiency of labor markets.) On the other hand, reliance on government debt also has a cost, since raising taxes to finance interest payments distorts labor and capital markets.

The choice between financing future benefits from general revenue (which pays the interest on the bonds) or from a payroll tax (that is, from within the pension system) also has important distributional effects. A central issue is the extent to which the fairness of different distributions of burdens and the incentive effects of the different methods of financing result in a preferred mix of relying on assets versus relying on future contributions. A key question is the extent to which coverage of the pension system will be expanding. In countries that already have fairly complete coverage, the choice between general revenue and a payroll tax is primarily whether to tax all income, including the return to capital, or to tax only earnings. In countries where coverage is expanding, there is a further issue: workers who were in the system early tend to have higher incomes than those coming into the system later, as coverage expands. Details of how benefits reflect the process of coverage play a key role in the distributional implications of different choices, as illustrated in Box 7.2. We express no views about the right mix, which depends partly on unknown parameters that will vary from country to country, and partly on the country's political economy.

Transfer of shares. In some countries an alternative to transferring bonds is to transfer shares in newly privatized state-owned enterprises. This was done on a small scale in Poland and is being contemplated in China. This is another way of using resources from other areas of government to finance pensions. The role of such shares is similar to the role of bonds: the trust fund holds them, using the dividends to finance benefits and possibly engaging in some sales in the distant future. There are significant differences between transferring bonds and transferring shares, however:

- Equities and non-inflation-indexed (nominal) bonds react differently to inflation. Although inflation tends to reduce equity values in the short run, the earnings of corporations tend to catch up with inflation in the long run, so that shares tend to catch up as well. The distinction is less important if the government uses inflation-indexed rather than nominal bonds.

- The value of shares is likely to follow a different time path from that of bonds, although it is not possible to tell exactly how investment in one will compare with investment in the other.

- Within the government, the initial sources of funds will be different: the treasury in the case of bonds, and the ministries currently holding shares (and so receiving dividends) in the case of shares. Although the political process could make offsetting transfers to reduce the differences, there is no reason to think that this would happen fully, and so no reason why the two approaches would be identical. Public economics recognizes that the politics of different kinds of funds are different.

- There may be concern about the governance of privatized state-owned enterprises. Whether the transfer of shares strengthens or weakens corporate governance depends on the country in question but is an important issue, discussed in the context of China in section 15.2.2.

- A key issue is whether the transferred shares are planned to be held for the long term, or intended to provide an initial portfolio for active fund management. The latter would undercut the governance issue and might take place in a setting with expensive transactions that are hard to monitor.

7.3   RISK SHARING WITHIN AND ACROSS GENERATIONS

All pension systems face the risk of macroeconomic shocks, demographic shocks, and political shocks (section 4.3). Funded plans face additional risks, notably management risk, investment risk, and annuities market risk.[10] Different pension designs share these risks among beneficiaries differently: some have little risk sharing beyond, possibly, the use of annuities to spread the longevity risk; others have risk sharing only within a generation; and others can share risks both within and across generations. It is useful to recognize the different underlying philosophies of risk sharing in different systems, since the philosophy behind a system bears directly on its design and may influence policy.

Pension design and risk sharing. In a pure defined-contribution plan based on private financial assets, an individual's pension, given life expectancy and other factors, is determined by the size of his or her lifetime pension accumulation. Thus the individual faces all the risks noted above, associated with varying real rates of return to pension assets, the risks of future earnings trajectories, and the future pricing of annuities because of uncertainties about life expectancy and future interest rates. Since the contribution rate is fixed, these risks manifest themselves through adjustments in the individual's monthly pension benefit.

Practice frequently deviates from this pure case. Employer defined-contribution plans may have adjustable levels of contribution, so that workers can increase their contributions if the returns on their pension savings are below expectations. The outcomes of individual accounts can be altered by government transfers (for example, to protect the pension rights of unemployed workers) or by government guarantees that offset low asset returns for some workers (and thus encourage riskier portfolios, if that is an option). Moreover, after a severe drop in asset values or the failure of a large

---

10. We omit discussion of some risks, including the important risk of disability, on which see Reno et al. (2005).

pension fund for other reasons, a government will be pressured to bail out those near retirement, pressure to which it may or may not respond.

If a defined-contribution plan involves the purchase of an annuity, funding after its purchase is generally on a defined-benefit basis; that is, future risk falls on the seller of the annuity. That risk, however, can also be shifted on the supply side by contracts between insurance and reinsurance companies. Or the risk can be shared with the annuity holders: in what is called a CREF annuity, offered by TIAA-CREF,[11] benefits are adjusted in the light of both the realized returns on the assets funding the annuity and the realized mortality experience of the cohort of beneficiaries.[12]

In a pure defined-benefit plan with funding, the risk of varying rates of return on pension assets falls in principle on the sponsor. In an employer-sponsored plan, the risk can be spread over several groups: current workers (through effects on wage rates), the company's shareholders and the taxpayer (through effects on profits), its customers (through effects on prices), and its future workers (if the company uses surpluses from some periods to boost benefits in others). The ability of a defined-benefit plan to spread risks across cohorts allows it to share those risks more widely than a defined-contribution plan, which can spread risks only among current market participants.

In a public defined-benefit system, adjustment to adverse outcomes may come from changes in a dedicated tax (usually a payroll tax), so that risk is shared with current workers; if the trust fund is allowed to accumulate assets or to borrow, risk can be shared also with future workers; if benefits are financed partly from general revenue, risk is shared with taxpayers, including pensioners and, through government borrowing, future taxpayers.

In practice, risks are shared even more widely. When defined-benefit plans get into financial difficulties, the sponsors, both firms and governments, often adjust not only contributions but also benefits. Although governments typically have the power to change both current and future benefits, legal restrictions usually limit the ability of employers to change accrued benefits (but not prospective benefits), short of bankruptcy. In addition, some countries provide guarantees for employer pensions, shifting some of the risk to other employers through mandated insurance contributions, as in the United States and the United Kingdom, and perhaps also to taxpayers if the insurance arrangement requires an infusion of government revenue. Insurance generally covers less than 100 percent of a worker's benefits, so that current and future beneficiaries bear some of the risk as well.

A central point is that if a public system is less than fully funded, it can be financed from past government or trust fund surpluses or by government or trust fund borrowing, thus sharing risks with future cohorts. Because of this ability to redistribute and to

---

11. TIAA-CREF (Teachers Insurance and Annuity Association—College Retirement Equities Fund) is the major private pension provider in the education sector in the United States.

12. Theoretically, risks can also be shifted through rolling annuitization, that is, purchasing annuities annually rather than accumulating assets toward a single purchase date (see Sheshinski 2008).

share risks across generations, it is generally optimal to have a PAYG element; there is no parallel result that the optimum should necessarily include some funding.[13] Box 7.3 (which of necessity is somewhat technical) explains how, if done well, sharing risks more widely through a PAYG element raises welfare, a specific example of the more general point that, in many circumstances, insurance raises people's welfare.

Risk and pension reporting. The optimal portfolio for an individual financing his or her own retirement wholly from accumulated assets will generally include equities. There are, however, exceptions: a person who is extremely risk averse with respect to his or her retirement income, or one who has only a small account and hence faces transactions costs (including learning costs) with a sizable fixed cost component, may prefer to invest entirely in bonds or other safe, low-transactions-cost assets.

Whatever the economic advantage of portfolio diversification, it is clear that any description of the impact on workers should adjust for risk in reporting the impact on lifetime utility. A risk-averse person derives more welfare from a certain, constant return of x percent than from uncertain, varying returns that average x percent; hence, to presume that the return workers receive is equal to the expected (that is, the average) return on a diversified portfolio is to overstate the pension's value. The simplest way to adjust for risk is to assume a bond rate of return on stocks, although, as noted in Box 7.3, this significantly understates the value to those with no outside assets. But it is an accurate measure for those with sufficient outside assets in a portfolio that has been optimized.[14]

A similar issue arises with defined-benefit systems that are adjusted for asset returns. If this is done optimally, as discussed in Box 7.3, workers in such systems bear some risk. Yet presentations commonly treat the benefit formula as if it will never be changed. If the formula is set at the expected value of benefits given the adjustments that will follow, the presentation depicts the pension plan as more valuable than it is. Historically, benefits in immature PAYG systems have often been increased beyond the level in the initial formula. Currently, however, with many systems unsustainable, benefits are likely to be less than given by the current formula, at least for younger workers. A key question for a sustainable system is what political outcomes are likely to follow in response to asset returns that differ from what was expected. Analysts have

13. Formally, the ability to adjust a pension benefit on the basis of changes in earnings levels that take place after benefits start makes the pension benefit unlike any asset to which retirees have access. Similarly, workers do not have a means of shifting the risk in their earnings to others. Whenever a potentially beneficial mutual trade (swap of assets) is not available in the market, an arrangement that implicitly makes it available provides gains that are similar to the gains from trade. Thus some use of such an adjustment can make everyone better off (Merton 1983). A similar outcome could be achieved through the market by the government selling bonds indexed to future aggregate wages (Valdés-Prieto 2005a).

14. The set of opportunities is not changed by giving a worker the opportunity to diversify the pension portfolio, if the same option was already available with outside assets. Reversing the logic: if the pension system requires workers to purchase stocks in place of bonds, a worker with enough stock outside the pension system can sell some stocks and buy bonds, ending up with the same overall portfolio allocation. This equivalence is approximate, not exact. Inside and outside options may differ in transactions costs and in the requirement or opportunity to annuitize.

▶ Box 7.3 Contrasting the potential for risk sharing in defined-benefit and defined-contribution plans

Assessing the value to workers of alternative pension portfolio arrangements requires a calibrated model of lifetime utility. One such analysis is by Gollier (2007). He considered the retirement utility for a hypothetical rational, well-informed worker in a mandatory retirement savings program with no other savings, who makes constant annual real contributions for forty years and adjusts his portfolio as he ages.* The analysis assumed no uncertainty about future earnings and a fixed retirement age, so that the only source of uncertainty is returns to pension assets.

Defined-contribution pensions. First, Gollier considered such a worker saving in a pension system with access only to a safe asset. Naturally, the higher the safe rate of return, the higher the worker's utility. Gollier used the relationship between lifetime utility and rate of return as a device for comparing different settings, calculating the measured safe rate of interest that gave the same lifetime utility in this setting as the expected utility in the other settings he analyzed.

Gollier then examined optimal lifetime utility for a worker with access to both a safe asset and a risky asset, the latter assumed to have independent and identically distributed annual returns modeled to resemble an investment in an S&P 500 index fund. With an optimized portfolio, the expected retirement utility (and so the measured safe rate of return) with access to two assets was higher than the rate of return available on the safe asset. When the safe rate of return was 2 percent, also having access to the equity asset produced an expected lifetime utility equal to what could be achieved with the safe asset alone if it paid 3.33 percent. Thus, for a worker whose only saving is through a pension plan with individual accounts, access to stocks is a large improvement, provided the worker invests optimally. Of course, workers with sufficient assets outside the system do not gain by having access to the same asset within the system.

Defined-benefit pensions. Next Gollier calculated the value to workers of having a defined-benefit system that optimally adjusted the portfolio of the system as a whole and adjusted the benefits of different cohorts in response to realizations of the risky rate of return. He assumed that each of forty birth-year cohorts working at any time are of equal size and optimized the present discounted value of the utilities of all cohorts, with the utility discount rate chosen so as to avoid ex ante redistribution. He found that the ability to spread stock market risk more widely raised expected utility enough to be equivalent to the utility achievable with a safe asset alone yielding 4.39 percent— a substantial gain.

Implications. These results illustrate two important points:

• Section 6.4 argues that it is necessary to adjust for risk when comparing different pension systems. The Gollier results make it clear that that adjustment is substantial.

• Because they can spread risks across cohorts, defined-benefit pensions, with an equivalent risk-free return of 4.39 percent, are significantly better at sharing risk than defined-contribution pensions with access to the same assets, whose equivalent risk-free return is 3.33 percent. This difference would be larger if the analysis incorporated the increase in administrative costs that occurs when individuals rather than a single trust fund investor make the investment decisions.

These calculations assume that both the individual and the pension plan hold optimal portfolios. Neither assumption is fully realistic. And the importance of deviations from optimality is likely to vary from country to country. Nevertheless, the calculation illustrates the value of wider risk sharing. ◀

---

*Leaving aside other savings, comparing retirement utilities across environments is equivalent to comparing lifetime utilities. After forty years of accumulation, retirement utility is taken to be a constant relative risk aversion function of the accumulation, with a risk aversion coefficient of 5.

little to go on in addressing this question. This focus on asset returns should not ignore the fact that both defined-benefit and defined-contribution pensions will also adjust to demographic changes that alter wages, rates of return, and the growth of the labor force.

Alongside market risks are political risks, by which we mean changes to benefits in response to political forces, not only to a consistent optimization of pension design. These risks are present with both PAYG and funded systems. Formal analysis of such political risks and how they differ across systems has not advanced very far. It will be interesting to follow developments in the Latin American countries that have introduced individual accounts and to contrast them with their histories with defined-benefit systems. Chile moved from a system where politically powerful groups could demand and receive benefit increases to one where legislation has so far not altered account accumulations for political reasons.[15] But not all countries have succeeded in insulating pensions from short-run politics. The case of Argentina is discussed in Chapter 11.

Who chooses pension portfolios? Gollier's analysis (Box 7.3) assumes an individual who is well informed and not liquidity constrained, who thus can borrow and save at a market rate of return so as to maximize lifetime utility. The analysis of pensions, however, has to consider the series of deviations from first-best discussed in Box 4.2, including pervasive information problems on the part of workers and possibly political motivations in the choice of investments by central funds or restrictions on private investments. In a pure defined-contribution plan with individual asset choice, there-fore, the individual faces not only the range of risks set out at the start of the chapter, but also the risk connected with the choice of pension portfolio or the selection of an agent who will make portfolio choices. In a private defined-benefit plan, it is the sponsor—usually a firm or industry—that chooses the portfolio directly or selects a portfolio manager, who is likely to be more sophisticated about investment than the average worker and to have access to some assets (particularly illiquid ones) that are not available to individual workers. Decisions about who chooses the portfolio, discussed in sections 9.2 and 9.3, have a major bearing on the distribution of risk.

Other aspects of risk. As discussed in section 5.3.4, different ways of indexing pensions, both during working life and in retirement, have different risk characteristics. Indexing pensions to prices protects pensioners' real standard of living but, in a growing economy, means that over time retirees fall behind average living standards. Wage indexation avoids the latter problem but confronts pensioners with the risk that wage growth turns out to be less than expected. And both approaches will have different effects for different groups of workers.

As discussed in section 6.1, financing from a dedicated revenue source may offer pensioners better insulation against short-term budgetary pressures than financing from general revenue. This is a risk better borne by current workers, who have more time to adjust and more options for doing so.

---

15. There has been frequent legislation concerning the pension system in Chile, but it has focused on governance of the market for individual accounts administration and on portfolio regulation, not on benefit adjustment. See Chapters 12 and 13.

8

▷

Gender and Family

Living arrangements are diverse, and a person's living arrangements change over time. At any given time there are adults who are single and living alone, others who are single and sharing housing and other consumption, and others who are married or in other unions that governments recognize in different ways.[1] Married couples differ in the extent to which they share resources. Some stay married until one of them dies, other marriages end in divorce after varying lengths of time, and many people remarry after a divorce or the death of a spouse.

Governments have three types of programs that recognize living arrangements in different ways, both across programs within a country and across countries:[2]

- *Transfers of income or of goods and services in kind (or both) to poor people:* Such programs take into consideration the incomes of spouses and in some cases also the presence of others sharing living arrangements.

- *Taxes to provide general revenue:* Countries differ in the extent to which taxes are based separately on the individual earnings and capital income of each spouse, or allow or require recognition of the earnings and capital incomes of both spouses, so that couples pay different amounts of tax than if they were single.

- *Pension systems:* Countries differ in how their public pension systems treat couples. Some require joint-life annuitization (see glossary); in others decisions about the type of annuity are voluntary. In some the public pension is based only on a person's individual record; in others it may take account of a person's marital status.[3]

---

1. Children also live in a variety of settings—an issue related particularly to provision for poor adults, which we do not explore.

2. In addition, rules affecting the distribution of estates commonly depend on family structure, and these rules differ across countries. See, for example, Cremer and Pestieau (2003).

3. Pension systems also affect demographic groups differently. Although concerns have been voiced about the different impacts on different racial groups, and on immigrants relative to native-born workers, we discuss only gender issues.

All these programs need to combine various equity and efficiency concerns. As the 2006 Report of the Chilean Presidential Advisory Council, discussed in Chapter 13, put it, there is a need to recognize both personal autonomy and solidarity within the family, "recognizing that women have their own rights as citizens and not only rights derived from their position in the family."[4]

In this chapter we examine how the rules of pension systems can affect men and women differently, focusing on three aspects:

- Whether the pension system has different rules for men and women (this was common historically, but many countries have changed their rules in the direction of uniformity);
- How, even if they are uniform, rules can affect men and women differently; and
- How governments recognize that many individuals live as couples, sharing resources to varying degrees and later bequeathing them.

Because the labor market behavior and outcomes (labor force participation and wage rates, for example) of men and women tend to differ, uniform pension rules typically lead to different distributions of pension outcomes for the two sexes. For example, in the United Kingdom in 2005, about 85 percent of recent male retirees were entitled to a full basic state pension; the comparable figure for women was 30 percent (U.K. Department for Work and Pensions (2006a, Executive Summary, para. 28). In addition, the overall financial positions of men and women in old age tend to be quite different. In most countries elderly poverty is more common among women, especially single women who were previously married, both widows and divorcees.[5] Since women have longer life expectancies and are typically younger than their husbands, women are more likely then men to be the survivor of a couple, and so the pension treatment of survivors matters greatly to differences in the impact of pensions by gender.

As Figure 8.1 shows, labor force participation trends have been different for men and women in many countries. Although their experience has become more similar over the postwar period, it is still far from the same and is likely to remain so.

This chapter explores some of the causes of these outcomes and some policies that influence the observed patterns. It also seeks to move discussion away from workers as individuals to thinking about workers (or pairs of workers) in families. The tension between principles relating to individuals and principles relating to families is a longstanding issue in the analysis of income taxation and antipoverty programs. Here we discuss this issue in terms of pensions.

A worker's contributory pension depends on his or her earnings, which determine contributions, and on the benefit calculation. Earnings, in turn, depend on three sets of variables: the worker's hourly wage, the number of hours worked in a given year, and

4. "Reconociendo que las mujeres tienen derechos propios por su condición de ciudadanas y no sólo derechos derivados de su posición en la familia" (Chile Presidential Advisory Council 2006a, p. 12).

5. On the incidence of elderly poverty among U.S. women, see Karamcheva and Munnell (2007).

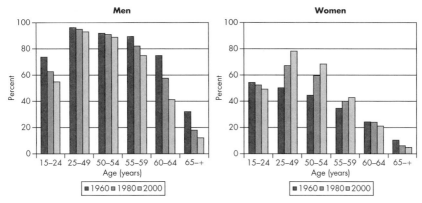

FIGURE 8.1.
Labor force participation rates in industrialized countries, by gender and age group, 1960, 1980, and 2000. *Source:* Sigg (2005, Figure 1).

the number of years in which the worker participated in the covered labor market. Hourly wages are themselves strongly influenced by experience in the labor market. This chapter therefore frames the issue, in section 8.1, by discussing some factors that affect wages, hours of work, and labor force participation. Section 8.2 discusses the different effects on men and women of annual taxes on earnings. This topic, although on the face of it outside the remit of this book, illustrates in a simpler context some issues that arise in the design of pension systems. Pension issues related to gender, including survivor pensions, are discussed in section 8.3. The final section offers some conclusions.

8.1   FRAMING THE ISSUE

A large literature examines the economic effects of gender differences.[6] We start with two factual observations:

- There are differences in the economic and social positions of men and women, some of which can be influenced by policy interventions.
- There are differences in the economic positions of individuals, couples, and families. Although some of these differences can be modified by policy, some cannot. Because of economies of scale in the production of some important household consumption goods, for example, family membership changes consumption opportunities.

6. On the changing nature of marriage, see Lewis (2001); on gender and the welfare state, Orloff (1996), Lewis (2002), and Stier, Lewin-Epstein, and Braun (2001); and on gender and motherhood pay gaps, Budig and England (2001), Davies and Pierre (2005), Joshi, Paci, and Waldfogel (1999), and Paull (2006). On gender wage inequality in the post-communist transition countries, see Trapido (2007).

Wages and labor supply. Women's wage rates on average are lower than men's, for several reasons. In poorer countries women frequently have less access to schooling,[7] and in many countries they receive less job-relevant training. In addition, there may be unequal access to jobs, and women may receive lower pay for equal work. Many countries outlaw overt wage discrimination, yet women's wages remain lower than men's even after controlling for differences in training.[8] Although of central importance to pensions, the determinants of wages lie outside the scope of this chapter, not least because they raise issues well beyond those of economic policy design.[9]

Besides having lower average wage rates, women on average spend fewer hours per year in paid work than men and participate for fewer years, in part because, on average, they spend more time caring for children and elderly dependents. In some countries, moreover, women are more likely to work in the informal sector, where they do not normally build entitlement to pension benefits. Spending time looking after others can be a matter of choice or of constraint. Some women have the option of long-term paid employment but make an active, well-informed, and unpressured choice to forgo paid work to care for children. But women's weaker labor market attachment is often the result of constraints and social pressures. These include deeply rooted social attitudes, for example about the division of caring responsibilities. Outcomes are also heavily influenced by economic policies, of which four stand out: the design of the income tax, the form in which care for children and the frail elderly is subsidized, the length of the school day, and flexibility in working hours.[10]

Consumption in the family. It is common for young adults in a wide variety of personal circumstances to share accommodation, recognizing the net economic advantage from doing so. Married couples also share housing. Beyond housing costs, there are further financial advantages in sharing food, automobiles, and consumer durables more generally. Although these advantages can be realized without a long-term commitment, and with or without marriage, society does not base policies on the expectation that (charitable donations apart) people will share with strangers. Thus measures of poverty as well as benefits in antipoverty programs are commonly set at different levels per capita for single individuals than for married (or otherwise legally recognized) couples. An antipoverty program would not be well targeted if it gave benefits to the nonworking spouses of high earners.

Within families there is obvious sharing of resources to some degree. But the division of control over income and wealth within the family typically influences consumption patterns (Lundberg and Pollak 2007). Although historically many

---

7. "Women remain disadvantaged, especially in the poorest countries. Their opportunities for educational, social, and economic advancement are usually markedly inferior to those of men, and they often face barriers in gaining access to good education and health care for both economic and cultural reasons. The end result—in low and some medium human development countries—is a lower level of education attainment for girls than boys" (Stotsky 2007); see also Buvinic and King (2007) and Lewis and Lockheed (2007) in the same symposium.

8. On gender wage differences in the United States, see Blau and Kahn (2007).

9. On policies for higher education—generally applicable also to tertiary education and training more broadly—see Barr (2004*b*). On wage discrimination, see Hakim (2004).

10. See Apps and Rees (2004) and, for discussion in the context of Germany, Rees (2006).

governments severely limited the economic rights of married women, as discussed in Chapter 1, governments in developed economies today generally intervene very little in resource allocations within the family, apart from rules about bequests and rules to protect children (for example, mandatory schooling). Yet the division of income and wealth within the family matters when thinking about the impacts of policies.

Value judgments. Some countries have gender-neutral, or unisex, pension (and other) policies, which affect men and women differently because on average their circumstances are different. Others have different policies for men and women. Historically, pension rules were often financially advantageous for women, for example when they set lower ages for full benefits. The individual accounts in Chile have earliest eligibility ages of 60 for women and 65 for men. But such a seemingly advantageous rule can also have negative effects. Since workers may contribute to their accounts only until they reach retirement age, women are favored by having earlier access to their retirement funds, but simultaneously injured by restricted opportunities to contribute.

Globally, there has been a steady trend toward removing differences in pension rules between men and women. As pension systems have wrestled with cost issues, raising the age for full benefits for women to that for men has been a common response.[11] Among the perceptions driving this trend is a recognition that different rules set up social expectations that influence both the opportunities for some women and the responses of some women to the opportunities that are present. Thus a move toward uniform rules, generally by decreasing the pension opportunities of women, has been viewed as appropriate. The move to uniform treatment is also viewed as a matter of securing human rights (for example, EU legislation sets a common retirement age, derived in part from decisions by the European Court of Human Rights) and as an element in horizontal equity (equal treatment of equals), which implies that rules should be gender neutral. Adherence to horizontal equity is thus a restriction on allowable tools. For example, men's labor supply is less elastic than women's; thus, were horizontal equity not a consideration, an optimal taxation approach would impose a lower tax on women than on men.[12] Adhering to the principle of horizontal equity, this chapter rules out such policies and, in doing so, makes a value judgment that rules should be gender neutral but designed to make sense for both men and women.

Policy impacts. The design of taxes and pensions inescapably affects the behavior of family members in a wide variety of ways, of which the following are only examples (to put it more bluntly, it is not possible to have a policy that does not affect incentives in these and other areas):

- Gender-neutral tax rates have different effects on husbands and wives on average, because, as noted, men and women have different labor supply elasticities.

11. In contrast, in 1961 the United States *lowered* the earliest age for benefits for men from 65 to 62 to match that for women.

12. In other words (ignoring cross-elasticities and the distinction between the decision about whether to participate in the labor market and the decision about how many hours to work), there is an efficiency argument for taxing men and women differently: a tax on men, because of their inelastic response to taxation, creates less inefficiency than the equivalent tax on women. This efficiency argument, demonstrated in a representative-agent (Ramsey) model, might be offset by distributional issues, however (Boskin and Sheshinski 1983, Kleven and Kreiner 2005, Apps and Rees 2004, 2007).

- Consumption behavior can differ depending on whether benefits are paid to the husband or the wife. For example, evidence suggests that if child benefits are paid to the mother rather than the father, a greater fraction will be spent on children (Lundberg, Pollak, and Wales 1997).
- Policy design can encourage or discourage marriage. Taxes may be higher or lower on two people if they remain single than if they marry. Similar issues can arise with pensions.
- Policy design can encourage or discourage mothers with young children from taking paid work, depending on the design of child care subsidies or income tax deductions, the length of school hours, and the employment rules applicable to people with small children. Also relevant is the subsidized provision of pension credits for those caring for young children.

Many of these issues are discussed in sections 8.2 and 8.3.

Resulting questions. These policy impacts suggest a series of questions, the answers to many of which are outside the remit of this chapter:

- How is consumption shared within the family? How should it be shared?
- How should the earnings of husband and wife be taxed?
- How much should taxes, current benefits (such as subsidized child care, or child benefits), and future benefits (such as pensions) encourage mothers with young children to accept paid work or discourage them from doing so?
- Should taxes and benefits be designed to encourage marriage? If other policy goals can be met only by rules that discourage marriage (for example, if some benefits are lost upon marriage), how much weight should be given to that disincentive when designing such policies?
- How do the policy rules affect the outcomes for children?
- How should survivor pensions be organized?
- How should pensions be arranged for couples who are divorced?

Implications. Our main reason for posing these questions is to make it clear that none of them has an unambiguous answer. Adopting horizontal equity as a starting point restricts the range of policy options, but the remaining set of policies is still very wide. As with other aspects of pension design, therefore, the task is to optimize in terms of the weights given to different objectives; and since those weights reflect differences in individual tastes and in social values (for example, between paid work and care activities), views about policy are likely to differ much more over gender issues than for other aspects of pensions. The matter is complicated because it is often not clear whether a particular outcome, for example a woman forgoing paid work to look after young children, is the result of choice or constraint.

The conclusion to which this leads is that, in this aspect of pensions as in others, there is not—and cannot be—a single optimal policy that applies to all countries. The rest of this chapter has the more modest aim of discussing policy options that make sense in different contexts, with no pretense at identifying a definitive set of answers.

8.2 ANNUAL TAXES ON EARNINGS

As an approach to gender issues in a simpler context than pensions, this section discusses the design of a tax on earnings in a single year.[13] There are two basic questions: How should the tax system treat couples relative to single individuals? And how should it treat couples with the same total income but different relative incomes of husband and wife? Tax design needs to consider the impacts on labor supply, marriage, and consumption and child raising within families.

Tax theory as applied to individuals and couples. With some recent exceptions (see footnote 12), optimal tax theory has focused on individual taxpayers, not recognizing the role of families. Nevertheless, the underlying principles for a well-designed tax system are relevant for thinking about taxing families and indeed contain elements that must not be ignored. When examining the impact of a small increase in a tax rate, the theory recognizes two key aspects: the additional revenue generated and the taxpayer's ability to pay.

How much additional revenue would be collected with a slightly higher tax rate? With a proportional tax (that is, one that is neither progressive nor regressive), the analysis incorporates the response of the tax base to a higher tax rate and interactions with other taxes. For example, people can respond to a higher rate of payroll tax by reducing their hours worked, hence their taxable earnings, hence the direct yield of the payroll tax; as a follow-on effect, with lower earnings, people will reduce their consumption spending. Thus the gain in revenue from a higher payroll tax rate is partly offset by reductions both in the payroll tax base and in the consumption tax base. With a progressive income tax, it is necessary also to consider the effect on higher earners of raising the marginal tax rate on a lower income bracket: the higher earners do not face an increase in their marginal tax rates but do pay more tax. The revenue yield of an increase in the tax rate is the increase in revenue in the absence of any behavioral responses minus the revenue loss from any such response. The latter incorporates the efficiency cost of the tax increase.

The question with respect to taxpayers' ability to pay (taxable capacity) is whether the higher tax is being paid more or less by people with a greater ability than others to bear taxation. More precisely, optimal tax calculations need the relative weights on taking another tax dollar from person A or person B in the light of their different economic positions, for example differences in their incomes.

Taking into account both revenue raising and ability to pay, linear tax theory (the theory that applies, for example, to a uniform tax on some good or service) looks to tax more heavily those tax bases that are relatively unresponsive to a tax increase and that relate to people with greater taxable capacity. In doing so, it is important to bear in mind that any tax change will affect groups of taxpayers that are heterogeneous in terms of their responses and their situations; analysis needs to reflect all of them.

---

13. Throughout this section we abstract from the complications that arise where marginal taxes on earnings depend also on the level of capital income. Our focus on a single year allows us to ignore the role of expectations of future taxation.

When moving from individuals to couples, the same analysis carries over but is complicated by additional elements:

- There are two different labor supplies, which taxes can affect differently.
- Taxes affect the consumption of husband and wife in ways that depend on how taxes on each affect decisions within the family.
- Taxes interact in important ways with other determinants of the arrangements for child care, such as subsidies for child care and school hours. Taxes may also influence fertility, an effect we do not consider.

Labor supply decisions. In a context that allows flexibility over how many hours to work, that decision (sometimes referred to as the intensive margin) depends on the marginal rate of taxation. The decision whether to work at all (the extensive margin) depends on the average tax on the change in income as a result of the change in labor supply.[14] Empirical evidence suggests that the major difference in the elasticity of labor supply between prime-working-age men and women comes through threshold effects on participation (full time versus part time versus out of the labor force) rather than on smooth adjustments in hours of work.[15] A different approach would compare the labor supply responses not of husband and wife but of the higher and the lower earner in a couple, thus introducing the possibility of setting tax rules differently for the higher and lower earner in a way that is gender neutral.[16] We are not aware of any empirical studies that take such an approach.

Joint versus individual taxation. In a system of individual taxation based on earnings, each spouse faces both an average tax rate and a marginal tax rate determined only by his or her own earnings. (Again we ignore the possible impacts of capital income on the taxation of earnings.) If the system is progressive, those rates are low for a spouse with low earnings. If, further, the individual tax schedule is the same for single individuals as for married individuals, then a worker faces the same tax rate whether married or not, so that there is no marriage bonus or penalty, and so (setting aside the possibility of arranging a shift of taxable earnings between spouses) no incentive for or against marriage. Some countries, however, have different tax schedules for individuals living alone, individuals who are heads of households (single parents), and individuals who are married. If the schedules are different for single and married people, marriage can affect a person's tax liability, and so taxes can be an incentive or disincentive to marriage.

With joint taxation of couples, both average and marginal taxes for each spouse may depend on the earnings of both; whether it does depends on the detailed design of the tax system. Reflecting what has been done at some times (but sidestepping undue complexity), Box 8.1 spells out a variety of ways in which taxes can depend on

---

14. On taxation with both extensive and intensive margins, see Kleven and Kreiner (2005) and Kleven, Kreiner, and Saez (2007).

15. The extensive margin is important also for young people considering whether to pursue their education, and for older people considering retirement.

16. In 2001 about a quarter of U.S. married women earned more than their working husbands, and for roughly 60 percent of such couples this situation persisted over three years (Winkler, McBride, and Andrews 2005).

the earnings of both spouses. In keeping with the principle of gender neutrality for tax rules, we refer to taxes of the primary and the secondary earner, where these are based simply on which spouse has higher earnings.

To sum up Box 8.1, with joint taxation the incentives for the lower earner to work or not and, if so, for how many hours depend on three things: how the tax base is

▶ Box 8.1 Different tax structures for couples

Denote the taxable earnings of the primary and secondary earners in a couple by I_p, I_s. Denote their taxes by T_p, T_s. If there is individual taxation, with tax function $T = F(I)$, which is the same for both primary and secondary earner, then we have

$$T_p = F(I_p)$$
$$T_s = F(I_s).$$

If there is joint taxation, the tax can depend on both incomes in ways that differ from a straightforward $F(I_p) + F(I_s)$. We can write this general structure as

$$T_c = F(I_p, I_s).$$

We focus on the taxes paid by the couple and do not explore their perceptions of who is "responsible" for different amounts of tax, although these perceptions may affect the allocation of consumption within the family.

As an example, the tax might depend on the sum of their earnings, $T_c = F_{sum}(I_p + I_s).$* Or there might be earnings sharing with individual taxation:

$$T_p = T_s = F_{share}\left(\frac{I_p + I_s}{2}\right).$$

These two examples would be identical if the tax rates are the same in both tax functions and the tax brackets are twice as wide when taxing the sum. In these cases both earners face the same marginal tax rate, but when contrasting the actual earnings level with nonparticipation in the labor force, each faces a different average tax rate: higher for the lower earner if there is a rise in marginal tax rates over the relevant range because of progressivity. The impact on a marriage penalty or bonus, again, depends on whether the tax structure for a single person is the same as the tax structure for the couple, or different.

But joint taxation can be more complex. For example, the tax base might count only a fraction a of the lower (secondary) earnings. Or the tax base could have an exempt amount of earnings, E, for the lower earnings. Or both might apply, in which case we can write

$$T_c = F\{I_p + a[\max(I_s - E, 0)]\}.$$

In this case, although the marginal tax rate of the higher earner is F', the marginal tax rate of the lower earner is either 0 or aF', depending on the size of the exempt amount relative to earnings. The average tax rate of the lower earner also differs from that of the higher earner, depending on the fraction a included and on earnings relative to the exempt amount.

Joint filing might be optional or mandatory; if optional, the tax structure for a married person filing separately can be different from that for a single person. ◀

---

*Until the end of the nineteenth century, women in the United Kingdom could have neither income nor wealth in their own right. Although that position changed, a woman's income, other than a tax-free allowance, continued normally to be taxed in the hands of her husband until 1990, so that tax was applied to the aggregate income of husband and wife. In 1990 the United Kingdom moved to individual taxation (see James and Nobes 1988, pp. 170–71).

defined (for example, whether or not there is a difference in the way higher and lower earnings are taxed), the pattern of tax rates (for example, the extent to which higher earnings face a higher marginal tax rate), and the earnings of the higher earner (for example, whether the two people have fairly similar or very different earnings). Since the responsiveness of hours worked to changes in net wages is plausibly not very different for men and women, whereas their extensive margins (that is, the decision whether or not to work) are very different, there is a case for lower average taxation of the lower earner. (The separate issue of child care costs is discussed below.) Alongside the effects on labor supply is the question of whether there is a tax penalty or a tax benefit from marriage; the answer will depend both on the relative tax treatment of the lower earner and on the tax structure for couples compared with that for single people. In addition, rules for secondary earners apply to all couples, those with young children and those without. Thus some tax policies are imperfect substitutes for child care policy; the two should be analyzed together. For example, a deduction or credit for children might be made equally available to one- and two-earner couples.

At this time, although we are aware of some exploratory work, the optimal tax analyses we know of do not go very far in clarifying the choice of tax parameters. Moreover, these studies assume a unitary structure of decision making within a couple and assume, moreover, that the preferences underlying that structure are ones that policymakers would find acceptable. But the evidence is clear that decisions within a family about consumption by the adults and about child raising do depend on the relative positions of husband and wife. Thus a more satisfactory theoretical basis would incorporate a model of decision making within a family.[17]

The tax treatment of and direct subsidies for child care. The discussion thus far has concerned the taxation of single people relative to couples, and of couples with different divisions of earnings, setting to one side issues raised by the presence of children. We turn to those issues now in the context of a very specific issue, namely, subsidies for child care in connection with labor supply. We begin by exploring the logic behind the treatment of the cost of earnings and then turn to the incentive to participate in the labor market.

Consider a self-employed person. If the chosen base of taxation is earnings net of the cost of those earnings, what costs should be deductible from gross earnings? There is no simple answer. A person's job might require special clothing that he or she would not buy if the job were different. However, such clothing substitutes for other clothing, and so not all of its cost is a cost of earning income. Similarly, work that involves travel will entail eating in restaurants while traveling, which is more expensive (but possibly more or less enjoyable) than eating at home. The tax system has no way to assess accurately the additional costs associated with work that overlap with the costs of living. Thus rules of thumb are typically used to decide what items are deductible and, if so, whether wholly or in part.

Child care raises similar issues. In principle, child care should be deductible if the parent could not work without it. But in practice, behavior is diverse: some parents are self-employed and work at home and make no use of paid child care (either combining work and child care or relying on others without paying them, for example relatives, or

---

17. On the need for such analysis, see Pollak (2007).

neighbors in a swap arrangement); others do not work but nevertheless make some use of paid child care. How much parents rely on paid child care may vary with the different jobs that are available. Thus any tax treatment of child care costs as part of determining net earnings is somewhat arbitrary, because it imposes a uniform tax rule across a diverse population.

The issue is slightly different for employees than for the self-employed. To the extent that the added costs of work apply to anyone holding the job, one would expect the market wage to cover those costs or the employer to pay for the goods or services needed. To the extent that costs vary across individuals (some employees have small children, some do not), the market wage is a blunt instrument. In either case the logic from the case of the self-employed carries over. In practice small expenditures may be ignored to hold down the complexity of tax collection.

For a single parent, the incentive to stay at home to look after a child comes from the effects on labor supply of the tax on earnings, the extent of any subsidy for child care, and the value of any tax deduction or credit for pensions given for child care activities. The comparison is more complex for someone considering jobs with different degrees of compatibility with childrearing responsibilities; for example, some jobs but not others may conflict with school hours.[18] Different countries will have different views about the social value of having a single parent stay at home with a young child.[19] For the secondary earner in a couple (defined as the one more likely to stay home), although the underlying logic of economic effects and social attitudes is the same, the analysis is complicated by the need to consider the tax treatment of couples.

8.3   THE DESIGN OF PENSION SYSTEMS

Annual taxes on earnings affect the supplies of labor by household members, the extent and division of care activities, decisions about the allocation of consumption, and patterns of marriage and divorce. Pension design affects decisions in the same realms during working years, although plausibly the effects are generally smaller.[20]

Pension design has additional effects because benefits depend on a long history of earnings, because one member of a couple will generally outlive the other, and because of divorce. These effects include

- Significant effects on decisions about when to retire, discussed in Chapter 5
- Effects on allocation within a family through decisions that affect the financial position of the surviving member of a couple

18. A further complication is that child care might cost twice as much for someone with two children under school age (once at school, child care during school hours in most countries is publicly financed). The United Kingdom, fairly typically among developed countries, recognizes the presence of two children by paying a child benefit for each, but pays only one child care subsidy, based on an income test, not a family-size test.

19. In addition, the degree of subsidy (along with other policies) will affect the incentive to have children and the distribution of income between those with and those without children.

20. On gender and pensions see Ginn (2003) and James, Cox Edwards, and Wong (2003); in the context of the European Union see Leitner (2001) and Zaidi, Grech, and Fuchs (2006) and, in a U.K. context, Rake, Falkingham, and Evans (2000) and U.K. Department for Work and Pensions (2005); on Chile see Arenas de Mesa and Montecinos (1999).

- Complications from different patterns of marriage, divorce, early death, and remarriage over working years, and possibly retirement years as well.

In addition, although a full analysis of annual taxation would recognize a role for expectations about future taxation, such a role has not been incorporated in the literature we have seen and is plausibly less salient and less important than issues of future pension benefits.

The overrepresentation of women among the elderly poor arises in part because of their lower earnings and fewer and smaller contributions while of working age, and in part from their greater likelihood of surviving their husbands than vice versa. The latter is important because the fraction of the family's pension benefits that continue after the death of a spouse may not be sufficient to maintain the survivor's consumption, and because ill health in old age—particularly if it involves long-term care—can be financially costly for the family. In this context, the design of survivor pensions matters.

This section compares the relative impact on men and women of different choices about pension design. We start with some general aspects of old-age pensions and then consider pension credits for child care, the pros and cons of organizing pensions on an individual versus a family basis, survivor pensions, and the treatment of pensions upon divorce.

8.3.1 Old-age pensions

As noted in section 8.1, we believe that gender neutrality in pension rules is appropriate, but that attention should be given to the details of the rules for their relative impact on men and women. These rules can influence the incentive to work when younger and the level of benefits when older.

Contributory pensions versus noncontributory universal pensions. Some countries provide a pension benefit for which eligibility or the size of the benefit is conditional on the number of years of residence in the country; in others the benefit depends on the number of years of contributions to the pension system. Rules based on residence tend to result in larger pensions for women relative to men than rules based on contributions.

Contribution requirements. Some countries give no benefit unless a person has contributed for at least a minimum number of years (ten years in the case of U.S. Social Security), whereas others provide benefits after any contribution. Since women on average contribute for fewer years than men, the latter approach tends to provide at least some pension for more women. For the same reason, the fewer the years of contributions necessary to qualify for a full benefit, the (relatively) higher the pensions that women tend to get. In Chile eligibility for the guaranteed minimum pension required twenty years of contributions, a level reached by relatively more men than women. (On proposed reforms of the Chilean system, see Chapter 13.)

A provision that years spent in child care count toward meeting contribution requirements, discussed in section 8.3.2, helps women, relatively speaking. The U.K. government has announced that it "will radically reform the contributory principle, by recognizing contributions to society while retaining the link between rights and responsibilities" (U.K. Department for Work and Pensions 2006a, Executive Summary, para. 38). As a result, "all those who have worked or cared for 30 years will get full entitlement to the basic State Pension" (para. 47).[21]

Benefit formulas. Details of benefit formulas affect men and women differently. For example, the formula used in the U.S. Social Security system relates benefits to the average level of indexed earnings over the highest-earning thirty-five years of a career, with zeros included if needed to reach thirty-five years. In response to a proposal to extend the averaging period to thirty-eight years, analysts noted that, on average, women would add more zeros to reach thirty-eight years than men, subjecting them to a relatively larger decrease in benefits. On the other hand, unlike most countries, Social Security has a progressive benefit formula. Since, on average, women have lower earnings than men, this progressivity benefits them relatively.

Retirement age. Although it is less common today, many countries have in the past set the statutory retirement age for women lower (typically by five years) than that for men. A lower earliest eligibility age favors women, assuming that the pension at that lower age is the same as that at the higher earliest eligibility age for men. Past thinking included this option to reflect in part different social perceptions of the roles of women and men, and in part the typical pattern of women being younger than their husbands. (A lower earliest eligibility age for women allows a typical couple to retire more nearly simultaneously.) However, this opportunity can generate social pressure for women to retire early and can lead to lower actual retirement ages, which may not be in the best interest of some women. In contrast, a lower *mandatory* retirement age unambiguously disadvantages women, in terms of both earnings opportunities and pension benefits if the latter would be higher with longer work. A lower actual retirement age for women than men, either because retirement is mandatory or as a consequence of social attitudes, will reduce benefits for women in many pension arrangements. Also relevant is whether other rules, such as eligibility for disability benefits and the opportunity to contribute to tax-favored retirement accounts, are based on the earliest entitlement age. In such respects also, a lower retirement age can place some women at a disadvantage.

Retirement incentives also depend on the incentives to continue work past the earliest entitlement age; these can vary between men and women depending on the structure of the benefit formula and the differences in the typical earnings histories of men and women. For example, if there is a large jump in benefits upon crossing some threshold number of contribution years, and if more women than men are just below the threshold when reaching the earliest entitlement age, the incentive to work up to the threshold will be more important for women than for men. And systems that incorporate family structure in benefit determination create different incentives for the lower and the higher earner in a couple. (Box 8.2 discusses the case of U.S. Social Security.)

21. Under the U.K. proposal, a person is entitled to a full basic (flat-rate) state pension upon satisfying two conditions: thirty years of actual or deemed contributions *and* attaining state pensionable age, currently 65 and set to increase in future years. Thus someone who starts work at 18 and contributes continuously is not eligible for a pension at age 48.

Where pension benefits depend on the number of contribution years, as in many defined-benefit systems, earlier retirement implies fewer contribution years and hence a smaller pension. Where benefits are actuarially related to a person's pension accumulation, as in defined-contribution systems, women's benefits can be lowered in multiple ways. First, if a woman retires earlier, she contributes for fewer years, and so her accumulation and hence her monthly pension benefit are smaller. Second, having retired earlier, she collects a pension for longer than an otherwise identical person who retires later, further reducing her monthly benefit; if the pension calculation takes account of women's longer life expectancy, the effect is even stronger. Separately, women may prefer not to be forced or pressured to retire at a younger age than men. In many countries the pressure to raise women's eligibility age came from women.

Gender-specific versus unisex mortality tables. Governments can provide annuities based on uniform pricing for a given birth cohort or require private providers to do the same. In such a system a man and a woman with the same pension accumulation and retiring at the same age receive the same monthly pension, and a man and a woman with the same accumulation who happen to have the same life expectancy receive the same expected lifetime benefits. On average, however, men receive less in present discounted value of pension benefits per dollar of accumulation than women because of their lower average life expectancy.[22]

Alternatively, governments may allow pension providers to base annuities on gender-specific mortality tables, in which case, given their different life expectancies, pensions for men and women will be priced differently: a man and a woman with the same accumulation and retiring at the same age would receive different monthly pensions, the man receiving a larger one. This practice occurs in countries in Latin America but is outlawed in employer-organized systems in the United States and the European Union, and many countries require unisex life tables not only for the mandatory system but also for voluntary pensions.

In sum, different pricing rules result in different patterns of benefits, hence different patterns of returns relative to contributions—a part of the redistribution occurring in a plan. Since higher earners tend to live longer than lower earners of the same gender, uniform pricing will tend to benefit them;[23] additionally, market pricing will reflect administrative costs, so that people with higher benefits will get better pricing. Because women tend to live longer than men, an additional pattern of redistribution arises from uniform pricing relative to nonuniform pricing. Such outcomes need to be viewed within the context of the entire system, which will generally contain other redistributive elements, notably for poverty relief (for example, if pensions are partly financed from progressive taxation) or where there is a flat-rate benefit or a minimum guarantee.

8.3.2   Pension credits for child care

A system in which entitlement to a pension recognizes years spent caring for children or for elderly dependents helps women relative to men, because women in general bear

22. A careful calculation of the extent of difference would have to note that, within each gender, higher earners receive larger pensions and live longer. Different relative distributions of earnings among men and women would then affect the magnitude of the effect.

23. Simonovits (2006) analyzes the same argument in the context of NDC pensions.

the greater share of the care burden. We discuss first the different ways in which such entitlements might be organized, and then the broader question of whether this approach is good policy.

Different forms of pension credit. There are different ways of recognizing care activities, with different distributional and incentive effects. One approach is to credit a woman's pension record with a fixed amount for each year she provides care, as in Sweden's NDC system. Sweden also credits a caregiver's individual funded account. Thus her pension is larger because of additional deposits into her account, paid out of general revenue. In some countries pensions are based on career average earnings, typically incorporating people's highest earning years. In this case a uniform level of credit per year of child care raises the pension of someone with a short career or sufficiently low earnings, and many offer less (or no) help to someone with a long career and high earnings. In other countries, including Canada and the United Kingdom, years spent in caregiving may be dropped from the calculation, thus reducing the number of years used in calculating career average earnings. With an earnings-related pension, this approach implicitly credits a higher-earning woman with a larger amount than a lower-earning woman.[24]

There are other types of pension credit. Some countries give credits for time spent in college, thereby giving an advantage to those who obtain more education. Since more education tends to generate higher incomes, it is not clear that this is a good rule. Some countries protect people in military service; this can be done either by counting years of military service as contribution years, or by making explicit pension contributions from the defense budget during a person's military service.

The broader question is when credits for time spent in caregiving are good policy. Note first that a pension credit is a blunt instrument, which does not distinguish between cases where labor supply is affected by the credit and cases where it is not. For example, some parents in well-off households may have no paid work, and hence are eligible for a credit, but also employ a full-time nanny. That is, a pension credit for people with young children and low or no earnings does not distinguish between those who look after the children themselves and those who do not. And unless the credit is added to any pension contributions paid by working parents, it does not distinguish between those who look after children and do not work and those who manage both to look after children and to work.

In assessing pension credits for child care, one needs to consider several dimensions: the extent to which society should share in the costs of raising children; the balance between providing income at the time of caring and providing pensions in the future; the desired balance of incentives between labor market activities and caring for children; and the relative treatment of different types of families.

---

24. To see this, suppose a pension is normally based on a person's forty highest earnings years. For someone who has thirty years of earnings and spent ten years caring for children, the average will be based on those thirty years of highest earnings, with the next-highest ten years of earnings dropping out of the calculation. Thus those ten years are credited with the average of the highest-earning thirty years rather than zero. This is worth more to a woman with higher earnings in those thirty years than to one with lower earnings. For women with more than thirty years of positive earnings, the gain depends on earnings in the highest-earning thirty years relative to earnings in lower years.

Supporting the costs of childraising. Raising children has costs, in terms of both expenditure and possibly forgone earnings; forgoing earnings also reduces future pension benefits. Two questions arise: *where* those costs should fall, that is, the division between parents and taxpayers; and *when* those costs should fall, that is, the extent to which parents should be helped when the children are young rather than, through a pension credit or similar instrument, in later years.

Many countries provide income to families with children in order to share the costs of childrearing more broadly across society. They may do so out of concern for equity across family types, or to protect children, or to encourage fertility. The incomes of families with children can be raised through a deduction in the income tax or through a refundable credit, which is equivalent to a nontaxable child benefit, that is, a weekly or monthly or annual cash payment to the caregiver.[25] (Or a child benefit might be included in taxable income to be even more progressive. We ignore more complex treatments.) Countries also share childrearing costs with parents through free services, such as free schooling. All these instruments have an income effect but provide no incentive effect for work, except perhaps when they move the taxpayer to a lower income tax bracket.

Balancing money now and money in the future. For any level of budgetary support for child care, a general question facing policymakers is whether such support should take the form of income at the time the care is provided (often a time when family resources are stretched) or future income in the form of pension. A more specific question is whether, as with earnings, the child benefit should be considered as income that should be subject to mandatory retirement saving. If one ignores the cost of raising children, the answer is yes, for the purpose of consumption smoothing. But raising children does have costs, and so the question is how the presence of those costs changes that conclusion.

In the simplest case, the income that is relevant for consumption smoothing is the amount that parents can spend on their own consumption, after their spending on child care, out of given total spending. This simple case assumes that the presence of children does not change the parents' marginal utility from spending on themselves relative to the marginal utility they derive from spending when older.[26] The presence of a child benefit will reduce the net costs of bringing up children and thus mitigate

---

25. This assumes that the person receiving the tax credit is the same as the person who would receive the child benefit; in many countries the child benefit is normally paid to the mother. Child benefits (also called family allowances) are common throughout Europe and in many other countries (see Bradshaw and Finch 2002). The United States does not offer child benefits but does allow an income tax exemption for dependent children.

26. One can argue that what should be smoothed is not consumption but utility, but parents' utility is affected over time by many factors, including the presence of children and (perhaps) grandchildren and (perhaps) the early loss of a spouse; it is not clear what it means to try to smooth utility across such uncertainties. More formally, optimizing lifetime utility involves equalizing the marginal utility of consumption across time. Setting to one side such complications as intertemporal nonadditivity, age-varying period utility, and nonadditivity of children's consumption, and assuming that the utility discount rate equals the real interest rate, we have the simplified Modigliani model of optimal constant consumption.

the decrease in income that is relevant for consumption smoothing. This logic suggests that, for a person with children, the earnings base for mandatory saving should be reduced to reflect some measure of the costs (net of any child benefit and other subsidies for children) of bringing up the children. In principle, the deduction from the earnings base should be smaller, the higher is the child benefit and the greater the extent to which the utility from having children lowers the parents' marginal utility of spending on themselves when the children are young relative to when the children (and the parents) are older.

Balancing incentives between paid work and caring. Decisions about the optimal design of consumption smoothing have to be set alongside policy preferences about the balance between paid work and caring for children. Incentives to take paid work are stronger where subsidies for child care are conditioned on the caregiver being in paid work, and where taxation of secondary earners is lower. Incentives to take paid work are weaker where caregiving is recognized through a pension credit. In contrast, a child benefit paid independent of work (as is typical) has an income effect on labor supply but no substitution effect.[27]

The relative sizes of these elements determine the balance of incentives between paid work and caregiving. To maintain a given level of incentive for paid work, the presence of a pension credit needs to be balanced by an offsetting change in one of the other incentives. Policy design needs also to consider the balance of incentives between paid child care and care by the parents themselves or other family members. The following are some options:

- The incentive to stay at home to care for children can be strengthened by making child benefits or pension credits, or both, available only to people with no (or little) earnings.

- To strengthen the incentive to take paid work, a subsidy for child care costs could be conditioned on working at least a minimum number of hours. Such a subsidy encourages the use of paid child care by those who earn income and therefore the willingness to accept work that will have them use paid child care.

- It is possible to separate the incentive to work from the incentive to use paid child care when working. A pension credit for part-time earnings (and lower taxation of secondary earners with children) can encourage part-time work that limits the need for (and the use of) paid child care. Thus policy can encourage such work by limiting the child care subsidy but not the net encouragement to paid work.

Of course, in practice the desire to avoid undue complexity will affect the design of policies that support children and encourage (or do not encourage) paid work.

Balancing the relative treatment of different family types. The choice of balance between different instruments has important distributional effects. A greater emphasis on pension credits or child benefits assists families with children relative to those

---

27. By increasing parental income, the child benefit reduces the incentive to take paid work; however, the benefit has no effect on the net return to additional work, and thus creates no disincentive via the substitution effect.

without (assuming the tax on secondary earners is the same whether or not the family has young children). A greater emphasis on lower taxation of secondary earnings benefits couples with children relative to single parents. Unless the lower taxation of secondary earnings is available only to those with small children, it does not match a pension credit. And a pension credit does not perfectly match a child care subsidy, since use of child care is not universal among those who work. Thus the distributional effects of the various instruments are diverse and complex and may require some offsetting adjustments.

There are also potential distributional effects between better- and worse-off families. A critical question is the overall financial position of recipients of a pension credit. If the credit goes primarily to members of high-earning families (perhaps because they are the most likely to be able to afford to have someone not in paid work) who will have sizable pensions, the situation is very different from one where the credit goes primarily to low-income single parents, who would otherwise have very small pensions. Thus the case for a pension credit needs to be evaluated on a country-by-country basis, with a focus on who receives it and on the extent to which that fits policymakers' distributional objectives.

Political arguments. It is conventional to consider each part of the pension system (in this case a pension credit for caregivers) in the context of optimizing across all the elements in a pension system. However, in a democracy, pension design may reflect a compromise of different views. Thus it may happen that policymakers think that pension benefits are too low overall, and are unable for political reasons to increase them, but are able to achieve a targeted increase for some groups. If policymakers choose this route, the following question arises (with both economic and political implications): if the only politically available tool is a pension credit for those with children, is it better to give it to all people with children or only to those who do not work when their children are young? The former does not reduce the labor incentive to work, whereas the latter does.

In sum. The pension credit has a multidimensional role in optimizing the balance between current and future consumption, the balance of incentives between paid work and child care, and the balance of redistribution across families of different types. As noted earlier, it is not possible to have a policy that does not affect incentives in these and other areas.

8.3.3 Individual versus family pensions

The design of pension systems, like the design of an income tax, is no accident but depends heavily on the social philosophy that underpins it. Specifically, does policy regard a woman primarily as an adjunct of her husband, hence covered by his pension contributions, or primarily as an autonomous individual, earning a pension in her own right? The former view was common in the past but has been rejected in many countries in favor of a view that recognizes autonomy but also a woman's role as part of a family. The latter view prompts a policy drive to adjust labor market and pension institutions to strengthen women's earnings and encourage labor force participation; it also influences views about how an equitable pension system might look. Such views are in part a matter of social values, on which countries differ, just as they differ in the mix of one- and two-earner couples and the prevalence of marriage.

As with an income tax, a related social consideration is whether to think of the family or the individual as the economic unit. This is a major issue in any program aiming at redistribution. Should people with low earnings or low pension benefits in rich families be eligible for the same redistributions as those with low earnings or low benefits in poor families or on their own? Most people would say no, but one thing that complicates this evaluation is that family structures have become more fluid: more than in the past, the family at the time of benefit receipt may be different from the family at the time when its members worked and made pension contributions. And divorce settlements may or may not have taken into account future pension benefits.

Organizing pensions on an individual rather than a family basis, with women having pensions *only* in their own right, is argued by some to be a better fit for societies with such fluidity in structure. On the other hand, as discussed above in the context of income taxation, family structure affects available resources and the demands on those resources. Moreover, adjusting pension benefits after a divorce (discussed below), which is a way of recognizing family structure, may be important for relative pension levels. As an example of the role of family structure, Box 8.2 discusses the current public pension arrangements for spouses in the United States and the resulting labor market incentives (see also Favreault and Steuerle 2007).

▷ Box 8.2 Auxiliary and surviving spouse benefits in the United States

In the U.S. Social Security system, persons 62 and over with at least ten years of covered earnings are entitled to a worker benefit, provided their current earnings are not too high (in other words, there is a retirement test; for details on how the benefit is determined, see Chapter 11). If a worker has claimed benefits and is married, the worker's spouse, if also at least 62 and with low or zero earnings, is entitled to a spouse benefit equal to one-half of the worker's benefit, adjusted for the age at which the benefit starts. However, a person may receive only the higher of the spouse benefit or a worker benefit based on his or her own record. So, if a couple are both over age 62 and both claim benefits, the husband receives the higher of a benefit based on his earnings record or half of the worker benefit to which his wife is entitled (both adjusted for the age at which benefits start). Similarly, the wife receives the higher of a worker benefit based on her earnings or a spouse benefit equal to half of her husband's benefit. (Technically, each spouse receives a worker benefit based on his or her own earnings, plus an additional benefit to reach the higher of the two benefits. A person with ten years of coverage whose spouse benefit exceeds his or her worker benefit is referred to as a dual-benefit recipient.)

When one member of a couple (say, the husband) dies after retirement, there is a new calculation, giving the survivor the higher of the worker benefit based on her own earnings record or a survivor benefit equal to 100 percent of her deceased husband's worker benefit; again, these benefits are subject to adjustments for the ages at which they start. When a covered worker dies before retirement, there is a similar calculation once the survivor reaches the eligibility age for benefits.

With this structure, a married person with sufficiently low average lifetime earnings compared with the earnings of the spouse receives no additional benefit as a consequence of additional earnings. Thus the implicit tax on earnings (the payroll tax minus the value of additional future benefits) is equal to the full payroll tax rate for pensions, with no offset for anticipated benefits. With somewhat higher earnings, so that there is

(continues next page)

(continued from previous page)

potential eligibility for a survivor benefit (based on 100 percent of the deceased worker's benefit) but not to a spouse benefit (based on 50 percent of the deceased worker's benefit), the implicit tax is still quite high. This system, which goes back to the early days of Social Security, thus creates adverse incentives for labor market participation and for additional hours of work for a person with low career earnings and a spouse with much higher earnings, since additional earnings bring no additional pension benefit, given eligibility for a spouse pension. The labor market incentives for the higher earner in the couple also depend on the earnings level of the spouse, being greater if a higher worker benefit also raises the benefit received as a spouse benefit.

The Social Security benefit formula is progressive (see Chapter 11), to provide a higher replacement rate for those with lower earnings, who on average are more needy. This underlying logic calls for comparing the degree of need of an individual with that of a couple with the same total earnings. Consistent with this approach, some adjustment is called for when two people rely on benefits rather than one. As with our discussion of tax treatment of couples in Box 8.1, more complex systems are possible that would do a better job of combining fairness and incentives.

Note that, with this structure, a survivor receives between one-half and two-thirds of what the couple were receiving when both were alive (ignoring adjustments for the ages at which benefits start). If husband and wife had the same average earnings, the survivor receives one-half. In the case of a one-earner couple (or with a spouse receiving a spouse benefit), benefits go from 150 percent of the higher earner's benefit to 100 percent of the worker benefit—a reduction of one-third. This pattern of survivor replacement rates has no apparent logic.

A further set of incentives relates to remarriage if a person who remarries loses his or her pension based on the previous spouse's earnings (Baker, Hanna, and Kantarevic 2003; Brien, Dickert-Conlin, and Weaver 2004). ◀

8.3.4 Survivor pensions

Studies find that a single survivor of a couple typically needs more than half of the couple's income—commonly 65 to 70 percent—to maintain a broadly constant standard of living. Thus, in the absence of other resources and survivor benefits, if two spouses are the same age and have identical earnings histories and identical pension benefits, the death of one will lower the living standard of the other. This is part of the mechanism that results in higher poverty among widows than among married elderly women.[28] Survivor pensions are therefore an important element in preserving the living standards of the elderly. (The U.S. system is described in Box 8.2.) Although we discuss only the case of surviving spouses, the issue is broader: a well-designed system also has benefits for young survivors, notably young children (see Baker, Hanna, and Kantarevic 2003).

There are many ways of organizing and financing survivor pensions. In a funded defined-contribution or NDC pension, the accumulation could be used to purchase a joint-life annuity, with a suitable fraction for the survivor. In a two-earner couple this can be done by both earners. Of course, with mandatory annuitization, differences in

---

28. For analyses of the impact of widowhood in the United States, see Holden and Zick (1998) and Karamcheva and Munnell (2007).

the perceived life expectancy of people who are the same age imply that there are perceived winners and losers from such a mandate. In contrast, if joint-life annuitization is voluntary, there are issues of adverse selection: couples who think that the spouse will live considerably longer than the worker are more likely to purchase such annuities. Voluntary joint-life annuitization is the approach taken with the funded portion of the pension system in Sweden (although not with the NDC portion, which does not allow that option). The balance of influences on the decision could be tilted toward a joint-life annuity by making that the default, and more strongly by requiring both members of a couple to agree before the default is replaced by a single-life annuity for the worker. Regulation of employer-provided pensions in the United States includes these rules. A further step would be to make joint-life annuitization mandatory.

A defined-benefit system could offer a similar set of options, based on the actuarial conversion of a single-life annuity into the relevant joint-life annuity. Alternatively, survivor benefits might be provided out of the overall revenue of the pension system, as in the U.S. Social Security system, thus benefiting couples at the expense of single people. Such an arrangement involves transfers to couples that are greater, the higher the worker's pension benefit, a feature that has been much criticized. Thus it may be better to use a more complex rule covering survivor benefits, such that they are partly financed out of the worker's benefit and partly out of the resources of the pension system, with the proportions depending on the level of benefit.

If pensions are proportional to earnings, the underlying logic is that the pension system does not attempt to adjust for differing needs at different levels of earnings; that is, it makes no attempt to redistribute between richer and poorer pensioners. Any redistribution takes place outside the system, and so the pension system itself does not need to adjust redistribution where there is joint-life annuitization. Thus, when benefits start for a couple of given ages, the expected present discounted value of benefits, including benefits when both are alive and when only one of them survives, should be determined by the defined-benefit formula or the balance in a (funded or notional) defined-contribution account.

In contrast, with a progressive benefit formula as in the United States, the system adjusts replacement rates to reflect need. Under an income tax, a couple is seen as less able to pay taxes than a single person with the same aggregate income; analogously, a couple has a greater replacement need than a single person with the same aggregate earnings history. Thus the replacement rate for a couple (reflecting the earnings of both) might be matched with that of a single person judged to have the same need. But a further complication arises because one member of a couple generally survives the other. Thus "replacement need" should be considered on a lifetime basis, including recognition of the "survivor replacement rate," the ratio of the benefit paid to the survivor to the benefit paid when both were alive. It is common in employer plans for the worker to receive some benefit independent of the survival of his or her spouse, whereas the spouse receives a smaller benefit if he or she survives the worker. It is not clear that such an arrangement makes sense.

8.3.5   Divorce

The increased fluidity of marriage raises the salience of rules for pensions when a couple divorces. There are social rules, often involving the courts, on the division of accumulated assets (including sometimes human capital) of the couple upon divorce, with particular focus on accumulations during the marriage. Entitlements under a public pension system might be part of what gets divided as part of the general settlement, or they might be regarded as implicit assets that cannot be divided. The rules of the pension system might determine the division, or they might merely limit the division that a divorce settlement or divorce court ruling may make. The issue is important: without some adjustment, divorce after many years of marriage can result in very low benefits for a person with a limited earnings history. Indeed, poverty rates for divorced women who do not remarry are high in the United States.

There are different strategies for providing benefits after a divorce, implemented through decisions at the time of retirement or at the time of divorce. One strategy is to provide benefits when a divorced person reaches retirement age. This can be done as a transfer of benefits between spouses. For example, when a worker starts to draw a pension, benefits are adjusted to provide some benefits not only to a current spouse, but also to previous spouses, using a formula relating to the lengths and timing of the marriages. Future availability of such benefits could be factored into a divorce agreement. Alternatively, benefits for a divorced spouse could be financed from the resources of the pension system generally, without reducing the benefit of the worker entitled to the pension, as in the United States (see Box 8.3).

A second strategic approach is to transfer explicit or implicit pension wealth between spouses at the time of a divorce, based on their earnings records (and realized rates of return if there are assets) during the marriage. In Canada, when a marriage or common-law partnership ends, the entitlements to the Canada Pension Plan built up by the couple during the time they lived together may be divided equally between them as part of a divorce settlement.

A third approach is to divide earnings records on an annual basis during the marriage. Kotlikoff and Sachs (1998) have argued for individual accounts, where each year the earnings of husband and wife are divided evenly between them. These accounts

▶ Box 8.3 Auxiliary and survivor benefits for divorced spouses in the United States

In the United States, if a couple divorces after being married for ten years or more, and at least one has not remarried before starting benefits, a Social Security benefit may be payable to one spouse based on the other's earnings record. The rules parallel those for the spouse and survivor benefits described in Box 8.2: a divorced person is entitled to the higher of a worker benefit based on his or her own earnings record, or a divorced spouse benefit equal to 50 percent of his or her spouse's worker benefit. (An amendment to the Social Security Act in 1965 provided benefits to divorced wives and widows if they were dependent upon the wage earner's support and if their marriage had lasted twenty consecutive years or more; this was reduced in 1977 to ten years). Because the system does not decrease a worker's benefits because of auxiliary benefits provided on the basis of his or her earnings record, such payments come from the pension system as a whole, subject to a maximum family benefit for a single earnings record. If that maximum applies, the worker benefit is not affected, but the other auxiliary benefits are reduced. Similarly, there is a surviving divorced spouse benefit of 100 percent of the worker's benefit, again subject to a family maximum. ◀

▶ Box 8.4 Dividing earnings records between husband and wife

Consider a couple where the husband is five years older than the wife and both plan to stop working and start collecting benefits at age 65. Assume they participate in a funded defined-contribution system with identical benefit rules for all individuals, both married and single, in which the earliest age for claiming a benefit is 65. (Analogous issues can arise under a defined-benefit system with similar rules.) Assume also that the husband's accumulation at age 65 is X, which would result in a monthly benefit of x, of which he gets $x/2$, based on $X/2$ at age 65. Once the wife reaches 65, she is entitled to a benefit based on the other $X/2$, which will have grown over the intervening five years, probably yielding a larger pension (but not necessarily, because it might be subject to annuitization with a different mortality table and a different interest rate).

In addition, because of earnings sharing, the husband is entitled to a benefit based on half of his wife's earnings up to the time his benefits start. With continued sharing, he receives further increases as she goes on earning. Since the husband retires when his wife is 60, not 65, his benefit is lower than what she would receive on her earnings at age 65 if she did no further work since her account continues to accumulate.

In the case of a one-earner couple where the earner is the older, the availability of only half the benefit may represent a liquidity problem that makes it hard for him or her to retire at 65. ◀

belong to the individual and would be carried through a divorce. However, when the ages of husband and wife are significantly different and they have had very different earnings (and the higher earner is older), such a division of pension assets undercuts their ability to finance their retirement if they remain married. This is clearest in the case of a one-earner couple. When the worker reaches retirement age, only half of the benefit is available until the younger spouse has reached retirement age. Box 8.4 identifies some additional complexities.

8.4 CONCLUSION

This chapter has put forward three sets of arguments about gender and family issues in pension design:

- There is no unambiguously best design. But some designs are unambiguously bad.
- Policy should not focus only on the design of the pension system itself, but should also be cognizant of the impact on eventual pension benefits of other policies concerning, for example, the taxation of earnings, subsidies for child care, all-day schools, and regulations about flexibility of work for parents of young children.
- We do not argue that women ought to work or ought to care for children; rather the argument is that tax and pension systems (and other policies) inevitably create incentives that affect decisions about paid work, care activities, and leisure and therefore should be chosen to reflect diverse social values, individual preferences, and constraints, all of which will differ within a country and across countries.

More concretely, pension design needs to be sensitive to the differing impacts on men and women. To that end it should

- Consider what recognition is appropriate, and in what form, of years spent in socially valued activities such as caring for children, disabled people, and elderly dependents, balancing such recognition with incentives to participate in paid work
- Set common rules for pension eligibility and determination
- Require the use of unisex life tables if the system converts account balances to annuities
- Ensure that satisfactory pension arrangements are in place for surviving spouses and after a divorce.

9

▷

Implementing Pensions

Chapters 4–8 set out the economic theory that underlies good policy design, recognizing that many different designs are possible and identifying examples of poor design. Moving beyond general economic analysis, this chapter emphasizes that what constitutes good design for a particular country depends also on the country's capacity to implement it. A system that cannot be implemented more or less as designed is not a good design. Numerous cleverly constructed reforms—of pensions, the finance of health care, student loans, and many others—have failed because their administrative requirements were underestimated or exceeded what was possible, or because political support for the reform was lacking. The issue is not unique to developing countries. Examples abound of government projects in developed countries that were late, over budget, or failed altogether.[1]

This chapter considers the conditions for the feasibility of pension designs. The analysis is selective, both for reasons of space and because neither of us is an expert in implementation: neither of us has ever run a pension system or studied implementation in detail. Our central point—obvious but often overlooked—is that a country's choice is constrained by its fiscal, political, and institutional capacity. Ignoring or underestimating the task of implementation dramatically increases the likelihood that a reform will fail to achieve its objectives.

Effective reform requires at least three sets of skills: in policy design, administrative and technical implementation, and political implementation. Although we will have less to say about the last of these, it is of coequal importance with the more technical aspects. Experts in one set of skills frequently do not grasp the importance of the other two. There is much lip service but little real understanding. Experts in policy design tend to ignore implementation or to underestimate its difficulty; politicians may give insufficient weight to the coherence of policy or to meeting its administrative requirements,

---

1. For example, Hendy et al. (2005) reported that the development of a nationwide computer system for the U.K. national health service was at risk because health care staff had not been consulted sufficiently. Separately, the time scale and costings were claimed to be unrealistic.

for example by not allowing enough time or by not including an adequate administrative budget. Administrators and other technical experts may overestimate the difficulty of change, may take a blinkered approach, or be reluctant to reform for other reasons.

A key point is that implementation requires skills additional to and different from policy design. The idea that if one understands the policy, one can establish a program for implementing it, is generally false. Implementation skills are an integral element in reform, not an add-on. They must be involved at the stage of policy design, not bolted on after policy is set. There is a deeply flawed view that policy involves "higher" skills: higher-level people design policy, which is then handed over to the apparatchiks to implement. This is, quite simply, wrong: the three sets of skills—policy, technical, and political—are neither hierarchical nor sequential. Effective implementation needs the right skills, and from the outset.

Section 9.1 sets out the tasks that a government must be able to carry out if a pension reform is to succeed, tasks that clearly vary with the type of pension system. Section 9.2 describes the capacities that private pension providers need to have to implement voluntary or mandatory individual accounts effectively—that is, to ensure that the supply side is working well. Section 9.3 considers the demand side of the market for individual accounts, notably the extent to which workers are well informed about the decisions they need to make, about the characteristics of different pension arrangements, and about the quality of different pension providers.

9.1 THE CAPACITY OF GOVERNMENT

Pensions—large or small, simple or complex—must respect three sets of constraints: financial capacity, administrative capacity, and a series of broader institutional requirements.

9.1.1 Financial capacity

Consumption by retirees is at the expense of consumption by workers, or spending on investment, or both. From a macroeconomic perspective, therefore, pensions are in part a device that helps to divide output between workers and retirees. Clearly, total spending on pensions must be compatible with a country's financial capacity. This emphasis is not ideological. A central goal of policy is to increase living standards. And there is no dispute that beyond a certain point high taxation is harmful. Thus public spending and, within that, public pension spending, must be compatible with economic growth.

It is important, however, to be clear what that statement means and what it does not mean. It is a mistake to proceed from "excessive public spending is harmful" to "public spending should be minimized"; the first statement does not imply the second.[2] In the context of pensions, the taxes or contributions that finance pension benefits should limit labor market distortions and be compatible with economic growth. The size and coverage of a pension system should depend on the state of the macroeconomy and of the government budget. As other chapters have noted, different economies

2. Although it is common for some commentators to assert that the government spends too much, generally analysts think that governments spend too much on some purposes and too little on others; and analysts disagree as to which is which.

can function well with public pension systems of very different sizes and designs. But since pension systems must have a reasonable degree of stability to fulfill their social purpose, there must be sufficiently wide and long-lasting political support to ensure that the probability of a sharp reversal of the policy is low.

9.1.2 Administrative capacity

Although all pension systems make significant demands on government capacity, some are considerably more demanding than others.

Publicly provided pensions

The following options are listed in ascending order of their fiscal and administrative demands. We focus on systems that pay benefits periodically (for example, monthly) rather than those that pay a single lump sum at retirement age.

Noncontributory systems. The limited budgets and administrative capacities of very poor countries restrict them to providing modest, administratively simple poverty relief, for example through locally based discretionary benefits, means-tested social assistance, or a flat-rate, tax-financed pension for the very elderly. Even the simplest of such arrangements requires that government have at least a limited capacity to collect tax revenue and be able to distribute benefits to the intended recipients (which requires, for example, that government can ascertain people's ages).

Simple defined-benefit contributory arrangements. A somewhat greater fiscal and public administrative capacity makes possible a national system of income-tested social assistance, or a simple PAYG pension (for example, a flat rate per year of contribution), or both. The pension can be financed in a range of ways: from a dedicated social insurance contribution or from a mix of general revenue and contributions; either is possible with a trust fund (that is, a partial accumulation to cover future pension liabilities) or without. Systems of this sort require a government that can collect contributions effectively, maintain records over the years for workers who will be mobile geographically and across firms, adjust benefit levels for the worker's age when benefits start (if the system allows a delayed start), and pay benefits in an accurate and timely way. Government also needs the ability to project future contributions and benefits so that the system can adapt slowly and with significant lead times to evolving financial capacity.

If the pension system incorporates a trust fund, government needs the ability to preserve and invest these claims on future output. Preservation starts with the ability to prevent widespread embezzlement. Also critical is a suitable macroeconomic environment. In particular, as discussed in Box 9.1, bouts of high inflation can erode or even erase the purchasing power of accumulations in the absence of full indexing—and the ability to fulfill indexed promises. Trust funds may hold a portfolio that consists entirely of government debt, or they may hold private assets as well. If funding is to strengthen the ability of the economy to provide consumption to pensioners in the future, any additional government borrowing through purchases of government debt by the trust fund must not be used wholly for current consumption. If private assets are purchased, there needs to be an adequate capital market in which to invest. Although investments abroad can substitute for investments in domestic capital markets, they may or may not be good choices at different stages in economic development.[3]

---

3. As discussed in section 6.3.2, developing countries may have to pay a country risk premium to induce capital inflows, and such inflows can increase vulnerability to capital flight by foreign investors. See also Box 4.1.

▶ Box 9.1 The importance of avoiding high inflation

Governments must have the capacity to avoid high inflation, because rapid, unanticipated inflation erodes the real value of nominal bonds, including those held in pension funds. The impact on stocks is generally negative as well, although stock values, like the value of the underlying companies, may return to the previous relationship to the economy. A single burst of rapid inflation at any time during a person's working life (if assets are not fully indexed) or during retirement (if annuities are not fully indexed) will cause a sharp decline in his or her pension benefits, as the example below illustrates.

Two points are noteworthy about inflation after retirement. First, any loss of value due to inflation is permanent; retirees have little opportunity to make up any of the lost ground, since they have far less ability than workers to adjust to inflation through additional earnings or increased saving. In addition, with rising life expectancy, people live much longer in retirement than previously. Thus, even low inflation can have a considerable cumulative impact on a retiree's standard of living. For example, with 2 percent annual inflation, the real value of a nominal benefit after ten years is only 82 percent of its original value, and only two-thirds after twenty years. Note that these losses are stated in terms of the original benefit, which as a proportion of the worker's previous real earnings, is the replacement rate; the decline relative to rising average real earnings of current workers is generally considerably larger.

As an example of the ill effects of inflation on pensions, the price index in the United Kingdom in January 1974 was 100; by September 1978, in the wake of the first oil shock, it was 200. Most individual annuities in the United Kingdom were not indexed to inflation at the time, and so their real value was halved. Most U.K. private pensions are now required to compensate for annual inflation of up to 5 percent (so-called limited price indexation). Had that rule been in place in the 1970s, the nominal value of pensions would have increased from 100 to about 133, still well short of the 200 needed to preserve their real purchasing power; in other words, pension benefits would have lost one-third of their value. ◀

Separately, pensions may require effective coordination between national and subnational levels of government if all are to have a role in supporting the elderly. This is a matter both of broader constitutional arrangements and of the specifics of pension design. As with all systems, it is also a matter of implementation. For example, the software to run the pension system should be provided centrally, with subnational levels of government unable to make any modifications except (if the system allows such variation) to set a local level of benefit within a nationally determined formula. Experience shows that excessive customization is a likely outcome unless strictly prevented.

Earnings-related public pensions. Earnings-related pensions require, in addition, that government measure people's earnings effectively and keep the more detailed records needed for calculating benefits. (Appendix 9.1 lists the specific tasks in the case of the U.S. Social Security system.[4]) Examples of such systems are notional defined-contribution (NDC) pensions (see glossary), which take into account all of a worker's earnings in all years, although the accumulated balance is a sufficient statistic

---

4. Communist countries avoided the need for such detail by basing benefits on a short earnings period at the end of a career. As discussed in section 5.2.1, such a system does not fit the needs of a market economy and should be avoided, notwithstanding the easier administration involved.

for calculating benefits. Without detailed records, however, it is difficult to correct errors once workers approach retirement and attempt to verify the accuracy of calculations. Hence earnings-related pension systems require that government undertake the following tasks:

- Track and record a worker's earnings accurately across his or her entire working life, which requires identification of and recordkeeping for each individual worker
- Do so for workers who are mobile across jobs, employment status (employed, self-employed, or unemployed), and geographical regions
- In the case of an NDC system, make actuarial calculations that accurately convert notional accumulations in accounts into benefit levels
- Assist workers' planning by keeping them informed through regular (ideally annual) statements of the relevant earnings records (or balances in their accounts, in an NDC system) and the implications for retirement income of those records or balances and future contributions, based on a range of assumptions
- Pay benefits accurately and promptly
- Make the calculations and adjustments necessary to keep the system financially sustainable, either automatically or by legislated changes.

Merely listing these requirements is sufficient to emphasize their stringency.

Publicly funded defined-contribution systems. This type of arrangement can vary greatly in the extent of administrative capacity needed. Such systems hold assets and therefore require the capacities discussed earlier to maintain trust fund investments. What the system needs beyond that depends on its design. Perhaps the simplest is a provident fund system, which has a single fund that determines all benefits on the basis of its realized earnings. Thus the administrative needs are similar to those of an NDC system. It may be possible to rely on private insurance firms rather than a government program to actually calculate and pay benefits. But this, in turn, relies on adequate regulation of those firms.

More-sophisticated systems can allow workers to choose different portfolios. This approach greatly increases the demands on communication and recordkeeping, since the government has to keep track of each worker's portfolio in order to credit accounts appropriately and must maintain a system that allows workers to change their portfolios, either by changing the mix of new purchases or by rearranging existing portfolios. The greater the amount of choice allowed, the greater the administrative complexity and administrative cost, as the discussion in Appendix 9.1 illustrates. And since some workers may fail to choose a portfolio, it is necessary to set up a well-designed default portfolio, as discussed in section 9.3.

Private pensions

Government has three interests in the functioning of employer-provided pensions and individual accounts: to ensure that the pensions fulfill the expectations reasonably held for them; to encourage lower earners to save for retirement; and, in many (but not all) countries, to encourage retirement saving generally, both to promote old-age security and to bolster economic growth.

The early history of voluntary private arrangements illustrates the need for government action to help pensions fulfill such expectations. As discussed in section 5.2.1, employers first offered pensions to attract and retain workers and to facilitate the timely retirement of less productive older workers. Early private pension systems sometimes operated without legal oversight. Thus nothing prevented firms from laying off workers shortly before they would have become eligible for a pension, thus defeating the workers' expectations. In some settings firms could simply terminate their pension plan, leaving covered workers with no legal recourse. And even firms that fully intended to pay could get into financial trouble and be unable to fulfill their pension commitments. To address these issues, governments intervened in a range of ways, as discussed in Box 9.3 later in this chapter.

Thus if private pensions, whether provided by an employer or arranged by an individual directly with a financial intermediary, are to provide effective consumption smoothing and insurance, a country needs not only adequate private sector capacity but also—and frequently overlooked—adequate government capacity. Secure pensions require macroeconomic stability, a well-designed incentive structure, and well-regulated financial markets and insurance markets—in all of which the government has a central role.

Maintaining macroeconomic stability. Sound macroeconomic policy is critically important if investment in domestic assets is to yield good returns. In particular, for the reasons set out in Box 9.1, it is important that government prevent high inflation. (Widespread inflation indexing can ease much of the cost of higher inflation but is itself a technically demanding institution). In addition, the ability of returns from investments abroad to finance retirement consumption domestically depends on exchange rate policies and on the other macroeconomic policies that set the environment for exchange rates (see the discussion in Box 4.1 and section 6.3.2).

Setting incentives. The financing of consumption from investments depends also on the tax treatment of gross returns. It is common for governments to tax capital incomes as well as labor incomes. It is also common to have special tax rules for retirement saving to make it more attractive. However, these rules sometimes constrain investment choices.

To encourage the spread of saving, rules may offer tax advantages only to plans with sufficiently wide coverage, withholding or removing tax advantages if a plan is established only for top management. In addition, as discussed in Box 9.6, recent analyses of behavioral economics have led to rules in the United States to encourage firms to set up structures that make it more likely that workers will take advantage of opportunities to save. Similarly, there is discussion (U.K. Pensions Commission 2005) of automatically enrolling U.K. workers in savings plans, so that they have to take positive action to opt out. Countries also have rules to assist the achievement of social goals, for example protecting family members by making joint-life annuities mandatory or by establishing them as the default.

Regulating the system. Government needs regulatory and supervisory capacity over firms, over financial institutions and insurance companies that handle individual retirement accounts, and over insurance markets and financial markets in respect of both employer plans and individual accounts. Such regulation is vital to protect consumers in areas too complex for them to protect themselves. This requires tightly drawn up procedures *and* administrators with the capacity and the will to enforce those procedures. Box 9.2 illustrates how regulatory problems can arise, using examples from the United Kingdom.

▶ Box 9.2 The U.K. mis-selling scandal and other problems

Even developed countries experience problems of implementation: in regulating the governance of private pensions, regulating how pensions are sold, and adequately announcing changes to public pension arrangements. A report from the U.K. Office of Fair Trading (1997, p. 7) discusses how "in the past legitimate expectations have been betrayed: the misappropriation of large sums from the Mirror Group Pension Scheme and the mis-selling of personal pensions to those induced to abandon existing entitlements in favour of less advantageous schemes attest to that."

The Maxwell scandal. A major financial scandal arose in the United Kingdom during the late 1980s, after Robert Maxwell, the owner of the Mirror Group of newspapers, illegally siphoned off £440 million from the group's pension funds to buttress business failures. Although workers' pensions were put at risk, the funds were largely recovered through £100 million from government resources and a £276 million out-of-court settlement with financial institutions and the remnants of Maxwell's media group. In the wake of the scandal, proposals to tighten regulation (U.K. Pension Law Review Committee 1993) led to the establishment of a new independent body, the Occupational Pensions Regulatory Authority, whose functions were subsequently subsumed in an overarching Financial Services Authority.

The mis-selling scandal. Until 1988 it was mandatory for workers to belong to the State Earnings-Related Pension Scheme (SERPS) unless their employer had an approved pension plan that it made mandatory for its workers. Beginning in 1988 it remained mandatory to belong to an earnings-related pension, but workers were allowed to choose among SERPS, an occupational plan (if one was offered), or a personal pension (that is, an individual account). The reform also created financial incentives for workers to choose the last option. As a result of a major sales drive, significant numbers of people, many of them women and poorly paid, were persuaded by deceptive advertising and face-to-face selling to move out of occupational pensions or SERPS and into individual accounts during the late 1980s and early 1990s.

Over time it became clear that many people who had made such a move were predictably worse off as a result, and over 500,000 such pensions were investigated for mis-selling. A decade later, the Director of the Office of Fair Trading could still write:

> Many personal pension plans are ... simply poor value. Their benefits are consumed in the high levels of expenses needed to support the marketing effort and the active management of the funds. These expenses are often loaded on the early years of the plan, so that they bear disproportionately on plans where the contributions are discontinued because of changes in personal circumstances. In comparison with most occupational schemes, the level of employers' contributions may be inadequate or non-existent. (U.K. Office of Fair Trading 1997, p. 8)

In response, the Financial Services Authority imposed on the pensions industry a requirement to offer compensation, the total cost of which exceeded £10 billion.

Problems with SERPS. Implementation problems are not restricted to private pensions. The 1986 act that brought in personal pensions also made the formula for SERPS less generous in two important ways: the accrual rate was reduced, and, beginning in 2000, surviving spouses were allowed to inherit only half of their deceased spouse's entitlement to SERPS (previously they had inherited the whole amount). However, until 1996 the leaflets and other documentation provided by the pensions administration

(continues next page)

(continued from previous page)
did not incorporate information on the changes, and staff were not advising people correctly. When the situation came to light in early 2000, the U.K. ombudsman and Parliament created pressure for action. As a result, the changes were cancelled for people who reached the official pensionable age before October 5, 2002, and thereafter were to be phased in for people who reached pensionable age between October 2002 and October 2010 (for details, see U.K. Department for Work and Pensions 2006*b*). ◀

The regulatory task is harder than it looks: precisely because pensions are such complex instruments, regulators need to be highly skilled—and the particular skills that are required command a high price in the private sector. There are at least four problems:

- The regulatory regime may be ineffective, either because of a lack of competence or because of regulatory capture, so that private pensions do not deliver benefits as expected.
- The regulatory regime may be too burdensome; in corporate defined-benefit plans, this may result in a decrease in coverage, as discussed in Box 9.3.
- The regulatory regime may become one of de facto government control, with the pension provider acting, in effect, as an agent of the state, which may lead to inappropriate design.
- The management and regulation of pension funds may crowd out other demands for scarce human capital.

▶ Box 9.3 Difficulties in regulating private defined-benefit plans

The long-run security of workers and retirees requires long-run financial stability of pension arrangements. When a firm or industry with an unfunded or inadequately funded defined-benefit pension gets into financial trouble, its workers and retirees lose much, and possibly all, of the pension they were expecting. Countries have found this highly unsatisfactory and have responded in a range of ways.

One approach is through government-provided guarantees. However, if guarantees are not generous enough, they do not protect workers and pensioners adequately; but if they are too generous, they may lower the incentive to manage funds prudently (that is, may create moral hazard). For example, risky pension investment may become attractive since, with defined benefits, the pension fund keeps for itself the high returns if the risk pays off, and the guarantee covers the losses if it does not.

A second approach is to impose requirements about coverage and funding. Some of these are not contentious: an example is vesting rules, which prohibit firms from denying a worker a pension after some period of employment if pensions are offered to other workers. More controversially, requirements about the degree of funding, and particularly about the speed with which any shortfall must be made good, can create problems. When asset values fall, firms need to increase their contribution rates if they are to restore adequate funding rapidly. But this demand on a firm's revenue typically comes at precisely the time when the firm is experiencing low profitability: low profitability and declines in asset values are highly correlated.

One outcome of stringent funding requirements is that sponsors may close defined-benefit plans. This trend is accentuated when other requirements are imposed that add more to the cost of the pension than firms think is worthwhile: for example, that the rights accrued by workers who have left a firm be fully protected, and that pension benefits cover spouses. This has been an important trend in the United Kingdom, where a series of requirements on corporate employer defined-benefit plans—all introduced for the best of motives and mostly sensible when taken alone—cumulatively placed a major financial burden on sponsoring firms. At least in part for that reason, many firms closed their plans to new members and, in some cases, moved future contributions of existing members to a defined-contribution basis. Blake (2006) concludes that a combination of piecemeal reform and inadequate regulatory impact assessments created a situation in which individuals ended up with weaker pension promises than thirty years earlier and firms faced solvency problems arising from their legacy defined-benefit plans.

In sum, policies designed to ensure the long-run stability of defined-benefit plans face an inherent tension: too little regulation leaves workers with inadequate protection, but too much imposes excessive costs on plan sponsors, often at inopportune times, leading to withdrawal of the plans, at least for new members. Given this tension, it is worth considering whether substituting employer-provided defined-contribution plans for employer-provided defined-benefit plans might improve the social outcome. ◀

In sum. Even voluntary private funded pensions require nontrivial government capacity to regulate and supervise financial markets, including insurance markets. Voluntary plans can contribute to a political environment that encourages better regulation of markets, as well as serve as a test phase in any move toward mandatory plans that will cover a much larger fraction of the labor force, including the more vulnerable workers. Moreover, the extent to which pensions fulfill social goals depends on how well the plans themselves are regulated. Mandatory private funded pensions require significant fiscal capacity, plus strong public *and* private institutional capacity, as discussed in more detail in section 9.2.

9.1.3 Institutional requirements

Alongside government financial and administrative capacity, a third set of requirements applies to the broader background. Property rights need to be sufficiently well defined, both in principle and in practice, to support an efficient allocation of resources by competitive markets. A related but separate point is that efficient economic activity is hindered by widespread corruption. A private market economy cannot function well without significant government intervention to secure property rights and combat corruption. Through legislation and the courts, the government sets rules for private property and contracts and sees that those rules are enforced. Through legislation, regulation, and the courts, the government sets rules for market interactions, including rules governing product safety, consumer information, and compensation where appropriate. Private markets function best when government has put in place good, clear rules and where enforcement is even-handed, honest, prompt, and predictable.

Institutional requirements also include a well-defined and well-designed division of responsibility between government and market. Although the choice of dividing line involves an element of ideology, it should rest mainly on technical considerations. Markets are efficient only in certain clearly defined theoretical circumstances, including the presence of well-informed buyers and sellers and of competition. Where these conditions broadly hold (for example, in markets for food and clothing), production and allocation are more efficient in the private sector; where they fail, and particularly where they fail badly (for example, in health care and primary education), there is a case for significant government activity, provided the government has sufficient capacity.[5]

Similar issues arise in certain activities widely recognized as best performed by government. There is often a choice between direct government production and government purchases from private providers (for example, in procurement of military supplies and support services, jails, street cleaning, and recordkeeping). Determining when it is likely that one mode of provision will perform better than the other involves some subtle considerations (Sheshinski 2003; Megginson and Netter 2001). Even when private provision is efficient, government is needed to enforce contracts, to limit fraud and deception, to preserve competition, and to protect consumers from poor-quality products.

Pensions occupy an intermediate ground. As the earlier discussion of financial and administrative constraints makes clear, all pension systems, whatever their design, depend critically on effective government. Beyond that, however, a wide array of options not only are possible but have been adopted, as illustrated in Chapter 11. Thus the extent of government involvement should be neither minimized nor maximized, but optimized; the optimum will depend both on a country's objectives and on its constraints. All countries need more good regulations and fewer bad ones.

9.1.4 The need to match design to constraints

The funnel of realistic options in pension design widens as fiscal and administrative capacity increases. As Chapter 11 illustrates, developed countries can choose almost any combination. Conversely, a reform whose design exceeds the fiscal and administrative capacity of government will fail to achieve the policy objectives and, if it causes a fiscal black hole, may cause much wider damage to the economy and to political stability.

Thus an early and essential task for policymakers is to locate their country—now and in the near future—on the spectrum of options identified in section 9.1.2, so as to determine the range of systems it makes sense for them to consider; the topic is taken up more fully in section 16.2.3. Complex reforms, such as the creation of mandatory, privately managed, privately funded pensions, should not be considered until the necessary economic and technical preconditions are in place.

9.2 THE CAPACITY OF PRIVATE PENSION PROVIDERS

Given the great interest in mandatory individual funded accounts since their introduction in Chile and their adoption in various other countries, we pay particular attention here to the implementation requirements for this type of arrangement. Alongside the various public sector capacities just discussed is a series of complementary private sector capacities. Two sets of questions arise:

- Is private sector capacity adequate? As discussed below, private pensions depend on administrative expertise to keep track of individual contributions and pension accumulations across a working life, and on financial market expertise to manage pension funds and payouts. A lack of either capacity runs the risk that administrative costs, administrative breakdowns, or incompetent or corrupt fund

5. For fuller discussion see Barr (2004a), Barr (2003, in Chinese), or, more briefly, Barr (1998).

management will erode the benefits to pensioners from investment returns. Since administering an individual account has a fixed cost element (it does not cost much less to administer a small accumulation than a large one), the issue is of particular concern for small pensions. At worst, deficient administrative capacity and expertise in fund management put at risk the viability of the whole system of private accounts.

• Even if private sector capacity is adequate, is its deployment in administering private pensions its most welfare-enhancing use? A key issue is whether a developing country is willing to let firms from developed countries take on tasks that domestic firms might find too demanding, thus avoiding a situation that risks the retirement security of vulnerable workers.

Fully funded individual accounts require more capacity than notional individual accounts. The major tasks, discussed below, include collecting contributions, keeping records and informing workers, selecting portfolios, investing funds, and determining and paying benefits. As discussed in section 9.3, the process of educating workers— about what they have at a given moment, what they can expect to have at retirement, and how to think about the choices they can make—is also important. In an economy where most workers have no experience in making such financial decisions, it is critical to provide education on the implications of different choices.

All these tasks have costs that vary with the design of the system and with the quality of services provided.[6] All involve government as well, but in different ways with different design features. Some of the features make sense only in combination with other features, but we present them in the sequence above, without focusing on the interactions. Moreover, insofar as asset prices are set by the market, any evaluation of the benefits that a given level of contributions can finance needs to take into account not only the costs of providing services but also the returns available given the state of the country's capital markets.

9.2.1 Collecting contributions

Contributions to individual accounts can be collected from employers by a tax authority (as in Sweden), by a separate government agency, by a centralized private agency (perhaps supervised or owned by the funds receiving the contributions), or by direct payments by employers separately to the different individual funds (as in Chile). Costs tend to increase as one moves down this list. A tax authority can exploit economies of scope, since it is already collecting other taxes from employers. A separate government agency is likely to have higher costs, unless it coordinates with the tax authority. Such an agency is similar to a centralized private agency, and the government could contract with private firms to carry out some tasks. In either case supervision is necessary to make sure that funds are collected in the right amounts and delivered promptly to the right places. Direct payment by employers to individual funds is the most expensive process and the most difficult for government to supervise.

---

6. There are significant one-time costs in setting up a system, and ongoing costs once the system is mature. This section discusses only the ongoing costs but also serves as a guide to the initial costs of creating the necessary institutions.

Inevitably, mistakes are made in allocating contributions in the right amount to the right account (not to mention embezzlements at the level of the employer, the collector, or the receiving fund). Robust mechanisms for correcting these mistakes contribute substantially to accuracy and so to confidence in the pension system, but they have significant costs. Error rates tend to vary with the type of recordkeeping and means of communication with funds. Electronic records and paper records differ in their error rates, types of errors to which they are prone, and ease of correction. Thus the general financial maturity of the formal sector matters for the efficiency of the system.

The key dimensions with respect to quality are the accuracy and completeness of collection and delivery, and its timeliness. Funds collected but not yet delivered earn little or no interest for contributors, but more frequent collection and delivery raise costs, and the greater the number of funds, the higher the costs.

9.2.2 Keeping records and communicating with workers

Recordkeeping and communication can be either centralized or decentralized. Here the main dimensions of quality are the frequency with which workers receive statements about their accounts, the quality and effectiveness of the education they are offered, and the availability of services to answer their questions. A separate issue is the extent to which workers can change portfolios or portfolio managers. As discussed in section 9.2.3, such choice might deliberately be constrained for any of several reasons. Latin American countries with individual accounts, for example, limit the frequency with which workers may make changes. This constraint saves on costs, both to the system and to individual investors, and may discourage unnecessary advertising and similar expenditure by competing providers.

As already discussed, government has an important regulatory role in protecting the accuracy of recordkeeping. Also important is whether the government guarantees the integrity of the system, for example by covering any losses due to theft or other illegal acts (but not those due to poor choice of investments by the worker). These supervisory requirements involve a significant cost, which varies with the number of accounts but very little with the value of the assets in the accounts.

9.2.3 Selecting the menu of portfolios

With any system of asset accumulation, the design of the institutions involved in making portfolio choices is important. It is important to ensure that the choices are made for the benefit of current and future retirees, not for other objectives. It is important to have rules that encourage efficient portfolio choices. Such rules will naturally differ in different circumstances. It is one thing to have a centralized trust fund run by professional fund managers, effectively insulated from political pressures and highly motivated to do a good job. But in some countries it may be necessary to restrict portfolio choices, so as to insulate portfolio managers from outside influences. And the rules will be very different if the portfolio choices are made by individual workers themselves: both the administrative costs and the difficulty inexperienced investors face in making good investment decisions call for restricted choices.

Three elements are important in considering how much choice workers should have. First, how well are they likely to choose (discussed in section 9.3)? Second, among workers with the capacity to choose well, how much are those choices likely to vary, and how much does the variation matter? Third, what are the costs associated with wider choice? The argument for limiting choice—in the number of portfolios made available to workers and in the frequency with which a worker may change funds—is precisely that consumers do not always choose well, so that transactions and other costs may outweigh the potential gains from wider choice. Since costs are a central part of the argument and raise complex issues of measurement, it is helpful to start by discussing different measures of cost as a prelude to discussion of choice.

Evaluating charges. The different arrangements described below tend to have systematically different levels of cost, as more choice tends to cost more. These costs need to be allocated across accounts (or outside the system of accounts). There are multiple options for allocating costs across different accounts (in a centralized system) or regulating charges (in a decentralized system). The charges could be made proportional to annual contributions or to a person's total accumulation, implying that all workers with the same portfolio receive the same rate of return. Alternatively, the charges could include a fixed component reflecting the underlying structure of costs, implying that workers with larger accumulations have higher rates of return net of charges. The importance of this choice depends on the dispersion in the earnings of the covered population.

For any given system of allocating costs to accounts, there are many ways to report the resulting charges. Some of these are described in Box 9.4. Consideration of costs and comparison across systems require recognition of the compounding nature of costs: different ways of allocating costs will affect workers with different lengths and timing of their careers. Because of the effects of compounding, it is easy to under-estimate the importance of charges. A comparison of up-front charges and annual charges is shown in Table 9.1.

The table reports charges for a forty-year career, evaluating the charge right at the end of the career. Many workers have shorter periods of covered employment, and those periods might be early or late in their careers. With annual charges, the length

TABLE 9.1

Cumulative effects on account value of sales load and management charges

UPFRONT OR ANNUAL CHARGE	CUMULATIVE DECLINE IN VALUE OF ACCUMULATION (CHARGE RATIO) AFTER FORTY YEARS[a]
FRONT-END LOAD (PERCENT OF NEW CONTRIBUTIONS)	
1%	1%
10%	10%
20%	20%
ANNUAL MANAGEMENT CHARGE (PERCENT OF ACCOUNT BALANCE)	
0.1%	2.2%
0.5%	10.5%
1.0%	19.6%

Source: Diamond (2000).

[a]Calculations assume real annual wage growth of 2.1 percent and a real annual return on investments of 4 percent. With a larger difference between the rates of wage growth and annual return, the charge ratio with annual management fees is slightly larger.

of time that a contribution is growing matters for the importance of the charges. For a dollar that is contributed one year before the start of benefits, a 1 percent annual charge takes only 1 percent of the accumulation. For a dollar contributed twenty or forty years before the start of benefits, the charge ratio is much higher, because that dollar's accumulation is subject to the annual charge each year for twenty or forty years. Of course, with positive real interest, a dollar deposited earlier finances a higher retirement benefit. But the point of this calculation is that, for a given gross return on assets, higher charges mean lower net returns, and the impact of higher annual charges is more important, the longer the contribution is accumulating and the more times it is subject to an annual charge. In the face of competing pressures between cost and choice, countries have adopted a wide range of approaches.

A single, centrally organized portfolio. The simplest and least expensive option is for government to choose the workers' portfolios for them, as was formerly done in Singapore.[7] Although this can be done by building a single, monolithic portfolio, it is also possible, without allowing individual choice, for portfolios to vary systematically

▶ Box 9.4 Measuring charges

Comparing the costs of individual accounts is complex. Some set-up costs are independent of the size of the system, whereas others depend on the number of participants. Ongoing costs are mostly fixed costs per account, and for that reason cost estimation is often approached in those terms. For all but the smallest plans, the cost of managing the aggregate portfolio is small relative to the costs of recordkeeping, including communication with account owners. For example, in the U.S. Thrift Savings Plan, described in Box 11.5, investment management fees represent about 10 percent of total administrative costs.

Account charges come in different forms in voluntary private markets. There can be charges when deposits are made (called a front-end load, or sales charge) or when money is withdrawn (a back-end load, or deferred sales charge); there are also periodic (usually annual) charges based on the value (and type) of assets in the account, or on the rate of return as is common with hedge funds. Similarly, costs can be measured in various ways, so that a common measure is needed to allow comparison of diverse systems. The following measures are potentially useful:

- *Percentage as a front-end load.* The Thrift Savings Plan reports the dollar cost of running the accounts. Dividing this annual dollar cost by annual deposits gives a *percentage front-end load*, that is, the annual cost as a percentage of a person's annual contribution. This may or may not match the way the individual accounts are charged.
- *Annual percentage management charge.* This is the annual charge as a percentage of the account holder's accumulated balance.
- *Reduction in yield.* If the rate of return in a given year was 5 percent before charges and is 3 percent after, the reduction in yield is 2 percentage points.
- *Charge ratio.* This is the percentage decrease in a person's total accumulation at retirement as a consequence of all administrative charges over the life of the account.

Table 9.1 shows the relationships among the percentage front-end load, the annual management charge, and the charge ratio, based on continuous time calculations. ◀

7. The Central Provident Fund Investment Plan in Singapore offers some limited choice, as outlined in section 11.3.

across workers of differing characteristics. For example, the mix of stocks and bonds in a worker's account can be selected to vary systematically with age; the default allocation of funds in Chile uses this so-called life-cycle approach. Given fixed costs per account, a single, simple, government-designed fund can be used for a worker's account until it exceeds some minimum size, at which point the cost of portfolio choice may be seen as worthwhile for workers who choose (but are not forced) to move to another arrangement, such as those described below.

Choice among a small number of centrally organized funds. The least expensive way to give workers some choice is for the government to establish a limited menu of investment funds and to select the managers for each. Workers then divide their contributions among the available alternatives and may change the allocation of new contributions or rearrange existing asset holdings (both of which affect costs), subject to specified limits. As discussed in section 9.3, a default fund is necessary for workers who fail to make a choice. Although the government might invest directly in assets, contracting with private providers to manage the funds takes advantage of the presence of existing firms, which plausibly have economies of scale. Moreover, the commingling of pension funds with private investments in the same fund contributes to insulation from political pressures on investment. The lowest administrative cost comes from a successful selection of efficient, low-cost providers for the different funds after a process of examining alternatives, perhaps involving an auction among firms judged capable of performing. (Box 11.5 discusses the example of the U.S. Thrift Savings Plan, the pension program for federal workers that illustrates this approach.)

Choice among competing providers of highly regulated funds (resulting in a limited set of funds). In Chile and some other countries,' pension assets may be invested only in a private. tightly regulated investment fund that engages in no other business. Entry to the business is open to any firm with the necessary capital, so that in principle the industry is competitive. As discussed in Chapter 12, however, in practice choice among funds in Chile has remained limited: a small number of firms transact most of the business, and there is continuing concern about the high level of charges.

Other Latin American countries have followed approaches similar to Chile, except for Bolivia (Box 11.2), which allowed only two firms to enter and initially gave workers no choice between them. Because firms had to bid for the right to be one of the chosen two, charges are lower than elsewhere in Latin America. However, it is important in settings like this, after a price has been set, to regulate the quality of the services provided, and this is not easy. Indeed, the quality of services has been a source of complaint in Bolivia. As Table 9.2 shows, costs vary widely even among countries following similar strategies. Apart from Bolivia, costs range from 12 to 36 percent of a person's annual contribution, reflecting, among other factors, the small size of the accounts.[8]

Choice among a wide set of centrally accepted funds with price regulation. In contrast with the limited options in Latin American countries, Sweden, discussed in section 11.4.8, makes available a wide array of funds. Sweden has both an NDC pension and mandatory participation in funded individual accounts, with 2.5 percent

8. For broader discussion of recent experience with pensions in Latin America, see Gill, Packard, and Yermo (2005) and Arenas de Mesa and Mesa-Lago (2006).

TABLE 9.2

Administrative costs (percent) of private investment funds in Latin America, December 2002

COUNTRY	ADMINISTRATIVE FEE AS SHARE OF SALARY[a](1)	CONTRIBUTION TO FUND AS SHARE OF SALARY (2)	FEE AS SHARE OF TOTAL CONTRIBUTION = (1)/[(1)+(2)]
Argentina	1.56	2.75	36.19
Bolivia[b]	0.50	10.00	4.76
Chile	1.76	10.00	14.97
Colombia[c]	1.63	10.00	14.02
El Salvador	1.58	11.02	12.54
Peru	2.27	8.00	22.10
Uruguay[d]	1.92	12.27	13.53
Average	1.60	9.15	16.87

Source: Gill, Packard, and Yermo (2005, Table 7.3).
[a]Includes only account and asset management charges that are set as a percentage of contribution or salary. Insurance premiums are excluded.
[b]Includes only the contribution charge; the asset management charge varies from zero to 0.23 percent, depending on the amount of assets in the portfolio.
[c]Refers only to the mandatory pension fund system for December 2000.
[d]Excludes an additional commission for custody, which averaged 0.293 percent of total assets under management in December 2002.

of payroll going into the latter. Funds meeting specified requirements may join the list of approved funds as long as they agree to pricing rules set by the government. In 2007 there were over 700 such funds. Workers allocate their contributions among up to five funds and inform the government of their choice. The government has put in place a central clearinghouse, which keeps the records, collects the contributions, aggregates the contributions going to each fund (and any portfolio transfers), and sends them to the funds. A potential problem with competition among a wide array of funds is that it encourages advertising, which adds to costs without necessarily improving consumer choice, not least because of the imperfect choices made by workers, discussed in section 9.3. After the initial startup period, the arrangements in Sweden resulted in limited advertising, in part because administration through the central clearinghouse means that firms do not know which workers have invested with them. Without price regulation, competition among many funds would be very expensive. Even with a central clearinghouse, arrangements in Sweden are significantly more expensive than the U.S. Thrift Savings Plan. It remains to be seen how well price regulation will work over the long haul: historically, price regulation has not worked well over extended periods.

Choice among a wide set of competing providers. In the United States, individuals saving in tax-favored retirement accounts can hold these funds with private providers, who are subject to standard capital market regulation. Analyses of the U.S. voluntary mutual fund industry have found a steady downward trend in charges for different kinds of mutual funds. Yet the impact of charges remains significant. In 2006 average annual charges were 83 basis points for bond mutual funds and 107 basis points for equity mutual funds (Investment Company Institute 2007). According to Table 9.1, the resulting charge ratio (loss of benefits due to the charges) for a mix of funds would be roughly between 15 and 20 percent. This includes annual fees and conversion of front-end loads to an annual charge, but not brokerage charges for transactions by the funds. Nor does it reflect the fact that many U.S. investors pay separately for investment advice, sometimes as much as 1 percent of assets per year in what are called wrap accounts.

The United Kingdom also allows workers who opt out of public and private defined-benefit systems to contract directly with firms in the investment and insurance markets, thereby making essentially all of the market available.[9] As in the United States, this approach has proved to be very expensive: Murthi, Orszag, and Orszag (2001) estimate the charge ratio for these pensions to be above one-third for the accumulation phase, not counting annuitization costs. That is, benefits are one-third lower than if these costs were avoided. Not least for that reason, reforms have been introduced, but administrative costs (shown in Figure 9.1) remain a concern. We are not aware of any country taking this approach to mandatory accounts.

Given the size of the fixed-cost element, the U.K. Pensions Commission (2004*a*, p. 224) questioned "whether [the level of costs] implies that there is a segment of the

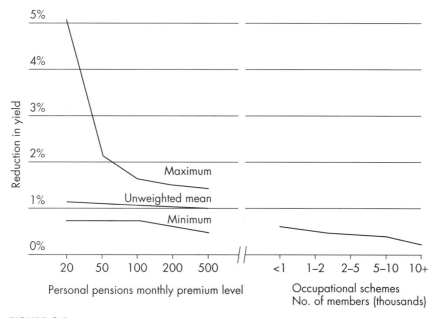

FIGURE 9.1.
Administrative costs of pension plans in the United Kingdom. Source: U.K. Pensions Commission (2004*a*, Figure 6.9).

9. In the United Kingdom these are an option for workers under the *mandatory* system; workers are obliged to contribute to an earnings-related pension, which can be the public pension (SERPS), or an employer pension, or one or more individual accounts. The United States also has tax-favored individual accounts, which allow individuals choice across the entire financial market; these are voluntary.

pension market, comprised of lower income savers and people working for small firms, to which a free market will never be able to sell pension products profitably except at [reductions in yield] which make savings unattractive." For those reasons the subsequent report (U.K. Pensions Commission 2005) recommended introducing low-cost savings plans, with centrally administered individual records and fund management on a wholesale basis.

In sum, systems that offer wide choice among competing providers face two strategic problems:

- Approaches that offer wide choice have proven to be expensive. The effect of charges, often overlooked, should not be underestimated. Table 9.1 shows that even annual charges as low as 1 percent of assets under management have a major impact on accumulations when the charges are made annually over a long period. Over a forty-year career, the typical dollar of assets remains in an account for roughly twenty years. Hence an annual charge of 1 percent reduces a person's accumulation after a forty-year career by roughly 20 percent (the charge ratio).

- In addition, as discussed more fully in section 9.3, many investors make poor choices.

9.2.4   Investing funds

Some investments are readily handled within the public sector. If, for example, a provident fund wishes to hold government debt, it can purchase government bonds paying market interest rates directly from the national treasury, without going through the markets. Much the same holds for shares in privatized state-owned enterprises, for example in the Central and Eastern European countries and China, insofar as the intent is to hold equity as a way of giving workers a good long-run rate of return. The same argument holds for the government bond portion of a portfolio when government establishes a set of alternative investments from which workers can choose.

If a fund wishes to invest in private stocks or bonds, transactions in the private market will be necessary. It is critical to have a transparent mechanism for choosing the assets, one designed to protect the interests of workers rather than to advance the public purposes of government or the private purposes of public or private officials. The use of index funds and of auctions for the right to manage funds may add to transparency. Nevertheless, auditing and possibly oversight by a government agency, perhaps a specialized one, are important to ensure that the large sums involved are not partly diverted to other uses.[10]

A separate issue is the use of pension resources for purposes other than providing pensions. For example, some governments require that pension funds hold government debt on which it pays below-market interest rates. Another example is provided by Mexico, where part of the funded accounts of workers is invested in housing—a move designed to benefit the residents rather than the investors. Such diversion of funds for other purposes detracts significantly from the workings of the fund management side

---

10. For discussion of the regulation of pension fund investors, see Davis (2002), and on good practice in fund management, OECD (2006*a*) and International Organisation of Pension Supervisors (2008).

of the pension system and casts doubt on the rest. And issues of corruption and embezzlement are always a concern.[11]

In some countries a critical issue is the timing of any decision to allow investments abroad as part of workers' portfolios. As discussed in section 6.3.2, in developing countries a tension exists between the shorter-term interests of workers, for whom some foreign investment can diversify risk, and those of the economy, in that premature investment abroad may increase the cost of capital domestically and so slow economic growth.

9.2.5   Determining and paying benefits

The simplest, least expensive way for a pension provider to pay benefits is as a lump sum when the covered worker reaches a given age. Two issues, however, complicate the choice of this approach. The first, discussed in section 5.3.5, is whether to pay benefits only to people who have largely or wholly stopped working. Such a policy requires reliable information on earnings. A second, critical issue is how beneficiaries handle the lump-sum payment. There are several reasons for concern. One is that retirees with few other assets, but potential eligibility for a guaranteed minimum income, may spend their lump sum rapidly in order to have earlier access to the minimum income payments. A second concern is that pensioners ineligible for a guaranteed minimum income may spend the money too rapidly for their own good—a particular issue with couples with different life expectancies. Further, if beneficiaries do not appreciate the insurance value of well-priced annuities—income that a worker will not outlive—they may make too little use of them. Annuities can be joint-life, to protect the families of workers in retirement (see section 8.3.4), and indexed annuities can provide basic protection against inflation, a critical part of retirement security (section 5.3.4). Thus there are good arguments for requiring at least some annuitization.

In response to these concerns, governments often limit the rate at which funds may be withdrawn, or they may require some degree of annuitization. In Chile workers have a choice between annuitization and monthly withdrawals that are limited in size, based on life expectancy. Alternatively, part of the accumulation may be taken as a lump sum if the person is entitled to a high enough level of benefits. In the United States, a commission appointed by President George W. Bush recommended requiring annuitization sufficient to keep beneficiaries above the official poverty line, with no requirement above that point. In the United Kingdom tax-favored voluntary accounts give account holders incentives to take at least 75 percent of accumulations as an annuity.

Annuities can be supplied by the government or, if the portfolio funding the annuities contains marketable assets, by private insurance companies, although the latter approach faces some of the problems noted in Box 9.5. Such companies need to be tightly regulated to ensure that they can continue to honor annuity contracts over the many years that some workers will live in retirement. Individually purchased annuities are considerably more expensive than group annuities. If the system relies on private

---

11. As noted above, transparency is critical. In the U.S. context, "the story at the state and local level is that while in the early 1980s some public plans sacrificed returns for social considerations, plan managers have become much more sophisticated. Today [1999], public plans appear to be performing as well as private plans" (Munnell and Sundén, 1999, p. 2).

▶ Box 9.5 Providing annuities: The problem of uncertainty

The providers of annuities face problems in predicting life expectancy. As the First Report of the U.K. Pensions Commission (2004a, 2004b) points out, the longevity risk comprises several different elements.

Specific longevity is the probability distribution of age at death of a given person at age 65 covered by a given cohort-specific mortality table. This risk matters for the individual and is the risk that an annuity is designed to cover. It reflects a risk that is readily quantifiable, like the risk when gambling at a casino.

Cohort longevity relates to the life expectancy of all men or women born in a given year and reflects the fact that future aggregate mortality rates are not known. (Of course, cohort uncertainty implies uncertainty about individuals as well. But it is analytically useful to separate these two aspects of uncertainty about individuals.) As with stock market returns, this is a risk for the aggregate economy and must fall somewhere; different institutional arrangements put the risk in different places. Life expectancy is known to be increasing, but there is uncertainty about how fast. Thus there is a "funnel of doubt," which, importantly, gets wider as the duration of retirement increases. For example, past official projections in the United Kingdom have been on the low side: they correctly identified a slowdown in the rate of increase of life expectancy in the second half of the twentieth century but mistakenly attributed it to a biological "maximum duration of life" rather than to the cumulative impact of smoking, an effect that has now been absorbed and, if anything, has reversed. More generally, there is considerable debate among demographers and actuaries as to the likely trend in future mortality rates. As a more extreme example, before the AIDS epidemic, it is unlikely that insurance planning would have incorporated the rising mortality rates in much of Africa, shown in the figure; mortality rates also rose sharply in Russia after the end of the Soviet Union.

If the institutional arrangement is to keep this risk on insurance companies holding conventional assets, then it falls ultimately either on their shareholders or, in the event

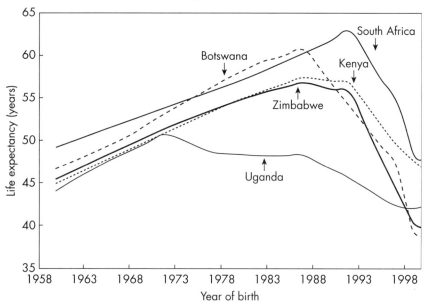

Life expectancy at birth in selected African countries, 1960–200.
Source: World Bank (2004).

that the insurance companies cannot meet their contractual obligations, on the annuity holders or the government guarantee fund, if there is one.* Moreover, the pricing of this risk will be reflected in the price of annuities. Insurance companies can shift this risk (and so avoid some of the pricing incentives) by using reinsurance or by investing in assets that help to hedge the risk, for example mortality-indexed bonds, if the government offers them.**

Alternatively, they can explicitly shift risk to the annuity holders through benefits that depend on realized mortality experience (as in CREF annuities; see section 7.3). Or government can insure the payments and charge insurance companies a premium, which will affect annuity prices. In all these cases the risks do not go away; they get allocated somewhere, with different mechanisms resulting in different outcomes, which will vary in efficiency.

Longevity over the longer term (that is, for future cohorts) is estimated with considerable imprecision, reflecting growing uncertainty about age-specific mortalities farther in the future and the fact that mortality rates are strongly correlated across birth years. Medical breakthroughs or new diseases will impact many cohorts. Because of the long duration of pension arrangements, adjustments can fall in different places, depending on how plans are organized and adjusted. We discuss risk sharing in Chapter 7.

In sum, policy must address the facts that the underlying problem is uncertainty and that uncertainty can create uninsurable costs. Those costs have to be borne somewhere. ◀

---

*The same problem arises for other long-term uncertainties, notably the high price and loosely-specified contracts offered by insurance policies covering the costs of long-term care (see Barr, 2001a, Chapter 5, on the analytics; see also "Aged Frail Denied Care by Their Insurers," *New York Times*, March 27, 2007).

**Mortality-indexed bonds are similar to an inflation-indexed government bond. Just as inflation-indexed bonds pay more interest the higher is inflation, so mortality-indexed bonds would pay more interest the lower the mortality rates of those of pension age.

insurance companies to provide annuities, the government may therefore consider organizing groups in order to hold down costs. Where individuals have a choice, either over the form of annuity or over the provider, potential problems of adverse selection will arise. Individuals expecting longer lives will be right on average and will choose more-backloaded annuities. Private providers of annuities, on the other hand, will try to find the shorter-lived customers. These issues are complex to evaluate and manage.

Benefit levels can be indexed to prices, wages, or a combination of the two, as discussed in section 5.3.4. Alternatively, the increase in annuity value from year to year can depend on the rate of return on some portfolio underlying the annuity. Annuity pricing, in particular whether annuities should be unisex or not, is discussed in section 8.3.1.

9.2.6 When do funded individual accounts become feasible?

Notional individual accounts and funded individual accounts are two ways of providing consumption smoothing for workers, alongside basic pensions. They differ in two strategic ways:

- They have different financing needs. Contributions to funded accounts are used to purchase assets and therefore cannot be used to pay benefits to current beneficiaries. As discussed in section 7.2, the choice between the two approaches has inevitable redistributive effects across generations and thus requires consideration of the economic position of current workers relative to that expected for future workers.

• They have different administrative requirements. For funded accounts to function properly, all the elements discussed above need to be in place; institutions need not be perfect, but they need to be robust. And we have noted that worker choice involves additional administrative burdens.

Here we turn to another dimension on which notional and funded accounts differ, namely, their interaction with capital markets.

Risks and gains. The assets that funded accounts require are best purchased in capital markets or through financial intermediaries such as banks and insurance companies. In considering the choice between funded and notional accounts, two questions arise: Will existing capital markets and financial intermediaries provide the necessary services effectively? And will the extra demand for market and intermediary services improve the functioning of both?

Whether capital markets will be effective depends on the country in question. As discussed in section 6.3.2, financial institutions in some countries are clearly too weak to put at risk the pensions of large numbers of workers by mandating funded individual accounts. In developed countries it is just as clear that the capital markets are up to the task. Many countries lie somewhere in between, with some degree of risk of poor functioning.

The extra demand generated by funded accounts might or might not improve the functioning of capital markets. In developing countries what is critical is a sustained effort to improve the regulation of markets and the functioning of the economy generally. In Chile individual accounts helped with the development of capital markets, not least by serving as an additional source of political pressure for effective regulation. Put another way, although additional demand can assist market development, the primary channel is the political one, in the form of greater support for effective regulation, and so a greater ability to legislate and implement a better regulatory regime. As we have noted elsewhere, the typical buy-and-hold investment strategies of pension funds will lead to greater market capitalization, through both increased issuance of shares and higher share prices, but will not add much to the volume of transactions and so to liquidity. This was the case in Chile: however, many other changes to the economy were occurring at the same time as pension reform, so that not all of the quality of Chilean growth should be attributed to it. In contrast, some countries lack the regulatory capacity to improve their capital markets sufficiently to take advantage of such an opportunity.

Thus, over a range of country capacities, there is potential for improving capital markets but also the risk that pensions will fare badly. Analysts disagree about where to draw the line in this intermediate range, between circumstances where the risk of loss is less important than the possibility of gain, and vice versa.

The role of voluntary pensions. Mandatory funded accounts may be able to stimulate market development. But so can voluntary pensions. The role of the latter depends on whether a country has limited the size of the mandatory system, leaving room for supplemental voluntary accounts. The magnitude can be influenced by tax-favored status for such savings, adequate supervision and regulation of voluntary pension financing, and an economy sufficiently large that economies of scale can be achieved out of the voluntary investments.

Creation of the accounts can be coordinated with improvement in financial and insurance markets. A potential market test of the suitability of existing institutions is the extent to which they are used by private voluntary systems.

9.3   THE CAPACITY OF CONSUMERS

Alongside government capacity and private sector capacity, a third set of questions concerns the capacity of individuals and, in particular, whether individual consumers understand the bases for good choices. It is argued that, by allowing greater choice, individual accounts offer two sets of advantages: they increase welfare through the increased economic growth that occurs via improved allocation of savings to investment; and they increase the welfare of individual workers, who can invest according to their different degrees of risk aversion.

The first potential advantage is assessed in section 6.3, which argues that such benefits may be real, but that this will depend on country specifics. The second potential advantage also needs to be tested. The conventional argument in favor of choice is that it maximizes welfare by accommodating differences in preferences across individuals. At least two sets of qualifications are relevant, relating to the costs of choice and to the extent of consumer understanding and information.

The costs of choice. Although the benefits from increased individual choice may be real, they may be offset by the costs of allowing such choice (Box 9.4). This is a serious issue for individual accounts: as already noted, charges tend to be high, and they tend largely to be a fixed cost, thus bearing most heavily on small accounts and in countries where economies of scale are not available. Depending on pricing rules, this cost may hit poorer workers especially, and those in poorer and smaller countries most of all.

Consumer understanding and information. These are central. It is a standard proposition in economics that the welfare gains from individual choice are contingent on efficient choices between consumption when younger and consumption when older. Given the extent of risk and uncertainty, and the complexity of many pension products, over what range, if any, does increased choice make workers better off?

One potential problem is myopia. The purpose of pensions is to ensure retirement income. But some workers pay too little attention to the future: they may not attend to making a good choice and may be influenced by current inducements when choosing investments, for example from sales pressure and possibly kickbacks.[12]

A second concern is that individuals often do not do a good job of looking after their own best interests when it comes to retirement planning, as discussed in Box 9.6. Many people are imperfectly informed about complex financial products and hence make a poor choice of financial intermediary for their retirement savings. (See the discussion in Box 9.2 of the U.K. mis-selling scandal.) Financial markets, like most retail markets, are marked by a diversity of prices for similar, indeed sometimes seemingly identical products. Some people end up with high-cost options because they lack the necessary information or capacity to make good choices. For example, many people

12. Higher consumption may come in part through kickbacks. For example, a fund manager may use part of the income from administrative charges to pay a large upfront commission to an agent for each new customer; the agent may in turn share the commission with the customer as an inducement to join.

do not understand the importance of portfolio diversification, as evidenced by heavy investments by some workers in the stocks of their employers.

▶ Box 9.6 Do consumers choose well? Lessons from behavioral economics

Box 2.1 set out the simple theory of saving in a first-best world. Two bodies of literature help to explain why choices about saving and about one's pension provider may be suboptimal: that on the economics of information, discussed in Box 4.2 and above, and a recent and growing literature on behavioral economics (see U.K. Pensions Commission 2004a, pp. 207–10, and Tapia and Yermo 2007).

Many people do not save enough voluntarily to maximize lifetime utility, and few buy annuities voluntarily despite their considerable value. Indeed, widespread manifestations of suboptimal behavior are observed. One type of problem is that people may fail to choose, or delay doing so:

- *Procrastination:* People delay saving, do not save, or do not save enough. There is considerable evidence (Choi et al. 2001) that, with retirement saving, as elsewhere, people agree that they should do more but put off the action itself.
- *Avoiding explicit choice:* In theory it should make no difference whether individuals face an opt-in or an opt-out provision; in practice, automatic enrollment leads to much higher participation. Participation rates in employer 401(k) plans in the United States differ sharply depending on whether or not enrollment was automatic with an opt-out (Madrian and Shea 2001).
- *Immobilization:* Complexity and conflicting information can lead to passive behavior. People presented with a larger range of 401(k) options have been found to participate less. Table 9.3 shows the large fraction of new workers in Sweden who make no choice.

In addition, when people do choose, their choices may make little sense:

- *Short-term gratification:* Many people retire at the earliest age permitted, which may be too early for their own good or that of their spouses. In the United States a large spike in retirements occurs at age 62, even though pensions rise for later retirement on roughly an actuarially fair basis for the average worker.
- *Framing:* Choices are influenced by how they are presented. Faced with a choice of four equity funds and two bond funds, people are more likely to choose an equity fund than if the choice were between four bond and two equity funds.
- *Familiarity:* Another poor but common choice is to invest heavily in the stock of one's own employer; if the firm goes bankrupt, employees invested in the firm lose both their wage income and much of their capital accumulation, as happened to many employees of Enron. Such behavior shows a failure to understand the benefits of diversifying risk.
- *Herd instinct:* People follow fashion, as, for example, in the technology stock boom of the late 1990s. A related phenomenon is excessive trading: many people appear to trade too much, on average worsening their position on the risk-return frontier while also incurring trading costs. Another is trying to time the market, moving between classes of assets in a way that increases risk relative to expected return, and indeed seems to lower the expected return on average as well.
- *Poor use of annuities:* Decisions about annuities also tend to be flawed, not least because most people do not understand the underlying idea of insurance.

Recent experimental evidence supports a tendency in some circumstances for people to have a high discount rate in the short run (that is, a tendency to instant gratification) and a lower one in the medium term. The problem is that when the future arrives, it becomes the present; hence short-term gratification continues, resulting in time-inconsistency.

These findings suggest a number of implications for policy design in both employer and public plans:

- To avoid immobilization, keep choices simple, for example by offering only a small number of clearly differentiated funds.
- Use automatic enrollment, thus turning inertia to the individual's advantage: once automatically enrolled, most people will stay with the plan.
- Design a good default option: an arrangement based on automatic enrollment plus worker choice of plans requires a default option for workers who do not make a choice. The existence and design of the default option are important (see Beshears et al. 2008 for a fuller discussion).
- In employer plans a further option is to design policy so that people commit now to action in the future, thus making use of procrastination to assist policy. People are happy to promise to save more in the future, as in the "Save More Tomorrow" plan of Thaler and Benartzi (2004). The essence of that arrangement is that people commit to save a given fraction of their salary, but starting only with the next pay increase; the fraction is initially small but, unless the individual takes explicit action to end the arrangement, rises with each successive pay increase. ◀

A related possibility is that workers will fail to make any choice at all; this, too, can happen when individuals are not well informed. In Sweden, despite a massive effort at public education at the launch of the system of funded individual accounts in 2000, about one-third of workers did not choose a fund and thus ended up in the default fund, a global fund with about 85 percent of its assets in equities (although a few of them, including some professional economists, may have consciously done nothing, viewing the default fund as the best option). As Table 9.3 shows, the number of workers making a choice was much lower after the initial period. By 2003 over 90 percent of new workers, most of them young and with little to invest at the start, did not choose a portfolio. Nor is there much evidence of people moving away from the default fund as they become older and have larger account balances.[13] The presence of a default option can itself influence choice, either because workers interpret its default status as a recommendation, or because the default leads them not to bother with informing themselves. Thus a well-designed default is considerably more important than would be the case if the standard economists' model of rational choice were fully accurate.

A third concern is that even where a person does have the necessary capacity to choose well, an individual account is an ongoing relationship, so that the benefits of smarter shopping (in the form of higher returns and lower charges) in any particular

TABLE 9.3

Share of first-time choosers investing in the Swedish default fund (Premiesparfonden)

	2000	2001	2002	2003	2004	2005
Percent investing in default fund	33.0	72.4	85.9	91.7	90.6	92.0

Source: Sweden Ministry of Finance (2005, p. 36).

13. In 2004 the government appointed a review panel to address the issue. Its report, drawing on survey results in which 50 percent of respondents said that they lacked adequate knowledge to make the choice, suggested reducing the number of funds and giving better guidance to savers. See Sweden Ministry of Finance (2005).

month are small, whereas the transactions costs in terms of time are significant. Thus workers, particularly low earners, for whom the gain in any month is smallest, have little incentive to stay on top of the changing details of alternative investments and alternative charges.[14] In the absence of detailed regulations, the risk is of a dizzying array of prices and arrangements.

In this setting it is important to move beyond the "average" worker and consider differences among workers in earnings and in the options they select. It is not an adequate analytical approach to base evaluation of a system only on a low-cost option, making the assumption that everyone who chooses a higher-cost option has sound reasons to expect to gain from that choice. Both positive political economy reasons and normative considerations call for a tightly regulated market, with its inherent benefits and costs.

Individual choices will vary in ways that a centralized formula cannot duplicate. Is this good or bad? Our answer is some of both—it depends on the quality and complexity of the centralized formula and on the quality of individual decisions. Some individuals will choose well (in an ex ante sense) given their degree of risk aversion and the risk-return frontier they face. Many of these are likely to be experienced investors with a sufficiently large portfolio outside the mandatory system that they can adjust, making options within the system of little consequence. Others will choose badly, ending up at points that are not on the frontier or that are do not match their risk aversion. The principles of finance—the advantages of diversification, the trade-off between risk and return, the identification of underlying stochastic structures, even the efficiency of markets—are not, after all, intuitively easy concepts. Indeed, cognitive psychology tells us that even much simpler statistical concepts are generally not intuitive. Given the noise in returns, moreover, it is difficult for anyone to tell good portfolio managers from bad ones.[15] With some organizational structures, efforts to prevent fraud and mis-selling are extremely important. Choices will be regulated, and policymakers need to recognize that, like the politics of direct government portfolio choice, the politics of portfolio regulation has its own potential shortcomings.

Conclusion. Box 9.6 suggests that there is good reason to be skeptical about the gains from individual choice in mandatory accounts. Will learning-by-doing take care of that? The evidence suggests not. U.S. experience with 401(k) plans shows that worker education must be substantial and expensive to have a noticeable effect on investment choices. This should not be surprising, since what is involved, it can be argued, is not an information problem but an information processing problem (Box 4.2) and, moreover, one that involves trading off current effort for future consumption, leading to the difficulties discussed in Box 9.6. More generally, the considerable difficulty in making investment choices even in countries with

---

14. This is true even for the simplest financial arrangements. Banks in some countries offer higher interest rates on new types of savings accounts while leaving the terms of existing accounts unchanged, relying on the inertia of existing savers, many of whom stay in the old, lower-yielding accounts. In some other countries regulation restricts the freedom of banks to offer different interest rates in this way.

15. Studying Swedish mutual funds, Dahlquist, Engström, and Söderlind (2000, p. 410) "find evidence of persistence in performance for money market funds, but not for the other fund categories."

generations of individual experience in investing is a major concern in countries with a limited history of individual investment.

In sum, the counterargument to the proponents of competitive pension provision is that the advantages of idealized competition are contingent on sufficiently good decision making. The scale of uncertainty, risk, and other consumer information problems does not *necessarily* rule out consumer choice as welfare improving, but should be seen as a counterpoint, especially in poorer countries where citizens have little financial market experience.

APPENDIX 9.1   IMPLEMENTING INDIVIDUAL ACCOUNTS IN THE U.S. SOCIAL SECURITY SYSTEM: A HYPOTHETICAL TASK LIST

This list looks first at the tasks that would be necessary to implement individual accounts within the U.S. Social Security system, and then considers which tasks would be different if the accounts were privately organized.[16]

Accounts organized by government

We assume that contributions are received throughout the year and are linked to individual taxpayers after the end of the year, when W-2 forms are filed.[17] It also assumes that the government receives the money and arranges for investment, recordkeeping, and benefit payments. Asterisks indicate tasks already done by, or similar to tasks done by, the Social Security Administration or the Treasury.

1. *Collect contributions from employers*
- Receive and record money from employers shortly after each payday.*
- Reconcile amounts received with employers' quarterly 941 forms and annual W-2 forms to detect missing payments or payments that appear to show discrepancies.*
- Segregate account contributions from other taxes paid by employers.

2. *Invest funds*
- Select a private fund manager or managers.
- Invest new contributions during the year according to government policy and account holder instructions.
- Designate a default investment portfolio for individuals not selecting a portfolio.
- Report investment returns to the record keeper: annual averages for new contributions, monthly or quarterly for valuations of account balances.

3. *Credit workers' accounts with new contributions*
- Identify missing or inconsistent reports from employers by reconciling annual and quarterly reports, and correspond with employers to remedy problems.*

16. This appendix is adapted from Diamond (2000, Appendix A).

17. In the United States, Form W-2 is the annual statement of earnings and withholdings of income tax and Social Security contributions that workers receive from their employers at the end of the tax year. Form 941 is the employer quarterly tax return. Form 1040 is the basic individual tax return.

- Record new contributions. Identify discrepancies between W-2s and Social Security files and correspond with employers or employees to resolve these.
- Set up a new information system of records needed to administer accounts: worker identification, portfolio choice, effective date of choice, interfund transfers and their dates, designation of death beneficiary, marital status, spouse identification, spousal consent code (depending on policy), current address.

4. Enroll workers and record their portfolio choices (and other new information)

These tasks depend on the nature and extent of employer involvement (mandatory or voluntary). Options include

- Ongoing requirement that employers enroll new employees and report their portfolio choices annually (on W-2s or W-4s)
- One-time employer responsibility to enroll workers in the plan and send data to the record keeper
- Do not involve employers but instead deal directly with workers through 1040 forms, correspondence, phone, website, or visits in person.

5. Educate and communicate with workers

- "Wholesale" tasks (such as in the U.S. Thrift Savings Plan; see Box 11.5) include developing educational brochures, videos, and training courses for employers to use to enroll workers.
- "Retail" tasks (performed by employers in the Thrift Savings Plan) include one-on-one communication with workers through Social Security field offices, a free phone number, and a website.

6. Pay death benefits

- Determine policy for death benefits, including registry of state laws on inheritance rights and rules for determining jurisdictions, if relevant.
- Set rules of evidence for determining the correct death beneficiary and maintain a record system to support it.*
- Resolve competing claims when they occur.*

7. Implement policy on treatment of accounts at divorce

Possible policies include letting the courts decide; automatically dividing equally the changes in account balances that occurred during the marriage; or automatically dividing contributions each year between spouses. Depending on policy, tasks include the following:

- Set policy for treatment of "qualified domestic relations orders" from the courts as part of court-supervised divorce settlements.
- Maintain historical records that can be used retroactively to combine and split the change in account balances of two individuals over a period of years or each year, to link accounts of husbands and wives and to transact a split. (This capacity is relevant if a divorce is accompanied by a redistribution of assets in individual accounts.)

- Set up systems for verifying marital status and the spouse's identity, and policies for resolving disputes and discrepancies and informing each party of transactions made on their accounts.

8. Pay retirement benefits

- Determine policies about the nature of withdrawal options.
- With annuities, determine whether the government or insurance companies will assume mortality and investment risks and administer the annuities.
- If insurance companies are involved, determine policy for their involvement, such as standards for participation, competitive bidding for group contracts, and some sort of reinsurance.
- Set policy on joint-and-survivor annuities and beneficiary designation for non-annuitized funds.

9. Retirement benefit counseling

Assuming a number of withdrawal options are available:

- Explain to pensioners what the choices are and what the terms mean, and present scenarios of how different choices would affect the particular pensioner and spouse.
- Set policies on who will provide the information and who will pay for it.

10. Early access to accounts in case of hardship

- Determine hardship rules and how they will be applied.
- If access is through loans, set up systems for how they will be repaid.

Privately organized accounts: Additional tasks

We assume that employers withhold funds and transfer them to the government and that employers send annual W-2s reporting the amounts belonging to each worker. The government's tasks in collecting contributions are then the same as in government-organized accounts. When W-2s have been submitted, the government sends each worker's funds to a financial institution of the worker's choice. The financial institution is responsible for all further dealing with the account holder, including investing the funds, crediting workers' accounts with new contributions, obtaining information about the worker's portfolio choices, obtaining data needed to pay benefits to the worker or his or her beneficiaries, educating and communicating with workers about investment choices, paying death benefits, implementing policy on treatment of divorce, paying retirement benefits under applicable rules, and providing retirement benefit counseling. It is also responsible for enforcing whatever policy applies with regard to early access.

New issues and tasks that arise under this model:

- Government maintains a default plan or default institution for workers who fail to designate a financial institution.
- Government sets rules on financial institutions eligible to hold Social Security accounts.[*]

- If workers are required to hold their funds in only one institution at a time, government and financial institutions put systems in place to ensure that this happens.
- Once money is sent to the financial institution, it is responsible for receiving portfolio choices from workers, correcting mistakes, and ensuring that the costs of error and delayed correction do not fall on the worker.
- Government policies might regulate financial institutions' fee arrangements, the terms on which institutions may accept accounts, and possibly the institutions' marketing practices.
- Government policies might regulate what kinds of portfolios are allowed.
- Government monitors institutions' compliance with whatever rules apply to the accumulation and distribution of account funds.*
- Auditing, trustee, legal, and related functions must be assigned, to the extent these are not included above.

10

▷

Conclusion to Part I

This chapter brings together the main analytical conclusions of Part I, starting in section 10.1 with discussion of principles. Section 10.2 considers the resulting lessons for policy.

10.1 PRINCIPLES

10.1.1 Principles of analysis

Pension systems have multiple objectives. The major objectives of individuals with regard to pensions are consumption smoothing and insurance. Governments may have additional goals, including poverty relief and redistribution. Analysis and policy design need to take account of all these objectives, and governments have to consider them alongside other goals of public policy, including economic efficiency and output growth.

   Analysis should consider the pension system as a whole. Pension design affects the labor market, economic growth, the distribution of risk, and the distribution of income, including by gender. Analysis of those effects needs to consider the entire pension system, and in particular whether a change in one part needs to be accompanied by a change in another. Similarly, analysis needs to consider the impact of any change over the short and the long run, including the time path from one steady state to another.

   Analysis of distributional effects should consider the progressivity of the system as a whole, rather than of each element. Thus benefits from different parts of the pension system should be considered together and, for many purposes, alongside the taxes that finance them. For example, suppose that everyone gets a flat-rate pension financed by a proportional tax; although the tax side, considered alone, is not progressive, the system overall is, because lower earners pay less tax than higher earners but everyone gets the same pension. Indeed, the pension system can be progressive even if the tax system is regressive, so long as the progressivity on the benefits side outweighs the regressivity on the tax side.[1]

Analysis needs to take account of major deviations from first-best. The simplest theoretical case, illustrated in Box 2.1, assumes that everyone is self-supporting on a lifetime basis and that labor markets, savings institutions, and insurance markets exist and function ideally.[2] However, pensions raise issues of choice over a lifetime, and pension products are generally complex. Thus progress in helping consumers to become better informed has been limited, even in developed countries, not least because consumers choosing specific pension products face not only information problems, which can be resolved by offering more information, but also information processing problems, that is, problems too complicated for most of them to resolve even when given the necessary information (many medical choices have a similar characteristic). As a result, people often fail to make choices that maximize their long-term well-being, and they often make no explicit choice at all—a common result where excessive choice or excessive complexity becomes overwhelming. The design of pension systems needs to take account of these problems of information and decision making. For example, in contrast with the simplest case, restricting choices can at times improve outcomes; it is also critical to design good defaults for people who make no explicit choice.

Alongside these problems in choosing among pension products, consumers also face problems in choosing the timing of retirement. If pension benefits bear an actuarial relationship to a person's expected duration of retirement, the combination of longer lives and retirement at the earliest possible date (a common occurrence) inescapably aggravates elderly poverty. The concern that some people are retiring too early for their own good matters for the choice of an earliest entitlement age and increases the importance of careful design of the incentives to work beyond the earliest entitlement age.

On the supply side, insurers also face information problems. An issue of particular concern, discussed in Box 9.5, is difficulties in predicting cohort life expectancy. In the absence of a government-organized mandate, insurers also face problems of adverse selection in the market for annuities.

In addition to these information problems, analysis needs to take account of other deviations from first-best, notably incomplete markets and taxation.

Analysis of funding needs to consider how the funding is generated. The impact of pension design on future output is a central element. One way to increase funding is to increase contribution rates (or reduce benefits) now in order to have lower contribution rates or higher benefits in the future; another is to place assets with the pension authority rather than hold them elsewhere. The first approach can raise national saving, and thus output, and so enhance the capacity to provide benefits in the future. The central point is very simple: to raise national saving, changes to pension arrangements have to lower someone's consumption, either that of workers, if contributions are increased, or that of retirees, if benefits are reduced. The transfer of assets does not

---

1. With a flat benefit financed by a proportional tax up to a cap, the system is progressive up to the cap but does not have further progressivity beyond the cap, because everyone beyond the cap pays the same tax and gets the same benefit, whatever their earnings.

2. For fuller discussion of the economic theory, including information problems, see section 4.2.2 and Box 4.2; on problems of consumer choice, including lessons from behavioral economics, see Box 9.6.

have that effect if the assets would have been saved anyway. It does not create additional output, but only changes the distribution of the burden of paying for benefits, including benefits that are a legacy of an older pension system.

These principles underpin good policy design. Failure to observe them, illustrated by examples in earlier chapters, leads to the analytical errors summarized in Box 10.1, which are thus the mirror image of the points above. These errors, besides being important in themselves, can—and do—lead to faulty policy design; hence we make no apology for any repetition.

▶ Box 10.1 Analytical errors: The World Bank and other culprits

Discussion of pensions is prone to analytical errors of which the following—by the World Bank, but certainly not only the World Bank—are prime examples. Section 11.3 discusses parallel policy errors.

Tunnel vision. As discussed in section 2.2, analysis that focuses, often implicitly, on a single objective such as consumption smoothing may be flawed because it pays inadequate attention to other objectives such as poverty relief. Similarly, it is generally mistaken to consider one part of the pension system in isolation, ignoring the effects of other parts. There is no efficiency gain from moving redistribution from one part of the system to another, even if the change leaves one part with no deviation from full actuarial principles.

Improper use of first-best analysis. It is a mistake to focus on the labor market distortions caused by a given set of pension arrangements while ignoring or downplaying the contributions of those arrangements to the various goals of pension systems—contributions that are not available without distortions. The central idea in Diamond (2003) is that any optimal program will necessarily induce distortions, because, starting from laissez-faire, distortions create second-order efficiency costs but first-order distributional gains. The argument (section 5.2.2) that an actuarial relationship between contributions and benefits is optimal in terms of labor market effects is generally mistaken. It is right to design pensions so as to avoid larger distortions than are justified by their contribution to goals, but it does not follow that minimizing distortions is the right objective.

Also mistaken is uncritical acceptance of the argument (see section 9.3) that competition among pension providers necessarily benefits consumers by increasing choice and driving down administrative charges. Although applicable in a wide set of circumstances, this line of argument understates the serious information problems and information processing problems that particularly affect pensions. These problems do not mean that there should be no consumer choice, but rather that options should be carefully designed, for example through constrained choice and well-crafted defaults.

Improper use of steady-state analysis. It is mistaken to focus on the design of a reformed pension system in steady state while ignoring or underplaying the steps that are necessary to get to that steady state. This issue becomes especially important when considering whether or not to move from PAYG toward funded pensions. As discussed in section 6.4, the argument that funding is inherently superior because stock market returns exceed the rate of wage growth is mistaken for several reasons, not least because it takes no account of how the move to funding is to be financed.

Incomplete analysis of implicit pension debt. As discussed in section 6.2, simple analysis that looks only at future liabilities (that is, future pension payments), while ignoring explicit assets and the implicit asset that is the government's ability to levy taxes, is misleading. Too narrow a focus on the cost side also ignores the considerable improvements in people's well-being from increased old-age security. Just as public debt

(continues next page)

(continued from previous page)

does not need to be fully paid off so long as the debt-to-GDP ratio does not explode, so publicly provided pensions need not be fully funded, as long as the unfunded obligations are not set to explode relative to the base for contributions. A related error is to treat implicit and explicit debt as equivalent.

Incomplete analysis of the effects of funding. A pensioner's living standard in old age will depend on his or her ability to consume goods and services produced by younger workers. PAYG and funding are both ways of organizing claims on that output. It is therefore mistaken to focus excessively on how pensions are financed while ignoring future national output and its division between workers and pensioners. A common example of this error, discussed in section 6.3.3, is to argue that funding necessarily assists adjustment to demographic change. The error in this claim is its failure to recognize that the effects of funding will depend on the answer to a series of questions, many of which are often addressed incompletely or ignored:

• Will funded pensions increase saving?
• Is increased saving the right objective?
• Will funded pensions strengthen the performance of capital markets?
• If so, are mandatory pensions necessary for this purpose?
• Are redistributive effects across generations—which are inevitable—desirable policy?

Ignoring distributional effects. Because pension systems can redistribute across cohorts of different birth years, it is necessary to consider both who gains and who loses because of the need to finance pensions at some time, possibly in the future. The most egregious error is to ignore the fact that any choice between funding and PAYG necessarily makes choices about redistribution across generations. As discussed in section 7.2, a move toward funding that increases saving redistributes from today's generation to future generations. Irrespective of the merits of the move, it is faulty analysis to ignore those distributional effects.

As discussed in Box 6.4, the error in ignoring distributional effects is profound: it makes an implicit assumption about the distribution of income across generations; it leads to mistaken claims for the Pareto superiority (see glossary) of some policies; and it ignores the fact that a PAYG element in a pension system is generally welfare enhancing because of the resulting possibility of intergenerational risk sharing. ◀

10.1.2   Principles of policy design

Policy should avoid changes not needed to achieve the government's objectives. It is, of course, a counsel of despair to argue that there should never be radical change. But it is equally mistaken to pursue reforms that are seen as innovative or radical as though that, of itself, contributes to achieving policy objectives. "If it ain't broke, don't fix it" is generally sound policy advice. The case for specific types of reform needs to be made carefully, because change is difficult, and because pensions affect many people for many years, and over many cohorts.

The system should aim to achieve the government's objectives in the simplest way possible. "Keep it simple, stupid," another important aspect of reform, is often overlooked. Simplicity is prudent even in developed countries,[3] but is particularly important in developing countries to ensure that the design of the system is compatible with a country's institutional capacity. For example, mandatory pensions should not rely

---

3. See the criticism of the complexity of the U.K. system in U.K. Pensions Commission (2004*a*, 2004*b*).

prematurely on privately marketed assets; consideration of such a system should wait until adequate regulatory structures are in place for the accounts and for annuity providers, for financial markets, and for accounting by firms. Reliance on privately marketed assets for a mandatory system for all workers should be based on demonstrated successful experience, either with voluntary private pensions or with some experimental group.

Pensions should be portable within a unified system. Mobility is essential to an efficient labor market. Thus, to the extent possible, pensions should be portable as workers move from one geographical area to another, from one public enterprise to another, from the public to the private sector and vice versa, from one private firm to another, and from the uncovered (informal or rural) to the covered sector, and in and out of self-employment,. Such portability is achieved most readily when the system has a uniform structure across the covered population, both across localities and across sectors. This does not rule out differences in benefit levels—indeed, such differences are essential in large countries with wide differences in living standards and living costs—but it does mean that the framework should be national. If a system has separate pension funds in different regions or industrial sectors, the contributions of mobile workers in their former region or sector should count toward their pension in the new. The system in the United States complies with these principles, and the issues are very much on the agenda in the expanded European Union, although progress thus far has been limited. And the question of a nationwide system is acutely relevant to a country as large and diverse as China. A uniform structure does not rule out supplementary pension systems (voluntary at the firm level) in private firms or for government employees.

Uniformity in structure has important political implications as well. A multiplicity of pension systems can give rise to political pressures to transfer resources to those systems that cover workers and retirees who are politically well connected. Uniformity offers some protection against political pressures that run counter to shared social goals.

Pension design should pay close attention to incentive structures. As discussed in Chapters 5 and 6, pensions have major effects on labor markets and saving. As discussed in Box 10.1, it is a mistake to seek to minimize distortions, since the achievement of some of the goals of pensions, notably poverty relief, insurance, and redistribution, inevitably involves distortions. Instead policy should seek to contain adverse incentives, bearing in mind their trade-off with the achievement of the goals of the pension system. That said, it is known that certain types of policy design create adverse incentives that can be avoided; as discussed in section 5.2.1, defined-benefit pensions should be based on a person's earnings over an extended period, avoiding heavy reliance on final wages.

Particular attention needs to be paid to retirement incentives. A national mandatory retirement age is a bad design and should be avoided. It is important to have adequate incentives for people to continue to work past the earliest age at which a pension can be claimed. This can be done by paying pensions even when a person continues to work, or by increasing benefits for a delayed start to retirement.

Policy design should pay close attention to administrative costs. Different types of pensions have very different costs, as Figure 9.1 shows for the United Kingdom and as illustrated more broadly in Table 9.1. Costs are generally highest where workers can choose their investment services provider or can purchase their individual portfolio directly in the market. Clearly, a major issue for policymakers is how to regulate pensions generally, and charges in particular.

Among the advantages claimed for funded individual accounts are that they increase individual choice and that they offer a higher return than PAYG pensions. Given the decision-making problems already discussed, the welfare gains from the first can be questioned. The second claim, as discussed in section 6.4, ignores important issues concerning the distribution of benefits, of costs, and of risks: as already noted, the move to funding inescapably redistributes across cohorts; in addition, the claim ignores the fact that funded individual accounts generally have higher administrative costs, which are largely a fixed cost per account; charges, if they parallel costs, thus bear most heavily on small accounts.

Sweden has sought to address these issues through a clearinghouse model, whereby the administration and maintenance of individual accounts are centralized. Like Sweden, the U.S. Thrift Savings Plan (Box 11.5) has centralized administration; it also limits the choices available to workers, further lowering costs. In both countries the delivery of funds to private firms for investment is done in aggregate by the government, not separately worker by worker.

The system should have the capacity to adapt and evolve. Any pension system will need adjusting over time. As incomes rise, reforms proceed, and institutional capacity grows, the system should adapt accordingly. It should therefore be designed with an eye to the future as well as the present. The system should have some degree of automatic responses to circumstances, particularly inflation and changes in life expectancy.

10.2   LESSONS FOR POLICY

This section summarizes the lessons of the previous chapters for pension design generally, for finance and funding, and for political and administrative implementation.

10.2.1   Pension design

Many countries have pension systems with three parts: a basic pension, mandatory individual accounts, and voluntary pensions. Each part, if well designed, helps the others fulfill their social goals. Other countries, such as the United States, address concerns about redistribution and consumption smoothing by integrating both into a single public pension. Either approach can be used to incorporate a good design that addresses the system's multiple goals.

A basic public pension is a vital complement to individual accounts. By themselves, individual accounts do not adequately provide poverty relief, income redistribution, or insurance against adverse labor market outcomes. Policy must address the fact that many people are poor; individual accounts alone would leave them below the poverty line even after contributing to the system throughout a lengthy career. And in many countries policymakers have redistributive ambitions broader than poverty relief. Thus there is unambiguous support on technical grounds, largely independent of ideology, for a mix of a basic pension and individual accounts, or some other integrated mechanism that addresses the various objectives. The relative size and specific design of each element will depend on the weights that policymakers give to these different objectives.

Since pension systems are designed mainly for workers who have worked for most of their adult lives, some other mechanism is needed to address poverty among people without a long record of covered employment or self-employment. Poverty protection for these people can be provided within the pension system (for example, through a noncontributory universal pension), or through a separate mechanism (for example, through income-tested social assistance), or both.

Countries can achieve major gains from improving the existing system of basic pension and earnings-related pension (sometimes referred to as parametric change), and many are adopting this strategy in the face of population aging, whether or not they are also pursuing other reforms.

Individual pensions are one way to facilitate consumption smoothing. In a country where most people are poor, an earnings-related element of the pension is relatively unimportant. But in countries where earnings are high or, as in China and the European former communist countries, where earnings are rising rapidly and the distribution of those earnings is widening, a separate element of consumption smoothing becomes an increasingly important complement to the basic pension. The design—whether fully funded, notional, or related to earnings in some other way—will depend both on the country's preferences and on its institutional capacity.

Voluntary pensions are essential to increasing individual choice. People have different needs, tastes, life expectancies, and careers: some are more risk averse than others, some care more than others about their standard of living in old age, some are more eager than others to retire early. Thus different people should be saving for retirement at different rates, and the optimum timing of that saving during a person's career varies. Some people have children early in life and some late, and so bear the cost of raising children at different times in their lives. Similarly, the pattern of housing costs, particularly purchase prices, varies both within and across countries. Yet national pension systems are limited in the degree of complexity they can usefully (and politically successfully) incorporate. Voluntary supplementary pensions offer a mechanism for accommodating these different preferences, although they need sound regulation to make sure that they serve their social purposes. The size of the mandatory system and the tax treatment of voluntary pensions are both important for the extent of their development.

Different systems share risks differently. In a pure system of individual accounts organized in the private sector and based on private financial assets, the risk of unsatisfactory outcomes is imposed on the individual worker (an exception is the longevity risk, if benefits are taken in the form of an annuity). The allocation of risk in the pure case can be altered by government guarantees or government bailouts. In a pure, privately organized, defined-benefit arrangement, the risk is borne by the employer, and thus ultimately by the employer's current and future workers and shareholders and by their customers if the costs of a deficit fall partly on prices; hence the risk is shared more broadly. This allocation, too, can be altered by government bailouts or if an employer fails to pay promised benefits. In a pure defined-benefit system financed out of social insurance contributions, risks are shared across contributors, that is, across the current working generation and, if benefits are adjusted, across beneficiaries. The allocation in the pure case can be altered by variations in partial funding, or by borrowing, which transfers risks across different generations, through adjustments of contributions or benefits. Finally, in a system financed out of general revenue as well as, or in place of, payroll taxes, the risks are shared across all taxpayers, and hence across generations (since future taxes as well as current taxes can change as debt varies). A central question for policymakers is how widely risks should be shared, a question with both efficiency and equity implications. (For a fuller discussion of risk sharing, see section 7.3.)

Different systems have different effects by gender. Pension systems, like other institutions, create incentives that affect decisions about paid work, care activities, and leisure. Analysis therefore needs to reflect diversity in social values, individual preferences, and economic situations within a country and across countries. As with the broader aspects of pensions, there is no single unambiguous best design, but some designs are unambiguously bad.

There are wide-ranging choices in pension design, and many ways to design good systems. The choices in different countries depend in part on policymakers' objectives and in part on initial conditions, notably the existing social security system and the existing level of market development. The design and relative sizes of different elements in a pension system depend on the income levels of the elderly, the role of voluntary pensions, and the degree of concern with social solidarity. Countries with reasonably well functioning systems have made very diverse choices, as the discussion in Chapter 11 illustrates.

10.2.2 Finance and funding

As the discussion in Chapter 6 makes clear, the finance and funding of pension systems raise issues that are both complex and controversial. They are also fruitful territory for some of the analytical errors discussed in Box 10.1.

Unsustainable pension promises need to be addressed directly. A frequently heard, but flawed argument runs, "PAYG pensions face major fiscal problems; therefore they should be privatized." This is a non sequitur—the "therefore" does not follow in logic. Whatever financing problems a pension system may face, privatization does little or nothing to alleviate them (as examples, see some of the recent U.S. proposals); indeed, it may exacerbate them (as it did, for example, in Argentina, and as, again, in some U.S. proposals; see Horney and Kogan 2005). It is important to distinguish between two questions:

- Is the fiscal cost of public pensions a problem?
- Would a move toward funding be beneficial?

These are separate questions, requiring separate answers. If a public pension is running a deficit that is regarded as unsustainable, the only solution is to make it sustainable by increasing contributions, reducing benefits, or a mix of the two. In contrast, if there are potential benefits from funding, a move in that direction may be sound policy even where the fiscal costs of a public pension are sustainable.

A move to funding generally has major fiscal costs. In a PAYG system the contributions of younger workers pay the pensions of older people. But if a country moves to a funded system, the contributions of younger workers will instead go into their individual accounts, and so the pensions of retired people must come from some other source: higher taxation, or additional government borrowing, or reductions in spending on other government programs. Thus a move toward funding generally imposes an added burden on today's workers, who have to pay not only their own contributions but also some or all of the taxes that finance current pensions (see section 6.3.1).

One way to spread (but not eliminate) the fiscal costs of the transition is to phase in funded pensions gradually. Another is to postpone the move to mandatory funded accounts. A country that wants to introduce individual accounts but cannot absorb the fiscal costs of transition, or one where institutions are not yet strong enough to support mandatory funded accounts, has the option of introducing mandatory notional defined-contribution pensions, supplemented by voluntary funded accounts. This approach maintains the structure of individual accounts but avoids the additional fiscal and administrative burdens of funding; it also keeps open the option of phasing in mandatory funded accounts at a later stage. The strategy is applicable to China, as discussed in Chapter 15, and potentially to other countries where mandatory funding might be premature or that might have adopted mandatory funding prematurely.

A move to funding has intergenerational effects. If funding is to raise output growth in the future, it has to increase saving today. But for saving to increase, consumption by today's workers must decline, through higher contributions, or consumption by today's retirees must decline, through lower benefits, or a mix.[4] Thus a move to funding generally imposes a burden on today's generation to the benefit of future generations. Depending on country specifics, this may or may not be sound policy. (For a fuller discussion, see section 7. 2.) More generally, introducing a new PAYG system allows the early cohorts to receive larger pensions than if the new system were fully funded. Thus any choice between PAYG and funding is also and necessarily a choice about the intergenerational distribution of income.

There is no automatic relationship between funding and growth. Funding will raise the rate of economic growth if it increases saving or improves the efficiency with which saving is channeled into investment (see section 6.3.1). But some methods of providing funds may not increase saving; others, such as increased mandatory pension saving, may be offset by declines in other saving; and funding may not be good policy in any case if the saving rate is already high. And the efficient channeling of saving into investment requires formal capital markets that are capable of allocating funds to good investment opportunities more effectively than informal capital markets (see section 6.3.2). Gains in the effectiveness of capital markets are possible but depend on effective administration and on political support for the deployment of that administration in regulating financial markets. Thus the economic case for funding has to be made in each country.

A related point is that funding is not an automatic solution to demographic problems (see section 6.3.3). Rather, its operation is indirect and its helpfulness contingent on whether it has beneficial effects on growth. Without additional resources, longer lives require either later retirement or reduced monthly benefits, however they are financed.

10.2.3   Political and administrative implementation

Implementation matters. Effective reform requires much more than good policy design; rather, it rests on a tripod of abilities: policy design, political implementation, and

---

4. An exception arises to the extent that a country can finance the transition by drawing down an accumulated general budget surplus—the case in Chile. Since these funds were being saved anyway, there is no increase in saving.

administrative implementation. The importance of implementation is often underestimated. It requires skills that are just as demanding as policy design, and those skills need to be involved when the policy is designed, not at as an afterthought.[5]

Policymakers need to ask a series of questions:

- What relative weights should be attached to the objectives of consumption smoothing, insurance, poverty relief, and redistribution? This is largely a political question.
- How tight are the fiscal constraints?
- How binding are the institutional capacity constraints; specifically, where is the country located along the spectrum discussed in section 9.1.2?

The discussion below sets out some of the main issues in implementation.

The scale of mandatory pensions must respect fiscal capacity. In macroeconomic terms, pensions are in part a device for dividing output between workers and retirees; they also influence how output is divided between consumption and investment. Thus spending on pensions must be compatible with a country's financial capacity, notably the ability to finance the consumption of retirees and the investment from which future economic growth derives.

Government is an essential participant in any pension system. All pension systems depend critically on public sector technical capacity (see section 9.1). With PAYG systems this includes the ability to collect taxes and contributions, to keep track for many years of the contributions of workers who are mobile and who may change names, and to project future contributions and benefits with reasonable accuracy so that government can adjust the system gradually to changes in financial capacity, avoiding sharp shocks for retirees or workers close to retirement.

It is a fundamental error to suppose that private pensions get government out of the pensions business. Given the major market imperfections discussed in Box 4.2, purely private arrangements for insurance and consumption smoothing will be either inefficient or nonexistent. Thus government has a major role in pensions in all countries, whatever the specific configuration of arrangements. Government must be able to enforce compliance with contribution conditions, to maintain macroeconomic stability, and to ensure effective regulation and supervision of financial markets, including insurance and annuities markets. Such regulation is vital to protect individuals in areas too complex for them to protect themselves. More generally, private markets function best when government has put in place good, clear rules and where enforcement is even-handed, honest, prompt, and predictable. Government also has an important political role in fostering an environment of stability for long-lasting institutions.

Private sector capacity is essential for private pensions. Alongside government capacity, private pensions also require considerable private sector capacity (see section 9.2). Administrative tasks include the ability to collect contributions, to keep individual records over long periods, to inform workers about their accumulations and expected benefits, and to determine and pay benefits. Financial tasks include the ability to manage large investment portfolios.

---

5. For fuller discussion see the start of Chapter 9 and, in the context of reforming the finance of higher education, Barr and Crawford (2005, Chapter 16).

The capacity of consumers is important. Participants in pension arrangements need to be educated about what they can expect to have at retirement and about how to think about the choices they can make. This task, difficult enough in developed countries, is even harder in an economy where most workers have no experience in making such financial decisions (see section 9.3).

Controversy is inescapable. No pension system anywhere has been able to avoid all controversy. Some controversies are about possible reforms in the pension system whose solution implies losses for some groups, and differences over values or politics about who should bear those losses. Many countries have systems with bad design features, giving rise to adverse labor market incentives and unsustainability, leading in turn to excessive and avoidable uncertainty for workers and financial markets. Controversy also arises in other areas, including the minimum retirement age, the balance between public and private pensions, the design of the public pension, rules for gender equity, and the size of any private sector mandate. Effective politics are therefore central to any successful reform.[6]

6. The politics of the recent reforms in Chile, discussed in Chapter 13, were handled very well by the Chile Presidential Advisory Council.

Part II

Policy Choices

11

▷

International Diversity and Change

Part I argued that sound policy design and the capacity to implement it are both fundamental. Building on that analysis, the central argument in this chapter is that countries have choices about pension systems, choices that widen as their economic and institutional capacities grow. Section 11.1 discusses some of the reasons that systems today rightly look different from systems fifty years ago. Section 11.2 considers developments in pension systems and their design and economic and political responses to long-term trends. Some of the responses in some countries worked well; others fared badly, not least because of policy errors, as section 11.3 illustrates. Section 11.4 offers brief descriptions of a number of pension systems, including those of Argentina, Australia, Bolivia, Chile, China, Hungary, the Netherlands, New Zealand, Poland, Singapore, South Africa, Sweden, the United Kingdom, and the United States, to illustrate the wide variety of possible choices. Two of these countries, Chile and China, are discussed in more detail in the following chapters.

11.1 CHANGES OVER THE PAST FIFTY YEARS

Pension systems have been changing, and with good reason: many of the earlier structures were no longer well suited to social and economic environments that have changed profoundly. Thus countries should continue to pay attention to current practice and what best suits their current situation, and not indulge in nostalgia for earlier approaches that have been appropriately discarded.

11.1.1 Long-term trends

The backdrop to the discussion that follows is the long-run trends discussed in Chapter 1: rising life expectancy, declining fertility, declining labor force participation among older males, and expanded rights for women.

Demographic change. Life expectancy has been rising for a very long time (as discussed in Chapter 1 and shown in Figure 1.1) and is projected to continue to rise (Figure 1.2), because of declining child mortality, declining mortality during working years, and longer life beyond working years. A second long-term trend, declining fertility (Figure 1.4), is evident not only in industrialized but also in poorer countries. Both trends have been significant and widespread, affecting the United States and Canada, Western and Northern Europe, the former communist countries of Europe, Australia and New Zealand, Japan, and many developing countries.

Declining labor force participation of older male workers. This trend is in large part a response to higher living standards. As people become richer, they can afford to choose a different balance of work and leisure. Figures 1.7 and 1.8 show the long-run trend. Figure 11.1 illustrates the situation in 2002: the labor force participation of older workers (men and women combined) is lower, and in many countries considerably lower, than that for younger workers. Many men are now retiring before they are 60, including a large number of civil servants throughout much of the world. Earlier retirement and longer life combine to increase the duration of retirement, which ranged from fifteen years for men in Japan in 1999 to nearly twenty-one years in Italy (Sigg 2005, Table 8.1); durations are even longer for women. In some countries, however, the trend to early retirement has halted (Scherer 2001; OECD 2002, Table V.1; Sigg 2005, Figure 3).

Increasing economic and political rights for women. This change, also discussed in Chapter 1, is a key part of the evolution of pension design and is central to pension design for the future. Increasing numbers of women work for pay, and for an increasing number of years, and the view that women's old-age security should come solely

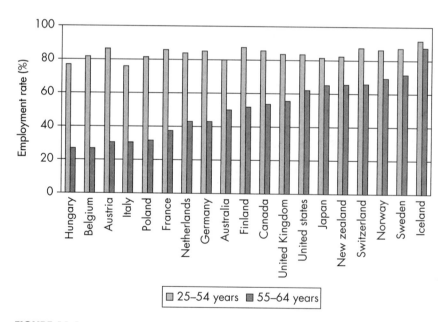

FIGURE 11.1.
Employment rates by age group in selected OECD countries, 2002. Employment rates are for both sexes. *Source:* Sigg (2005, Figure 8.2).

through their husband's pension contributions is increasingly regarded as out of place. For these reasons and others, more women have pensions in their own right. In addition, as discussed further below, pension design needs to accommodate a greater variety of living arrangements.

11.1.2   Changes over the postwar period

Superimposed on these very long term trends is a series of changes that have taken place since the end of World War II.

Growth in pension systems. Before the war, the typical system covered few workers beyond the urban formal sector. Those systems have since expanded rapidly in terms of both coverage and benefit levels, as discussed further in section 11.2.1.

The baby boom. The post-World War II baby boom, shown for the United States in Figure 1.10, is a fairly widespread phenomenon and, when combined with other demographic trends, has had powerful effects in some countries. But its importance should not be exaggerated: as Figure 1.5 shows, the age pyramids projected for 2050 are not strikingly different in the United States from those in India and China, which had no baby boom.

Growth of female labor force participation. The archetypal family structure comprising a male breadwinner and a female caregiver was never the entire story in the West, and female labor force participation was always high in the Soviet system. Throughout the Western countries over the postwar period, women in increasing numbers not only have taken on paid work, as shown in Table 1.2, but have pursued lifelong careers. One implication for pension systems is that the presence of more workers eases the short-term finances of a PAYG system by increasing the contributions base. Another is that many systems have needed to be redesigned to recognize the entitlements that a woman builds on the basis of her own earnings record.

All these elements—the long-term trends and the postwar changes—have direct and obvious implications for the costs of pension systems. Two further changes have important implications for other aspects of pension design.

A changing international environment. Alongside reduced restrictions on international trade and finance has come an increasing awareness of international labor mobility. The practice of migrating to another country, working there, and sometimes returning to one's country of origin has a longer history than these other manifestations of globalization: for example, many of the early English settlers in what is now the United States followed this strategy. How pension systems deal with prime-age immigrants, who naturally tend to have shorter careers in the destination country than the native born, has received relatively little attention. But as pension systems have grown, incomplete entitlements become a greater perceived problem. Thus the treatment of migrants and—a related issue—the international portability of pension rights are becoming, and will continue to become, more salient. A major manifestation is the unresolved issue today of how to organize pension rights within the wider European Union.

More-fluid family structures. In many countries the nuclear family has neither the stability nor the numerical dominance it had fifty years ago. In a world where most people married and stayed married, the most common reason for women being single was widowhood, which could be addressed by including widows' benefits in the pension system. Today, in addition, many women are single after a divorce or never marry at all. In the United Kingdom something like 40 percent of mothers can now expect to be single mothers for some part of their adult life. Of that total, about half will be single parents for more than five years (Ermisch and Francesconi 2000). Pension systems need to be redesigned to accommodate the greater diversity of living arrangements, both across individuals and across a single individual's life. In countries where, traditionally, support for the elderly was largely through the extended family, rural-urban migration and, in some countries (such as China), much smaller families increase the importance of pension systems in filling the growing gaps.

11.2 ISSUES AND RESPONSES

The economic and social context in which pensions operate today is thus very different from that of 1950: the economic and social environment is different; there has been a natural maturing of pension systems, altering the economic and political menus of feasible changes; and change is required to accommodate long-run trends. In this section we consider some issues arising from these factors that policymakers in many countries have faced over the last sixty years. We discuss in turn developments in pension systems and design (section 11.2.1), the menu of economic options for adjusting pension systems to long-term trends (section 11.2.2), and political aspects of adjustment (section 11.2.3).

11.2.1 Developments in pension systems and design

Notwithstanding considerable differences across countries, a number of developments since World War II are common to many, including growth in the scale of pension systems, measures to address gaps in coverage, the indexation of pension benefits to rising wages and prices, adjustments to achieve gender balance, and, in some countries, the introduction of notional defined-contribution pensions (see glossary). Alongside these changes, which mainly concern public systems, are two further developments: the introduction of mandatory individual accounts, along with measures to address their administrative costs, and efforts to strengthen the governance of private pensions.

Growth in the size and extent of coverage of pension systems. Even in the developed countries, most pension systems before World War II covered relatively few people and provided relatively modest benefits. Systems tended to cover urban workers but not workers in agriculture and often not the self-employed, a nontrivial omission since agriculture generally employed a larger fraction of the labor force than today. The first figure in Box 7.2 shows how small the transfer was to early cohorts in the U.S. Social Security system. The extension of pension systems, both in their coverage and in the replacement rate they offer, has been a widespread feature of postwar policy. Wider coverage has made systems more expensive and increased the importance of managing the politics of reform effectively.

Addressing gaps in coverage. A major goal of mandatory pension systems is the reduction of elderly poverty, often accompanied by decreased reliance on means-tested programs outside the pension system, which involve stigma and have higher administrative costs. Lower poverty rates have been an important accomplishment of systems with wide coverage, and the expansion of coverage beyond urban employees, mentioned above, was an important part of the accomplishment. But the need for income-tested support for the elderly remains. Part of this need derives from incomplete individual histories of employment in the covered labor market (that is, from incomplete contributions records). Incomplete coverage arises in countries with immature pension systems and in developing countries with limited institutional capacity, a large informal sector, or both. However, it also comes from fragmented careers even in countries with nearly full coverage. Thus it is no accident that even in developed countries not all workers have a full contributions record. In 2005 in the United Kingdom—a country with a mature system and strong capacity to enforce contributions—only about 85 percent of recent male retirees and 30 percent of female retirees were entitled to a full basic state pension.

As the Presidential Advisory Council in Chile correctly realized, it is thus mistaken to imagine that better administration is a complete solution to problems of coverage:

> The prevailing image at the time of the pension reform [in Chile in 1981], of a workforce composed mainly of male heads of household, with permanent jobs, contributing continuously throughout their active lives, has become less and less representative of the real situation of the country and will become even less so in the future. This means that the system designed at that point in time is also gradually losing its ability to respond to the needs of the population as a whole.[1]

The implication is that the design of pension systems should recognize that gaps in contributions will occur. One approach has been to adjust the rules of the contributions regime, for example by granting contribution credits, supplemented by income-tested poverty relief, to people who are unemployed or caring for young children. Another has been to reduce the number of years of work necessary to qualify for a pension. Also under this head, a few countries now take account of contributions to public pensions in other countries, to reflect migration.

A different approach, recognizing that gaps in contributions are unavoidable in a modern economy, is to introduce a noncontributory universal pension to assist in covering women, people with fragmented careers, and workers in the informal sector. Australia, New Zealand, and the Netherlands have adopted this type of pension, and Chile introduced one in 2008. South Africa (Box 11.3) illustrates how a noncontributory universal pension can work in a developing country and can be extended to the rural population.

Indexing benefits to rising wages and prices. The use of indexing to offset the impact of inflation on the purchasing power of pension benefits during retirement is key to ensuring that benefits can be relied on to maintain a given level of consumption. Many countries have incorporated such indexing, sometimes to prices, sometimes to wages, and sometimes to a mix as systems have matured. In its absence, inflation alone can "cure" the financial shortages of pension systems—and went a long way toward doing so in some of the former communist countries—but that is obviously bad policy.

---

1. "La imagen predominante en la época de la reforma previsional de una fuerza laboral compuesta mayoritariamente por hombres jefes de hogar, con empleos indefinidos, cotizando en forma continua a lo largo de su vida activa, se ha ido volviendo menos representativa de la realidad del país y lo será aún menos en el futuro. Esto hace que el sistema entonces diseñado también vaya perdiendo capacidad para responder a las necesidades del conjunto de la población." (Chile Presidential Advisory Council 2006*a*, p. 6)

In addition to indexing benefits during retirement, many countries now index contributions or earnings records during working life, usually to wages, thus taking account of wage growth over a worker's career when determining his or her initial benefit and avoiding the uncertain impacts of inflation on the real value of initial benefits. Again, as a result, the political process has to address explicitly any financial shortfalls in the pension system rather than rely on inflation to take care of imbalances.

A change in the basis of indexation can have significant effects. In the latter part of the 1980s, reforms in the United Kingdom indexed the basic state pension to changes in prices rather than (as previously) to wages. As a result, the replacement rate offered by the basic pension fell from around 20 percent of average earnings in the mid-1980s to 16 percent in 2002 (U.K. Pensions Commission 2004b, Figure F.3) and is anticipated to continue to fall as long as price indexing remains in effect.

Adjusting gender balance. The last half century has seen growing concern for the position of women, growth in labor force participation by women, a rise in divorce rates, and a shrinkage in marriage in many countries. This has led many countries to move their pensions either toward or all the way to gender neutrality in legal structure. The United Kingdom, for example, is moving toward a common retirement age for men and women. The increased fluidity of family structures means that basing a woman's benefits substantially on her husband's contributions is increasingly unsatisfactory. Because of changed attitudes, with increasing emphasis on the rights of women as citizens, it is also widely regarded as undesirable.[2] We argue in section 8.3 that pension systems should seek to be gender neutral but should also recognize the existence of families. Thus pension design should protect the rights of spouses in respect of the death of one member of a couple and of divorce. One example, that of the United States, is outlined in Boxes 8.2 and 8.3. A separate issue is whether, how, and to what extent a pension system should recognize years spent caring for children. Several countries have done so explicitly, including Canada, Sweden, and the United Kingdom. As discussed in section 8.3.2, there are different ways of designing such recognition.

Introducing notional defined-contribution pensions. A recent innovation in pension design, notional defined-contribution (NDC) pensions were invented and implemented roughly simultaneously (but somewhat differently) in Italy and Sweden. At their root, as discussed in section 3.4, NDC pensions are organized on a PAYG basis, but they mimic funded individual accounts in that benefits are strictly related to a person's previous contributions, using a government-selected notional rate of interest rather than a market rate of return. Several other countries have since introduced pensions organized on that basis, including a number of the reforming former communist countries. The innovative parts of this design are the use of a defined-contribution vocabulary within a PAYG system, and the related adjustment of benefits for life expectancy. Reliance on an indexed sum of all earnings has long been part of the system in France and Germany (Legros 2006).

---

2. In the United Kingdom until 1978, a married woman could opt to pay a greatly reduced national insurance contribution, which gave no entitlement to a pension, on the grounds that she was covered by her husband's contribution. Such an arrangement today would be unthinkable, as well as a violation of EU law.

Addressing the administrative costs of individual accounts. Administrative costs, although seemingly a narrow technical matter, have important policy ramifications. As illustrated in Table 9.1, an annual management charge of 1 percent reduces a person's pension accumulation, and hence that person's monthly benefit, by about 20 percent over a full career. When Chile introduced funded individual accounts in 1981, some analysts thought that market competition would result in low administrative costs. That has not been the case either in Chile or in the other countries that imitated Chile, except for Bolivia (Box 11.2), which did not follow Chile's reliance on the market but instead established government-organized bidding for the right to handle workers' accounts. As a result, policy in Chile has seen repeated changes in the regulations for individual accounts in the hope of reducing costs. As discussed in section 9.2.3, individual accounts that allow a choice of provider or of portfolio in the market have high administrative costs, which, moreover, consist largely of a fixed overhead per account and hence are a greater burden for smaller accumulations. Thus policies aimed at strengthening competition have been advocated and tried but, in the absence of stringent regulation, have not been very successful; for the reasons set out in section 9.3, this is not surprising.

In response to increasing awareness both of the existence of these costs and of their size, countries have explored other ways of reducing them, as discussed in section 9.2. Sweden has centralized much of the administration of pensions, which it combines with price controls. The United States has combined centralization with very limited individual choice, but only for federal civil servants, not the entire working population (Box 11.5). A similar proposal in the United Kingdom includes simple personal accounts (U.K. Pensions Commission 2005, U.K. Department for Work and Pensions 2006*a*).

A system with a government-selected portfolio can have lower transactions costs but can easily have a low rate of return as well. The approach can be implemented through individual accounts or through a trust fund for a defined-benefit system. The quality of investment historically has been very mixed. In the past some countries have done poorly with centralized investment.[3] But with a greater recent focus on the incentives and transparency of the process of such investment, some countries have seen returns comparable to those of private investors. Good-quality investment is more likely with full and transparent accounting, including a clear and explicit mandate, independent non-political management, and detailed, published, audited accounts (see, for example, Norway Central Bank 2006). However, it is inherently difficult to put in place a system that can ensure sound investment, particularly where experience with such investment is limited.

Strengthening the governance of private pensions. Strengthening the regulation of financial markets generally has been an ongoing and necessary process in all countries, including the most developed. (Box 9.2 illustrates some of the problems in the United Kingdom.) In parallel, many countries have increased the requirement that private pensions be funded and have strengthened their regulation. Some countries have introduced mandatory insurance.[4]

3. See, for example, World Bank (1994, Box 4.5), which shows negative real rates of return over extended periods in a range of countries, the worst being Peru, with a real loss of 37 percent between 1982 and 1988.

4. Examples include the Pension Benefit Guaranty Corporation in the United States, created by the Employee Retirement Income Security Act of 1974, and the Pension Protection Fund in the United Kingdom, established by the Pensions Act 2004.

Strengthening of funding requirements is meant to safeguard the future interests of current workers and to protect government revenue to the extent that the government insures pensions. On the face of it, stringent funding requirements will benefit workers, but as discussed in Box 9.3, it can be counterproductive to impose on employers too much of the cost or too much of the risk, or to require that shortfalls be made up too quickly. Attempts to do so can lead employers to close their plans to new participants and to further contributions from existing ones, and sometimes to replace defined-benefit pensions with a defined-contribution system. The changeover has worked to the detriment of some workers.

11.2.2 Economic adjustment to long-term trends

Over the period since World War II, countries have responded in a range of ways to financial imbalances in their pension systems, which have come primarily from demographic pressures and the long-run decline in labor force participation by older male workers. Few governments would claim that the process is complete.

Faced with ever-larger numbers of pensioners, some policymakers (for example, in some EU countries) at first ignored the problem, paying the increasing deficits out of general taxation. A range of other possible policy directions—higher contributions, lower monthly benefits, and later retirement—are generally more realistic. Economic growth also assists adjustment, and therefore policies to raise output, for example through increased national saving, are also an important part of the picture.

Higher contributions. Contributions have tended to rise in most countries, through higher contribution rates or higher ceilings on the income on which contributions are levied.[5] Although there is room for variation, contribution rates face the constraint of adverse incentive effects, an issue to which countries have recently become more sensitive in the face of international competition. Given the extent of population aging in many countries and high existing contribution rates, higher contributions on their own are not usually a complete solution. Indeed some countries have avoided significant further increases in contribution rates.

Lower monthly benefits. If people live longer and the average retirement age and available financing do not change, the average pension benefit will have to fall. This approach avoids fiscal problems but risks increasing pensioner poverty. In countries with NDC systems, such as Sweden and Poland, benefits fall automatically in response to increased life expectancy (see section 3.4). Because an NDC system is quasi-actuarial, people can offset the decline in benefits by working longer, an option that is relevant also in countries with defined-benefit systems that increase benefits sufficiently for a delayed start. Some workers will respond to lower benefits and actuarial (or nearly actuarial) benefit increases by working longer, mitigating some or all of the decline in replacement rates.

Key to lowering pensions is to spread the decline suitably across cohorts and to give adequate advance notice, while preserving the opportunity for increased saving, more work, or both, to raise replacement rates. The politics of benefit reduction are also easier when the reductions are not imminent—an opportunity when long-run problems are addressed early.

---

5. Ceilings on the earnings relevant for contributions and benefits are discussed in section 5.2.1.

Later retirement. If benefits are roughly actuarial, longer work does not affect the long-run finances of the system. But it does increase the replacement rate, affecting the adequacy of pension benefits. Concern remains about the replacement rates of some workers who would continue to retire as soon as they can. When pensions are being lowered for any given retirement age, it is possible to limit the decline in replacement rates by increasing the earliest entitlement age.

If we were designing a pension system for a new planet whose advanced life forms were living longer and longer, we would not choose an earliest entitlement age that was fixed for all time at some given age. What is needed is a process by which the earliest entitlement age bears a sensible relationship to life expectancy. Governments, lowering monthly benefits in response to cost pressures, are, or will soon be, looking for ways of increasing the employment rates of older workers and, to encourage that trend, will also need to seek ways of encouraging labor market flexibility so that older workers have greater choice over the move from full-time work to full retirement, both over its timing and whether it is immediate or gradual. The analytics of these issues are set out in section 5.3.

Pensions, saving, and growth. Policies to promote economic growth are an important part of the response to demographic trends. One approach is through higher saving out of additional revenue. The Norwegian Government Petroleum Fund (Norway Central Bank 2005, 2006) uses some of the revenue from oil taxation as a buffer against demographic change. The United States has built up a trust fund, with payroll tax rates set above what was needed to cover expenditure, to be drawn down as part of accommodating the retirement of the baby-boomers.[6] Chile switched to funded individual accounts while financing benefits under the old system out of general revenue.

A parallel concern is to devise broader strategies to promote growth:

- Measures that can increase worker productivity include policies that encourage investment in more and better capital equipment, improve the allocation of capital through better capital markets and tax policies, improve the quality of the labor force through more education and training, and improve labor mobility to allow a more productive allocation of labor.

- Measures that can increase the number of workers from each age cohort include policies to increase labor supply (for example, that of married women by offering better child care facilities), to raise the average age of retirement, to encourage higher fertility, and to import labor.

The message for policymakers is to consider the entire menu of pro-growth policies.

11.2.3   The politics of adjustment

Political cultures vary widely: politics can be more adversarial or more consensual, and more top-down or more grassroots; public willingness to become seriously engaged in debates about policy can be higher or lower. The United Kingdom and the United States share an adversarial tradition, whereas debates in countries like Norway and Sweden, with their more consensual political culture, have taken a different form.

---

6. The extent to which the build-up of the trust fund has added to national saving, given the politics of the rest of the government budget, is unclear and a matter of dispute.

The Swedish reforms that resulted in their NDC system in 1998 were based on a long period of political debate and public discussion. Interestingly, Sweden held two parliamentary votes: the first on the principle of moving to NDC pensions, and the second, at a later stage, on the specific system to be implemented. This approach is intended to avoid the situation where a reform fails because, although everyone supports the whole, a majority votes against the specific part that affects them negatively—by analogy, everyone supports the need for garbage dumps, but not in their own back yard. Norway adopted a similar process in debating pension reform, ending up with a consensus of all parties except one on each end of the political spectrum (see Grønvik 2006).

Pensions affect many people over many years, and therefore changes require a clear strategy supported by much detailed work. But raising taxes, reducing benefits (even future benefits), and increasing the earliest entitlement age are all politically difficult—and made no easier because public debate often fails to distinguish among an increase in earliest entitlement age, an increase in the normal retirement age, and any changes in the way benefits are determined for delayed retirement. Thus governments often find it useful—both to garner the necessary expertise and to provide political insulation—to set up a commission to assess the situation and make recommendations. The United States, the United Kingdom, and Germany, among other countries, have looked to commissions headed by persons other than elected officials to help with their adversarial political process. We briefly review four such commissions.

United States: The Greenspan Commission. From the creation of Social Security in 1935 until 1972, many rounds of legislation expanded coverage and raised benefits and taxes. The 1972 legislation included a real increase in benefits and the first automatic indexing of the system for inflation. As detailed in Box 5.6, however, this indexing was not done correctly. Thus by 1977 a projected Social Security deficit would have forced benefit cuts within five years, and the projected deficit over the standard seventy-five-year projection period would have required a 75 percent increase in the payroll tax rate to provide the scheduled benefits. The clear need for reform in the short term and the recognition of error in the 1972 legislation contributed to a bipartisan approach to reform, resulting in legislation in 1977 that created the basic structure of the current system. However, because the financial imbalance was so large, the intention was to squeeze through the short term and to cover a substantial period, but less than the full seventy-five years. The legislation might just have met this goal but for the deep recession of the early 1980s, which made the short-run finances untenable. It thus became necessary to review benefits and taxes only a few years later.

This time the process was more contentious, and several attempts to generate legislation failed. An initial proposal by the Reagan administration (elected in 1980) without adequate public and political preliminaries was met by a partisan political response that contributed to severe losses to Reagan's party in the 1982 congressional elections. By 1983 the long-run projected financial shortfall was roughly one-quarter what it had been in 1977, but the system was expected to run short of money, and hence to have to cut benefits, that spring. Some combination of benefit cuts and tax increases was needed quickly. Since the voters had already shown their strong disapproval of elected officials who propose such changes, a bipartisan approach was needed to leave neither party standing alone in the vulnerable position of having inflicted pain.

With that political stimulus, a compromise was reached, a key role being played by a bipartisan commission headed by Alan Greenspan—not yet the world-famous star of the Federal Reserve System. The commission included members appointed by both parties, who stayed in close contact with the party leaders.[7]

The bipartisan solution included measures to increase revenue and measures to reduce benefits in roughly equal proportions. Some of these changes were needed in the short run given the precarious short-run finances. Others were phased in over decades to achieve balance over the traditional seventy-five-year horizon.

This experience offers three possible lessons for countries with adversarial two-party politics. First, the political momentum to respond to a financial shortfall in the public pension system will generally be lacking until the impact on financing is imminent. Second, a bipartisan (or, in some countries, multipartisan) commission can be useful in breaking the political impasse. And third, the approach to legislation needs to be genuinely nonpartisan.

United States: The Commission to Strengthen Social Security. The 1983 legislation was barely sufficient to cover the standard seventy-five-year projection, and the years just beyond the projection horizon showed large deficits. Thus the rolling seventy-five-year projections soon showed deficits again, but very far in the future.[8] From the mid-1980s until the 2000 presidential election, there was considerable public discussion of Social Security shortfalls and various proposed reforms, but no serious attempt at legislation. The Clinton administration offered part of a plan to restore actuarial balance, and President Bill Clinton devoted considerable time to public education on the issue. Also, starting in the early 1980s, conservative think tanks pushed for the adoption of Chilean-type individual accounts.

During the 2000 presidential campaign, Governor George W. Bush said he would appoint a commission to propose a reform that complied with a number of principles, including funded individual accounts and no tax increases. After his election as president, Bush appointed a commission that was bipartisan in the sense that its membership included both Republicans and Democrats, but unlike the Greenspan Commission, all were appointed by the administration, and thus the commission did not really represent both political parties. Because of the terrorist attacks of September 11, 2001, Social Security reform was largely set to one side until after the 2004 election. President Bush then made it his primary domestic policy goal and launched an intensive campaign to present his approach to the public. Although he did not put forward a complete plan, Bush drew heavily on the recommendations of the commission and brought commission members to attend his public appearances. However, public support for his approach was never widespread or durable, and it decreased through the period of his public advocacy. Thus, in addition to confirming the three political lessons already mentioned, and redefining the meaning of "bipartisan" in "bipartisan commission," this experience may have

---

7. For a detailed description of the Greenspan Commission's work, see Light (1985).

8. This experience has led to a revision of the standard criterion of seventy-five-year balance, referred to as actuarial balance, to the criterion of *sustainable* actuarial balance, which supplements the standard criterion with the further condition that the trust fund not be declining at the end of the projection period. It also led to more attention to infinite-horizon projections to supplement the seventy-five-year projection. See the discussion of the open group method in section 6.2.1.

illustrated that replacing part of the U.S. defined-benefit system with individual accounts, with no additional funding, was not acceptable to the American public.[9]

The U.K. Pensions Commission. In 2002 a commission was established to address problems in the U.K. public pension system, notably the high rate of pensioner poverty, the heavy and growing reliance on means testing, and low rates of pension saving. The commission's core recommendations (U.K. Pensions Commission 2004*a*, 2004*b*, 2005) were a phased increase in the level of the basic state pension; a phased increase in the pensionable age to 66 in 2024, rising thereafter by one year every decade; and the introduction of simple personal accounts with many of the characteristics of the U.S. Thrift Savings Plan for federal employees (Box 11.5), including limited choice for workers from a small number of funds, centralized account administration, and wholesale fund management.

The commission offers some useful lessons:

- It took a strategic view, looking at the pension system as a whole; thus its recommendations were likewise strategic.

- It drew some of its staff from the Department for Work and Pensions and thus had a capacity for detailed analysis.

- The commission's first report, published in 2004, focused on diagnosis and potential options. This was politically astute. One of the options was an increase in the pensionable age, hitherto a political minefield. The measured tone of the first report and the commission's subsequent public discussion were instrumental in changing attitudes.

- The increase in the pensionable age recommended in the second report, published in 2005, was sufficiently far in the future that, in public briefings, the chair could say, "if you are over 50 this won't affect you; if you are in your forties you will have to work for an extra year." This long notice did a great deal to lower the political temperature.

- As part of its initial agreement with the government, the commission's finances allowed it to maintain a reduced staff for six months after its second report was published, to give it the capacity to respond—and to continue to respond—to the misinformation, disinformation, and special pleading that inevitably results from such reform proposals.

The German Commission for Sustainability in Financing the Social Security System. The German public pension system experienced a financial crisis in 2002, mainly because of the unexpectedly long and deep downturn after the unification boom.[10] To keep the system afloat, the majority partner in the governing coalition (the Social Democrats) proposed an increase in the contribution rate; this move was opposed by the junior partner (the Green Party), which had promised to improve the financial sustainability of the system. The coalition ended up agreeing on a package with increased contributions in the short run and a review of the entire system.

9. For further discussion of the commission's recommendations, see U.S. President's Commission (2001), and for a critique, Diamond and Orszag (2002).

10. We are grateful to Axel Börsch-Supan for providing the text on which this discussion is based.

The commission, chaired by a Social Democratic academic, Bert Rürup, comprised academics, businesspeople, representatives of public interest groups (including the employers' federation and the trades unions), and representatives of the public pension administration, a total of twenty-four people. The commission had three working groups: on public pensions, health insurance, and long-term care insurance, each with two co-chairs chosen to represent opposing views.

The subcommissions on health insurance and long-term care insurance quickly split into two camps, ultimately issuing carefully worded summaries of why they agreed to disagree. The pensions subcommission, however, succeeded in agreeing on a recommended reform package, building on the multipillar system introduced three years earlier by then labor minister Walter Riester.

The recommendations, published in 2003, had three elements:

- Future benefits would be indexed to a weighted mix of wages and the inverse system dependency ratio (the number of workers divided by number of pensioners). This would convert the traditional defined-benefit system into one that resembled an NDC system, in that population aging would automatically reduce pension benefits to keep the system in financial balance.
- The normal retirement age would be increased from 65 to 67 between 2011 and 2035.
- The rules for private pensions would be relaxed to encourage greater participation.

Unlike the proposals for health and long-term care insurance, these three elements were supported by a large majority in the commission and adopted by the Bundestag in 2004; only the unpopular increase in the retirement age had to wait until 2007 to be ratified.

The reform reduced the implicit debt of the German public pension system by about 50 percent, and savings in publicly subsidized private pensions tripled between 2004 and 2007. Retirement patterns changed as well, partly because of earlier reforms, and partly because of a change in attitudes about older workers brought about by the emotional public debate over later retirement that started after the commission's work had ended.

It is hard to assess why the pensions subcommission was successful in bringing about reform while the other two subcommissions failed. One reason may have been early agreement among the academic members not to entrench themselves in extreme positions; they then tried to pull the political actors toward the same middle ground. Another possible reason is that the press focused all its attention on the bitter debate over health care, leaving little room for public discussion of pensions. Finally, the arguments in the pension subcommission quickly turned toward how to rationalize the country's rule-bound pension policy, leaving little room for ideological debate.

11.3 POLICY ERRORS

The discussion of analytical errors in Box 10.1 is paralleled here by one of policy errors—often the result of analytical errors—which have affected adjustment to long-term trends. Once more, the World Bank, a highly influential actor in pension reform internationally, provides illustrations. The bank, however, was far from alone (see, for example, Piñera 1995). In addition, the bank was often right in diagnosing a clear need for reform of previous pension arrangements, which in many countries combined high fiscal costs with limited coverage and poor incentives. Finally, one of the most forceful recent diagnoses of errors, encapsulated in Box 11.1, is an assessment by the bank of its own pensions work.[11] In what follows we discuss policy errors and then point to some overoptimistic predictions.

11.3.1 Policy problems

Inadequate attention to poverty relief. This problem is largely a consequence of inadequate attention to the whole range of pension objectives, with distributional effects especially likely to be ignored. Policy discussion tends to focus heavily on fiscal sustainability, leading policymakers to take their eye off the ball of poverty relief. The problem has come to be recognized: "The main problem regarding Peru's pension system was not that it was spending 1.2 percent of GDP . . . but, rather, that coverage was so low that the basic goal of a pension system—to provide income security to the old—was far from being accomplished" (Rofman 2007, para. 5.4), and Gill, Packard, and Yermo (2005, p. 11) write, "First, and most important, the poverty prevention pillar should get a lot more attention than it has in Latin America during the last decade."

Similarly, the Presidential Advisory Council in Chile, discussed in more detail in Chapter 13, recognized that,

> If things go on as they are, it is estimated that within 20 years, only about half of all older adults will be able to count on a pension higher than the minimum . . . [leading to] about a million people with pensions below the minimum in 2025. Among those at highest risk of finding themselves in this situation are low-income workers, seasonal workers, the self-employed and a considerable proportion of women.[12]

Inadequate emphasis on implementation. The analysis in Chapter 9 places heavy weight on the preconditions necessary for effective implementation of a pension reform, especially such a demanding reform as a move to individual funded accounts. As discussed below, many reforms have taken a more optimistic view than we would about the extent to which a country meets the preconditions.

Individual funded accounts require financial institutions that are effective enough that the added weight of pension business will further strengthen them. Yet "the Bank persistently encouraged countries such as Ukraine and Russia to institute multi-pillar reforms even when financial sector conditions were weak" (World Bank 2006a, p. 56); it also encouraged such reforms in countries with poor corruption indexes (World Bank 2006a, Figure 3.5).

11. See, in particular, World Bank (2006a), summarized in World Bank (2006b) and Gill, Packard, and Yermo (2005). See also the background papers written for World Bank (2006a) by Rofman (2007) and Valdés-Prieto (2007a, 2007b). Also relevant are Devesa-Carpio and Vidal-Meliá (2002), Rofman and Lucchetti (2006), and von Gersdorff (1997).

12. "De seguir las cosas como están, se estima que dentro de 20 años sólo alrededor de la mitad de los adultos mayores podrá contar con una pensión superior a la pensión mínima. . . . Esto significa cerca de un millón de personas con pensiones inferiores a la mínima en 2025. Entre quienes se encuentran en mayor riesgo de encontrarse en esta situación se cuentan los trabajadores de bajos ingresos, los temporeros, los trabajadores por cuenta propia y una importante proporción de las mujeres." (Chile Presidential Advisory Council 2006a, p. 7).

▶ Box 11.1 World Bank diagnosis of errors in pensions policy

A 2006 World Bank study identified a number of policy errors committed by the Bank in its pensions work in a range of countries, powerfully summarized in the list of figures in the study's table of contents (World Bank 2006a, p. v), of which the following are examples:

Figures

2.1 More Sector Work Addressed Fiscal Issues and Transition Costs, and Fewer Reports Discussed Public Administration
3.1 Many Countries Had High Inflation at Reform
3.2 Several Countries Had High Budget Deficits at the Time of Their Pension Reform
3.3 Poor Financial Sectors Characterize Some Europe and Central Asia Multi-Pillar Reformers
3.5 Many Reformers Had Poor Corruption Indexes at the Time of Reform
3.6 Corruption Ratings Are Poor among Some Potential Reformers
3.7 Some Multi-Pillar Countries Already Had High Savings Rates
4.2 Fiscal Deficits Have Grown in Many Countries with Second Pillars
4.3 Savings Rates Increased Only in Kazakhstan
4.4 Market Capitalization Remains Quite Low
4.5 Post-Crisis Pension Portfolios in Argentina Fled to Government Bonds
4.6 Pension Participation Rates Have Not Changed in Latin America and the Caribbean ◀

Insufficient weight was given to the administrative costs of individual accounts, costs that are significant even in large, developed countries with long-established systems (such as the United Kingdom's personal accounts for people who opt out of the state earnings-related pension, and the voluntary Individual Retirement Accounts in the United States) and considerably higher for small accounts in small countries starting a new system.

The administrative capacity of government is also important, yet,

the limited quality of civil records in Bolivia allowed people to change their age and even to invent beneficiaries of the ... program. Second, the ... state did not have a bureaucracy in place that was capable of actually distributing the Bonosol [pension benefit] to the elderly, many of whom had to travel from the countryside on foot to collect the benefit in person. (Valdés-Prieto 2007b, para. 3.61)[13]

Political implementation is equally important. Yet,

The Bank, the designers of the Bonosol program and outside observers failed to see one pitfall. Future governments could increase the size of Bonosol payouts in electoral years. ... In fact, the government chose to maximize the electoral impact of this reform, by paying out the first Bonosol (a single annual lump sum) just one month before the 1997 election ... [so that] the 1998 payment had to be suspended. (Valdés-Prieto 2007b, paras 3.63-64)

13. Another example, although less important, illustrates the same point. We have mentioned the importance of adequate projections of future costs. The World Bank's Pension Reform Simulation Toolkit (PROST) model assists countries in doing this. Again, however, not enough attention was paid to government's technical capacity, so that, "some countries could not implement PROST because of too few trained professionals" (World Bank 2006a, p. xxv).

Failure to address acknowledged problems. When a system is on an unsustainable trajectory, delay in addressing long-run problems increases the size of the changes that will be required later. When a system has elements of poor design (for example, inefficient retirement incentives), the economy bears the resulting costs, as reform is delayed. Moreover, those costs are likely to continue for some time after a reform, since changes may be phased in slowly to benefit workers who anticipated gaining from the poor design elements, such as an unduly attractive early retirement option.

11.3.2 Overoptimistic predictions

How have outcomes compared with predictions?

Replacement rates. "The replacement rates envisioned by policymakers setting the contribution parameters of the new multipillar systems ranged from 60 percent to 70 percent of some average of earnings prior to retirement" (Gill, Packard, and Yermo 2005, p. 225; see also Piñera 1995). These projections often turned out to be optimistic, in part because financial returns were lower than predicted, in part because projections were often of gross returns (ignoring administrative charges), and in part because some predictions were based on naïve arguments about the beneficial effects of competition on costs and charges. Argentina is perhaps the most striking example. But Argentina is far from alone: "In Chile in early 2002 civil servants started demonstrations demanding to be allowed to switch back to the pre-reform PAYG regime as a result of disappointing projected replacement rates from individual accounts" (Gill, Packard, and Yermo 2005, p. 15).

Coverage. The predicted expansion of coverage from conversion to individual accounts has not happened. "Low rates of coverage of the working population under pure PAYG systems were a strong motivating factor for pension reform" (Gill, Packard, and Yermo 2005, p. 96), the argument being that "the close link between contributions and benefits... should discourage evasion, escape to the informal sector, and other labor market distortions" (James 1998, p. 276).

For the reasons set out in section 5.2.2, this argument does not hold in theory and has been falsified in practice. Arenas de Mesa and Mesa-Lago (2006, Table 1; see also Rofman and Lucchetti 2006) compare coverage in Latin America at the time each country reformed with coverage in 2004. Coverage actually declined in all countries: in Argentina from 50 percent to 21 percent, in Mexico from 37 to 28 percent, and in Peru from 31 to 12 percent. Coverage in Chile also fell, but only slightly. Thus,

> Stalled progress with ... increasing coverage, is cause for concern among the region's governments. The share of the workforce that contributes to a formal pension system remains low. ... In several Latin American countries the share of the elderly population receiving pension benefits is falling. For at least some individuals the new funded, privately managed individual savings pillars are not as attractive as they are made out to be. (Gill, Packard, and Yermo 2005, p. 125)

Transition costs. The fiscal cost of reform is important, yet there was a tendency to underestimate both the size and the duration of the costs of transition from PAYG to funded systems (see Devesa-Carpio and Vidal-Meliá 2002). Transition costs for Bolivia were projected in 1997 to peak in 1999 at about 2.6 percent of GDP and decline thereafter (von Gersdorff 1997, p. 20). In reality, "a major flaw in design encouraged a surge in early pensions and . . . a sequence of pension policy decisions raised the actual transition deficit by 2.6 percentage points of GDP (as of 2002) above the level planned in mid-1996" (Valdés-Prieto 2007a, para. 3.79).

Financing transition costs was a particular problem where a move to funding was initiated at a time of fiscal deficit: "Bolivia, Kazakhstan, Latvia, and Romania had budget deficits over 3 percent of GDP, an indicator that fiscal conditions for implementation of a funded system were not ideal" (World Bank 2006a, p. 22). Not least because of these fiscal costs, the International Monetary Fund has tended to be less enthusiastic in recommending funded pensions than has the World Bank.

Transition costs have been high and persistent. The system in Chile, although eminently sustainable, continues to require significant annual public spending, averaging 5.7 percent of GDP between 1981 and 2004, with projected spending from 2004 through 2010 of 5 percent of GDP, as noted in section 12.2.6. These costs are higher than were forecast during the 1980s (Devesa-Carpio and Vidal-Meliá 2002, p. 29).

Economic growth. Claims that pension reform would boost economic growth have mostly not been fulfilled: "The Bank has also emphasized the pro-growth aspects of multi-pillar reform—that is, increased savings and capital market development. But the . . . [bank's internal] evaluation found few countries in which these promised outcomes have been achieved" (World Bank 2006a, p. 56).

In sum. Its proponents predicted that

A mandatory multipillar arrangement for old age security helps countries to . . .

- Achieve a close relationship between incremental contributions and benefits in the private mandatory pillar. This should reduce effective tax rates, evasion, and labor market distortions.
- Increase long-term saving, capital market deepening, and growth, through the use of full funding and decentralized control in the second pillar. . . .
- Insulate the system from political pressures for design features that are inefficient as well as inequitable.

The broader economy should be better off in the long run as a result. So should both the old and the young. (World Bank 1994, pp. 22–23)

What happened? While some of this has occurred, it has been far from universal:

In many countries with multi-pillar systems . . . investments in privately funded pillars are not well diversified, although rates of return are high as a result of investments in government bonds. While these bonds offer high returns, they often just compensate for macroeconomic and investment risk. In addition, privately funded systems remained open to political influence, just like PAYG plans, particularly in times of economic crisis. (World Bank 2006a, p. xxiv)

11.4 PENSION SYSTEMS IN DIFFERENT COUNTRIES

Pension systems differ widely across countries. There is no dominant arrangement worldwide. At a strategic level, a country's pension arrangements reflect the relative

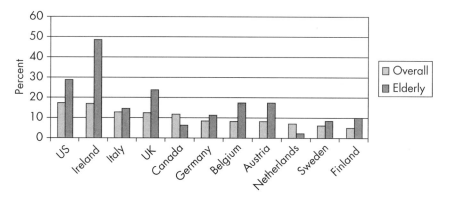

FIGURE 11.2.
Population living on less than half the median income in selected OECD countries, 2000. *Source:* Luxembourg Income Study.

weights attached to its various objectives. One reflection of the differences in these weights is the poverty rate among the elderly relative to that among the working-age population, which varies greatly, as shown in Figure 11.2.

Countries have chosen systems that vary from more or less pure consumption smoothing, in the form of mandatory saving with little or no insurance (for example, Singapore's publicly administered provident fund, which is in essence a savings plan), to a primary concern for poverty relief, achieved through a noncontributory flat-rate pension, with any consumption smoothing done on a voluntary basis (as in New Zealand). In between, a wide range of systems explicitly address both objectives, some with substantial reliance on funding (Chile), others with intermediate reliance on funding (Sweden, the United States), and others established mainly on a PAYG basis (France, Germany, Italy). The Netherlands has a noncontributory PAYG universal pension based on years of residence, together with funded occupational pensions. Reforms in Chile, discussed in Chapter 13, introduce a noncontributory PAYG basic pension alongside the existing system of individual funded accounts, thus strengthening poverty relief. In short, countries have successfully implemented pension systems using very different mixes of structures. This section briefly describes some of them.[14]

14. For an international comparison that classifies systems by the extent to which pensions are earnings related, see U.K. Pensions Commission (2004*b*, Appendix D); on the OECD countries and the European transition countries, see OECD (2004*c*), Queisser and Whitehouse (2006), and Whiteford and Whitehouse (2006). For recent assessments of developments in the United States and the United Kingdom, see Thompson (2006) and Hills (2006), respectively, and on the welfare state in the European Union, Pestieau (2006). On Latin America see Arenas de Mesa and Mesa-Lago (2006) and Mesa-Lago (2007). See also the other papers in the symposium in *Oxford Review of Economic Policy*, vol. 22, no. 1, Spring 2006. For useful institutional description see OECD (2007) and U.S. Social Security Administration (2007*b*). For links to descriptions provided by agencies and organizations, see "Social Security in Other Countries" at the U.S. Social Security website (www.ssa.gov/international/links.html). See also the resources in AARP's Global Aging Program at www.aarp.org/research/international/map/. For an overview, see Whiteford and Whitehouse (2006, Tables 2 and 3).

11.4.1 Argentina

Argentina reformed its pension system in 1994, using both a defined-benefit PAYG public pension and mandatory individual funded accounts. There is a statutory retirement age of 65 for men, 60 for women. The reforms made heavy demands on both financial and technical capacity, and the system was not able to withstand economic crisis in 2001.[15] As a response to the economic emergency, the government obliged the pension funds to swap the dollar-denominated bonds they were holding for newly issued peso-denominated bonds. The proper valuation of the new bonds created continuing problems, since their value depended on the credibility of government policies.

A further problem, largely inherent in a contributory system in a country with a large informal sector, is low compliance with contribution conditions. As a consequence, many workers are unable to meet the requirement in Argentina of at least thirty years of contributions to qualify for any benefit, and this limits the effectiveness of the system at providing poverty relief.

The Argentinean experience suggests three sets of lessons. It illustrates the risk of embarking on overambitious reforms, or on reforms that, although plausible on the basis of optimistic assumptions, are not sufficiently robust in the face of economic turbulence. It also shows the related danger of political interference during economic crisis, which can affect both defined-benefit and defined-contribution systems. Finally, it highlights the importance of compliance for ensuring that the coverage of the system in practice does not deviate substantially from that on paper.

11.4.2 Chile

Chapters 12 and 13 discuss the system in Chile, so the discussion here is brief.[16] The root of the system, similar to that in Singapore, is mandatory saving. Chile, however, relies on competitive private supply, with free entry for any firm that can meet the regulatory requirements, together with considerable regulation. The post-1981 system comprised privately managed, defined-contribution, individual accounts, with employees mandated to contribute 10 percent of covered earnings, plus contributions for disability and survivor insurance and fees for providers. Workers may take their pensions as inflation-indexed annuities or as phased withdrawals.

The individual accounts provide consumption smoothing, supported by various institutions to assist poverty relief. Until 2008 a minimum pension guarantee, financed from general revenue, was available for those who had contributed to the mandatory system for at least twenty years; in addition, a means-tested pension, also financed by general revenue, paid a benefit at about half the level of the minimum guarantee. Beginning in 2008, the minimum guarantee and the means-tested pension were progressively replaced by a noncontributory basic pension.

---

15. Some commentators argue that the financial demands of the pension reform contributed causally to the economic collapse, a conjecture on which the jury is still out. For fuller discussion of the Argentinean reforms, see Bertranou, Rofman, and Grushka (2003), Arza (2006) and, for a broader assessment of experience in Latin America, Gill, Packard, and Yermo (2005).

16. See also Diamond and Valdés-Prieto (1994), Edwards and Edwards (2002), and, for fuller discussion of Chile in the broader Latin American context, Gill, Packard, and Yermo (2005), Arenas de Mesa and Mesa-Lago (2006), and Mesa-Lago (2007).

▶ Box 11.2 Pensions in Bolivia

In 1996, using funds from the privatization of state-owned enterprises, Bolivia created a noncontributory pension (Bonosol) for resident citizens above age 65.* At the same time, like many other countries in Latin American, Bolivia followed Chile in setting up mandatory, funded, individual accounts for salaried workers. Bolivia broke new ground by organizing the mutual funds for these accounts in a way that took cognizance of administrative costs (section 9.2.3) and the small size of the Bolivian market. The system requires contributions of 10 percent of covered earnings, plus 1.71 percent for disability and survivor insurance, and 0.5 percent for administrative charges. As Table 9.2 shows, these administrative charges are considerably lower than in other countries in the region; the comparable figure for administrative charges in Chile is 1.76 percent, and in Peru 2.27 percent.

Rather than allow free entry (subject to regulation) to the industry, Bolivia decided to begin with only two pension providers, each covering half of the country, with competitive bidding for the right to be one of these two firms; the bidding was based on the average monthly management charge per account. The plan was to allow competition between the two starting in 2000 and regulated free entry starting in 2002 (von Gersdorff 1997).

This approach raises two major issues. One is whether the regulatory authorities can ensure an adequate quality of services. As a general proposition, when granting monopoly rights after a bidding process, it is hard to ensure the adequacy of dimensions of service that are not readily measurable and hence are hard to monitor. Second is the issue of whether, having started in this way, the introduction of competition, with the additional costs that will arise from marketing, will preserve the low initial cost structure. In a small market with entrenched incumbents, entry is likely to be limited or nonexistent, and the resulting duopoly is not likely to behave very differently from a monopoly. ◀

---

*For assessments, see Escobar and Osvaldo (2004), Leach (1998), Martinez (2004), and von Gersdorff (1997). The pension was stopped in 1998 and reintroduced in 2002. At the time of writing, Bolivia was planning to replace the annual Bonosol with a more generous monthly payment.

Notwithstanding the intentions of policymakers, private pension provision became highly concentrated, calling into question the plausibility of competition even in a medium-sized economy like Chile. The point is of particular relevance to smaller economies, as discussed in Box 11.2 in the case of Bolivia.

Thus the post-1981 system in Chile gave heavy weight to consumption smoothing, with some insurance through voluntary annuitization and with limited weight to poverty relief. The problems of the system—including a high rate of pensioner poverty, incomplete coverage, gender equity issues, and high administrative charges and fiscal costs—are discussed in Chapter 12. A major set of reforms to the system, including the introduction of a noncontributory basic pension, is discussed in Chapter 13.

11.4.3   China

Since 1997, China has moved from an enterprise-based system of defined-benefit pensions based on final salary toward a unified system for urban workers.[17] The new system

---

17. On China's pension system, discussed in Chapters 14 and 15, see also Drouin and Thompson (2006), Salditt, Whiteford, and Adema (2007), and Williamson (2004).

has three elements: a defined-benefit, PAYG, first-tier pension (the social pool); a mandatory, funded, defined-contribution pension; and voluntary, enterprise-based pensions.

From 1999 onward, coverage was expanded with the intention of including the employees of private and other types of enterprises in urban areas, the self-employed, and (it was hoped) the informal sector. The system is financed by dedicated contributions, mainly from firms and workers, with some financing also from the self-employed and workers in the informal sector.

This system makes long-run strategic sense but has not functioned as intended. The three elements together offer poverty relief, insurance, and consumption smoothing, with some allowance for differing tastes. Problems remain, however, of fragmentation, system financial deficits, problems with individual accounts, and administrative difficulties, as discussed more fully in Chapters 14 and 15.

11.4.4   The Netherlands

The Netherlands has a noncontributory universal pension (that is, one without a contributions or income test) payable at age 65. The full pension is set at a subsistence level, at 70 percent of the net minimum wage. The system differs in two respects from conventional systems of social security. First, the benefit is awarded on the basis of residence, not contributions.[18] Second, the benefit is financed through an earmarked tax, the AOW (*algemene ouderdomswet*, or general law for the elderly) premium, which is additional to, but integrated with, the income tax. The tax base for the AOW premium is income, not earnings, and the premium is paid only by people under 65. A person with insufficient years of residence for a full pension receives a partial pension and is eligible for social assistance if his or her income from all sources is below the subsistence level.

It is interesting to reflect on the nature of the arrangement. From one perspective the benefit is noncontributory, that is, part of a person's rights, hence addressing problems of coverage. On the other hand, it is financed from the AOW premium and so can be regarded as contributory, but through the income tax rather than a payroll tax, although there is no requirement to have had at least some level of taxable income. Each of these views is valid, and each has support from a different political perspective; thus it is perhaps not surprising that the system has remained broadly stable since its introduction in 1957. The trick, from a coverage perspective, is to require contributions, but not to make benefits conditional on a person's contribution record. Currently, policymakers are wrestling with the increasing cost of the benefit, given increasing life expectancy.

The noncontributory universal pension is combined with a system of occupational pensions by industry. Although in a formal sense such pensions are voluntary, once an industry chooses a plan, participation becomes compulsory for workers

---

18. The full pension is awarded at age 65 on the basis of fifty years of residence between the ages of 15 and 65; the full pension is reduced by 2 percent for each year of nonresidence. In 2005, 84 percent of beneficiaries received full benefits, although with increased international labor mobility that number is expected to fall.

in the industry.[19] Over 90 percent of the workforce participate in an occupational pension, of whom about one-third were in career-average defined-benefit plans in 2002 and about two-thirds in final-salary plans. Pensions are subject to negotiations among employers, trade unions, and the government and are required by law to be funded. The division of contributions between worker and employer varies from plan to plan. The combination of a noncontributory universal pension and an occupational pension for a fairly full career provides a total replacement rate of about 70 percent of an average worker's final salary.

Given the pressures facing defined-benefit plans—longer lives, financial market turbulence, increasing requirements for transparency in company accounts with respect to fund deficits—pension funds in the Netherlands are responding in ways that share risks among workers, employers, and pensioners more broadly than in either a conventional defined-benefit system (where the risk in a pure plan falls on the employer) or a conventional defined-contribution plan (where the risk in a pure plan falls on the worker).[20]

11.4.5 New Zealand

The pension system in New Zealand is in many ways the polar opposite of that in Singapore (section 11.4.7). The bedrock of the system is a noncontributory universal pension (New Zealand Superannuation) paid from general taxation to all persons over 65 who pass a residency test,[21] and included in a person's taxable income. The pension is allowed to vary between a floor set at 65 percent of the net average wage for a married couple and a ceiling of 72.5 percent of the average wage. For a single individual the level of payment depends on living arrangements. In 2003 the benefit for a single person sharing accommodation was 40 percent of the net average wage; for someone living alone the comparable figure was 44 percent. The basic pension is supplemented by voluntary savings, which, unusually among countries, for many years received no tax advantages.[22] The country is also an outlier in that there is no mandatory earnings-related pension. However, the flat benefit is high enough to represent a high replacement rate for a sizable fraction of the population, limiting concern about consumption smoothing.

The savings regime was reformed in 2007 with the introduction of KiwiSaver, a subsidized and tax-advantaged defined-contribution plan. Participation is voluntary, but workers are automatically enrolled, so that a worker who wishes to opt out has to take positive action to do so. The design is simple, in part in recognition of the problems of consumer choice discussed in section 9.3.[23]

---

19. If the social partners (the unions and employer organizations) in an industry agree on a pension plan or fund, they may ask the minister of social affairs to make the plan compulsory for nonorganized employers in that industry (and thus for employees working in such firms, since the pension plan is part of the employment contract). In this way the pension plan in fact becomes compulsory for all employers and employees working in the industry.

20. For fuller discussion, see Ponds and van Riel (2007).

21. The pension is payable at age 65 to all New Zealanders living in the country, subject to ten years' residency since the age of 20 and not less than five years' residency since the age of 50.

22. For a fuller discussion, see St John (2005).

23. On the 2007 reforms see St John (2007) and the New Zealand government KiwiSaver website www.kiwisaver.gov.nz.

As with arrangements in the Netherlands, the system is highly effective in relieving poverty. Since the pension benefit is universal, exceeds the poverty line, and is based on residence rather than a history of paid work, it is not surprising that only 7.6 percent of pensioners (typically those who do not meet the residency requirement) are below the poverty line (New Zealand Ministry of Social Development 2005, Table A.1). The approach also addresses the gender inequalities that often arise with contributory systems, and it accommodates diverse labor market arrangements and fluid family structures, since, for example, a woman's flat-rate pension depends neither on her own record of contributions nor that of her husband.

The system is popular. A referendum in September 1997 on replacing the tax-financed flat-rate pension with mandatory funded individual accounts (along Chilean lines) was easily defeated. Eighty percent of the electorate took part, and 92.8 percent of those voting rejected the proposal. Since 2000 the public plan has been partially prefunded so as to smooth tax rates as the population ages.[24] Box 11.3 discusses non-contributory pensions in a range of countries.[25]

▶ Box 11.3 Noncontributory pensions

High-income countries. Like New Zealand and the Netherlands, Australia also has a noncontributory pension. The benefit is paid from general revenue and subject not to an income test, designed to restrict benefits to the poor, but to an affluence test, which has the more limited purpose of clawing back benefits from the rich.* Since 1992, workers have in addition been subject to de facto mandatory participation in individual funded accounts, an outgrowth of the country's voluntary employer-based plans, which over time the government decided to systematize.**

Middle-income countries. The new noncontributory pension in Chile is discussed in Chapter 13. South Africa also has a noncontributory pension, the State Old Age Grant. Both countries use an affluence test. The South African case is interesting in that it reaches effectively not only urban pensioners but also the rural elderly and is well targeted. The last point should not be surprising, since old age is a good indicator of potential poverty (see the discussion of targeting in Box 7.1).

The pension, paid to men at age 65 and women at 60, is financed from general revenue with no contribution conditions. The benefit—around half of average household income—is high relative to the very low incomes of most nonwhites in South Africa, but low relative to the incomes of the better off. Originally introduced as poverty relief for whites during the 1930s, the plan was gradually expanded to cover all race groups.

(continues next page)

24. The intention is to allocate around NZ$2 billion of general revenue per year over a twenty-year period to a fund, on which the government can draw later to smooth the cost of providing pensions. The fund's mandate is to invest the money in a way that maximizes returns without undue risk, but in a responsible way. The fund began investing in 2003; as of June 30, 2007, its assets totaled NZ$13.1 billion. It is expected to grow to around NZ$109 billion by 2025, making it one of the largest funds in Australasia. See the New Zealand Superannuation Fund website at www.nzsuperfund.co.nz/.

25. For further discussion of noncontributory pensions, see Willmore (2004, 2006); in addition to the countries mentioned in Box 11.3, the latter discusses Canada, Denmark, Finland, Iceland, Norway, Sweden, and the United Kingdom and, among middle-income countries, Mauritius.

(continued from previous page)
Research findings suggest that it is highly effective both in terms of social policy and in the way the plan is implemented:

> The South Africa social pension is an example of a transfer plan where eligibility is determined by age. In spite of the simplicity of the targeting indicator, the pension is effective in reaching the poorest households and those with children.... The South African authorities have overcome the difficulties of making cash transfers to even remote rural areas, and of checking eligibility among even illiterate pensioners. (Case and Deaton 1998, p. 1359; see also Lund 2002, and Burns, Keswell, and Leibbrandt 2005)

The administration of the system is consolidated under the South African Social Security Agency (see South Africa National Treasury 2007). In most urban areas, people receive the pension through bank accounts or post offices. In rural areas government has outsourced delivery to the private sector, organized at the provincial level. The system at its best is effective and innovative. In some areas vehicles fitted with cash dispensers go to predesignated places at preordained times. Pensioners enter their ID number (or fingerprint), and their pension is paid out. Notionally there is a government official on hand to provide help, but this facility is patchy.

Problems remain, however, including the potential for private sector contractors to make excessive profits; attacks on vehicles; and the disincentive to banks to move into rural areas, since the system carries out what would otherwise be one of their major functions. Not least for these reasons, there has been a significant new shift to placing the cash machines inside supermarkets. Thus the cash-dispensing function of the banks is now available, as is the savings function (since pensioners do not have to withdraw the whole monthly benefit at one time), but not the other functions of banks.

Low-income countries. A number of low-income countries have noncontributory pensions (sometimes called social pensions), including Bolivia, Botswana, Namibia, and Nepal. Total spending is typically small (below 1 percent of GDP in Botswana, Namibia, and Nepal), and the benefit is also generally small (Willmore 2006, Table 1).

As discussed in Chapter 13, pensions of this sort have the great potential advantage of extending coverage to people with limited contributions records, especially women, and workers in the informal sector. In assessing their desirability and feasibility in a particular country, policymakers need to consider a range of factors:

- How well could the pension be targeted? The cost-effectiveness of a noncontributory universal pension depends on the accuracy of age as a targeting device. In principle, the more poor people a country has, the greater the importance of poverty relief and the better targeted a noncontributory pension will be. The extent to which age alone is a good indicator, however, will vary from country to country (see Kakwani and Subbarao 2007), depending, for example, on the extent to which old people live alone or as part of an extended family.
- Is administrative capacity sufficient? Even a simple pension has administrative requirements. The government must be able to establish people's ages and to guard against multiple claims by one person and claims by relatives on behalf of a pensioner who has died.
- Is the cost of delivery low enough relative to the size of pension being considered?

Where a government has the necessary implementation capacity, policymakers have a range of options to contain costs:

- The level of the pension can be kept low (for example, it is only 10 percent of GDP per capita in Botswana and Nepal).

- The age at which the pension is first paid can be set high (in Nepal only 1.1 percent of the population are older than the qualifying age).
- If administrative capacity permits, a further option is to pay a smaller pension to the younger old (for example, those aged 65 to 75) and a larger one to the older old (those 75 and over).

---

*For a fuller discussion, see Carey (1999), Whiteford and Angenent (2001), Mitchell (2002), and Borowski (2005) and, for gender aspects Jefferson and Preston (2005).

**In 1992 the Australian government introduced a tax surcharge, under which employers who did not pay contributions were liable to pay more in tax than they would otherwise have paid in pension contributions. The effect was to increase pension coverage from about 75 to 80 percent of the workforce to 92 or 93 percent. Contributions are not mandatory for self-employed workers or for extremely low paid workers.

11.4.6 Poland

The system of pensions that Poland inherited from the communist era was poorly suited to a market economy.[26] A strategic problem was the large number of pensioners, partly because coverage was close to universal—one of the strengths of the system—but also because the pensionable age was low. The latter had a series of causes: many people were allowed to retire early in the waning days of communism to preserve social peace, and the process continued during the early transition to absorb workers left jobless by restructuring; for similar reasons, access to a disability pension was relatively easy. A second strategic problem resulted: pension spending in the early 1990s reached 15 percent of GDP, a level incompatible with other demands on scarce fiscal capacity, particularly at a time when falling output was badly eroding that capacity. Pension benefits varied unsystematically and bore little or no relation to contributions or to need. Finally, although social insurance contributions were collected, there were no records of how much each individual worker had contributed, such records being largely unnecessary with universal full employment (so that the great bulk of workers had a full contributions record) and pensions based on final salary.

A major reform in 1998 established a mandatory system with two elements. The first is an NDC pension. A person's notional fund is indexed in line with the growth of total economy-wide wage bill, hence in line with trends in productivity and employment; in retirement the intention is that pensions are indexed to a pensioner price index.[27] Thus a person's public pension is strictly proportional to his or her (notionally) cumulated contributions (using the notional interest rate as the discount rate), with two significant exceptions: there is a minimum pension guarantee for people with an appropriate contributions record, and credits are paid for years spent out of the labor force raising children. The second element in the system consists of mandatory, privately managed,

---

26. For an overview of pension reform in the European former communist countries, see Barr (2001a, Chapter 15), Müller (1999), and Whiteford and Whitehouse (2006). On the Polish reforms specifically, see Góra and Rutkowski (1998), Golinowska, Pietka, and Zukowski (2003), Muturi, Zajkowski, and Chlon-Dominczak (2000), Chlon-Dominczak (2002), and Chlon-Dominczak and Góra (2006).

27. Indexation of benefits during retirement in the years after 1998 was supposed to be based on price inflation plus 20 percent of wage growth, but in reality benefits were somewhat volatile.

defined-contribution pensions, which are integrated with the first tier in a number of ways. Although the intention of the reform was to equalize the minimum retirement age at 62, the necessary social and political consensus was absent, and so the minimum retirement age remains at 65 for men and 60 for women. All these arrangements apply as described to younger workers, with transitional arrangements for older workers. Thus Poland offers the example of a system that provides consumption smoothing through NDC accounts and funded individual accounts, together with a poverty relief element (the minimum guarantee, pension credits for childrearing activities, and other forms of poverty relief for the elderly). Thus it resembles Sweden.

Poland's system is illuminating also in terms of its implementation. Notwithstanding the country's considerable institutional capacity and heavy emphasis during the reform process on building an adequate administrative infrastructure, the reforms almost came to grief because the system was initially unable to keep track of people's contributions. The roots of the problem were delayed implementation of the new computer system, initial compliance problems, and administrative inefficiency as a legacy of the past (Muturi, Zajkowski, and Chlon-Dominczak 2000). The situation was rectified, but from the outside it looked as though a collapse was narrowly averted.

Some other countries in Central and Eastern Europe—for example, Latvia—have adopted a strategy with similarities to that of Poland, with an NDC first tier and a mandatory funded second tier. Others have taken a different approach. The Czech Republic and Slovenia decided against mandatory funded accounts, instead choosing to reform their PAYG arrangements and encourage voluntary pension saving. Hungary adopted an intermediate approach, one that includes mandatory funded accounts, raising the significant concerns described in Box 11.4.

▶ Box 11.4 Pension reform in Hungary

Reform in Hungary affected two components of the pension system: parametric change to the PAYG element, and a new system of mandatory, funded, defined-contribution accounts. The existing system of voluntary funded accounts continued as before.

Participation in the new second tier was mandatory for workers entering the labor force after July 1, 1998, and voluntary for all others. The second tier started in January 1998 and by 2004 had assets equal to 4 percent of GDP.

The reforms raise a number of concerns, which echo the cautions about transition costs in Chapter 6 and about implementation and administrative costs in Chapter 9:

- Transition costs of 1.5 percent of GDP associated with the introduction of funded accounts contributed to a large budget deficit.
- A joint World Bank-IMF study found that "The average return performance of [pension funds] has been rather disappointing" (World Bank 2005, para. 30). Between 1998 and 2005 the average weighted real net rate of return was 3.75 percent (in some years real returns were negative), lower than the average rate of growth of real wages of 5.3 percent (World Bank 2005, Table 12), and lower than in any of the reforming countries in Latin America (World Bank 2005, Table 13).
- Administrative costs were high. Using the same methodology as in Table 9.1 for assessing long-run costs (that is, not giving excessive weight to high start-up costs), the World Bank-IMF study estimated an annual management charge of 1.18 percent (World Bank 2005, para. 48) and a charge ratio of between 18 and 30 percent (World Bank 2005, Table 20).

• For part of the period, administrative charges reduced the net real return to close to zero (Augusztinovics et al. 2002, updated in Matits 2004), to the great disadvantage of people who moved to the new system toward the end of their career. As Matits (2004, p. 11) noted, "[g]iven workers' low level of understanding of the new private pillar, it probably would have been fairer if older workers would have not been allowed to switch."

For these and other reasons, an occasional paper issued by the National Bank of Hungary concluded that

... the performance of the pension fund sector in Hungary can be regarded as unsatisfactory. ... [New] pensioners of the multi-pillar system are projected to receive significantly lower benefits than members of the pure PAYG system with an identical wage-profile and service years. ... And ... a major tension could arise from pensions being below any social minimum. (Orbán and Palotai 2005, p. 28) ◀

11.4.7   Singapore

The pension system in Singapore is built around mandatory, publicly managed, defined-contribution pensions, provided mainly by the Central Provident Fund.[28] Thus the core of the system is an individual savings plan illustrated by the simple model in Box 2.1, with little or no insurance in the form of annuities.

The contributions of participants are channeled into three types of account. The Ordinary Account accumulates funds for retirement but offers earlier withdrawals for approved purposes such as the purchase of a home. The Medisave Account covers hospitalization and allows the voluntary purchase of catastrophic illness insurance sponsored by the Central Provident Fund. The Special Account is in principle meant exclusively for retirement but can also be used in a limited way for mortgage payments. Contribution rates decline with age, on the premise that lower wages for workers older than 55 will encourage employers to hire them.[29] Alongside the Central Provident Fund, a preretirement Central Provident Fund Investment Scheme allows individual choice from worldwide portfolios, although management costs are high.[30]

Accumulations are hampered by substantial preretirement withdrawals and by low rates of return to pension savings. Although the government guarantees a nominal interest rate of 2.5 percent a year, the real annual return over the period 1987-2005 was only 1.3 percent. A small pool of funds (about 3 percent of total balances) are contracted out to private fund managers. The real return of these funds between 1987 and 2004 was 2.9 percent, more than twice that of the Central Provident Fund.

At retirement a person can choose to buy an annuity but is not required to do so. Only a small proportion of pensioners choose the annuity option; thus most elderly

28. For fuller discussion, see Asher and Amarendu (2006).

29. In 2007 the contribution rate was 34.5 percent of covered wages for workers under 50, 28.5 percent for workers between 50 and 55, 20 percent for workers between 55 and 60, 12.5 percent for workers between 60 and 65, and 10 percent for workers older than 65. The sum of participants' balances in March 2006 was equivalent to 63 percent of GDP.

30. The Central Provident Fund was introduced in 1955. The Approved Investment Scheme was introduced in 1986 and renamed the CPF Investment Scheme in 1997.

Singaporeans are exposed to longevity risk. Nor are there any arrangements to address inflation risk.

In sum, Singapore's pension system relies almost exclusively on mandatory savings to provide consumption smoothing. However, the replacement rate (estimated in one study at 20 percent of previous earnings) is inadequate, nor is there a tax-financed redistributive element to provide poverty relief. Mitigation of longevity, inflation, and political risks is limited. And the design and governance of the system are continuing concerns.

11.4.8 Sweden

After major reform in the 1990s, the pension system in Sweden comprises two elements: a partially funded system of NDC accounts combined with a generous guarantee that keeps all the elderly out of poverty, and a system of funded individual accounts, the Premium Pension.[31] The guarantee provides that a person who reaches retirement after forty years' residence in Sweden is eligible for a full minimum benefit. For fewer years of residence the benefit is reduced proportionately; there also is an income-tested minimum pension. In addition, credits are given during working life, both to the NDC pension and to the Premium Pension, for periods when a person is out of the labor force looking after young children or collecting unemployment or sickness benefits.

The system has an 18.5 percent contribution rate, of which 16 percentage points are for the NDC element and the remainder for fully funded individual accounts. The NDC element uses a notional interest rate equal to the rate of growth of average wages. However, if at any time the calculated financial balance of the system is unsatisfactory, that rate is lowered automatically; no legislative action is required. Each worker receives an annual statement with information about the notional account and the funded account, including the values in the accounts, the contributions made that year, and projections of future benefits under different assumptions.

Benefits may first be claimed at age 61, and this age is not scheduled to change; in practice, however, most people first claim benefits at age 65 (in contrast with the United States, where many people claim benefit at the earliest eligibility age).[32] The initial benefit is set by a quasi-actuarial calculation based on the mortality of the worker's birth cohort, the age at which he or she first takes benefits, and the anticipated rate of increase in benefits. Benefits increase each year after retirement based on the difference between the notional interest rate (normally the rate of wage growth) and the anticipated annual increase of 1.6 percent.

The 2.5 percent of payroll going to the funded individual accounts is collected by the government and distributed to the participating mutual funds in accordance with individual portfolio decisions. The number of funds is large, over 700 in 2007. Individuals may choose the funds in which to invest their individual account contributions, up to a maximum of five; as discussed in section 9.3, there is a default fund for the large

---

31. For fuller discussion, see Sundén (2006).

32. In Sweden in 2006, 7 percent of participants first took a pension at age 61, 4 percent at 62, 4 percent at 63, 4 percent at 64, 75 percent at 65, 4 percent at 66, and 1 percent at 67, by which age almost everyone was drawing a pension (although not necessarily stopping work). Those not working at earlier ages than 65 are typically on disability benefits.

number of workers who do not make a choice. The government transfers worker contributions to and between mutual funds based on the aggregate of worker contributions to each fund and portfolio changes. Funds must be approved by the government and must accept the charges established by a centrally set formula. On retirement a worker's accumulated assets in the fund must be used to purchase an annuity (individual or joint-life) provided by the government.

Sweden addresses the problem of administrative costs through a central clearinghouse, whereby the administration and maintenance of individual accounts is centralized. Contributions to the NDC pension and individual accounts are collected together, and the funds are then channeled wholesale to individual accounts; thus fund managers know nothing about individual contributors. The average annual charge (net) is 0.73 percent of assets, equivalent to a charge ratio of about 14 percent.[33] This central management of funds is similar to that in the U.S. Thrift Savings Plan, discussed in Box 11.5, but the latter severely restricts the choice of funds and incurs much lower costs for fund management. The costs of administering the accounts are also lower in the Thrift Savings Plan, but the costs are not fully comparable because the Thrift Savings Plan deals with a single employer, the federal government.

In important respects, Sweden is a semi-public analogue of the post-1981 system in Chile, but with more weight given to poverty relief. The experience of the system illustrates one way to organize a well-designed NDC system and shows that, even in a developed country, fully funded individual accounts can be expensive, and that many workers show no interest in a wide choice of investments.

11.4.9 United Kingdom

Pension arrangements in the United Kingdom have witnessed much change over the years.[34] Under the 1946 National Insurance Act, flat-rate contributions gave entitlement to a flat-rate benefit, including a retirement pension. The retirement age was set at 65 for men, 60 for women. For a full pension a man needed forty-four years of contributions; a woman needed forty. There was no statutory indexation of benefits, which instead were raised periodically.[35]

The 1975 Social Security Act replaced the flat-rate contribution with an earnings-related contribution, which gave entitlement to the flat-rate basic state pension and to a new State Earnings-Related Pension System (SERPS). The contribution conditions remained unchanged, with the important exception that a pension credit was introduced for care activities. Participation in the basic state pension was compulsory. Workers also belonged to SERPS unless their employer had opted out, in which case

---

33. Fees for the individual accounts in 2005 included an administrative fee charged to all accounts of 0.3 percent of assets; an average fund fee (including the default fund) of 0.43 percent of assets after a rebate (the average rebate is 0.37 percent of assets); and an average fund fee for the default fund of 0.16 percent of assets after rebate. Thus, on average the total fee is 73 basis points, which, as Table 9.1 shows, reduces accumulations over a forty-year career by roughly 14 percent.

34. For a description of the system as of 2004, see U.K. Pensions Commission (2004b, Appendix F).

35. The long-run trend of these ad hoc increases was to maintain benefits constant relative to pre-tax average earnings; shorter-term deviations from this trend often involved increases in the run-up to an election; see Barr (1981).

they belonged to their employer's approved occupational pension plan. Under the 1975 act, contributions were indexed in line with wage changes, and pensions during retirement in line with the greater of wage or price changes. (See Box 5.8 on the design flaws of this arrangement.)

Reforms announced in 1986 changed the indexation of benefits during retirement to changes in prices; they extended opting out by allowing individuals to choose to have an individual account in place of SERPS or an employer-provided pension; and they announced ways in which SERPS would be less generous from 2000 onward. (Box 9.2 describes some of the problems encountered in implementing these reforms.) A further reform consisted of a phased increase in women's retirement age to 65. As a consequence, projected public pension spending in the United Kingdom shows the unusual pattern of declining as a percentage of GDP, as shown in Figure 1.9, despite significant aging of the population.

By the mid-1990s, however, the U.K. pension system faced major problems. The cumulative effects of price indexation and the known failings of coverage in contributory systems created problems of pensioner poverty. Occupational pensions concealed many of the problems of the public system but provided inadequate coverage of lower earners. Further reform of the public pension was announced, and attempts were made to introduce individual accounts for lower-paid workers. These added to the complexity of the system but had little impact. Problems with occupational pensions aggravated the situation, partly because of adverse stock market conditions after 2000, and perhaps also because of heavy-handed regulation (see Box 9.3).

These problems were the background for the U.K. Pensions Commission (2004a, 2004b, 2005), whose main recommendations are discussed in section 11.2.3. In accepting those strategic recommendations, the government made a further change: beginning in 2010 a full pension will require only thirty years of contributions.

The U.K. experience exemplifies two strategic errors. First, the system was changed too frequently and with too short a time horizon. Since a central purpose of pensions is consumption smoothing over increasingly long lives, stability over long periods is important; changes should be made infrequently, announced long in advance, and phased in gradually. The second problem, excessive complexity, is in part a result of the first. A system that had originally been simple and well understood ended up not only too complex for many in the general public to understand, but complex to the point where many experts had difficulty understanding it.[36]

11.4.10 United States

The U.S. Social Security system has been gender-neutral since 1961. Retirement benefits are available to workers with sufficiently low earnings (that is, a retirement

---

36. As an example, different elements in the public pension embodied different accrual rates for delayed receipt of pension, so that projecting an individual's pension entitlement for retirement at different ages became a major exercise. Another problem is that if the basic pension retains an income-tested element (which is projected to be the case for many years to come), it may not be worthwhile for a low earner to build pension savings; whether it is worthwhile depends both on the worker's future earnings and on the details of the income test in force at retirement. Given that both are unknown, sellers of private pensions in the United Kingdom are concerned about giving advice that might in later years make them liable to lawsuits for mis-selling.

test) between age 62 and the age for full benefits, which is in transition from 65 to 67. There is no retirement test after the age for full benefits. Benefit determination is a four-step process. First, the worker's thirty-five best wage-indexed annual earnings are averaged (including zeros if needed to reach thirty-five years; wage indexing is done only up to the year that the worker turns 60, after which nominal earnings are used). Then, a three-piece benefit formula is used to calculate a benefit level. With replacement rates of 0.90, 0.32, and 0.15 for successively higher bands of income, the benefit formula is progressive. The third step is an adjustment for the age at which benefits start. The adjustment is roughly actuarially neutral between age 62 and the age for full benefits, but not large enough to be actuarially neutral after that, as Figure 5.1 illustrates. There are auxiliary benefits for spouses, described in Boxes 8.2 and 8.3. The fourth step is the increase in benefit levels in line with prices after a worker reaches age 62, whether benefits have started or not. For a worker starting benefits at age 65 in 2006 with indexed average lifetime earnings of $30,000 (a little below the median), the annual benefit would be $13,812, for a replacement rate of 46 percent (ignoring auxiliary benefits). The system's expenditures were 4.2 percent of GDP in 2006.

Revenue for both disability and retirement pensions comes from a 12.4 percent payroll tax rate up to a taxable maximum, which is high enough that roughly 94 percent of workers have all their earnings subject to tax each year (but roughly 15 percent of aggregate earnings escapes the tax). Revenue also comes from some of the income tax revenue derived from taxing pensions. Currently revenue exceeds expenditure; the excess goes into a trust fund, which holds U.S. Treasury bonds paying market interest rates. At the end of 2007 the trust funds for retirement and disability benefits held just over $2.2 trillion, equal to just below 3.8 times expenditures in 2007.

There is no mandate to participate in any pension except the public pension, but workers contribute to a wide array of employer and individual schemes. The Thrift Saving Plan for federal civil servants, which supplements Social Security and is discussed in Box 11.5, offers an interesting example of a simple plan with inexpensive administration.

▷ Box 11.5 The U.S. Thrift Savings Plan

The U.S. government established the Thrift Savings Plan for federal civil servants (see www.tsp.gov) in 1986. The plan offers participants a very limited choice of portfolios. Initially there were three: a stock market index fund, a fund holding bonds issued by private firms, and a fund holding government bonds. In 2007 workers could choose from six funds, including a life-cycle option. A government agency keeps centralized records of individual portfolios. Fund management is on a wholesale basis. Investment in private sector assets is handled by private financial firms, which bid for the opportunity (and which manage the same portfolios in the voluntary private market).

As a result, administrative costs are astonishingly low: as little as 6 basis points annually, or 60 cents per $1,000 of account balance. By 2007 the program had grown to include 3.8 million participants and held assets of $225 billion. The commission appointed by President George W. Bush to propose reforms for Social Security recommended that it adopt the same approach, which should also be of wide interest to other countries considering reform, in particular to developing countries where institutional capacity is limited. As discussed in section 11.2.3, the United Kingdom is considering a similar plan. ◀

11.5 CONCLUSION

Although the institutions supporting pension systems are complex, the conclusions we draw are simple:

- Systems today look very different from fifty years ago. This is no accident. This is as it should be.
- There are many different ways of achieving the various objectives of pension systems. The diversity of (more or less) well-run systems is considerable. This, too, is as it should be.
- A number of countries have badly designed structures, and those with good ones often have some features that would benefit from change.

12

▷

Chile: The Pension System

Chile's pension reform of 1981 has fascinated commentators and influenced other countries. The system has been a work in progress, with frequent legislated changes since the original reform. In 2005 Chile's newly elected president appointed an advisory council to consider what further changes might be necessary. The council's analysis is the basis for the latest round of reforms, which were enacted in 2008, shortly before this volume went to press, and which are discussed in Chapter 13. This chapter describes and assesses the post-1981 system (that is, the arrangements prior to the 2008 reforms). That system is based on mandatory saving, with competition among providers both for the savings element and for annuities. Successful emulation of this approach is harder than many policymakers realize, as shown by the experiences of other Latin American countries attempting to follow a similar path.[1]

12.1 DESCRIPTION OF THE POST-1981 SYSTEM

12.1.1 Individual accounts

By the late 1970s the pension system in Chile faced major problems, notably a multiplicity of PAYG defined-benefit plans (see glossary), with unreliable benefits and arbitrary differences across plans. The major change in 1981 was to introduce mandatory individual accounts for workers employed in the formal sector. Workers are required to place 10 percent of covered earnings into these accounts and to make a market-determined additional payment for mandatory disability and survivors' insurance, plus a commission to the firms that administer the individual accounts, collect contributions, and manage the pension funds. Retiring workers may take their pensions as inflation-indexed annuities purchased from insurance companies, but they are not obliged to do so. Instead they may draw down their accumulation through

---

1. See Diamond and Valdés Prieto (1994), Edwards and Edwards (2002), and, for fuller discussion of Chile in the broader Latin American context, Gill, Packard, and Yermo (2005), Arenas de Mesa and Mesa-Lago (2006), and Mesa-Lago (2007).

phased withdrawals; constraints on the rate of withdrawal reduce the risk of their outliving the money. In this case the funds remain with a pension management firm, which handles investment of the funds and payment of benefits. Annuities and withdrawals are subject to mandatory protection of family members.

To handle the individual accounts, Chile organized a regulated market in which fund management firms (called *administradoras de fondos de pensiones*, or AFPs), originally restricted to handling a single mutual fund each, compete to manage funds. Entry into the business was (and remains) open to any firm meeting sufficient capital and managerial criteria (for example, the firm's managers must have no criminal record). Chile later allowed firms to manage up to five fund portfolios each, varying in their mix of stocks and bonds. Thus, although the exact makeup of the portfolios is left to the private market (unlike with firms participating in the Thrift Savings Plan in the United States, described in Box 11.5), the range of choice has remained limited.[2]

Having experienced considerable inflation over its history, Chile has more indexed assets, both public and private, than most other countries; their value is based on an inflation index published daily. Many government bonds are indexed by this means, as are some mortgages and corporate bonds as well as some labor contracts and many types of commercial contracts. Since 2002, however, the Central Bank of Chile has promoted the emergence of long-term nominal bonds, both public and private. Pension funds in Chile hold both indexed and nominal bonds, and about 40 percent of pension fund portfolios are invested in equities, about half of them abroad, offering medium-term protection against inflation.

12.1.2 Poverty relief

The individual accounts, intended to provide consumption smoothing, are supported by two sets of institutions that predate the 1981 reforms. First, for low earners who have contributed to the pension system for at least twenty years, a subsidy from general revenue brings their pension benefit up to a minimum guaranteed level. Second, there is a means-tested welfare pension for the elderly poor, financed by general revenue at about half the minimum pension guarantee. As discussed below, both the low level of such benefits and their incomplete coverage raise continuing concerns.

12.1.3 Voluntary pensions

In parallel with the mandatory system is a system of voluntary pension savings (*ahorro previsional voluntario*, or APV). This system may be used by the self-employed, by workers whose attachment to the formal labor market is patchy, and by employees who wish to make contributions beyond the mandatory 10 percent.

The voluntary system has grown quickly since 2002, when the set of authorized providers was expanded, but remains small relative to the mandatory system.[3]

---

2. As discussed further in section 12.2.5, regulations require a guaranteed minimum return, which is structured in a way that encourages firms to hold similar portfolios. Further regulations affect the process by which account holders may switch between pension funds.

3. In December 2005 total APV savings were $1.9 billion (unless noted otherwise, dollar figures are in U.S. dollars), equivalent to about 2.7 percent of the total of the mandatory system. At the same date there were about 323,000 savers with APV balances, equivalent to 4.4 percent of participants with an AFP account and 8.5 percent of active AFP contributors.

Participating workers contribute, on average, 6.4 percent of the relevant contributions base, compared with the 10 percent contribution to the mandatory system. Employers are not required to make contributions but may choose to do so.

12.1.4 Funding

As discussed in Box 6.2, moving to a funded system meant that each worker's contributions had to go toward his or her own pension; thus the government had to finance the pensions of existing pensioners and the cost of pensions earned under the old system by continuing workers. To finance the transition, Chile set aside an amount equivalent to 5 percent of GDP at the time of the reform. Substantial and systematic fiscal surpluses from 1987 onward made it possible for the government to take over those legacy obligations without going deeply in debt or reducing benefits. Compared with using those surpluses either for lower taxes or higher (noninvestment) public spending, this resulted in higher national saving, a key ingredient if a pension reform is to increase economic growth. In this respect Chile's experience contrasts sharply with that of most countries, where recommendations for similar reforms were made in a context of budgetary deficits,[4] which the pension reform made worse, thus contributing to further financing difficulties insofar as the reform resulted in higher interest rates on government debt.

Some advocates of this approach emphasize the very high real rates of return earned on the assets. Several points are worth noting. One is that in the early years the funds were held completely in government bonds and government-backed bank deposits. Thus the high rates of return reflected high interest rates in Chile, not the acumen of fund managers. Second, since the permitted range of portfolios was expanded, studies have found that, once account is taken of legal restrictions on portfolios, the portfolios have been on the risk-return frontier. A recent official report, discussed in the next chapter, stated that

> the claim that the pension system has produced real yields of 10% per year does not provide an adequate reflection of the system's performance. More realistic estimates of the actual yield on the worker's contributions, in other words, the return up to the moment of retirement, net of commissions, indicate that this would be between 4.5% and 6.5% per year.[5]

The central point is that the return on the portfolio and the return on deposits differ because of administrative charges; thus it is important to calculate returns net of administrative costs. Also relevant is the expectation that future returns are likely to differ from those from a period when the stock and bond markets underwent such large changes.

---

4. For example, Bolivia, Kazakhstan, Latvia, and Romania had budget deficits over 3 percent of GDP at the time they initiated reform; see World Bank (2006*a*, Figure 3.2).

5. "La afirmación de que el sistema de pensiones ha generado rentabilidades reales del 10% anual no refleja adecuadamente el desempeño del sistema desde la perspectiva de los afiliados. Estimaciones más realistas de la rentabilidad efectiva de los aportes del trabajador, es decir, del retorno neto de comisiones hasta el momento del retiro, indican que ésta se ubicaría entre un 4,5% y un 6,5% anual" (Chile Presidential Advisory Council 2006a, p. 23).

12.1.5 Regulation

Chile is often described as relying on unrestricted markets, with little role for government. This is a misreading. The AFPs holding the money and the stock and bond markets in which they invest are subject to tight regulation, including restrictions on portfolios, on the structure (but not the level) of charges to workers, and on how firms compete. Indeed, Chile created a new regulatory body just to supervise the AFPs. The insurance companies that provide annuities are also tightly regulated, with respect to both their investment portfolios and their practices in selling annuities. Such regulation is standard in developed countries for both mandatory and voluntary pensions. The Chilean experience illustrates the workings of government and markets in tandem in producing a well-functioning pension system that relies on markets. The political pressures to ensure that mandatory savings invested in stock and bond markets were invested well apparently also contributed to the political effort to regulate those markets. Indeed, the bond market did not exist in its present form until faced with increased demand from mutual funds and insurance companies, which needed to hold indexed bonds as backing for indexed annuities.

12.2 ASSESSMENT

The benchmark against which this section assesses the post-1981 system is not the system that existed before, but what a pension system should offer citizens today. The discussion in this chapter looks in turn at pensioner poverty, completeness of coverage, issues of vertical equity and gender equality, administrative charges, competition and fund diversification, fiscal costs, and economic growth. All of the criticisms offered here have also been made within Chile itself.[6]

12.2.1 Pensioner poverty

On the face of it, elderly poverty in Chile is not severe: measured poverty among older people (about 10 percent of the elderly population) is half the national poverty rate. That conclusion, however, should not be overstated as an assessment of the success of the post-1981 system. For one thing, older workers were allowed to continue under the pre-1981 system if they chose, and many did. Also, many of today's retirees spent far less than their full career under the post-1981 system: only women over 35 and men over 40 in 1981 had reached the retirement ages of 60 and 65, respectively, by 2006. Thus today's figures on elderly poverty only partly reflect the effects of the new system.

Looking to the future, "Many workers have saved little or nothing through the pension system."[7] This outcome is hard to avoid in a middle-income country with limited fiscal resources and a relatively large informal sector. But for several reasons poverty remains a potential problem even for workers who spent significant time in the formal sector: the contribution rate for pensions (net of charges) of 10 percent of

6. For example, at a seminar in Santiago in 2004, a Chilean senator spoke of the "seven deadly sins of Chile pensions": low coverage, low pensions, high administrative costs, high fiscal cost, lack of gender equality, weak competition, and political tests for appointment to the boards of directors of AFPs.

7. "Muchos trabajadores han ahorrado poco o nada a través del sistema de pensiones" (Chile Presidential Advisory Council 2006a, p. 5).

covered earnings is low compared with that in other countries;[8] coverage is incomplete as people moved in and out of covered employment, as discussed below, affecting both individual accumulations and eligibility for the minimum guarantee; and, the minimum pension guarantee apart, defined-contribution pensions by their nature are an instrument for consumption smoothing, not primarily for poverty relief. The first two roots of the problem are in principle remediable by raising the contribution rate and extending coverage. The third is an inherent consequence of the 1981 strategy and calls for reexamination of the design of the minimum pension guarantee. The other antipoverty instrument in the system, the income-tested welfare pension, provides limited benefits (about half of the minimum pension guarantee, as noted above) and was rationed until 2006.[9] Notwithstanding the relevance of these two sets of benefits to a significant fraction of the elderly, continuing and probably increasing pensioner poverty is an unsurprising outcome and a key driver of the reforms discussed in the next chapter.

Alongside poverty, a separate problem is uncertainty. An important element of old-age security is that, as a worker ages, he or she should develop a fair measure of certainty of the pension available at retirement. Individual accounts face fluctuations in yields and changes in the price of annuities, leaving considerable uncertainty, and, at least historically, there has been an element of political risk about the level of the welfare pension. Evidence that workers regard insecurity as a significant problem is another driver of the reforms.

12.2.2   Coverage

The coverage of the system remains incomplete for two sets of reasons. Part of the problem is the design of the system: contributions are mandatory only for employees, and thus voluntary for self-employed workers, and no allowance was made for years spent caring for young children. Yet in practice many workers move through periods of formal employment, unemployment, and self-employment, or leave the labor force for care activities or education. Separately, compliance is imperfect in that not all who are supposed to contribute do so. For both sets of reasons, many workers have significant gaps in their contributions record.

Coverage, measured as the ratio of contributors in a particular year to the total workforce, was around 64 percent in 1980; that figure has remained at about 60 percent—low, but one of the best in Latin America (Mesa-Lago 2005, Table 1). Like the problem of pensioner poverty, the coverage problem is common to middle-income countries. What is noteworthy, however, is that problems of coverage persist despite Chile's solid administration. The outcome in Chile thus offers little support to earlier arguments that a tighter relationship between contributions and benefits would generate a large improvement in compliance. For the reasons discussed in section 5.2.2, this result is predictable.

Problems of poverty relief and coverage are aggravated by adverse incentives, a topic explored by Gill, Packard, and Yermo (2005, Chapter 8). Since workers are

8. Although many countries have worker contributions of around 10 percent, these are accompanied by employer contributions of broadly equal size.

9. The welfare pension also faced design problems. In principle, when a recipient's living standard crossed a threshold, the entire benefit was withdrawn, creating incentives for corruption at the municipal level at which benefits are administered.

entitled to the minimum pension guarantee on the basis of twenty years of contributions, there is an incentive for low earners to limit contributions to twenty years; similarly, the incentive to make additional contributions for the many workers who will never reach the twenty-year requirement is just the benefit that can be financed by their contributions. Thus, for low-earning workers with twenty years of contributions, "housing, household enterprise, and even the education of children are among alternative investments being pursued by individuals" (Gill, Packard, and Yermo 2005, p. 184). Hence the density of contributions of low earners tends to be low. A separate incentive is to underdeclare earnings, since entitlement to the minimum pension guarantee is based on years of contributions, not on their size.

12.2.3   Vertical equity

The minimum pension apart, Chile's individual accounts provide fully actuarial benefits, as befits an instrument for consumption smoothing. That it gives higher benefits to individuals with higher earnings is part of the design. Such a system does not redistribute from rich to poor, but, among those purchasing annuities, from people whose life span falls short of the anticipated life expectancy used in annuity pricing to those who exceed it. Not surprisingly, the density of contributions rises across income deciles. Thus a better-off person not only makes higher contributions per month, appropriately reflecting higher earnings, but also on average contributes for more months than a lower earner.[10]

The argument is not that actuarial benefits are inequitable, but rather that they need to be part of a system that includes effective poverty relief. Chapter 13 discusses reforms that replace the guaranteed minimum pension with more powerful poverty relief.

Additionally, voluntary contributions enjoy tax advantages. As in many countries, the design of those tax advantages gives the greatest benefit to the best off.[11]

12.2.4   Gender equity

Gender and family are discussed in Chapter 8.[12] There is a clear conflict between two approaches: the pension system can treat women as dependents and try to offset any resulting disadvantages, or it can make little or no distinction between men and women. The developed countries are increasingly drafting legislation that takes the latter route. In considering gender in the context of pensions, it is necessary to look both at a woman's earnings record, which determines her contributions, and at the design of the pension system, which determines benefits.

---

10. For fuller discussion, see Gill, Packard, and Yermo (2005, Figure 8.1 and surrounding text).

11. If taxes are progressive and contributions are deductible at a person's marginal tax rate, better-off contributors will generally contribute more than people with lower incomes and receive tax relief at a higher marginal rate. If, in addition, benefits are taxed at the same rates as the contributions were deducted, taxpayers gain from deferring taxes until benefits are received rather than paying tax on an accrual basis. The higher the tax rate, the more valuable is deferral. It is possible to offer tax relief in other ways, for example with a tax credit or matching amount for deposits instead of a deduction. The credit or matching rates can be uniform or higher for lower earners.

12. See also Arenas de Mesa and Montecinos (1999).

In Chile, as in other countries, women's wages on average are lower than men's, because on average women have less training and because they may receive lower pay for equal work. Separately, women's labor force participation is more sporadic than men's, in part because women experience higher rates of unemployment and are more likely to work in the informal sector; both factors unambiguously contribute to lower pensions. In addition, women typically spend more time caring for children or elderly dependents. This is benign where it results from well-informed choice, but, at least in developed countries, it is regarded a manifestation of gender inequality where it derives from social attitudes about the division of care responsibilities, particularly where they interact with inflexible labor markets that do not facilitate part-time work. Several policies to encourage women's labor supply are discussed in Chapter 8, of which two are relevant to Chile:

- Child subsidies have different effects depending on their design. Family allowances, which are paid whether or not a woman works, do not encourage labor supply.[13] Subsidies for child care conditioned on work, in contrast, strengthen incentives to work and thus increase labor force participation.[14] In Chile child rearing is subsidized through family allowances, but there is no national system of subsidized child care.

- All-day schools directly assist women's participation. The school day in Chile has lengthened since the mid-1990s but remains shorter than the working day. This creates problems because labor market institutions in Chile do not facilitate part-time work.

In part for these reasons, women in Chile tend to have smaller pension accumulations than men. In addition, the design of the pension system places some women at a disadvantage:

- Women have a lower eligibility age than men and, as an empirical matter, tend to retire earlier. The ability to start benefits sooner is not per se a disadvantage, although the combination of earlier retirement and actuarial benefits means that women in practice receive smaller benefits. Voluntary contributions can only be made until the eligibility age, disadvantaging women who would like to make a later contributions.

- Reinforcing the previous point, because the minimum pension guarantee is paid only if a worker has contributed for at least twenty years, those who have contributed for fewer years have to rely on the (lower) welfare pension. Women tend to participate in the labor force for fewer years then men, and the pension system does not count years spent in care activities; it follows that a twenty-year rule leaves out more women than men.

13. Indeed, through the income effect, family allowances may encourage leisure and so discourage labor supply. On the other hand, the added income may permit financing of better-quality child care, which can make work more attractive.

14. For example, the child tax credit in the United Kingdom (Barr 2004a, Chapter 10; U.K. Treasury 2005) includes subsidies for child care.

- Pension providers are allowed to use gender-specific mortality tables for annuities and programmed withdrawals, and hence pay lower benefits to women for a given accumulation, to reflect their greater life expectancy.[15] The rationale for this arrangement is that in poor families it is mainly the man who participates in covered employment, and therefore unisex tables would put low-income families at a disadvantage.

These factors in the labor market and pension design are independent of each other and mutually reinforcing. As a result, nearly 70 percent of working women in Chile lack the twenty years of coverage needed to qualify for the minimum pension guarantee, a much higher figure than for men (Berstein, Larraín, and Pino 2006) and an outcome that can be inferred qualitatively without even looking at the data. There is some protection for surviving wives, since men are required to buy annuities that pay 60 percent of their pension to a surviving spouse; women are not required to make the same arrangement for their husbands. The intention is deliberately to provide an advantage to women,[16] and the system does so in a range of other ways as well: for example, the arguments, just noted, for using separate life tables and adjusting life tables for pension accumulation. Clearly, there is a major difference between this approach and that outlined at the start of the section, which largely disregards gender.

12.2.5 Administrative charges, competition, and fund diversification

Although administrative charges in Chile are at the lower end of the range in Latin America, they remain a concern (Arenas de Mesa and Mesa-Lago 2006, p. 155). Idealized competition, in a simple model, maximizes consumer choice and exerts downward pressure on prices. Real-world competition combines price competition with advertising and kickbacks and reflects the slow responses of consumers to changing circumstances. It is difficult to distinguish high mutual fund returns that are due to better management from those that are due to luck (and so unlikely to be predictive of future returns), and some investors do not appreciate that a higher return might be due to taking on higher risk; thus it is not surprising that in many countries investment firms advertise returns and that some investors give these returns undue weight. In mutual fund markets generally, one finds hallmarks of real-world, not idealized, competition in the variety of rates charged for similar investment options, and in the gaps between prices and marginal costs. Chilean workers are not different from investors elsewhere, and these problems appear in many markets aimed at small individual investors.

Notwithstanding actions that have been taken to strengthen competition, charges in Chile remain high for several reasons. First, as an empirical matter, workers are not sensitive to price differences: "The low elasticity to price variations arises from various factors, one of them being the mandatory and complex nature of the product.

---

15. Annuity providers are also allowed to use mortality tables that vary with the size of the pension accumulation at retirement. Since those with higher accumulations are, on average, financially better off, this is designed to capture the fact that those who are better off tend to live longer. In the absence of such a measure, actuarial benefits, which redistribute from short-lived to long-lived people, would thereby redistribute from poor to rich.

16. Nevertheless, where the husband was the only earner, the surviving wife receives only 60 percent of what the husband would receive if he outlived her.

Thus the vast majority of workers do not bother to find out or react to the differences in commissions between AFPs."[17]

This should not be surprising given the information problems discussed in Box 4.2 and the fact, as explained in section 9.3, that the resulting savings in charges in any one month are small, whereas the transactions costs in terms of time and effort are significant, so that workers' responses are sluggish; thus the incentives to engage in competitive behavior are muted. The sluggishness of consumer responses is reinforced by the fact that the portfolios of different firms have been very similar, in part the result of a government-mandated guarantee that no firm should perform significantly worse than the average.[18] Thus the choices workers face are limited.

Second, although entry to the industry is theoretically free, the number of firms has shrunk considerably: in 2004 only six firms were still active in the market, with the top three holding 80 percent of assets (Mesa-Lago 2005, Table 3). In part this concentration is an indirect result of regulation, in particular the requirement that AFPs have no other business, which restricts sharing facilities and hence reduces the opportunities for new entrants capable of exploiting economies of scope.

When relying on competition to keep down costs, it is important to regulate competition so that it manifests itself as much as possible through price competition rather than through selling efforts. This is not easy. The law requires AFPs to charge all their participants the same percentage contribution rate. Since costs are largely a fixed element per account, clients with high, stable incomes are very attractive: "Marketing based on gifts and discounts makes it possible to reach these clients, side-stepping the obligation to bring prices down for all participants."[19] Thus experience in Chile illustrates that competition is not something automatic, even in a country large enough to sustain enough mutual fund firms to generate credible competition. The issue is even more important in smaller economies (see the discussion of Bolivia in Box 11.2). That said, however, high costs are in part an inherent consequence of a system that seeks to give workers individual choice over their pension provider (see section 9.2.3).

The value of Chile's stock market relative to GDP has increased notably over the years. Credit for this improvement is shared among the pension reform itself, the reform of regulation of the stock market, and the opening of the capital account to foreign equity investors. However, since the funds handling the individual accounts mostly pursue a buy-and-hold strategy, this growth in value relative to GDP has not been accompanied by a matching growth in transactions, so that liquidity has not risen in step. The long-term bond market, meanwhile, has grown and is important for

17. "La baja elasticidad a variaciones del precio se origina en varios factores, entre ellos, la obligatoriedad y complejidad del producto. Esto hace que la gran mayoría de los trabajadores no se informe y no responda a las diferencias de comisiones entre AFP" (Chile Presidential Advisory Council 2006a, p. 21).

18. For the lower-risk funds (multifunds C, D and E), the return each year may not be less than the lower of 2 percentage points (200 basis points) below the average return of all portfolios in the same class over the preceding thirty-six months, or 50 percent of the average return of all AFPs over the same period.

19. "La comercialización basada en regalos y descuentos permite llegar a estos clientes, soslayando la obligación de bajar el precio a todos los afiliados" (Chile Presidential Advisory Council 2006a, p. 21).

financing both government and firms. Credit for this goes to the pension reform and to successful indexing for inflation.

12.2.6 Fiscal cost

The fiscal costs of pensions in Chile have been high and continuing. Direct government pension spending in 2004 was 5.5 percent of GDP, close to the 1981-2004 average of 5.7 percent, with official projections for 2005–10—nearly thirty years after the reforms were introduced—of 5 percent of GDP (Arenas de Mesa and Mesa-Lago 2006, Table 2). Part of this is the legacy of financing the transition to a funded pension.[20] But there are several other reasons for high spending. One of these is poverty relief: the minimum pension guarantee and the welfare pension together cost slightly less than 1 percent of GDP in 2003, with additional spending on disability pensions for people under 65. There is further public spending on pensions for the military and the police (about 1.7 percent of GDP in 2003), which were not part of the 1981 reform.[21] These high fiscal costs are not in themselves a defect, but they serve as a reminder to other countries that pension systems inescapably involve public spending and that the time horizon of transition costs is likely to be long.

12.2.7 Economic growth

Chile has shown good economic growth since the 1980s, and some commentators talk as though that growth were due mainly to the pension reform. Such attribution is wrong; a range of other reforms were also essential. The pension reform contributed to growth in two ways: by increasing national saving (assuming that the surplus used for the transition would otherwise have been consumed, not invested) and by improving the functioning of capital markets. Determining the total effect on growth and how much each cause contributed to economic performance is inherently difficult, perhaps impossible, notwithstanding some cross-country regressions that claim to have done so (Beck, Levine, and Loayza 2000, cited by Holzmann and Hinz 2005, pp. 34 and 47).

12.2.8 Voluntary pensions

Voluntary pensions have allowed further options. In 2006 about forty firms sold voluntary pensions, of which only six were AFPs. As noted earlier, however, the system remains small. For the majority of the population, voluntary pensions are not a major element in their pension wealth, partly because of the nature of the product, in particular its illiquidity, and partly because tax incentives to participate are smaller for lower-income workers. And a big part of the story is that, as in most countries, the very poor do little or no voluntary retirement saving.

---

20. For an estimate of public spending attributable to the move to funding, see Valdés Prieto (2005*b*).

21. In addition, changes in government accounting, in compliance with revised IMF procedures (International Monetary Fund 2001), have acted to increase the measured deficit in the pension system prior to 2000. The changes concern the way recognition bonds appear in the public accounts; the revised accounts include, as an above-the-line item, interest accrued on the stock of unpaid bonds rather than the cash disbursement of bonds at the time of retirement. This increases the deficit in the earlier years of the reform and lowers the deficit after 2000.

The voluntary system is used mainly by better-off workers. In 2005, 26 percent of workers in the top quintile of AFP contributors also made contributions to the voluntary system; the comparable figure for contributors in the lowest quintile was 2.7 percent. The average income of workers contributing to the voluntary system was $1,350 per month; the comparable figure for the mandatory system was $635. Again, this outcome is not surprising: higher earners face fewer liquidity problems, and tax relief is more generous since it is given at the worker's marginal tax rate, which is higher for higher earners.

12.3   CONCLUSION

Covered workers in Chile enjoy a pension system that is stable and effective at providing consumption smoothing for workers with a fairly full contributions record, and pension reform has been an important part of the process of improving capital markets. But Chile's overall program of economic reform, of which the pension reform is only one element, has required sustained successful political action supported by sound macroeconomic policies. Furthermore, there is continuing concern in Chile about low pension benefits, low coverage, gender inequality, and high administrative charges. Moreover, because the transition to a funded system takes a long time, and because of existing antipoverty programs, the pension system makes a continuing and substantial claim on general revenue.

These results, it can be argued, are predictable outcomes of two core elements of the 1981 strategy: the focus on individual accounts and the underlying model of competitive supply. On the first, individual accounts are directly related to a person's earnings history. Thus they provide consumption smoothing but by definition do little by themselves to relieve poverty in old age for someone with low lifetime covered earnings. Another instrument is needed to provide poverty relief. Two such instruments, the minimum pension guarantee and the income-tested welfare pension, are in place but have the major deficiencies noted earlier. Continuing elderly poverty is thus a direct result of the strategy.

Competition and consumer choice work best when consumers are well informed and highly responsive to market conditions. The failure of these assumptions in the case of pensions, summarized in section 10.1.1, calls into question the welfare gains from competition and is part of the explanation for high administrative charges, continued high AFP profits, and the concentration of the industry. (See also the discussion in section 4.2.2, Box 4.2, and Box 9.6.)

For these and other reasons, "the system of individual accounts created by the 1981 reform is not presently capable of meeting the pension needs of all Chileans."[22] Poverty relief calls for strengthening the guarantees that supplement the individual accounts. With rising life expectancy and no changes in the mandatory saving rate or the age at which pensions start, replacement rates will inevitably decline, unless interest rates rise considerably, which there is little reason to expect.

---

22. "El régimen de capitalización creado por la reforma de 1981 no es actualmente capaz de resolver las necesidades previsionales de todos los chilenos" (Chile Presidential Advisory Council 2006a, p. 17).

This analysis has focused on the basic workings of the system as it actually operates, omitting the harder-to-quantify role of the pension system in distributing risk. Risk arises in two ways. One is the sharing of capital market and aggregate labor market risks. As discussed in section 7.3, funded individual accounts forgo the potential for intergenerational risk sharing offered by other approaches.

Second is the much-discussed issue of political risk. Governments in Chile frequently intervened in pension outcomes under the old (pre-1981) arrangements, resulting in a system that tended to favor those with more political power at the expense of other workers and taxpayers. Similar problems have arisen in other countries. Since the 1981 reforms, frequent legislation affecting the structure of the system has not been accompanied by bailouts of low returns or transfers among groups based on political power, and the assets in the system have remained available for the financing of benefits. These outcomes are not an automatic result of this type of system but a consequence of the quality of the political process in Chile as well as the design of the system.

That said, the politics of basic pension design may not be settled: "The limited commitment shown by the population toward the pension system is a problem that may become deeper over time. This limited commitment, due to lack of information, the complexity of the system and its low political legitimacy ... may turn into more outright rejection in the future if its benefits fail to meet the population's expectations."[23]

The primary lessons are threefold:

- Mandatory funded individual accounts can be part of a good reform, but such a reform is not easy.
- Private supply plus competition are not on their own sufficient to keep down transactions costs or charges.
- Unless accompanied by a robust system of poverty relief, individual accounts are not a pension system, but only a part of a pension system.

---

23. "La limitada adhesión que la población revela hacia el sistema previsional es un problema que puede ir profundizándose en el tiempo. Esta escasa adhesión, originada en la falta de información, la complejidad del sistema y su baja legitimidad política ... puede transformarse en un rechazo más abierto en el futuro si sus beneficios se encuentran muy por debajo de las expectativas de la población" (Chile Presidential Advisory Council 2006a, p. 7).

13

▷

Chile: Proposed Directions for Reform

In 2006 the Presidential Advisory Council on Pension Reform, appointed in response to the problems discussed in the previous chapter, issued a carefully written report examining the circumstances of the pension system in Chile, presenting criteria for evaluating improvements and putting forward seventy proposals for reform. At the end of that year, President Michelle Bachelet sent a pension reform bill to the legislature containing many but not all of the council's recommendations. The bill, with some amendments, was passed into law in January 2008, shortly before this book went to press.

This chapter sets out and evaluates some of the council's recommendations. In our eyes, and in those of the council, Chile has done a good job of implementing a system of market-based, funded individual accounts providing consumption smoothing,[1] but has not adequately developed its distributional and antipoverty institutions. Thus the problem was more one of strategy than of implementation, and the council's recommendations sought to address the shortcomings of the strategy. Moreover, we agree with the report's starting position of avoiding radical change where it was not necessary for the achievement of important goals, both because change is difficult and because any reforms need long-run political support.

Section 13.1 briefly summarizes the council's strategic thinking. Section 13.2 sets out the council's recommendations about a new basic pension, section 13.3 summarizes recommendations concerning individual accounts, section 13.4 discusses mandatory coverage, section 13.5 looks at the proposed reforms to strengthen gender equity, and section 13.6 offers some strategic conclusions. Appendix 13.1 briefly summarizes some other aspects of the reforms. Throughout the chapter, the recommendations in italics are those of the council.

1. As noted in section 9.2.3, a market-based system where workers choose their providers is more expensive than a system organized by the government; the design adopted in Chile added further to costs by not creating a centralized mechanism for collecting contributions (Diamond and Valdés Prieto 1994). Within this framework, however, Chile has not had the implementation problems that have arisen in some other countries.

13.1 THE CORE STRATEGY

The council's report identifies three fundamental challenges facing the pension system in Chile: "to make social security protection a universal right, to minimize the risk of poverty in old age, and to transform pensions into a fair payment for the contribution that people have made to society through productive and reproductive work, both paid and unpaid."[2] In short, the council called for action to ensure that the pension system provides wide coverage, poverty relief, and efficient consumption smoothing that takes account both of work and of family responsibilities. It judged that the existing system would not, on its own, be able to meet those challenges:

> If the 1981 reform produced an unbalanced system that placed too many responsibilities on the system of individual accounts, it is unlikely that this system will of itself be able to correct the problems and cope with the changes that the country will continue to experience in the near future. It is not the responsibility of the AFPs [the private firms that manage the individual accounts] to correct the limitations of the system, nor does it seem wise to wait for the problems to present themselves and for the state then to improvise countermeasures. The aim of the pension reform must be to prevent frustration and avoid improvisation.[3]

Thus,

> the Council proposes to move from a system dominated by individual accounts to a pension system capable of balancing and integrating its various components, including that scheme. Instead of giving preference to one pension scheme over another or developing parallel systems, the proposed system would be structured on three pillars: a solidarity pillar, a contributory pillar and a voluntary pillar. These pillars must be capable of complementing and integrating with one another to ensure that older people have a decent life in old age.[4]

The key strategic reform proposed by the council is to introduce a "solidarity pillar." In addition, the council proposed an innovative reform to try to lower the cost of

---

2. "Universalizar el derecho a la protección de la seguridad social; minimizar el riesgo de la pobreza en la vejez y transformar a las pensiones en una retribución justa al aporte de las personas a la sociedad a través del trabajo productivo y reproductivo, remunerado y no remunerado" (Chile Presidential Advisory Council 2006a, p. 11).

3. "Si la reforma de 1981 generó un sistema desequilibrado, que hizo recaer demasiadas responsabilidades sobre el régimen de capitalización individual, difícilmente esta sistema podrá, por sí solo, corregir los problemas y hacer frente a los cambios que el país seguirá experimentando en el futuro próximo. La responsabilidad por corregir las limitaciones del sistema no es de las AFP y no parece prudente esperar a que los problemas se presenten para improvisar compensaciones desde el estado. Prevenir la frustración y evitar la improvisación debe ser el objetivo de la reforma previsional" (Chile Presidential Advisory Council 2006a, p. 7).

4. "El Consejo propone pasar desde un sistema dominado por el régimen de capitalización individual, a un sistema previsional capaz de equilibrar e integrar sus distintos componentes, incluido dicho régimen. Esto significa que, en lugar de privilegiar un régimen de pensiones por sobre otro, o desarrollar sistemas paralelos, se propone estructurar el sistema en base a tres pilares: un pilar solidario, un pilar contributivo y un pilar voluntario. Estos pilares deben ser capaces de complementarse e integrarse, y contribuir a que los adultos mayores tengan una vida digna en la vejez" (Chile Presidential Advisory Council 2006a, p. 13).

funded individual accounts. Those changes are part of a wider set of reforms, taken up at relevant points in the later discussion. In 2000 the government implemented a structural surplus of 1 percent of GDP, which in 2006 it decided to institutionalize in the Fiscal Responsibility Act 2006. That act established a number of funds, including a Pension Guarantee Fund, to smooth the burden of taxes needed for pensions, and an Economic and Social Stabilization Fund, intended, among other things, to protect social expenditure in times of fiscal stringency.

A separate set of reforms, together called the Social Protection System, is intended to address social exclusion. The system has three main elements: a system of income-tested poverty relief (Chile Solidario), created by the previous government; the Childhood Protection System, relating to children under 8; and the Labor Protection System, of which the pension reforms are part. We discuss only the pensions element.

13.2 THE BASIC PENSION

This section starts by listing the recommendations concerning the basic pension, with some brief discussion; section 13.2.2 offers an assessment.

13.2.1 Benefits and finance

Council recommendation: A new solidarity pillar should be established, to provide a basic pension, together with disability and survivors' benefits. The basic pension should replace the minimum pension guarantee and the welfare pension.

This is one of the council's central recommendations. The basic pension (with parallel benefits for disability and survivors) is to be payable at age 65 (the same for men and women), and not subject to any contribution conditions.[5] The council's report set as an explicit objective that the basic pension benefit should be above the poverty line. The basic pension replaces the minimum pension guarantee, which in 2006 was just below 88,000 pesos per month, and the welfare pension, which can be taken as an approximation to the poverty line, at about 44,000 pesos per month. In line with the council's recommendations, the legislation of January 2008 introduced a basic pension benefit of 60,000 pesos per month (approximately $125, about 21 percent of monthly GDP per capita) from July 2008 onward for someone with a small (or no) pension accumulation and with income in the lower part of the family income distribution. The benefit is set to rise to 75,000 pesos per month beginning in July 2009.

The basic pension is withdrawn at higher levels of individual and family income, based on a dual-test:

- The basic pension is gradually withdrawn as the contributory pension income of the *individual* rises.
- The basic pension is also withdrawn as the total income from all sources of the *household* rises, and withdrawn completely from a household that does not belong to the poorest 40 percent of households (legislated to rise to 60 percent).

---

5. Thus the system is universal in the sense that "noncontributory universal pension" is defined in the glossary.

Thus there is an individual contributory pension income test and a household income test.[6] The system has analogies with that in Australia, which provides a tax-financed pension with no contribution conditions, subject to an affluence test (see glossary).

Since the income test is partly based on household contributory pension income, not just individual pension income, the treatment of married couples raises important issues of horizontal equity. Importantly for gender equality, and discussed further in section 13.5, husband and wife in a poor family are each entitled to the full basic pension in his or her own right. On the other hand, a woman with little or no pension entitlement of her own but a rich husband will not get a basic pension.

Council recommendation: Establish a Solidarity Fund for pensions.

To meet the costs of the basic pension, the report recommends establishing a trust fund, the Solidarity Fund (Fondo Solidario de Pensiones), supported mainly from current revenue with only a small accumulation as a cash flow reserve. There are two arguments for such a fund: its existence as an explicit item in the public accounts may help to protect pensioners' interests, and it strengthens the transparency of the government's commitments to the pension system (transparency being a major concern of the advisory council). The Solidarity Fund would cover the cost of both the basic pension and subsidies to individual accounts (discussed in section 13.5), for example to a mother for each child. Thus the recommendation is to use this fund on a flow basis, not to add to the funding of the overall pension system beyond what accumulates in the funded accounts.

13.2.2 Assessment

There is much in these proposals that is noteworthy.

Poverty relief: Strengthening the underdeveloped element. The basic pension directly addresses the central problem of the old strategy, identified at the end of chapter 12. By itself, a system of individual accounts is primarily a vehicle for consumption smoothing and thus constitutes only part of a complete pension system. The missing elements are insurance and poverty relief; the inadequacy of the minimum pension guarantee and the welfare pension in providing poverty relief is discussed in section 12.2.1. Moreover, given the high implicit taxes they impose on recipients, both the minimum guarantee and the welfare pension provide poor incentives for participation in the system. The basic pension addresses the strategic problem in three ways.

First, it is awarded without a contributions test. Anyone who meets the affluence test is entitled to the pension, including formal and informal sector workers, urban and rural workers, the self-employed, and those outside the labor force. Thus the basic pension assists workers with low or sporadic income. By implication, it also recognizes care responsibilities: someone who cares for young children or elderly dependents and consequently has no paid work will make fewer contributions to an individual account and have a small accumulation upon retirement; such people are entitled to the full basic pension, subject to the level of their spouse's pension. Thus the basic pension

6. Once the system is phased in, the withdrawal rate is intended to be fairly low, in the region of 30 percent, thus avoiding major disincentives to work and saving. The detailed operation of the income test is complex, not least because it includes the inflation rate.

disproportionately benefits women. As discussed below, further proposed changes to individual accounts are also intended to recognize care responsibilities.

The basic pension benefit is significantly above the poverty line. This is desirable as a matter of social policy but raises questions about fiscal sustainability, discussed below. The role of effective actuarial projections is clearly crucial in this context.

In sharp contrast with the post-1981 system (Figure 13.1), benefits under the basic pension are well coordinated with those of the contributory pension (Figure 13.2), so that the two elements fit together as a system.[7]

Incentive effects. The basic pension raises questions about incentives for work effort and saving. As we have argued repeatedly, it is not possible to have a pension system with no distortions; the right way to frame the issue is to consider jointly the distortions caused by higher taxation and the welfare gains from the poverty relief that that taxation finances. A low basic pension benefit would have minimal incentive effects but would provide little poverty relief; a high basic benefit might do more than is necessary to relieve poverty, would cost more, and would create a greater disincentive to work effort. Similarly, a rapid phase-out of the basic pension as income rises would have larger incentive effects over a narrower range, whereas a slow phase-out creates smaller incentive effects over a wider range and, because of higher costs, larger

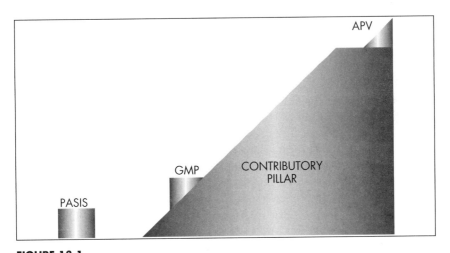

FIGURE 13.1.
Structure of the post-1981 pension system in Chile. PASIS (*pensión asistencial de ancianidad*) is the country's means-tested welfare pension; GMP is the guaranteed minimum pension; APV (*ahorro provisional voluntario*) is the system of voluntary pension system. Source: Chile Presidential Advisory Council (2006*a*, p. 18).

7. A person is not eligible to receive a contributory pension and a welfare pension (*pensión asistencial de ancianidad*, or PASIS) simultaneously. A person who has a small accumulation in the AFP system and who does not meet the twenty-year contribution requirement for the minimum guaranteed pension is required to draw down a monthly pension equal to the minimum guaranteed pension until the accumulation is exhausted. At that stage, with no remaining pension, the person becomes eligible for PASIS.

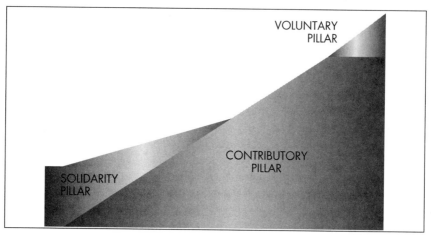

FIGURE 13.2.
Structure of the reformed pension system in Chile. Source: Chile Presidential
Advisory Council (2006*a*, p. 18).

incentive effects from having to raise the revenue to finance the benefit.[8] The choice
of the basic pension benefit and the rate of phase-out needs to balance the gains from
poverty relief against the adverse incentives from taxation.

Will a basic pension discourage work effort by lower earners? Qualitatively, the answer
is yes: a benefit reduces the work effort of potential recipients via the income effect; it also
does so via the substitution effect since, as Figure 13.2 shows, the basic benefit is reduced
as the contributory pension increases. Thus, by imposing an implicit tax on income from
the contributory pension, the basic pension imposes an implicit tax on covered earnings.

Will a basic pension discourage voluntary saving by lower earners? Qualitatively,
the answer is again yes: a benefit reduces the incentive to save via the income effect; for
some workers, it also does so via the substitution effect, since the reduction in the basic
pension benefit depends on the benefits received from both the mandatory and the
voluntary portions of the pension system. However, the accumulation of assets outside
the pension system does not affect the basic benefit. Hence the system discourages the
use of the pension system as a savings device, although this effect is not relevant for
poorer workers with very low savings. This disincentive against using the pension
system for voluntary saving needs to be evaluated in terms of the relative saving opportunities inside and outside the pension system, and the magnitude of the tax incentive
inside the system at different levels of earnings.

The report argues that everyone is made better off by higher earnings and saving.
Since an increase in the contributory benefit by $1 reduces the basic benefit by less
than $1, this is factually true after 2010, but not a complete analysis. Depending

---

8. More precisely, what matters is not the overall progressivity of the tax system but the
change in taxes to finance different possible costs of a basic pension. Since such hypothetical
alternatives are not really measurable, it is standard simply to assume that increases in revenue
resemble average revenue collection.

on the rate at which the basic benefit is clawed back, and on the importance of tax favoring, there will be a disincentive to saving in a voluntary system and an incentive to lower earnings and noncompliance in a mandatory system.

There is no effect from the link between the basic pension and the individual account balance for two groups of workers: those with very low or irregular earnings, whose contributory pension will never be large enough to cause a reduction in their basic pension; and those with high, regular earnings, whose contributory pension is well above the limit for any basic pension. Workers between the two extremes face disincentives, as they do under any arrangement to provide redistribution or insurance. There is no reason to think this one is unusually costly, but fuller judgment must await detailed analysis based on empirical estimates of covered labor supply and the elasticities of voluntary tax-favored saving. Since the value of tax favoring and of access to the mutual funds through the system, rather than outside, will not be great for those with low marginal tax rates, the link is likely to preclude voluntary saving by those in the range where the basic pension is being offset. This is probably not costly in terms of efficiency for two reasons: those with incomes in this range are not likely to do much voluntary retirement saving in any event, and the low tax rates mean that those who do save will not be much affected by saving outside the system rather than inside, if they have access to mutual funds with comparable returns net of charges.

Distributional effects. Within a system of contributory social insurance, solidarity is manifested by higher earners subsidizing lower earners. In the proposed solidarity pillar, net benefits (that is, benefits after the offset from the contributory system) are financed outside the contributory system through general taxation, and hence taxation on income, including income from capital. The proposals are progressive and, as discussed above, offer powerful poverty relief.[9]

Finance and funding. In thinking about the Solidarity Fund, three issues are noteworthy: the noncontributory nature of the basic pension, its fiscal sustainability, and the role of partial funding. The arguments for and against financing with dedicated revenue versus financing with general revenue are set out in section 6.1. The powerful advantage of a noncontributory system is the potential for wide coverage; the disadvantage is the potential vulnerability of the system's finance to short-run budgetary pressures and changes in political philosophy. As noted, a strong case can be made for either approach, the choice being as much political as economic.

Is the system affordable? The council's report projected the cost of the basic pension at 1 percent of GDP in 2025, about double the level of spending in 2006 on the minimum pension guarantee and the welfare pension. According to the report, these commitments can be met over time as the legacy costs of the old (pre-1981) system start to decline.

The Solidarity Fund could be financed entirely from current revenue or could have a funded element. In 2006, as part of the Fiscal Responsibility Act, which institutionalized a budget surplus of 1 percent of GDP, the government established a Pension Guarantee Fund, which receives 0.5 percent of GDP from general revenue in years when there is a fiscal surplus, with a minimum of 0.2 percent of GDP if there is no surplus.

9. There is a potential caveat. If the tax system is progressive but benefits are restricted mainly to white-collar, urban workers in the formal sector, a tax-financed system will be regressive. Since the basic pension in Chile applies to all sectors—formal and informal, urban and rural—that caveat does not apply.

(A parallel Innovation Fund derives its revenue from a royalty imposed on private copper companies.) At the time that the Pension Guarantee Fund was established, part of the fiscal surplus derived from a combination of high copper prices and the resulting large transfers to general revenue from Codelco, the state-owned copper company. The main purpose of the Pension Guarantee Fund is tax smoothing rather than economic growth;[10] in particular, its purpose is to assist higher pension spending until such time as the legacy costs of the pre-1981 commitments have been extinguished. It is thus comparable to the temporary surplus in the U.S. Social Security system designed to help to finance the costs of the baby-boomers' retirement. However, the fund's revenue may not be touched for its first ten years, so that paying a basic monthly pension benefit from 2008 onward will require additional public spending for at least the first few years.

Although the Pension Guarantee Fund has been established, the report left important details to be determined, including details of its management. One possibility is to follow the governance model of the Norwegian Government Global Pension Fund, in which a fraction of government oil revenue is deposited each year (Norway Central Bank 2005, 2006). The Norwegian fund is publicly accountable, has a socially responsible mandate, and is internationally invested, with the idea of smoothing the effects on taxation of future pension spending. The Chilean government studied the Norwegian fund closely in connection with the potential for adverse macroeconomic effects stemming from natural resource discoveries (the so-called Dutch disease),[11] but not in relation to fund management. The example is potentially of interest to other countries rich in natural resources.

13.3 INDIVIDUAL ACCOUNTS

The council's report devotes considerable attention to strengthening the system of individual accounts, through assistance to low-income workers (section 13.3.1), action to improve the overall operation of individual accounts (section 13.3.2), and a series of additional measures (section 13.3.3).

13.3.1 Assisting low earners

The report proposes a series of measures, of which the following are the most important.

Council recommendation: Subsidize the pension contributions of people on unemployment benefits.

10. As discussed in section 6.3, the economic impact of pension funds depends on whether or not they represent an increase in saving.

11. The term "Dutch disease" originated from a crisis in the Netherlands in the 1960s resulting from discoveries of large natural gas deposits under the North Sea. It is primarily associated with the discovery of natural resources, but it can result from any large inflow of foreign currency, whether from foreign direct investment, foreign aid, or a substantial increase in natural resource prices. The condition arises when foreign currency inflows cause an appreciation of the affected country's currency, reducing the country's competitiveness. In the long run, the lower competitiveness can result in jobs being moved to lower-cost countries. The end result is that nonresource industries are hurt by the increase in wealth generated by the resource-based industries. A similar problem occurred in the United Kingdom in the 1970s, for similar reasons. The pound sterling appreciated sharply, but the country fell into recession when British workers demanded higher wages and exports became uncompetitive.

The council proposed that the unemployment insurance program pay the pension contributions of people on unemployment benefits. In line with what has been done in some other countries, this mechanism contributes to consumption smoothing.

Council recommendation: Subsidize the initial contributions of low earners.

The council proposed a subsidy for the contributions of all low-income workers for the first twenty-four months of contributions. Presumably the idea is based on the behavioral insight that getting workers started in the system may help overcome noncompliance associated with inertia (see the discussion in Box 9.6).[12] Given a mandate for coverage of the self-employed (see section 13.4), the subsidy encourages compliance with the new mandate rather than offering encouragement to participate in a voluntary system.[13]

Council recommendation: Increase the visibility of charges.

The council proposed that commissions to pension providers be listed as a separate deduction from the worker's wage rather than included in the overall pension deduction. This may to make the charges more visible and hence strengthen downward pressure on them. Alongside measures to assist low earners, a further series of proposed reforms to individual accounts were directed toward ameliorating gender disparities. These are discussed in section 13.5.

13.3.2 Improving the operation of individual accounts

Most of the measures discussed thus far address income distribution and aim to increase workers' accumulations directly. A further set of policies aims at improving the operation of individual accounts generally.

The council was acutely aware of the lack of price sensitivity in account holders' choices of funds:

> The challenge for the Council was to propose mechanisms to make members more aware of prices, to allow greater competition and, possibly, the entry of new actors. These mechanisms must aim to achieve reductions in the commissions paid, without sacrificing other relevant attributes, such as the quality of the financial management and service provided, and without reducing the productive efficiency of the industry.[14]

12. Employers will receive a monthly subsidy from general revenue for each worker between the ages of 18 and 35 whose wages are less than 150 percent of the minimum wage. A subsidy of 50 percent of the mandatory contribution is paid for the first twenty-four months of contributions. The worker receives an equivalent subsidy to his or her individual account.

13. The United States subsidizes contributions by low- and moderate-income workers to voluntary retirement savings through the so-called saver's credit, an additional tax credit for such contributions.

14. "El desafío para el Consejo era proponer mecanismos que sensibilizaran a los afiliados al precio, permitieran una mayor competencia y, eventualmente, la entrada de nuevos actores. Estos mecanismos deben apuntar a conseguir rebajas en las comisiones pagadas, sin sacrificar otros atributos relevantes como la calidad de la gestión financiera y la del servicio prestado, y sin reducir la eficiencia productiva de la industria" (Chile Presidential Advisory Council 2006a, p. 22).

To that end, recommendations focus on reducing administrative costs and improving real returns.

Reducing administrative costs

Council recommendation: Widen legal options for exploiting administrative economies of scale.

Under the post-1981 arrangements, a pension provider must not be involved in any other business; this implied restrictions on administrative collaboration. The council's report notes that it should be possible to separate account administration (for example, keeping individual contribution records) from fund management (choosing portfolios of financial assets) and recommends lifting restrictions on subcontracting functions relating to the former. The idea is to allow pension providers to exploit the potential economies of scale in account administration.

It is noteworthy that the proposals to eliminate restrictions on administrative functions include "allowing bodies connected with social security to participate in these functions."[15] Thus the measures allow public authorities to assist in administration, opening the possibility of exploiting considerable economies of scale. Whether the exercise of such an option will be beneficial clearly depends on the quality of government actions.

Council recommendation: Introduce competitive tendering for new entrants to the labor force.

A system where firms in the market compete for individual workers is inevitably an expensive one, although it maintains good incentives for the quality of services. A system like that in Bolivia, where firms bid for the exclusive right to provide services to a segment of the population, is less expensive, but suffers from inadequate incentives to provide good service. The Chilean council proposes an experiment involving a mix of bidding and individual choice, which might result in lower charges while maintaining quality of service. The report recommends a system in which pension providers bid for all new entrants to the labor force over a one-year period, who then would have to stay with the winning bidder for at least eighteen months.[16] The provider would be obliged to offer the same commission to its existing participants, if lower than they are already being charged, and to any others who wish to enroll to benefit from the low charges. After eighteen months the provider would be allowed to increase its commission for all participants, preserving uniformity.

Part of the appeal of this process is the likelihood that new entrants, who have not yet accumulated funds, are not likely to be sensitive to the differences across firms. Thus the experiment is based on workers who, it is thought, contribute little to competitive price pressures. What will in fact happen over time is an interesting question that will merit exploration. But the experiment needs to be designed and evaluated carefully. Although not our area of expertise, it is natural to consider a randomized experiment where only a fraction of the new entrants are bundled into this bidding mechanism, to explore the longer-run implications.

---

15. "permitiendo la participación en estas funciones de entidades vinculadas a la seguridad social" (Chile Presidential Advisory Council 2006*a*, p. 22).

16. An identical mechanism is used in some countries for preferred providers of health care or pharmaceutical drugs; see Barr (2001*a*, Chapter 4, section 2.2).

A further reform aimed at lowering charges is to allow AFPs to offer discounts to participants who continue beyond eighteen months, to encourage them to stay. This would relax the rule that each pension provider have a single scale of charges for all its participants. It is likely to reduce prices for ongoing AFP users in the short run; however, it runs the risk of raising prices for those without sufficiently long participation, including, of course, new entrants. The process also runs the risk of decreasing competition in the long run by introducing a cost (the lack of a discount) to switching firms if all firms use such a discount. Thus it may be that, after the effect of bidding, the discounts are not helpful. Hence these two experiments—bidding for new entrants and discounts for continuing participants—need to be considered together and monitored closely to see if either or both are worth maintaining. It might be useful not to make both changes simultaneously, so that it is possible to distinguish their separate effects.

The purpose of these measures is to make the market more competitive in the face of consumers' sluggish response to price differences. The bidding mechanism is an incentive to lower prices, at least temporarily, and is intended to encourage new entrants who can bid low without having a current pool of affiliates for whom the price must be lowered. Entry is made easier because the possibility of decoupling account administration from fund management is thought to reduce the minimum profitable scale of an AFP from about 1 million participants to an estimated 250,000.

The council recognized the inevitable tension arising from the fact that most of the cost of maintaining accounts is a cost per account, not a cost that is proportional to the size of the account balance. The council made no recommendation on whether the option to set a fixed charge along with the proportional charge should continue. The legislation eliminated the flat charge.[17]

Improving real returns

Council recommendation: Simplify the legal restrictions on investment.

The report recommends simplifying the law constraining the types of securities that pension funds may hold, including the type and mix of stocks and bonds, and liberalizing the law's restrictions on the fraction of holdings that may be in overseas assets, leaving the exact nature of such restrictions to regulation. The design of such regulation and its modification over time are to be delegated to a new Technical Investment Committee.

Council recommendation: Change the focus of regulation to reflect risk.

Regulation of portfolios has focused on the mix of assets a fund may hold rather than on the primary purpose of such regulation, which is to optimize the combination of risk and return to which the pension savings of workers are exposed. The report recommends that regulation focus more explicitly on risk per se. As an example, it recommends that, over time, regulation replace the limits on foreign investment with limits on exposure to currency risk.

Council recommendation: Adopt policies to strengthen competition in fund management.

As discussed in section 12.2.5, a government-mandated guarantee that no pension provider will offer a return significantly lower than the average has led to fund managers

---

17. Although regulation has set the form of allowable charges, the levels have been left to the AFPs.

adopting very similar investment strategies. This has muted competition based on different strategies to achieve better returns, while plausibly increasing price competition, since that has become the major element of difference between firms. The report recommends redesigning these regulations to strengthen competition in investment management. Since it is difficult to judge the quality of such management, as opposed to taking on more risk or simply being lucky, it is not clear to us that this is a worthwhile goal in the context of firms that are already offering five different mutual funds.

13.3.3 Other reforms

Council recommendation: Develop a market for early life annuities.

The idea behind this recommendation is that workers who are within ten years of retirement should have the option to buy annuity "modules" in advance, payable from the date of their future retirement. Provided the annuity is indexed to price changes, this "early life annuity" arrangement gives the worker certainty about his or her future benefit, while shifting risk in the future pricing of annuities from the worker to the annuity provider. Of course, such a shift will influence the pricing of annuities. Economists have recognized the value of rolling annuitization as a mechanism for shifting risk in an idealized market setting (Sheshinski 2008). Of course, allowing workers to make multiple smaller transactions instead of one larger one may influence both the equilibrium pricing of annuities and the market for advice on annuitization. But this is a valuable idea whose implementation should be monitored closely.

Council recommendation: Introduce measures to give workers more-flexible choices about retirement.

Arguments about the appropriate earliest entitlement age are set out in section 5.3.2. As people live longer—and particularly if fertility is falling at the same time—the age at which people first collect their pension is an important variable in balancing the adequacy of pensions with their cost.

Under the post-1981 system, people do not have to start taking benefits on reaching the earliest entitlement age. And since the system is based on funded defined-contribution individual accounts, any delay in the start of benefits results in an actuarially fair increase in benefits once they do start. But the system has several aspects that matter for the ability of people to adapt to longer expected lives. One issue is that women's earliest age for access to benefits is less than that for men (60 rather than 65); as discussed in section 13.5, the council proposes eventual equalization.

A second issue is that opportunities for tax-favored retirement savings end at the earliest entitlement age. Adaptation to longer lives should include the opportunity for tax-favored voluntary saving beyond the earliest entitlement age. The council makes no recommendation on this aspect of policy.

A third issue relates to the fact that under the post-1981 arrangements people are allowed to draw their pension early, provided that their accumulation is large enough to provide a replacement rate of at least 70 percent. Thus the system combines an earliest entitlement age with a provision that it can be overridden by a replacement rate condition. The report proposes to lower the minimum required replacement rate for workers nearing retirement age: the rate would decline smoothly from 70 percent at age 60 to 54 percent at age 64, thus facilitating early retirement by older workers. Easing the rules for access to retirement benefits is thought to be useful for low-income workers, who are most likely to face adverse labor market conditions and shorter life expectancies. Combining a replacement rate test with an earliest age without a replacement rate test is an interesting innovation, although the earliest age of access to pensions needs to be chosen carefully. It is necessary to monitor whether allowing people with smaller accumulations to retire earlier results in much lower replacement rates later on. A worker who retires early will have to wait until age 65 to be awarded any basic pension. It is not clear how the basic pension would be integrated with a contributory pension that is taken early and is therefore smaller. To avoid excessive incentives to retire early, the integration should be based on what the contributory pension benefit would have been had the pension started at age 65, not on what it was when taken at an earlier age.

Many of the recommendations aimed at improving individual accounts are worthwhile in their own right and relatively uncontentious. What remains an open question is the effect of the measures that seek to strengthen competition, such as the arrangements for competitive tendering in conjunction with separating account management from fund management; as discussed in Box 9.4, administrative charges have a considerable impact on one's pension accumulation; competitive tendering, to the extent that it reduces charges over a full lifetime, is helpful. The possible impact on the quality of services also needs to be monitored. This is not an argument against competition, but it suggests that it will be important to monitor the effectiveness of the new measures and to make adjustments where necessary.

As noted previously, the report's starting position was to avoid radical change where it was not necessary, both because change is difficult and because any reforms need long-run political support. Not least for these reasons, the recommendations stay clear of more radical reforms, such as one that would mimic the U.S. Thrift Savings Plan (Box 11.5). Specifically, the report did not recommend a publicly run AFP, the subject of one of the most intense debates over pension reform in Chile (the other being women's retirement age). Although Sweden has a publicly run fund alongside the many private funds, it is available only as a default, not as a fund to which a worker can switch an existing account. Competition between public and private providers, provided that the public option is offered on a level playing field, seems potentially useful.

13.4 MANDATORY COVERAGE

As discussed in the previous section, the introduction of a basic pension without a contributions test has a dual purpose: to raise the incomes of people who otherwise would have little pension entitlement, and to extend coverage to people largely or wholly left out of the system. In addition, some of the recommendations relating to individual accounts, particularly those aimed at assisting low earners, are intended, among other things, to improve coverage.

Council recommendation: Extend the mandatory system to cover self-employed workers on the same basis as employed workers.

The report recommends that the distinction between employed and self-employed workers be abolished, so that self-employed workers become entitled to the same benefits as employed workers and face the same tax regime. Thus self-employed workers would be eligible for the basic pension, and the basic pension would interact with the contributory pension in the same way as for employed workers.

As regards individual accounts, the report recommends phasing in arrangements over the next five years such that self-employed workers would make mandatory contributions in the same way as employed workers. Although the move is potentially a good one, national pension systems face two complications in dealing with the self-employed.

First, as Figure 13.2 shows, over a range of low earnings the basic pension benefit will be partly clawed back in respect of a person's AFP pension. Thus extending the mandate would, in effect, require self-employed workers to finance part of their basic pension, particularly to the extent that they disproportionately have low earnings; some form of earned income tax credit would be helpful in this context.[18] Second, the reporting of self-employment earnings is much more difficult for the authorities to monitor, making concern about compliance a larger issue. The more a system is redistributive, the larger the concern about compliance.

For the long run it is valuable for a national system to cover all workers, a key question being timing: when will institutions be ready and resources available to take on the large task of extending mandatory coverage? If Chile is ready, this is a good step to take.

Council recommendation: Equalize eligibility for voluntary pensions for self-employed workers.

The report stresses the importance of voluntary pensions for workers with an inadequate record of contributions to the mandatory system, for high earners with income above the ceiling for tax concessions, and, more generally, as a means of enhancing individual choice. The post-1981 system gives little encouragement for self-employed workers to join voluntary pension plans: the tax advantages are limited, and confidence in such plans is lacking. Rectifying these problems is clearly necessary and desirable.

13.5 ADDRESSING GENDER DISPARITIES

An important series of recommendations, some relating to the overall system, others concerning individual accounts, were explicit moves toward greater gender neutrality.

13.5.1 Measures affecting the overall system

Council recommendation: Husband and wife are each entitled to a basic pension.

As noted in section 13.2, husband and wife in a poor family are each entitled to the full basic pension in his or her own right. Although this is desirable in terms of gender equity, policy design faces a dilemma, in the case of well-off couples where the husband is the sole or main earner, between treating women on a strictly individual basis, on the one hand, and targeting benefits to the poorest families, on the other. As discussed in Chapter 8, if a woman's basic pension takes no account of her husband's accumulation, she is treated as an individual, but targeting is not tight. Alternatively, if a couple is treated as a single entity, a woman with a rich husband will not receive a basic pension and is thus treated as a dependent. This would not in itself be a violation of gender neutrality if the arrangement were symmetrical, with couples with one high earner and one low earner treated identically, whether the husband or the wife was the low earner. As noted above,

18. See Ellwood (2000), Barr (2004a, Chapter 10), and U.K. Treasury (2005).

the affluence test is based on household income; thus a spouse with only a small contributory pension in his or her own right will not be entitled to a basic pension if household income is high. And the report proposes symmetry and so gender neutrality.

Council recommendation: Equalize the retirement age for men and women.

Women will receive a solidarity pension at age 65, the same age as men. Contingent on the gender measures discussed in this section having been put into place, the report recommends that, after a ten-year grace period, women's retirement age for contributory pensions should rise gradually until it equals that of men. If properly implemented, this approach conforms with the principles for raising the retirement age set out in Box 5.10.

Council recommendation: Introduce symmetrical rules for survivor and disability benefits.

The report recommends symmetrical rules for survivor benefits, thus including the husband as beneficiary of a survivor pension on his wife's contributions. As noted in section 12.2.4, in the post-1981 system survivor benefits were available to women but not to men.

Another recommendation under this heading is to equalize the maximum age for disability and survivor insurance at 65 for men and women. No recommendation was made about the timing and phasing of this change.

Council recommendation: Extend the social security system to include child care.

The idea behind this recommendation is to facilitate women's labor force participation by ensuring that all workers have access to child care, which can be private or public. Private child care tends to be more expensive. Currently the government provides child care for people with lower incomes; the charges depend on family income and are zero for the least well off.[19] The council's goal is ambitious in terms of ensuring sufficient quantity and good quality. The point is nontrivial given increasing understanding of the centrality of early child development (see, for instance, Feinstein 2003) and the need therefore to ensure adequate infrastructure and the education of qualified personnel. As discussed in section 8.3.2, the availability of child care also matters for female labor force participation.

13.5.2   Gender-related proposals concerning individual accounts

The report sets out a series of measures designed to increase the accumulations of women.

Council recommendation: Provide government-financed pension rights during maternity leave.

As legislated in 2008, women in the poorest 60 percent of the population are eligible upon the birth of a child for a contribution to their individual account based on one year's minimum wage, the contribution to be financed from general revenue. The provision is intended to preserve pension rights that a woman would otherwise lose when leaving the labor market for maternity reasons. Sweden has a similar policy.

---

19. A childhood council, which reported in parallel to the advisory council on pension reform, recommended the creation of a comprehensive policy for children up to 8 years old.

Council recommendation: Allow pension contributions by third parties.

The idea behind this recommendation is, for example, to make it possible for a husband to pay pension contributions for a wife who is caring for children or an elderly relative and receive the same tax treatment as for his own contributions.

Council recommendation: Allow the division of account balances upon divorce.

The post-1981 system does not allow redistribution of account balances. The proposal in the report is to allow (but not compel) such divisions as an option in the financial settlement in the case of divorce or annulment.

Council recommendation: Consider using different life tables for men and women in different parts of the pension system.

In some areas the report argues unambiguously for separate probabilities, for example separating disability and survivorship contracts for men and women. The argument is that women have fewer accidents than men, and hence are less risky and should pay a lower premium. The report is more cautious on whether annuities should be based on separate or unisex life tables. It proposes that a study be conducted into the desirability of unisex tables but that their use not be made mandatory at this stage.

This recommendation appears to conflict with the recommendation, discussed above, of making the treatment of survivor and disability benefits symmetrical. We think the approach of gender neutrality calls for uniform treatment of pricing of different insurance elements within the pension system. If the study were to find unfortunate distributional effects from a change in annuity pricing, these should be addressed directly (and presumably more efficiently) through measures relating to the size of pension benefits rather than through a blunt instrument of overall pricing.

13.5.3   Summary

The council's package of measures relating to gender addresses many of the sources of inequality identified in Chapter 8:

- Greater commitment to the provision of child care makes opportunities for labor force participation more equal.
- A series of transfers—taxpayer subsidies after maternity, the possibility of contributions from third parties, and the option of transfers upon divorce—will boost women's pension accumulations.
- Equalizing retirement ages will extend the period over which women accumulate savings and, in parallel, reduce their time in retirement.
- The provisions to help low earners and to mandate coverage of the self-employed will also matter disproportionately for women.

The report leaves to the future the decision about whether pension benefits should continue to be based on gender-specific life tables or use unisex tables. Many countries, including the European Union, outlaw the use of gender-specific tables in pricing annuities in mandatory systems and have uniform rules in defined-benefit systems. The United States outlaws such pricing in group annuities made available through tax-favored, employer-provided, defined-benefit plans. Thus this aspect of the recommendations can be regarded as cautious, perhaps for political reasons in an area that generated huge political debate in Chile. This is not per se a criticism: the best policy design will fail if it is not politically sustainable.

13.6 CONCLUSION

The reforms in Chile are based on a number of explicit and implicit principles. The first is to plan reforms reflectively, when the system is not in crisis, and when the inadequacies of the system of poverty relief, although clearly visible, are not as large as they will be. Thus the advisory council argues that Chile need not reform opportunistically but can instead put in place measures, some of them for the medium term, to address predictable future problems. Second, the council rejects a complete overhaul of the system, on the grounds that it is not necessary. A third principle is that of shared responsibility:

> The operation of the pension system is the responsibility of the state, the private administrators and insurers, the workers and the employers. . . . *In particular, the state has the final responsibility for the integrity of the system.*[20]

Taken as a whole, although there is much that can be discussed about the detail, the package of proposals is a genuine strategy that recognizes the need to strengthen poverty relief: "The Council has concentrated its efforts on putting together a harmonious set of reforms, capable of complementing one another to produce an integrated pension system."[21]

More specifically, the package addresses many of the problems of the present system outlined in Chapter 12:

- Pensioner poverty is addressed by the basic pension; through measures, including subsidies for low earners, to increase benefits from individual accounts; and over time by making the system mandatory for self-employed workers.
- The package addresses vertical equity: the post-1981 system works best for those who are best off; those who make higher contributions and have a greater contribution density receive greater tax benefits. The basic pension and the changes to the system of individual accounts to benefit the poor act to reduce the variation in pension benefits.
- Gender inequality is addressed by a series of measures. Making child care more easily available assists women's labor force participation. Raising women's retirement age over time to equal that of men will act to increase their accumulations. The minimum pension guarantee, which requires twenty years of contributions, will be replaced by the basic pension, which has no contribution conditions. The question of separate or unisex life tables remains an item for discussion.

20. "La operación del sistema de pensiones es responsabilidad del estado, de los administradores y aseguradores privados, de los trabajadores y de los empleadores. . . . *En particular, el estado es el responsable último de la integridad del sistema*" (Chile Presidential Advisory Council 2006a, p. 12, emphasis added).

21. "El esfuerzo del Consejo ha estado puesto en articular un conjunto armonioso de reformas, capaz de complementarse para generar un sistema previsional integrado" (Chile Presidential Advisory Council 2006a, p. 31).

- Chile has legislated changes in the competition rules for AFPs in repeated attempts to attain an equilibrium with lower charges. This has been difficult to accomplish. The council is making another attempt through competitive tendering (section 13.3.2) and by widening the legal options for exploiting administrative economies of scale, in particular by unbundling the administration of individual accounts from fund management so as to allow public authorities to assist in administration.

Most important, the fundamental weakness in the post-1981 system, identified at the end of Chapter 12, is that it provides consumption smoothing but only weak poverty relief. The reforms, by introducing a noncontributory basic pension alongside individual accounts, directly address this problem.

APPENDIX 13.1   FURTHER REFORMS

Benefit design

Council recommendation: Continue the process of enhancing some portability of benefit entitlements across countries.

This recommendation relates to a long-term continuing process. Under a series of international agreements, pension benefits are portable across a range of countries, notably among Chile, Peru, and Sweden. These agreements established portability of a range of entitlements, illustrated here in terms of a Chilean citizen, but applying equally to citizens of the other countries involved:

- A Chilean living in Peru is entitled to all of his or her Chilean pension at the same level as if living in Chile, and the pension can be paid in Peru.
- A requirement to contribute for a minimum number of years can be met by adding up the number of years of contributions in each country; for example, someone who has worked and contributed for ten years in Chile and ten in Peru is counted as having twenty contribution years.
- A Chilean living in Peru who wishes to apply for a Chilean disability pension may be given a medical examination in Peru.
- A Chilean worker may transfer his or her Chilean individual account to a Peruvian pension fund, provided that the worker has contributed in Chile for at least five years, that the entire individual account is transferred, and that the transfer is permanent.

Management of the system

Council recommendation: Take action to improve the public's knowledge about and understanding of the pension system.

The report recommends creating a fund to provide for pension education, its financing to be shared between private pension providers and the taxpayer. The central role of consumer information is discussed in section 9.3, which argues that it is both possible and desirable to improve citizens' understanding of the general way in which pensions operate, but naïve to assume that such education is a complete solution. The details of specific pension plans are highly complex in ways that even financially literate people find hard to grasp fully. Thus, as explained in Box 4.2, pensions raise both information problems, which are soluble, and information processing problems, which generally are not. In particular, the principles of optimal investing (such as the concept of a risk-return frontier) are subtle, as are the choices between annuitization and phased withdrawal and of the right time to start benefits. Moreover, understanding the interaction between the benefit from the individual account and that from the new basic pension involves a degree of numerical literacy.

Council recommendation: Develop a system of accreditation of independent financial advisers.

Where people are incompletely informed, for example about personal finance or medical care, one solution is to seek advice from experts. Thus the report recommends developing a system of accreditation for independent financial advisers that would apply to all types of pension provision. The idea has much to commend it. People will seek financial advice anyway, and, almost by definition, they will seek advice about those areas in which they are not well informed. Thus it is important to provide effective training of advisers and sound regulation of the advisory profession. Making such regulation effective, however, is not easy: the distortionary effects of different forms of payment for advice are well known.[22] The system of accreditation will thus require considerable care, and although this approach can be helpful, it should not be viewed as a panacea. Moreover, it should be accompanied by education on how best to use advisers.

---

22. In systems of medical care, the combination of fee-for-service and retrospective reimbursement of medical providers by insurance companies is well known to create an inefficient upward bias in medical spending (Barr 2001a, Chapter 4); upfront commissions for financial products can create similar biases. For analyses of the activities of financial advisers in developed countries, see OECD (2004a) and, in the United States specifically, Bodie (2003).

14

▷

China: The Pension System

This chapter describes the pension system in China (section 14.1), with a brief discussion of its antecedents, and assesses its strengths and weaknesses (section 14.2). The next chapter sets out our proposals for reform.[1]

14.1 DESCRIPTION

14.1.1 The inheritance

Although economic growth and development in China have been explosive, the country has features in common with other developing countries: income per capita is relatively low and inequality high; there is a dual economy, with most of the growth in urban areas; and institutional capacity is limited.

China also has features in common with the reforming former communist countries of Central and Eastern Europe. Before the economic reforms, the state was the major actor in almost all walks of life. There was near full employment, and most benefits were rooted in the enterprise and thus based on a model of formal sector, lifetime urban employment in state-owned enterprises. Social insurance contributions were paid mainly by the enterprise, but enterprises faced soft budget constraints: shortfalls on output targets were penalized, but financial losses were not. Given the predominance of agriculture and other rural activity, employment in the state-owned enterprises was only a small fraction of total employment, resulting in a pension system with very low coverage. The strategic incompatibility of this system with the needs of a competitive market economy with growing formal employment is clear. As the reforms in China gathered pace,

- Open unemployment emerged on a large scale. Tens of millions of people in China lost their jobs, creating an urgent need for unemployment benefits, an institution previously nonexistent because unnecessary.

1. Both chapters draw on the report of a group of which we were members (Asher et al. 2005; http://www.oup.com/us/pdf/social_security_study_2005). For other assessments and proposals for reform, see Drouin and Thompson (2006), Salditt, Whiteford, and Adema (2007), and Williamson (2004).

TABLE 14.1
Economic growth and saving in China, 1981-2005

PERIOD	AVERAGE REAL GDP GROWTH (PERCENT A YEAR)	GROSS DOMESTIC SAVING (PERCENT OF GDP)
1981–90	9.3	n.a.[a]
1991–1995	13.1	40.9
1996–2000	8.6	37.1
2001–05	9.5	39.6

Source: World Bank data.
[a]Not available.

- Poverty increased sharply, creating the need for more fully developed poverty relief; income disparities also increased sharply, both within and across regions (OECD 2004*b*).
- Financing of benefits by enterprises created problems for their viability in an internationally competitive environment, and problems for enterprise workers, whose benefits are not portable to private sector jobs.

In other respects, however, China stands out positively. Economic growth has been strong and sustained over the past twenty-five years, and the saving rate is exceptionally high, as shown in Table 14.1. Around that trend, however, is considerable regional variation, in both the level of income and its rate of growth—and given the size of the country, individual regions can be very large. China is experiencing rapid aging, as shown in the population pyramid in Figure 1.5, both because of rising life expectancy, as in other countries, but also because of China's policy of one child per family. Although the one-child policy has an important bearing on the ratio of the older population to the working-age population, it is less important for the flow of contributions relative to the flow of benefit payments because the pension system still covers such a small fraction of the labor force. However, as shown by Table 14.2 and discussed further in section 14.2.2, the system dependency ratio (see glossary) has deteriorated rapidly.

Fundamental reform of the pension system in 1997 sought to transform the old, enterprise-based arrangements into a nationwide system consistent with the needs of

TABLE 14.2
Retired worker population and pension system dependency ratio in China, 1980–2002

YEAR	NO. OF RETIRED WORKERS (MILLIONS)	SYSTEM DEPENDENCY RATIO (ACTIVE COVERED WORKERS PER RETIRED WORKER)
1980	8.2	12.8
1985	16.4	7.5
1990	23.0	6.1
1995	30.9	4.8
2002	36.1	3.1

Source: Zheng (2004*a*, Table 2), based on data from the Ministry of Labor and Social Security.

a market economy. The resulting system has three elements: a basic pension (section 14.1.2), individual accounts (section 14.1.3), and voluntary pensions (section 14.1.4). Section 14.1.5 briefly describes other forms of poverty relief.

14.1.2 The basic pension

The basic pension, sometimes referred to as the social pool, is a primary element in poverty relief in China. Subject to contribution conditions, all urban workers are eligible. Benefits are different for different cohorts. Workers who joined the workforce in 1997 or later ("new people") are entirely in the reformed system. Under this system the basic pension is a PAYG, defined-benefit pension, in principle payable to all urban workers at 20 percent of the local average wage after fifteen years of contributions. In practice, the level of benefit can fall short of the target, and coverage, even within the urban sector, is low.

Workers who retired before 1997 ("old people") are fully covered by the prereform system. Their entire pension comes from the social pool, in many cases from their former enterprise.[2] A third group ("middle people") consists of those who were working in 1997, having joined the covered labor force earlier. This group receives part of its pension under the new arrangements plus a transitional benefit at a level decided by the provincial government. Someone who joined the labor force in 1992 at age 20 thus had five years under the old system and so might be on the books for sixty years or more as a transitional case. This is not a problem per se, but emphasizes the importance of considering pensions in a full context, and not only in long-run steady state.

There is considerable discretion in the system, particularly in the way pensions are adjusted as prices and earnings rise, the magnitude and frequency of such adjustments being a matter for provincial governments. There are mandatory retirement ages for men (at 60) and women (55 for those in white-collar and 50 for those in blue-collar jobs); in what are classified as hardship jobs, the respective retirement ages are 55 and 45. Pensionable age is the same for the basic pension and for pensions from individual accounts. In practice, however, many people are allowed to retire early without any reduction in either element.

Since 1998, costs have been shared among workers, employers, and different levels of government. The contributions base is the standard wage, a narrower definition of income than typical taxable earnings in market economies. Alongside dedicated contributions, central and local governments provide substantial subsidies from general revenue, since not all regions receive sufficient contributions to finance all benefits. And in 2000 the State Council set up the National Social Security Fund to create a strategic reserve. Finally, as discussed in section 14.2.3, some of the finance of the basic pension has been through the use of funds meant for the individual accounts.

14.1.3 Individual accounts

Since 1998, urban workers in the state and nonstate sectors are expected also to contribute to a system of funded, defined-contribution individual accounts.

2. Such workers are entitled to a pension of 90 percent of their standard wage if they joined the labor force before 1945; for workers who joined between 1945 and 1949, the replacement rate was 80 percent, and for those who joined after 1949, 75 percent.

The case for a defined-contribution benefit centers on its capacity to provide a vehicle for consumption smoothing, an element of growing importance as earnings, which are increasingly market determined, become much more differentiated than previously. The case for funding has to be argued to an important extent on the basis of its contribution to economic growth, either through increased saving or by improving the operation of financial markets, or both. The analytical basis of this claim is assessed in section 6.3 and applied to China in section 15.3.1.

Each worker's benefit from his or her individual account is a monthly pension of 1/120th of the account's accumulation at retirement; that is, pensions are based on the assumption that average life expectancy at retirement age is ten years, and interest is ignored. Workers allowed to retire early receive a pension from their individual account without actuarial reduction.

14.1.4 Voluntary pensions

Operating alongside the national mandatory system, which has a uniform structure with provincial and local variations, voluntary pensions are a potentially important complement to the basic pension and individual accounts. Indeed, a uniform national system is most valuable when it coexists with a sizable voluntary system. Voluntary pensions accommodate different preferences and constraints, as discussed in section 5.1; they can help in developing capital markets and regulatory expertise, as discussed in section 6.3.2, thereby enhancing the long-run role of the private sector in providing pensions; and they can accommodate different working conditions across industries and across the wide regional differences that exist in a country as large as China.

Currently, voluntary plans are enterprise based, with no provision for individual plans. In China both approaches are likely to develop over time, once there are legal arrangements for individual plans.[3]

14.1.5 Other forms of poverty relief

Alongside the pension system is a minimum livelihood guarantee scheme (*di bao*), which started in Shanghai in 1993 and subsequently became a national urban policy, administered by the Ministry of Civil Affairs (a rural version of the scheme, which exists in some provinces, is not discussed here). The system grew rapidly, reaching about 22 million people, about 6 percent of urban residents, by 2003.[4]

The basis of the system is a minimum income (the *di bao* level) provided at the municipal level. In principle the system aims to make up the gap between the income of an urban household and the *di bao* level. The concern with such a policy design (see the discussion of income testing in Box 7.1) is that households face a 100 percent marginal rate of benefit withdrawal (if a household earns an extra 100 yuan, it will lose 100 yuan of benefit), a clear disincentive to labor supply. However, Ravallion and

---

3. At year-end 2003 the assets of such funds were about 35 billion yuan ($4.2 billion), a negligible amount compared with deposits in commercial banks. The Trial Measures on Enterprise Annuities, which took effect in May 2004, moved toward a more fully fledged system of enterprise-based voluntary retirement plans.

4. For an overview of poverty trends in China since 1980, see Ravallion and Chen (2007); for an overview of the *di bao* system, see O'Keefe (2006); and for an assessment of the effectiveness of the system, see Ravallion and Wang (2006).

Wang (2006) find that the practical operation of the system significantly mutes this rate of withdrawal. The system's main deficiency is less one of incentives than of coverage. At least half of the potentially eligible population receive no benefit, and the program covers only a small fraction of the aggregate income gap below the *di bao* line. Although in principle the design of the system should result in nobody receiving less than this amount, in practice the impact on poverty is small.

14.2 ASSESSMENT

The 1997 framework, combining a basic pension (social pooling) with individual accounts, offers a clear strategy. The basic pension provides higher replacement rates for lower earners and thus plays a key role in reducing poverty and providing insurance against low lifetime earnings. Individual accounts, linking pensions to earnings, become increasingly important as the distribution of those earnings widens. And both parts provide longevity insurance by paying benefits in the form of an annuity. The combination of a basic pension and individual accounts thus provides poverty relief, insurance, and consumption smoothing. Voluntary pensions allow for differences in preferences across workers and in the constraints they face.

At a practical level, the system is more unified than previously: at least in principle, contributions and benefits are brought together at the municipal level. In principle the system extends to private sector employment and self-employment in urban areas. And the administrative responsibilities of enterprises for pensions have in theory been removed.

In the course of implementing the new pension system, however, problems have emerged. At a strategic level, four stand out: fragmentation, system deficits, problems with individual accounts, and the embryonic nature of voluntary pensions.

14.2.1 Fragmentation

Despite the objective of unifying the pension system at least at the provincial level, organization remains highly fragmented, largely at the municipal or county level, and in some areas pensions are still enterprise based. Provincial unity has been achieved in very few regions. At the municipal level, governments have often been unable to enforce contributions, not least because of adverse incentives, discussed below.

In addition, coverage is limited, extending to fewer than 20 percent of urban workers. Despite the announced extension of the mandatory system to all urban workers, contributions from employers and workers outside the state sector remain very limited. Thus pensions, and social protection more generally, are heavily focused on urban, formal sector, state employees and employees of foreign firms. The problem is aggravated because compliance is incomplete.

Why does fragmentation matter? In equity terms, it matters because it vitiates the effectiveness of the pooling element in pensions. It matters also because many people regard it as horizontally inequitable if different groups are treated differently, for example if coverage is better for workers in some enterprises than others, or if rural workers have little or no social protection. And it matters for efficiency, because fragmentation violates one of the central features of good design, namely, a well-running, nationwide labor market, uniformity and portability being two essential ingredients of a system designed to assist economic development.

14.2.2 System deficits

Pensions in most parts of the country run a deficit, the joint result of high pension spending and limited capacity to collect contributions. Current rules and the antici-pated rise in the dependency ratio suggest that deficits are likely to persist.[5] High pension spending has multiple causes.

A generous replacement rate for older workers. The target replacement rate of the combination of the basic pension and individual accounts is 60 percent of the local average wage. In practice, however, "the pre-retirement wage replacement rate in China is one of the highest in the world, averaging around 80 percent and is as high as 100-130 percent in some regions" (Williamson and Zheng 2003, p. 10). This result is explicable in terms of the inherited system: workers received publicly funded wages, which were generally fairly low; upon retirement they received a publicly funded pension in place of those wages. Indeed, the pension was considered part of a lifetime wage. Seen from that perspective, high replacement rates seemed natural. In a market economy, however, wages will rise, the fiscal costs of pensions matter, and workers have additional options for financing old-age security, including private wealth. In such a world a replacement rate considerably below 100 percent is normal.

A high system dependency ratio. The pension system's high dependency ratio (Table 14.2) results in part from the limited expansion of coverage of the system beyond the state sector, together with the shrinkage of employment in many state-owned enterprises. Thus the number of contributors is small relative to the number of pensioners, all of them from the inherited system. The high dependency ratio also derives from certain features of the pension system itself, in particular the low pension-able age and large-scale early retirement, which together lead to a long average duration of retirement. At the official mandatory retirement ages of 60 for men and 55 for women, remaining life expectancy was nineteen years and twenty-six years, respectively.[6]

The trend is aggravated because many people retire at younger ages. In part, this is a predictable outcome of the prevailing incentive structure:

- Workers face incentives to retire early, particularly if they work for failing enterprises with wage arrears, and because the most productive workers will be able to find a new job even if they are receiving a pension.

- Enterprises going through hard times encourage early retirement so as to shift the burden of wages to the pension authorities.

- Local governments face incentives in the same direction: effective policing is costly and may be politically unpopular, whereas the costs of the extra pensions do not fall on their budget.

---

5. This assumes that a rising age dependency ratio is not offset by extending the system to the entire urban workforce, which would improve the finances of the system in the short run by introducing large numbers of younger non-state sector workers.

6. In 2001 remaining life expectancies for men aged 55-59 and 60-64 were 21.1 and 17.3 years, respectively; for women aged 50-54 and 55-59 the comparable figures were 27.9 and 23.6 years. The figures in the text are simple averages across the two age groups. See World Health Organization, Life Tables for WHO Member States (www3.who.int/whosis/life/life_tables/life_tables_process.cfm?path = whosis,bod,life,life_tables&language = english.

Thus it is not surprising that a survey of thirteen provinces (reported by Jiang Shi Ming 2004, p. 13) found that nearly 28 percent of total pension spending in 1997 was connected with early retirement, even though many of the recipients continued to work while collecting a pension.[7]

Generous indexation. Pensions are in principle indexed to changes in wages, but not fully, as discussed below. Although there are statistical issues about the definition of the wage index, the method of indexation can be costly during periods when real wage growth is rapid and inflation low.

Separately, the methodology of indexation is faulty. As discussed in section 5.3.4, the real value of pensions should not vary unsystematically with the level of inflation. Yet that is exactly what happens in China because pensions are not indexed in a properly weighted way. Currently, the increase in benefits is supposed to be somewhere between 40 and 60 percent of nominal wage growth. That makes the real value of benefits erratic. To illustrate, workers can have 5 percent real wage growth either with 5 percent nominal wage growth and zero inflation or with 10 percent wage growth and 5 percent inflation. If nominal benefits increase at half the rate of nominal wage growth, these two circumstances produce very different outcomes: with zero inflation, nominal and real benefits grow by 2.5 percent (half of 5 percent), or half the growth in real wages; with 5 percent inflation, nominal benefits grow by 5 percent (half of 10 percent), which means no growth in real benefits. Thus real benefits do not grow at half the rate of real wages. Higher inflation can make this more severe. With 15 percent wage growth and 10 percent inflation, nominal benefits grow at 7.5 percent—a *decrease* in real benefits of 2.5 percent. Proper indexing avoids this erratic response to inflation. The topic is taken up in section 15.5.2.

Faulty actuarial calculation. As mentioned above, the monthly pension from a worker's individual account is calculated as 1/120th of his or her accumulation. Ignoring interest, this parameter implicitly assumes that life expectancy at retirement is ten years. In fact, as just discussed, life expectancy is nearly double that figure for men and considerably more than double for women. The resulting cost falls on the social pool, since the finances of the two parts of the system are not separate, further contributing to cost pressures.

The error is important. Suppose that the retirement age is 60 and life expectancy at birth is 70. In that circumstance it is mistaken to assume that retirement for a typical person will last ten years: the relevant statistic is not life expectancy at birth, but life expectancy at the retirement age of 60. If life expectancy at birth is 70, expectancy at age 60 will be more than ten years unless the mortality rate at all ages below 60 is zero, which obviously it is not.

Incomplete collection of contributions. The system deficit arises also on the contributions side. In part this is a matter of enforcement capacity, but in part it results from disincentives due to the high contribution rates necessary to finance the system. Failing firms face incentives to delay contribution payments, to understate liabilities, or to default. More successful firms, being reluctant to subsidize the less successful ones,

---

7. A similar phenomenon occurred in Central and Eastern Europe. In Poland in 1990, for example, one-third of spending on old-age pensions benefited individuals below the normal pensionable age (World Bank 1993, Chapter 4).

face similar incentives. And both factors are exacerbated because workers in badly performing enterprises disproportionately seek early retirement.

14.2.3 Problems with individual accounts

As discussed in Box 6.2, a move from PAYG toward funding incurs inescapable upfront cash flow costs because it is necessary simultaneously to finance the PAYG pensions of the current retired generations and to pay contributions into the funded individual accounts of current workers. In China the deficits just described meant that it was not possible to meet these cash flow costs, resulting in "empty individual accounts" as local governments often used the contributions of workers to their individual accounts to finance deficits in the social pool, replenishing the account with IOUs, which are, in effect, government bonds. In practice, therefore, the empty individual accounts have some features in common with an NDC arrangement: they are run on a PAYG basis, in that contributions are used to finance current benefits, and the interest payments and redemption of the bonds both come from current public revenue, yet pension benefits bear a strict relationship to accumulations.[8]

Further problems are that the accounts lack a suitable institutional structure for holding private assets, and there is in any case an inadequate supply of suitable private sector assets. Thus, where individual accounts are funded, their main holdings are low-interest government bonds and bank deposits.

There are also problems of corrupt misuse of pension funds, exemplified by a major scandal in Shanghai in 2006.[9] Corruption, which is a serious problem in China, also aggravates the problem of incomplete compliance with contribution conditions.

14.2.4 Embryonic voluntary pensions

As already noted, voluntary pensions in China are limited to plans run by enterprises; there is no legal provision for voluntary individual plans, although individual savings are an option. Since voluntary pensions are in their infancy, the following are more questions than diagnoses of existing problems.

Coverage. The mandatory contribution rate to the basic pension and individual accounts is a relatively high 28 percent (albeit on a lower base than the usual wage measure), which discourages participation by covered workers in voluntary plans. Thus the workers most likely to be attracted to enterprise-based plans are, first, those in the township and village enterprises (TVEs), who are outside the mandatory system. Many TVEs are large and capable of implementing such arrangements. Second, some

8. The main difference from an NDC pension is that, in China, the interest rate on the accounts is whatever rate the different governments pay on the IOUs in the empty accounts, rather than a rate established by law in a way that supports the long-run sustainability of the system.

9. In August 2006 investigators discovered that about one-third of the Shanghai Social Security Fund had been invested in speculative real estate projects, and suspicions were that officials had benefited personally. The city's Communist Party chief (who was also a member of the Party's twenty-four-member Politburo) was jailed for corruption, as was the head of China's National Bureau of Statistics. See "Beijing Probes Shanghai Pension Scandal," *Financial Times*, August 27, 2006; "Chinese Real Estate Executive Detained in Shanghai Pension Fund Case," *International Herald Tribune*, November 7, 2006, and Salditt, Whiteford, and Adema (2007).

enterprises in better-off and fast-growing cities like Beijing and Shanghai might contemplate offering additional retirement benefits as part of labor retention. One way to expand the voluntary system in these circumstances would be to establish the legal framework for individual accounts, creating an avenue for voluntary retirement saving for the self-employed and others. Given the high saving rate in China, there is limited present need to introduce tax advantages for voluntary pension savings, although tax favoring might become relevant at some point in the future.

Administrative costs. Under current regulations each enterprise must set up its own annuity council, with worker representation. Small and medium-size enterprises, because of their limited capacity, are likely to contract out such operations to specialized agencies. Whether pension administration is handled in-house or contracted out, transactions costs are acutely relevant to the net rate of return, as discussed in section 9.2. Not the least of the implications is the need for regulation.

Regulation. Voluntary retirement plans require a strong regulatory and supervisory framework. Under present arrangements this is the responsibility of the Departments of Labor and Social Security in the central ministry and local governments.[10] Regulatory effectiveness is crucial in two ways: to ensure that voluntary pensions run as intended, and because the intimate involvement of government in private pension plans raises issues of contingent liabilities on central and local government, even if these are not specified in law. Moreover, multiple regulatory bodies create complexity and higher cost for firms subject to multiple oversight.

We have emphasized the importance of institutional capacity, a point of intense and direct relevance to voluntary retirement plans, whose expansion should be calibrated to the development of regulatory capacity and of financial and capital markets. Presumably the voluntary nature of these accounts implies that firms will not go into financial markets in which they have little confidence. This presumption, however, must be backed by a strong regulatory regime, with a parallel regime developed as the system is eventually extended to individual accounts.

14.3 CONCLUSION

The combination of basic pension and individual accounts introduced in 1997 potentially provides poverty relief, redistribution, insurance, and consumption smoothing; voluntary pensions, as an emerging third tier, allow for differences in preferences and constraints. Thus the strategy is sound. As implemented, however, the system faces difficulties in the form of fragmentation, system deficits, problems with individual accounts, the embryonic nature of voluntary pensions, and limited coverage in the urban sector and minimal provision for the rural population.

As a result of these problems, the urban pension system offers workers benefits that are patchy. Whether workers actually receive their basic pensions in full depends on the extent to which the relevant level of government—frequently the municipality, and in some cases still the state-owned enterprises—can finance them. The issue is less a

---

10. The general principle is that the responsible level of government (central, provincial, or municipal) depends on whether the organization sponsoring the pension plan is national, provincial, or local.

question of taxable capacity than of the ability to collect taxes and contributions from the rapidly growing private sector.

Individual accounts are affected by these collection difficulties and by aspects of the basic pension, for instance the early pensionable age, that add to the cost of the system. Both factors help to explain the phenomenon of "empty accounts," which arise because the limited contributions received are needed to pay today's benefits and hence are not available to fund current workers' individual accumulations.

If these problems can be resolved, a further series of questions then arises: are fully funded individual accounts desirable given present and projected economic conditions in China, and are they feasible given current regulatory capacity and the current state of financial markets? These questions are discussed in the next chapter.

15

▷

China: Potential Directions for Reform

The previous chapter argued that China's strategy for its pension system—a combination of basic pension and individual accounts—is sound, but that in practice the system faces a series of problems. This chapter, based on the report of a panel on which we served (Asher et al. 2005; http://www.oup.com/us/pdf/social_security_study_2005), sets out a series of recommendations (our summary recommendations are in italic) designed to address those problems and, more positively, to strengthen the ability of the pension system to achieve its objectives in ways compatible with economic theory, with international experience, and with China's capacity to implement reforms effectively. Section 15.1 discusses overall structure and administration. Sections 15.2, 15.3, and 15.4 consider options for the basic pension, individual accounts, and voluntary pensions, respectively. Section 15.5 discusses issues connected with the age of retirement, and section 15.6 considers ways of extending coverage to more of the population. Section 15.7 sets out the main conclusions.[1]

15.1 OVERALL STRUCTURE AND ADMINISTRATION

15.1.1 A National Pensions Administration

In operational terms, the proper starting point is the administrative structure of the system.

Recommendation: There should be a single set of regulations on mandatory pensions, preferably in the form of legislation that is enforceable.

A unified national system is essential to the portability of pension rights and hence to labor mobility. It is necessary also to maintain equity in the way regions share a national pool of contributions. Thus the rules on contributions and benefits should be set centrally by formula, and interpretation and enforcement of the pension law should be the responsibility of a central ministry. Those rules, however, should include room for regional variation in basic benefit levels. Local variation is a necessity in a country

1. For other assessments and proposals for reform, see Drouin and Thompson (2006), Salditt, Whiteford, and Adema (2007), and Williamson (2004).

with great regional disparities in prices and living standards, but that variation should be compatible with a national system.

Recommendation: There should be a single pensions administration with national responsibility and a single national pool to receive all pension revenue.

A national administration has certain core requirements. First, a national database with information on each worker's account is essential, both to foster a national labor market and because that is the only way to control pension spending by localities (which could otherwise pay pensions at whatever level they wanted out of the national pool). Second, there needs to be a single system of recordkeeping and standard software. That software needs to be constructed in such a way that localities cannot customize it with local variations other than those allowed under the central rules.

These administrative arrangements all need to be mandatory for localities. Maintaining a contributions record for each individual worker is a major task. It is necessary to identify each individual, keep track of his or her identity over time and from location to location, and attribute all of his or her contributions each year over an entire career. For many workers, records will need to be kept for forty years, and workers will increasingly hold a succession of jobs in multiple locations around the country.

The national pensions administration should be part of the central government and financed from its budget. It should administer both the basic pension and individual accounts. Administrative needs should be given significant weight, with a realistic time frame for implementation.

To achieve national pooling, it is important that the national pensions administration receive all pension revenue. Pooling lies at the core of the redistributive and risk-sharing element of the system. Given China's size and diversity, national pooling of the mandatory system is particularly important. This should not, however, preclude local initiatives with voluntary pensions.

Recommendation: The central authority should create an institution to be tasked with projecting the financial position of mandatory pensions and carrying out ongoing research on pensions.

Because pension systems operate over many decades, projections of future spending are essential periodically, so that mid-course adjustments can be made to ensure that contributions and projected benefits are broadly in balance. Such projections can also play a role in the political process if they achieve a reputation for being honest and nonpolitical. Understanding how the pension system is working in practice, not just on paper, is critical for improving it, particularly in a country where wide-ranging changes are taking place. Keeping abreast of developments in economic theory and foreign experience is also valuable.

15.1.2 Funding and revenue sources

Recommendation: The pension system should continue to be financially separate from the national budget, with financing from dedicated revenue sources.

As discussed in section 6.1, there are solid arguments for financing the basic pension from dedicated contributions rather than general revenue:

- Dedicated contributions help to depoliticize financial planning by insulating benefits from short-run fiscal volatility. A dedicated revenue stream and separate administration can also help to depoliticize pension projections, offering a process of political balancing of benefits with available finance over the long term. That is, a perceived need for long-run balance improves the politics of benefit legislation, by making salient the cost of higher benefits and the need for adequate contributions for the long-run planned level of benefits. Substantial reliance on taxpayer subsidies, in contrast, can leave pensions vulnerable to the fluctuating needs of the rest of the budget.

- They assist worker security by making benefits more predictable.
- A contributory system may have political economy advantages, if people think (rightly or wrongly) that contributions are a more secure source of future benefits than general taxation, which indeed they may be.

Two additional points are noteworthy. First, the question of whether or not to have a dedicated revenue source for the basic pension is logically separate from whether or not basic benefits should depend on a person's contributions record (as in China) or not (as newly legislated in Chile). The design of the system in the Netherlands (section 11.4.4) is instructive: there a noncontributory universal pension (see Glossary) is based on residence, but financed from a dedicated revenue source. Second, a noncontributory pension, as in the Netherlands and Chile, is less suitable to a country with the huge urban-rural disparities of China, unless, perhaps, benefits are set very low.

Recommendation: Contributions should be collected by the tax authority and passed on to the pensions administration.

The most cost-effective way to collect contributions is alongside the personal income tax. The tax authorities in China have the technical capacity required for the task (although it will be necessary to ensure that they have adequate resources). However, since pensions present the separate and demanding administrative tasks outlined above, it is appropriate for the tax authorities, having collected the contributions and identified the individual worker to whom each contribution should be credited, to pass the revenue and the information on to the pensions administration—a division of tasks seen in many countries.

Recommendation: Contributions and benefits should be calculated using the same earnings base as the income tax, but allowing variation within a formula set nationally.

It is important to align the incentives facing the income tax authorities with those facing the pensions administration, to avoid a situation where the tax authorities concentrate on total collections at the expense of accurately tracking the contributions of each individual worker. The problem is minimized when the tax authorities and the pension authorities both need broadly similar information on individuals.[2] Thus there are both economic and administrative advantages if the contributions base for pensions and the tax base for personal income tax are the same.

Contributions are currently based on the standard wage, which is a narrower measure than total earnings in a market economy. This basis encourages workers and employers to adopt forms of compensation that are not included in the standard wage.

---

2. In the United Kingdom, where student loan repayments are collected alongside the income tax, the student loans administration takes part in the process of reconciling its own accounts with those of the tax authorities. The effect is to improve enforcement of the income tax and national insurance contributions as well as of student loan repayments.

It is also regressive, because nonwage earnings are received disproportionately by higher earners. The contributions base should therefore be changed to a measure of earnings that approximates the measurable portion of total compensation, and the same measure should be used in determining income tax liability;[3] the contribution rate should be adjusted so that total contributions are broadly unaffected by the change. Such an approach also improves consumption smoothing, since broad earnings are a better measure of consumption opportunities than is the current contributions base.

Similarly, the basic pension benefit from the social pool should remain at approximately its current level but should be calculated on the basis of average local earnings, using the same definition as for determining contributions. Using the same definition limits attempts to manipulate reported earnings so as to increase benefits without increasing contributions. Thus benefits should vary with location, but within a formula set by a national authority.

15.1.3 Setting replacement rates and contribution and benefit levels

Recommendation: In the short run, replacement rates and the contribution rate and benefit levels should be broadly maintained, subject to some technical corrections.

Over the coming years, major changes will emerge in the finances of the pension system, particularly when reforms necessary to make the system sustainable are implemented and coverage is extended more broadly among urban workers and possibly beyond. Until those major reforms have been decided upon and long-term financial projections are available, it would be prudent to keep the basic parameters of the system—the replacement rate, the contribution rate, and benefit levels—broadly unchanged. Frequent changes would be disruptive and mistakes would be made. Finally, as discussed in section 14.2.2, the actuarial basis of calculating benefits from individual accounts is incorrect and should be rectified at an early stage.

Recommendation: The mechanism for setting contributions and benefits should address both simultaneously.

The relevant replacement rates for the mandatory system are those of the system as a whole, for the basic pension and individual accounts together. The balance between the two elements should reflect policymakers' preferences about the extent to which pensions should be related to earnings. The overall target replacement rates should reflect a balance among affordability, adequacy, coverage, and the age at which benefits start.

Once selection of further reforms is complete and cost and revenue projections are in place, the government should consider the trade-off between the basic pension benefit and the contribution rates for the basic pension and individual accounts. If contributions and benefits are set nationally without local variation, the government needs to set them consistent with sustainability as shown by the cost and

---

3. A common income base for income tax and pensions does not imply common thresholds. In most countries the two systems have different thresholds. In particular, there is almost invariably a ceiling for pension contributions, but none for the income tax. Some employer-provided benefits are very hard to measure on an individual basis. Employer self-insured group health insurance is an example, where different workers have different ex ante medical expenses, and simply adding to taxable income the average cost per worker would not give an accurate picture of what a young, healthy worker is receiving in compensation.

revenue projections. If there is scope for local variation, it needs to be either within centrally determined limits that preserve balance, or primarily financed locally, the underlying principle being that benefits should generally be financed by whichever level of government sets them. That is, the system needs to align the incentives that administrators face as they make decisions about contributions and decisions about benefits. That principle can be modified, but only with care, for example through block grants (that is, a lump sum) rather than matching grants.[4]

15.1.4 Public information

Recommendation: Improved public information is a priority, both about the changes in the overall pension system and, over time, about the individual position of each worker.

Workers should be informed in at least three ways. First, they should be well informed about the rules of the pension system as far as it affects them individually; for example, they should know how many years they must contribute in order to receive a full basic pension. Second, there should be a start to the process of informing workers of their accumulations from contributions and about their anticipated benefits, to assist their choices about consumption and financial planning and to help them monitor the accuracy of the system. Finally, it is necessary to educate workers more broadly about financial planning, since imperfect information and understanding are pervasive in an area as complex as pensions (see the discussion in section 4.2.2 and Box 9.6).

15.2 OPTIONS FOR THE BASIC PENSION

It is important to consider the basic pension (this section) and individual accounts (section 15.3) together. On their own, individual accounts do not adequately address poverty and distributional issues. Although income is rising rapidly, so are income disparities. Many people in China remain poor, and the system of individual accounts on its own would leave them in poverty despite a lengthy career. Thus the basic pension—the social pool—is an essential complement to individual accounts, the relative size and the specific design of each element depending on the objectives of policymakers.

---

4. A block grant from the central to provincial governments can be either tied (that is, available for spending only on the basic pension) or untied. If it is tied, a provincial government faces the marginal cost of additional pension spending over and above the block grant (for example, if it offers a generous pension or is lenient about early retirement). If the grant is untied, the provincial government faces the entire marginal cost of pensions (since it could spend the grant on other things). With a matching grant, in contrast, the central government agrees to pay (say) 50 percent of a province's pension costs; thus provincial governments face only half of the cost of any increase in pension spending; this creates incentives for inefficiently high spending. In the extreme, if provincial governments set benefits but these are financed from the center, the resulting incentives create a powder keg: the provincial governments face no incentive to moderate their pension spending, and indeed can treat it as cost-free; hence they may increase benefits, not least for reasons of political popularity. Such an incentive structure, a form of moral hazard, is well known to cause cost explosions. It explains part of the high level of medical spending in the United States; similar effects have been observed, for example, in the Czech Republic in 1992, after the funding and delivery of health care were separated.

15.2.1 Determining benefits

In addition to the accounting changes described above, it is appropriate to adjust the way the basic pension is determined to reflect labor mobility, which will inevitably increase in China. This will include the recognition that different people want and need to retire at different ages.

Recommendation: The basic pension in broadly its existing form should be retained.

There are two arguments for retaining a flat-rate basic pension broadly in its present form. First, the system already in place is strategically sound and commands broad acceptance. Second, a flat-rate pension makes less stringent demands on administration than other forms of organization, for example a basic pension with an earnings-related element, as in the United States.

Recommendation: The basic pension should be adjusted for individuals with less than a full career, for those who have worked in different locations over their career, and for the age at which benefits start.

Given the speed of change in economic conditions in China and the country's increasingly fluid labor markets, it is important to avoid sharp discontinuities in benefit entitlement. Thus the basic pension should be pro-rated with respect to the duration of a person's covered contributions record, with no minimum contribution period for receiving a pension. (Very small entitlements can be paid as a lump sum.) In addition, where a worker has made contributions to the basic pension in several locations, the initial value of the basic pension benefit should be a weighted average of benefit levels in the different regions, the weights reflecting the number of years in each location. Finally, the basic pension benefit should be adjusted on an actuarial basis for the age at which it starts.

Pro-rating for short careers and averaging across regions for mobile workers strengthen the link between contributions and benefits and limit opportunities for workers to manipulate the system. The obvious advantage of not pro-rating or averaging is simplicity: for example, a worker with a full contributions record could simply receive the basic pension benefit in the area where he or she retires. Such an arrangement, however, creates incentives for workers to move (or appear to move) to a high-wage location late in their career. An even greater problem arises if, late in her career, a person can migrate from a region with low earnings and low prices to (say) Shanghai, qualify for a basic pension at the Shanghai level, and then return to her original region and collect (legally or illegally) the Shanghai-level benefit. The arguments against such a system are broadly similar to those about final-salary plans, discussed in section 5.2.1, and apply with particular force in a country such as China with its wide regional income disparities.

The absence of a minimum contribution period avoids the horizontal inequity between a worker who has contributed for just long enough and a worker who just fails to meet the minimum requirement and therefore gets no pension at all.[5] It also means that workers with a partial contributions record are entitled to a partial pension; this feature is particularly important in a country like China, in which coverage is gradually being extended to new groups of workers.

---

5. In Chile, for example, a worker with twenty years of contributions has been eligible for the minimum pension guarantee, but a worker who has contributed for one month less than twenty years is not.

15.2.2 Funding legacy obligations from assets

The basic pension is relevant not only to people working today but also to those who retired under the old system. An important question is how to finance these inherited obligations, and hence how to measure them sensibly.

Implicit pension debt. Net implicit debt considers benefits and contributions together. A system's actuarial balance is defined as the present value, over some time horizon, of annual pension payments less annual contributions under the current rules. Three measures of net implicit debt are discussed in section 6.2.1. The most appropriate measure in this situation, the shutdown method, reflects the intention to honor past promises by continuing to pay benefits to people who have already retired, and to pay benefits accrued to date of current workers when they finally retire. This is the most useful measure of the legacy obligations of the old system at the time a reform takes place, and it is clearly the most relevant to China, as it was to Chile at the time of its 1981 reform.

Countries reforming their pension systems can finance these obligations either from inside the pension system (from future contributions) or from outside, or through a mix. Poland and Bolivia used proceeds from the sale of public assets to create a social security trust fund. Chile issued "recognition bonds" to individuals as a way of recognizing the obligations of the old system being dismantled, relying on later general revenue to finance the bonds as they matured. Thus the legacy burden in Chile falls on all taxpayers.

A country need not fully fund its legacy obligation from outside the pension system, just as it need not fully pay off its national debt. However, if an ongoing legacy obligation remains within the pension system, future workers receive lower benefits than could be financed by their contributions had the obligation been paid off by someone else. Thus it may be sound policy to pay off part of the legacy obligation.

Funding from assets. China's legacy obligations consist of the pensions of workers who retired before 1998 and the accrued pension entitlements of current workers for employment prior to 1998. These obligations were built up not only under pension arrangements that have been superseded, but under a very different economic system. Today's retirees and those who will retire shortly devoted most of their lives to building up the state sector. In return, they expected that the state-owned enterprises, or other public entities, for which they worked would provide for them in their old age. In the past this "lifetime wage" was provided from the current income of enterprises, but that approach is incompatible with a competitive market economy: if enterprises pay pensions on a PAYG basis, the older ones, with their larger numbers of retired workers, will no longer be able to compete with newer firms.

Currently, fiscal subsidies and contributions to individual accounts cover part of the deficit. If this continues, the rest of the legacy obligation will be financed by some mix of taxpayers and current and future workers in the form of lower pension benefits. As discussed in section 7.2.2, one alternative is to finance the legacy obligation by transferring assets. Many state-owned enterprises have been privatized, and the shares in those enterprises represent wealth, for which a market price has already been established by the sale of part of the government's holdings. That market price reflects current dividend payments on those shares plus expectations about future dividend payments. Thus an option for governments is to place shares in the privatized state-owned enterprises into a trust fund. Since the market for these shares is currently thin, the proposal is not that the trust fund would sell shares to pay benefits; rather it would use the flow of dividend payments as a source of ongoing finance. Any question of selling some of the shares would remain a matter for the future. Indeed, the government could, if it wished at this stage, transfer to the trust fund the financial rights in the shares but not the ownership rights.

As a step in this direction, recognizing the legacy obligation, the government of China decided in 2003 to transfer some of its shares in state-owned enterprises, particularly those listed on stock markets and those not listed but already organized as joint-stock companies, to the National Social Security Fund. Progress has been slow, however, and only a small quantity of shares have been transferred.

Recommendation: To assist with the cost of the legacy obligation, transfers of shares in state-owned enterprises to the National Social Security Fund should continue.

Such transfers have two potential advantages: they assist the financing of the basic pension, and they may contribute to the quality of corporate governance. On the first point, shifting the dividend flow from the government agencies currently receiving them to pension spending reduces the need for a separate fiscal subsidy to the pension system, thus improving the reliability of the system's financial balance (although it makes other government finances more difficult). Without such transfers—or to the extent that such transfers are not enough to fund legacy obligations fully—the obligations from the old system fall on current and future workers and thus contribute to low compliance, particularly among workers outside the state sector being added to the pension system. On the other hand, removing a revenue flow from the government is likely to result in higher taxes at some point than would otherwise be the case, creating an alternative source of inefficiency and potential problems with compliance.

How large should the trust fund be? The larger the fund, the lower the contributions necessary to finance a given level of benefits (improving the deal for younger workers and for those brought into the system as coverage expands), or the higher the level of benefits that can be financed from a given contribution (potentially improving the deal for current and future pensioners). Decisions about the size of the fund and the mix of bonds and shares in state-owned enterprises clearly have major efficiency, equity, and political ramifications.

In addition to assisting with finance, adding the National Social Security Fund as a shareholder can contribute to improved corporate governance of state-owned enterprises, a key ingredient in economic efficiency and growth.[6] As already noted, given the underdeveloped state of capital markets in China and the need for long-term investors, the National Social Security Fund should not sell its shares but instead hold them over the longer term, relying on the flow of dividends to help finance pension obligations. Good-quality governance needs good legislation, good oversight by regulatory authorities, and good oversight and exercise of voting rights by shareholders. The transfer of shares gives the National Social Security Fund the opportunity to

6. See the symposium on corporate governance in *Oxford Review of Economics Policy*, vol. 21, no. 2, Summer 2005. For a skeptical view of the robustness of corporate governance in China, see Hutton (2007).

function as a long-term strategic shareholder in these companies, with a major interest in protecting shareholder rights, including the right to a reasonable level of dividends. This interest could be pursued by monitoring firms, exercising shareholder voting rights, and obtaining representation on the boards of some companies. In many countries pension funds play an important role as a long-term strategic shareholder, overseeing the performance of companies and improving corporate governance generally. Moreover, the interest of the National Social Security Fund in corporate governance would lend more weight to the entire process of enterprise reform, including better legislation and better regulation, just as in Chile the investment of mandatory individual accounts in the stock market assisted the reform process by contributing to efforts to improve the regulation of the stock market. Given that the State Asset Management Bureau will continue to own substantial shares in state-owned enterprises even after the transfer of some shares to the National Social Security Fund, the ownership roles of the two bodies, with their different perspectives, can complement and reinforce each other.

Worldwide experience with investment by government agencies in diversified portfolios of assets shows that good-quality investment is far more likely with full and transparent accounting of the operations of these agencies. Thus, if the transfer of shares is to accomplish the goals of improved fiscal balance and stronger corporate governance, it is important that the National Social Security Fund have a clear and explicit mandate, independent nonpolitical management, and detailed, credibly audited accounts that are published regularly (as an example, see Norway Central Bank 2006). Such an approach may help to prevent the loss of public assets in the process of reform, as happened, for example, in Russia.

15.3 OPTIONS FOR INDIVIDUAL ACCOUNTS

Individual accounts, introduced in 1997, are a central element in the pension system. Their actual operation, however, has been unsatisfactory. Although designed to be funded, with accumulation of financial assets in each account, most accounts are "empty," containing only government IOUs, as discussed in section 14.2.3. Whether or not funding is the right policy—a question we discuss below—empty accounts undermine the credibility of the system. Moreover, little has yet been done to establish an institutional structure with the capacity to keep individual records on a national basis, buy assets in capital markets, and manage assets, much less to arrange for individual portfolio choice.

15.3.1 Funding individual accounts

The analysis in Chapters 6 and 7 suggests that funding is desirable if it leads to one or more of the following: increased national saving in a country with a shortage of savings, improved allocation of saving to productive investment, and desired intergenerational redistribution. In addition, funding needs to be administratively feasible. We argue below that none of these appear to apply in China today.

Increased saving. Will funding increase saving in China? Other things equal, the accumulation of real assets in individual accounts requires an increase either in contributions or in the government subsidy. As discussed in section 6.3.1, these policies may or may not increase national saving, depending on the extent to which increased saving in individual accounts is offset by reduced saving either by individuals or by government (for example, government borrowing might have to increase to finance the transition to funding). As Table 14.1 shows, China already has a very high saving rate—not surprising given the relatively short experience with a booming economy, an under-developed social safety net, and only one child per family in many areas. Thus higher saving through mandatory contributions to individual accounts is likely to be considerably offset by reductions in other forms of saving.

Is an increase in saving the right objective for China? Increased saving requires a drop in consumption today in order to have even higher consumption tomorrow. But, again, current saving is already high, and economic growth is rapid, so that future workers are likely to be considerably better off than today's workers. Thus a policy leading to yet higher saving does not seem attractive. Indeed, a priority of policymakers in recent years has been to raise the level of consumption. This suggests that the assets in the individual accounts should be financed through additional government debt, so as not to increase saving. But in that case what is the point of putting government bonds into the accounts or providing government bonds that can be sold to finance the purchase of other assets? Although in general such diversification is useful, the approach seems premature given the state of financial markets in China.

Improved allocation of saving to investment. China's future growth will depend not on an increase in the saving rate but on improved allocation of saving to investment. Improving efficiency in this way is a major objective. As discussed in section 6.3.2, funding can improve allocation if the activities of individual accounts strengthen the functioning of capital markets or of financial intermediaries. There is evidence that that has happened in Chile. However, three points about Chile at the time of its reform are noteworthy:

- There was a budget surplus that could finance the introduction of funded individual accounts.
- Chile had a long-standing market system and a system of administration that was strong for the country's level of development.
- Significant action was taken to strengthen market supervision in tandem with the introduction of individual accounts; that is, the pension reform added political will to strengthen regulation.

Irrespective of the state of its budget, China does not currently meet the second and third of these conditions. Financial markets are at an early stage of development. Although reform of the banking system has started, interest rates are not yet determined by the market, effective regulation is only now being established, and credit-rating agencies—a necessary institution for financial markets trading in risky products—do not yet exist.[7] With saving rates very high, a largely unsatisfied demand already exists for long-term and relatively risk-free investment vehicles, and the constraints to further deepening of the financial markets are mainly the lack of effective intermediation and regulation. It is therefore not clear how increased demand, through the accumulation

---

7. The importance of sound credit rating is highlighted by the problems created in the United States by unrealistically high ratings of securities based on subprime mortgages.

of financial assets in individual accounts, would contribute to further financial market reform. In the short run, funded individual accounts are likely to experience low returns or high risks. At a given saving rate, broad funding of individual accounts, by taking more money from workers, reduces direct lending and own investment by these workers, which at the moment are perhaps more efficient at channeling saving to investment.

Reform of the financial sector is desirable for reasons much broader than pension design. At some point, funding individual accounts may well contribute to further improvements in financial markets, particularly if it strengthens the pressure for improved regulation and greater reliance on market forces in allocating saving to investment. A mandatory, government-run pension system, however, should not be the pilot for major innovations, given the condition of financial markets in China today. It would put at risk the retirement incomes of a large population of workers, and any mistakes would set back reform of the pension system as well as financial institutions more broadly. Financial sector development can better be pursued by using voluntary pension arrangements to stimulate these changes and by subjecting them to a market test to check their effectiveness. As explained below, voluntary pensions should be funded. Although they are still small compared with the mandatory system, in an economy as large as China their absolute size is substantial and can have a significant impact on financial markets.

Improved intergenerational distribution. As discussed in section 7.2, different ways of organizing pensions distribute benefits and costs differently across generations. Would mandatory funding have desirable intergenerational redistributive effects? A decision to introduce funding would benefit a future generation of workers who, other things being equal, can then pay lower contributions. The question is whether there is a good reason to impose a higher contribution (because of the move to funding) on today's workers in China so that future workers can pay a lower contribution. Today's workers are relatively poor and subject to great economic uncertainty; meanwhile growth rates are high, so that workers in future generations, increasingly holding jobs in the covered sector, are likely to be much better off. Imposing higher contribution rates on today's workers in order to have lower contribution rates or higher pension benefits for future workers does not seem a reasonable objective for China.

Feasibility. Can large-scale mandatory funding be implemented now? As discussed in Chapter 9, there are considerable hurdles to successful implementation of mandatory individual funded accounts with individually chosen portfolios. The requirements are stringent and do not seem yet to be in place in China. Centralized investment with no worker choice is administratively less demanding, but, as also discussed in Chapter 9, outcomes in some countries—particularly those with limited experience in centralized investment—have not been good.

In light of the preceding arguments, funded individual accounts

- Are not necessary to encourage saving
- May be counterproductive in assisting efficient investment, particularly since voluntary funded pensions can help to develop capital markets
- Have perverse intergenerational redistributive effects
- Are likely to exceed scarce implementation capacity.

These conclusions apply to China today; they do not necessarily apply to China in the future (or necessarily to other countries). Ten or twenty years from now, China may wish to raise its saving rate, the financial system may be able to provide individual accounts that improve overall resource allocation relative to that available elsewhere, redistribution to future generations may be considered desirable, pension administration and private investment managers may have the capacity to cope with the heavy demands of funded individual accounts, and regulatory capacity may have been established. It is therefore important that the individual accounts of today be designed to allow a smooth transition to funding if and when policymakers regard that as desirable.

The notional defined-contribution (NDC) approach, discussed in the next section, offers such a smooth transition. An alternative approach, based on additional government debt that also prepares for future funding, is discussed in section 15.3.3.

15.3.2 Notional defined contributions and individual accounts

Recommendation: Future accumulations in individual accounts should be organized on a notional defined-contribution basis.

Given the conclusions above, NDC pensions (see section 3.4 and the discussion of Sweden in section 11.4.8) are a more promising avenue for the present. Pensions of this type have been adopted by countries seeking to retain the usefulness of a defined-contribution approach without the necessity of funding. Each worker accumulates a notional fund, comprising his or her contributions over the years, which is credited each year by the pensions authority with a notional interest rate defined by law. At retirement the worker receives a pension based actuarially on his or her accumulation. As with the pro-rated basic benefit, there is no need for a minimum contribution period for eligibility for benefit.

Organizing individual accounts on the NDC approach has significant advantages in China's current circumstances:[8]

- It offers consumption smoothing to today's contributors in a manner similar to funded defined-contribution plans, and hence is consistent with the purpose of individual accounts.
- However, because no fund is built up, it does not require today's (poorer) workers to make higher contributions so that future (richer) generations of workers can make lower ones; it thus avoids unsatisfactory intergenerational redistribution.
- It does not require the considerable private sector financial and administrative capacity of funded arrangements, since the system is run by the public authorities.
- It is less risky for workers, since the rate of return avoids exposure to the short-run volatility of assets in the capital market. This is particularly important at a time when banking and financial market institutions are still developing.
- The NDC model can be the basis for a future move to partial or full funding, since individuals could hold both notional and actual assets in their account portfolio.

---

8. Other writers have reached the same conclusion; see, for example, Williamson and Zheng (2003) and Zheng (2004*b*).

In addition to organizing future accumulations on an NDC basis, the pension authorities should credit the "empty" individual accounts for contributions since the start of individual accounts in 1998, including notional interest.

Recommendation: The notional interest rate in the NDC system should equal the growth rate of national average earnings of covered workers.

An important element in the design of an NDC system is the definition of the notional rate of interest with which accounts are credited. Two definitions are commonly used: the increase in average wages per worker (w), and the increase in total earnings (wL, where L is the number of covered workers). Particularly in a country like China, where coverage will grow rapidly but in uneven spurts, wages per worker seem a better choice. This would roughly preserve replacement rates across cohorts, apart from the adjustment for life expectancy. The relevant definition of earnings should be the same as for the contributions base.

Recommendation: The determination of full benefits from individual accounts should be based on actuarial principles, using the notional interest rate and the mortality table for the birth cohort to which a pensioner belongs.

The present method of calculating the monthly benefit available from individual accounts —1/120th of a person's accumulation—is technically incorrect. It is consistent with a combination of ten-year average duration of retirement and a zero inflation-adjusted interest rate. An actuarially accurate benefit would yield roughly half as much per month.[9]

Without actuarially accurate adjustment for longer retirements, finances that are adequate for a shorter life becomes inadequate for longer lives. Actuarial adjustment is also important for preserving labor market incentives for older workers: benefits grow the longer one works, as discussed in section 5.3.3. To put individual accounts on a sound actuarial footing, the expected present value of benefits for a cohort should equal the cohort's notional accumulation at retirement. This parallels the way that assets in funded accounts are used to purchase annuities at market prices and is an important element in a system capable of adapting to increasing life expectancy.

Both the basic pension and the pension from the individual accounts need to be adjusted over time—at a minimum for inflation, and possibly to give retirees a further increase that incorporates some of the growth in wage rates as well. The need to index the basic pension properly is discussed in section 14.2.2, and the choices among different weights of price and wage increases in section 5.3.4.

15.3.3   Funding individual accounts with newly issued government bonds

If the government wishes to retain the principle of mandatory, fully funded individual accounts, one approach would be to place into workers' accounts newly issued government bonds paying a market interest rate. Any bonds transferred should be indexed for inflation, and consideration should be given to making indexed bonds available to insurance companies as backing for indexed annuities, and possibly to the public. Another approach would include allocation of government-owned foreign bonds to the accounts, including the interest actually earned on these bonds. This approach differs from the

---

9. This calculation assumes an annual interest rate (adjusted for inflation) of 3 percent, annual growth of benefits in force of 1.5 percent, and a retirement duration of twenty-five years.

current practice of placing IOUs in "empty" accounts in that it would provide explicit assets with a rate of interest that can be determined in the market.

Since the bonds would represent additional net debt, the immediate impact on national saving would be similar to that with an unfunded NDC system.[10] There would be no actual purchase of bonds. The government would simply credit the individual accounts with its bonds, and the contributions of the current generation of workers would continue to finance the payment of pensions to the current generation of retirees. The approach is thus similar to that in an NDC system, except that the accounts would accumulate the value of actual securities rather than notional credits, with the interest rate set by the bond market rather than on NDC principles.[11] The two approaches would have the same impact on the current year's national budget, very similar effects on national saving in the near term, similar administrative burdens, and similar intergenerational effects, since in both cases the costs of pensions would fall on future generations.

There are, however, important differences. In particular, the NDC approach allows the government to retain flexibility. First, the government can adjust the notional interest rate to maintain the long-term balance of the pension system—indeed, that is one of the core purposes of determining the interest rate in that way. The funded approach allows no such flexibility short of repudiating the property rights in existing bonds or requiring the accounts to accept bonds that pay less than market rates. Because of the difference in commitment for future payments, and possibly other perceptual differences, the increase in outstanding net government debt inherent in a government bond approach may raise the interest rate at which the government can borrow. As discussed in section 6.2, implicit debt and explicit debt are not perfect substitutes.

A second source of flexibility is that the NDC approach leaves open the option of a move to mandatory funded accounts in the future, rather than forcing the decision now. In contrast, the funding-with-bonds approach effectively makes the judgment now that mandatory funding to increase saving will be desirable in China in the future, leaving open only the timing of portfolio diversification or of increased contributions to increase saving.[12]

15.4   OPTIONS FOR VOLUNTARY PENSIONS

Voluntary pension plans—whether individual or employer plans—are an important complement to the basic pension and individual accounts. They allow individuals to exercise different preferences about the time path of saving for retirement and different

10. In broad terms the increased saving by workers in their funded individual accounts is offset by additional government borrowing, represented by the bonds in those accounts.

11. In practice, there would be a single central portfolio of government bonds, and each account would be credited with the interest rate earned on the portfolio. Until contributions are no longer sufficient to pay benefits in force, the interest could be paid by issuing more bonds. Once contributions are no longer sufficient to pay benefits, revenue would need to be transferred from the general budget.

12. In the debate over Social Security in the United States (see Diamond and Orszag 2005*a*, 2005*b*), some advocates present portfolio diversification as a substitute for increased contributions, even though diversification does not directly increase saving. With the funding-with-bonds approach, a similarly mistaken analysis might result in diversification when it is not appropriate and a failure to increase contributions when it is appropriate.

degrees of risk aversion; they allow firms to respond to worker preferences; they enable industries where people work in harsh conditions, or where working life is short for other reasons, to provide for earlier retirement; they accommodate regional and private initiatives; and they promote innovation, particularly in financial markets. Such responsiveness is of considerable importance in a country as large, diverse, and rapidly changing as China.

Recommendation: Voluntary pensions should be encouraged and their regulation strengthened.

Voluntary retirement arrangements may be enterprise based or comprise individual plans managed by approved financial institutions. In China both types of plan are likely to develop and should be encouraged, although the timing of their introduction should take full account of the necessity for effective regulation and supervision. A start has been made on the regulation of enterprise-based plans with the issue of "Trial Measures on Enterprise Annuities." Similar regulations will eventually be needed for other types of voluntary pensions.

The regulation and supervision of voluntary pensions should be strengthened to safeguard accumulations, and simplified in organizational terms so that a single regulatory authority oversees any given employer or individual retirement account. Such regulation should cover employer-provided pensions, individual pensions, and pensions organized by regional governments. Enhanced regulation is needed also for insurance companies that provide annuities.

Recommendation: Supplementary voluntary pensions should be fully funded defined-contribution pensions, with their income tax treatment clarified and set on a consistent basis.

The history of voluntary corporate pensions in developed countries illustrates the different options for the design of voluntary pensions. Some have been defined-benefit arrangements and some defined-contribution. Some have been at the company level and some at the industry level, for example through trade unions. Whereas true defined-contribution pensions are by their nature fully funded, corporate defined-benefit pensions have been funded to varying degrees over time, across countries, and across firms within countries.

Some of the history of private defined-benefit plans has been unsatisfactory. In particular, if the defined-benefit plan of a firm or industry is inadequately funded and gets into financial trouble, either the firm has to add resources, or workers and retirees lose some or all of their expected pension, or the government has to bail it out on an ad hoc basis or through a government-mandated system of insurance. The problem is aggravated because, as we have noted elsewhere, shortfalls due to falling asset values tend to occur at exactly the time when sponsoring firms are experiencing declining profits, since falling asset values and declining profitability are highly correlated. Government policies to strengthen the long-run robustness of private defined-benefit plans face a potential contradiction, discussed in Box 9.3: too little regulation leaves workers and retirees insufficiently protected, but excessive regulation imposes heavy costs on the sponsoring firm or industry, often when it is least able to bear them. As a result, many defined-benefit plans in the United States and the United Kingdom have been closed to new participants.

In a country with a well-developed defined-benefit system, a combination of a government guarantee and a funding requirement may preserve the system while addressing the worst problems. In a country with few or no existing voluntary pension plans, there seems no reason to go down a route that is known to be difficult to maintain. The need for sophisticated regulation of funding levels adds to the case against such pensions in China today. Thus all voluntary supplemental pensions that receive tax-favored treatment should be defined-contribution plans.

Although defined-contribution plans subject workers to financial market risk, they may be a better approach than trying to shift the risk to employers and the government. First, the attempt may not succeed, leaving workers with risks they did not anticipate rather than ones they should have anticipated. Second, a government guarantee may create incentives toward risky investment decisions, which regulation may not be able to prevent. Third, in a country where the mandatory system is primarily unfunded, having a funded voluntary system diversifies the risks that workers bear, since fluctuations in the contribution base for a mandatory system and fluctuations in the returns to assets, although correlated, are not perfectly so. Because the system is voluntary, this diversification, although not as thorough as with a funded portion of the mandatory system, avoids the difficulties that arise from increasing mandatory contribution rates, which would be necessary in a system seeking to build funded accounts while simultaneously financing existing pension liabilities.

The tax treatment of voluntary pensions should match that of mandatory pensions up to a ceiling. One common feature is to make them tax-favored compared with other savings, for example through a widely accepted measure (for example, in the United States and United Kingdom) known as EET tax treatment: pension contributions should be from pre-tax income (thus exempt from tax, E); the earnings of pension accumulations should be tax free (again exempt from tax, E); and the pension, when paid, should be treated as taxable (T) income on the same basis as earnings. The choice of ceiling and the design of tax advantages should take into account the tendency for deductions at a person's marginal tax rate to be regressive, because the best-off workers tend to make the highest voluntary contributions, and because these workers can generally deduct those contributions at a higher marginal rate of income tax than lower earners; regressivity remains even if marginal tax rates at retirement are the same, since deferral of taxation is more valuable, the higher the tax rate.

It is not clear how rapidly the financial system will be able to accommodate significant quantities of retirement savings. Leaving decisions to the judgment of employers, which can choose to create or not to create such a pension, offers the hope of aligning pension growth with growth in financial and regulatory capacity.

15.5   RETIREMENT AGE AND BENEFITS AT AND AFTER RETIREMENT

In China the mandatory retirement age for workers in state-owned enterprises (60 for men, 50 or 55 for women, depending on type of job) derives from an earlier time when life expectancy was shorter and employment arrangements were on a lifetime basis. The typical actual retirement age is even lower because early retirement has increased sharply—a predictable outcome of the incentive structure described in section 14.2.2. In contrast, the median retirement age of men in the United States is 64.6, and that in Japan is 68.5 (1999 figures; see Sigg 2005, Table 8.1).

Longer life expectancy and large-scale early retirement together result in longer average retirements (as noted in section 14.2.2, the estimated life expectancy at retirement age in China is nineteen years for men and twenty-six years for women). As Table 14.2 shows, the combination of limited coverage, the decline of some state-owned enterprises, and lengthy retirement has raised the pension system's dependency ratio dramatically, from 1:13 (one retiree for every thirteen workers) in 1980 to 1:3 in 2002, and it is projected to reach 1:2 in 2030. The combined effect on pension finance of reduced working years and increased years in retirement is obvious and should be addressed.

15.5.1 Determining benefits at retirement

With individual accounts, whether funded or notional, the benefit should be determined on an actuarial basis from the accumulation in the account. There needs to be a minimum age for claiming benefit, which section 5.3.2 refers to as the earliest eligibility age; above that age, the pension should increase roughly actuarially. For a defined-benefit pension, such as China's basic pension, it is common to use different terminology, with an age for full benefits. In some countries (for example, the United Kingdom) the earliest eligibility age and the age for full benefits are the same, with higher benefits for those who retire at a later age. In other countries (for example, the United States) there is an earliest eligibility age and a higher age for full benefits, with more or less actuarial adjustment between the two.

Recommendation: The age for full benefits from the basic pension should be slowly increased to 65 for men and women; the earliest eligibility age for the basic pension and individual accounts should also be the same for men and women.

Although most Western countries historically have had a lower retirement age for women, the trend is to have a common retirement age, a process accelerated by EU legislation against gender discrimination. As discussed in Chapter 8, there is a strong case for a common pensionable age. Women typically live longer than men, so that there is no equity case for a lower retirement age for women. Separately, a lower pensionable age is widely regarded as discriminatory against men, who have to work longer in most public pension systems for the same benefit as a woman with fewer contribution years and, particularly when combined with a mandatory retirement age, may also be discriminatory against women. Thus the earliest eligibility age should be the same for the basic pension as for individual accounts, and should be the same for men and women.

The way change is managed is important: as discussed in Box 5.10, those close to retirement should not face a sharp increase in the number of years they must work to earn a pension. Similarly, there should be no large "steps" in the earliest entitlement age, requiring some workers to work much longer than others who are only slightly older. Finally, the changes should be rules based rather than discretionary, and they should relate to date of birth, not to date of retirement.

Recommendation: There should be no mandatory retirement age on a nationwide basis.

Policymakers are frequently concerned that raising the retirement age will increase unemployment. This is based on the belief that if workers stay in their jobs longer, there will be fewer job opportunities for new entrants to the labor force. As explained in section 5.3.1, however, in a market economy it is incorrect to think about the labor market in terms of a fixed number of jobs; the number of jobs is responsive to the availability of labor. In any case, many workers receiving pensions will continue to work, either for a different employer or in self-employment. In China a further consideration is that the availability of jobs in urban areas invites mobility from rural areas. There may be a weak, short-run relationship between the number of additional older workers who retire and the number of new labor force entrants who can be hired (although we are aware of no empirical evidence of such a relationship), but there is certainly no long-run relationship in developed countries, and no reason to think the results would be different in developing countries. Although the labor market is not yet working efficiently in China, pension systems need to be designed for the long run.

A separate line of argument against a mandatory retirement age is that workers have different tastes and constraints: some want to retire as soon as possible, whereas others enjoy their work and want to continue, and still others may want to continue in order to increase their pension when they do retire. Employers, similarly, have different views about how long they want individual workers to continue.

Since there is no gain in terms of reduced unemployment from a mandatory retirement age, and considerable gain for individual workers and firms from flexible arrangements, there should be no mandatory retirement on a nationwide basis. Many other countries have concluded that the government need not establish a mandatory retirement age; if worker and employer both wish it, a person should be able to continue working.

Recommendation: If a worker retires earlier or later than the age for full benefits, the benefit should be adjusted on actuarial principles.

Reductions in pension benefits for earlier retirement and increases for later retirement are both needed to ensure appropriate labor market incentives, neither overencouraging nor underencouraging different retirement ages, as discussed in section 5.3.3. If a worker retires early, his or her pension should be actuarially reduced. However, workers should not be allowed to retire even on an actuarially reduced pension significantly earlier than the age for full benefit of the basic pension: given the propensity for short-term gratification discussed in Box 9.6, some people may retire at the earliest eligibility age even if that leaves them eventually in poverty. The earliest entitlement age should be within approximately three years of the age for full benefits and should rise over time in line roughly with the age for full benefits. Nor should early access to a pension be used as a substitute for unemployment or disability benefits.

As discussed in section 5.3.5, any worker who continues in employment beyond the age for full benefits should either receive an actuarially higher benefit upon retirement or should start receiving benefits while working.

Recommendation: Receipt of voluntary pension benefits should be allowed at a younger age than the earliest entitlement age for basic and NDC pensions.

The sharp constraints on the age at which *mandatory* pensions may be paid do not apply to voluntary arrangements. As discussed earlier, a central purpose of voluntary pensions is to allow for differences in people's preferences and to extend the options of those who work in harsh or otherwise life-shortening conditions. Thus voluntary pensions can be particularly targeted to fill a gap between earlier retirement and the earliest entitlement age in the mandatory pension system.

15.5.2   Adjusting benefits after retirement

The previous section discussed the level of benefits a worker receives at the time he or she starts receiving benefits. A separate issue is how those benefits should change subsequently.

> *Recommendation: Pension benefits during retirement—both basic pensions and NDC pensions—should be indexed by a formula that applies nationwide, although with local parameter values.*

In developed countries, benefits during retirement are sometimes indexed to inflation, sometimes to changes in average wages, and sometimes to a weighted average of the two (see section 5.3.4). Price indexation preserves real purchasing power, but pensioners fall increasingly below average living standards as they age. Wage indexation preserves the relationship to average living standards but costs more for a given benefit at the start of benefits (or requires a lower initial benefit to cost the same). For given initial benefits, price indexation places greater emphasis on the affordability of the system, wage indexation on the adequacy of benefits. Policy needs to strike a balance between the two.

Another way to consider the growth of benefits is to recognize that, for a given present value, a trade-off applies between the initial level of benefits and the growth of benefits after retirement. For a given long-run cost, the more rapid the growth of benefits, the lower the initial replacement rate has to be. Different countries make different choices depending on a range of factors: views about the initial level of pension benefits, the relationship between benefits and average wages over time, the pattern of poverty by age among those above retirement age, and available finance. Either price indexation or wage indexation, or a weighted average of both, is appropriate, depending on the objectives.

The real value of pensions should not vary unsystematically with the level of inflation; as explained in section 14.2.2, however, the method of indexation in China has exactly that effect. The problem can be resolved without altering long-run projected costs by setting the growth of benefits as a proper weighted average (where the weights add up to 1.0) of wage growth and price growth, the weights being chosen to keep expected costs at the same level as projected under the current rule. Alternatively, the weights could be chosen to protect the ratio between real benefits and real wages, perhaps with a one-time change in the initial benefit level if any change in projected costs is to be avoided. Alternatively, the change in costs could be absorbed as part of the overall reform.

15.6   EXTENDING COVERAGE

As noted earlier, coverage of the mandatory pension system is patchy in urban areas and does not extend beyond them. A priority for the future should be to extend the system to uncovered urban workers and to the rural population.

15.6.1   Urban areas

> *Recommendation: The extension of the basic pension and individual accounts to all urban workers in all sectors, already decreed, should be implemented over time.*

The intention of the 1997 reforms was that the system of basic pension and individual accounts should cover all urban workers, whether employed in state-owned enterprises or the private sector or self-employed. The aim is entirely the right one, but implementation of the policy has been slow.

Enforcing the extension of coverage to all workers in urban areas will make additional demands on administrative capacity. In addition, a sudden imposition of a high contribution rate on earnings can disrupt young, growing businesses. For both reasons, change should be phased in carefully, perhaps starting with the largest firms. Compliance should be enforced by the income tax authority.

Extending coverage to workers outside state-owned enterprises will significantly improve the short-run finances of the pension system, since nonstate workers are much younger on average. This will particularly be the case if coverage is extended to new arrivals in urban areas, who will disproportionately be young workers. Thus the growing migration to urban areas mutes the effects of demographic change—but only in those areas. The mirror image will be even faster population aging in rural areas, where the aged have the least economic security and are at the greatest risk of severe poverty. It is important to avoid the mistake of using a period of surplus revenue due to the expansion of coverage to set benefits at a level that is not sustainable.

Recommendation: The decision eventually to include civil servants in the mandatory and voluntary systems should be implemented.

This change does not require a reduction in civil servants' pensions, since their participation in the national system should be supplemented by a government-organized pension, just as private firms are encouraged to supplement the mandatory pension. The supplemental pension should be a fully funded, defined-contribution pension that is part of the regime described for voluntary pensions generally. Including civil servants in the mandatory system would make eventual labor mobility between public and private employment straightforward. One way to phase in the system would be to implement it for newly hired civil servants.

Recommendation: The existing minimum income guarantee for urban residents (di bao) should be enhanced for the elderly.

Since the amount of labor provided by elderly people is not a primary issue for policy, it is possible to offer them a minimum income guarantee, such as the present *di bao*, discussed in section 14.1.5, on less restrictive terms than offered to the rest of the population. Such an element would widen and deepen poverty relief in China.

Such a guarantee can be designed and integrated with the pension system in a variety of ways. One approach is simply to set the minimum income level and other rules of the existing minimum income guarantee differently for older than for younger people. Another simple arrangement is a flat-rate pension, financed from general taxation and paid to everyone over a certain age, as in the Netherlands and New Zealand. Such arrangements have the great advantage of coverage and administrative simplicity, but at a higher direct fiscal cost than benefits that do not offer universal coverage. An alternative is a tax-financed pension paid to all but the best off (as in Australia and South Africa, and more recently in Chile); such a system is administratively more complex but fiscally somewhat cheaper. On the other hand, any system with an income test contains a disincentive to saving for old age. Any such system needs to be concerned with workers who are mobile between the formal and the informal sector and between part-time and full-time work, and not just with urban workers with formal, full-time jobs. Moreover, since the basic pension is the redistributive portion of the public pension system, an issue is whether some part of the basic pension should be an offset against a tax-financed pension that is paid to everyone. That is, a universal noncontributory pension might be offset at least partly by the basic pension, but not by other sources of income. In keeping with general tax treatment of pensions, the benefits may be made subject to income tax.

15.6.2   Rural areas

Recommendation: Enhancing old-age security in rural areas should be a high priority. An eventual aim is to unify urban and rural pensions under a single structure, and to unify minimum income guarantees similarly, although levels may vary.

This chapter has concentrated on urban pensions, which at best would cover one-third of the population. A high priority should be old-age security for the remaining two-thirds of the population, whose traditional forms of economic security have eroded over the past decade and who, with migration of younger workers into urban areas, face an aging problem more severe than the average for the country as a whole.

China might wish to study the experience of other countries in addressing the old-age security of a large poor population, particularly through noncontributory universal pensions (discussed in Box 11.3) and the minimum income guarantee (section 14.1.5). The introduction of such an arrangement in urban areas could serve as a pilot for rural areas; unified noncontributory pensions and minimum income guarantees for the elderly could be the beginning of the unification of the social security system.

The problem is much larger than poverty relief narrowly defined. Millions of people in rural areas cannot afford basic services. Access to education requires students to pay for books and in some areas also for heating. Access to health care is impeded by the absence of pooling arrangements to finance such care. Access to basic education and health care is an important part of economic development. These alternative uses of general revenue need to be kept in mind when considering rural pensions.

Within pensions specifically, one policy direction is to extend existing urban arrangements to embrace the more developed parts of the rural economy. The township and village enterprise sector is one of those parts.

Recommendation: Township and village enterprises (TVEs) and other rural enterprises should be encouraged to establish voluntary enterprise pension plans.

Some TVEs are large, with average income well above the poverty line and with significant institutional capacity, and thus meet the prerequisites for establishing voluntary pension arrangements. As noted in Chapter 14, although legislation does not cover voluntary individual pensions, the institutions exist for voluntary plans set up by enterprises and local areas. Encouraging larger TVEs and other rural enterprises to set up such plans would be a natural evolution of what already exists.

Recommendation: Consideration should be given to including some rural regions within the urban system.

Some areas designated as rural are increasingly hard to distinguish from areas designated as urban, a convergence that is likely to become more common as economic development proceeds. A natural and highly desirable extension of the existing system would be to facilitate and encourage the redesignation of such areas to allow them to become part of the urban system. A more radical approach would introduce institutions specifically aimed at rural areas.

Recommendation: Introduce a simple system of rural poverty relief.

A core question is how to address poverty in the face of fiscal constraints and a shortage of administrative capacity. Administrative problems are particularly intractable. Targeting via an income test is administratively demanding even in the West, and more so in a country like China with a large informal sector in both urban and rural areas, and where a large part of the income of the rural population derives from home-produced goods, in particular food. Thus it is difficult to measure income accurately or cost-effectively, reducing the usefulness of income testing as a mechanism for targeting.

Perhaps the simplest approach is through local discretion plus block grants. Localities are better informed than central government about who is genuinely poor and thus better able to target on a discretionary basis. However, if central government underwrites the costs of local poverty relief, localities have no incentive to contain costs. Thus local discretion should be combined with block grants from the center to localities, with levels based on anticipated numbers of needy. Some monitoring by the center is needed to encourage concentration of the benefits on the needy rather the well connected.

Whatever simple institutions are introduced, it is important to have in mind an upgrade path. In the medium term more-ambitious policies become possible, including a move toward income testing, a move from discretion toward a rules-based system, and eventually the possibility of unifying the rural and urban systems.

Recommendation: Consider a universal pension in rural areas.

An alternative to income testing or local discretion is indicator targeting (Box 7.1), which awards benefits not on the basis of income but on other, more easily measurable characteristics that are highly correlated with poverty, notably, in the Chinese context, ill health and sufficiently old age.[13] For such reasons, as noted elsewhere, tax-financed noncontributory pensions exist in a number of countries, most recently including Chile. Perhaps more relevant for China, South Africa (Box 11.3) has a noncontributory pension, financed from general taxation and payable at age 65 (60 for women), subject to an affluence test designed primarily to screen out middle-class recipients. South Africa illustrates that it is both fiscally and administratively possible to have simple income transfers that cover a large rural population. As discussed in Box 11.3, some low-income countries also have such systems.

15.7 CONCLUSION

The combination of a social pool and individual accounts provides a structure that addresses the basic objectives of a pension system: poverty relief, income redistribution, insurance, and consumption smoothing. Voluntary plans organized by enterprises, industries, or localities are a further component; such plans, alongside yet-to-be-developed voluntary individual pensions, are particularly necessary in a country as large and diverse as China. These three elements, if properly designed and administered, can complement and strengthen each other and together provide a basis capable of standing the test of time.

13. In countries like South Africa, with a higher birth rate, the presence of large numbers of children in the family is another useful indicator.

In the course of implementing the 1997 reforms, however, problems have emerged. Fragmented organization and limited coverage contribute to financing difficulties and to incompleteness of social insurance. The deficits contribute to "empty" individual accounts, because local governments often use the contributions made by workers to their individual accounts to finance deficits in the social pool. Moreover, a system has not yet been developed for organizing investment through individual accounts in the capital markets, nor are the capital markets in a satisfactory condition for such investment. Over time, if nothing is done, these problems create a vicious circle, as the deficits are likely to persist, requiring continuing large fiscal subsidies, while the "empty" accounts and other systemic problems continue to undermine the credibility of the system, making further implementation—enforcing compliance and extending coverage—increasingly difficult. Thus the emerging problems are serious.

Our recommendations for further reform in China are based on the principles of design, the constraints of implementation, and the lessons from international experience discussed in earlier chapters. The recommendations include

- Creating a single national system, with a single national pool
- Continuing the system of basic pensions, with some reform
- Continuing individual accounts, but organized as notional accounts rather than as funded accounts
- Over time, increasing the age at which a worker may first receive a pension from the social pool, that increased age to be the same for men and women
- Over time, increasing the age at which a worker receives a full pension from the social pool, that increased age to be the same for men and women
- Adjusting the basic pension and pensions from individual accounts on an actuarial basis for the age at which the pension starts
- Strengthening encouragement and regulation of voluntary, supplementary pensions, through employer plans and eventually individual plans
- Continuing the transfer of state-owned enterprise shares to the National Social Security Fund, using the dividend flow to improve the system's financial balance and involving the fund as a long-term shareholder in the interest of improved corporate governance
- Enhancing old-age security in rural areas.

These measures would strengthen poverty relief, extend coverage, increase the coherence and economic efficiency of the system, and substantially reduce the financial deficit of current arrangements. Depending on the magnitude of the adjustments and the speed with which they are phased in, the need for fiscal support will be substantially reduced—in time, possibly even eliminated—although it will take a number of years for these reforms to be implemented and their effects to be visible. Indeed, some combinations of the reform measures above would put the system into long-run surplus. If in the future careful quantitative projection of the mandatory system does show a long-run surplus, a mix of further opportunities could be considered:

- Reducing contribution rates, thus reducing the financial shock for private firms, reducing their resistance to the mandatory system, and creating more room for voluntary pensions

- Increasing benefits from the social pool
- Enlarging the notional individual accounts
- Using revenue to add some funding of individual accounts
- Strengthening poverty relief by introducing some form of minimum pension or by accelerating extension of the system to the rural population.

In sum, the 1997 strategy of a pooled element and individual accounts was a sound one, but the decision to implement individual accounts as fully funded was mistaken given economic conditions in China. Retaining the strategy but instead implementing individual accounts as notional accounts is a better strategy for China today.

Part III

Conclusion

16

▷

Policy Questions, and Some Answers

Drawing on the principles set out in Part I and the lessons from international experience in Part II, this chapter brings together the main themes that are strategically relevant to policymakers in any country where pension reform is being considered. Section 16.1 poses a series of questions about pension design. None has a definitive answer, although many have wrong answers. We list the questions mainly to illustrate the array of choices.[1] Section 16.2 sets out the key messages and conclusions we want to leave in readers' minds.

16.1 QUESTIONS ABOUT POLICY DESIGN

We consider in turn questions about poverty relief, consumption smoothing, the role of funding, and a range of other issues.

16.1.1 Poverty relief and consumption smoothing

How can the elderly be protected from poverty? Countries vary in the resources they devote to relieving poverty among the elderly, and in the ways they combine different instruments in doing so.[2]

All developed and many developing countries have a means-tested guaranteed minimum income for the elderly, but its level relative to the country's average income varies considerably.

Some countries have noncontributory pensions for the entire elderly population. New Zealand and the Netherlands, for example, provide income in the form of a

---

1. There are many ways to build systems that work reasonably well. Our judgment that a given country's system works reasonably well should not be read as an endorsement of all the details of that system. Indeed, we have never studied the system of a country without finding some elements we would change.

2. For brief descriptions of a number of countries' systems, see section 11.4. The systems of Chile and China are described in more detail in Chapters 12 through 15.

tax-financed, flat-rate pension available to everyone beyond a given age.[3] In Australia and South Africa a uniform pension is awarded subject to an affluence test (so that it screens out the best off), and as discussed in Chapter 13, Chile introduced such a program in 2008.

In addition, mandatory contributory pension systems address poverty by requiring covered workers to contribute resources when working, after which they receive benefits in retirement. This reduces poverty insofar as they might not otherwise have provided as much for themselves.

Some countries, but not others, incorporate redistribution in their contributory pension systems, further reducing poverty. For example, the systems in Argentina and China include a basic pension that pays a flat rate per year of contributions, along with a proportional earnings-related system. Mexico provides a tax-financed, flat-rate annual contribution to funded individual accounts. Chile has had a guaranteed minimum pension for workers with at least twenty years of coverage. The U.S. Social Security system has a progressive benefit formula, providing a higher replacement rate for those with lower lifetime earnings histories. In other countries pension credits for those caring for children raise the benefits of some workers with shorter earnings histories; rules affecting spouses after divorce can do the same.

Many of the elderly poor are widows. In addition to the elements described above, policies that encourage women to have a career and so receive a larger pension also serve to address poverty. Survivor benefits are another key element in reducing poverty among widows.

A good system, one that alleviates poverty while accomplishing other objectives, can be constructed with different mixes of these general approaches. And we think countries with different mixes of objectives and different economic and demographic circumstances ought to rely on different approaches in different degrees. The appropriate extent of reliance on noncontributory pensions depends largely on the level of labor force participation of women and the degree of coverage of the pension system. All systems that involve redistribution and provide insurance distort the labor market. Good systems do not distort more than is needed to achieve these goals, and they recognize the cost of distortions when balancing goals. Systems with means testing also distort saving decisions. But different systems distribute the distorted incentives differently, making the choice of design dependent on observed behavioral parameters and the distribution of earnings.

What types of pension systems and formulas are good at consumption smoothing? The design of the mandatory contributory element of the pension system ranges widely, from fully defined-benefit to fully defined-contribution, with some countries having one of each. Any of these arrangements can be structured to function well. France, Germany, Italy, and Sweden have linear benefit formulas, in which benefits are an almost constant proportion of earnings. Other countries have progressive, earnings-related structures, either within a single system, as in the United States, or through a combination of a flat-rate element and a linear element, as in Argentina and China. Whatever the approach, benefits should depend on all or at least a large part of

---

3. The benefit level does not vary with past earnings, but does vary with length of time in residence.

a worker's earnings history. As discussed in section 5.2.1, formulas based only on earnings during the last few years before retirement do not work well for a national system.

How high should the mandatory contribution be? Different countries have different rates of mandatory contributions and accumulated funding, with corresponding differences in replacement rates. Countries differ also in the maximum level of earnings subject to contributions (see the discussion in section 5.2.1). Another variation is to exempt workers with low earnings from contributions, or to give them an income tax credit that at least partly offsets their contributions.

Compulsory earnings-related pensions play two key roles. The first is to limit the consequences of people making bad choices about saving and annuitization (Box 9.6). This concern extends well above the usual poverty line, but not to the very well off. The second role, if a country has a means-tested minimum income guarantee, is to reduce the distortions to saving caused by the means testing.

Mandates have uniform rules, which are not efficient for some workers, given that the sensible level and timing of saving and the appropriate age of retirement vary from worker to worker. Voluntary arrangements can be flexible but give greater room for poor choices, and they typically have higher administrative costs than well-run mandatory arrangements. Thus a mix of mandatory and voluntary is often a good solution, and different proportions can be appropriate in different settings.

How strongly should voluntary pensions and individual retirement saving be encouraged? The importance of voluntary pensions also varies widely across countries, depending on prevailing attitudes and on the size of the mandatory system. The choice has significant distributional implications if voluntary contributions, generally made by the better off, receive tax advantages. The magnitude and design of tax provisions can be chosen so as to improve the workings of the voluntary system and limit adverse distributional effects. Voluntary pensions need to be funded and carefully regulated. Systems can be voluntary for the individual or can be provided voluntarily by firms; in the latter case, participation by the firm's workers may be mandatory or not. Some countries, for example the Netherlands, have systems that grew from voluntary beginnings but have over time become de facto compulsory.

All private retirement savings plans (and mandatory private individual accounts) rely on financial markets. Good regulation of those markets is thus a key component of good pension policy. Countries with poorly functioning markets for individual savings need to improve their regulation and enhance the development of simple savings instruments with low administrative costs. Additionally, countries need macroeconomic stability as a precondition for financial markets and the pension system to work well.

16.1.2   Sustainability and funding

As the discussion in Chapters 6 and 9 makes clear, the funding of pension systems raises major questions, of which the following are only the most basic.

What methods support long-run sustainability? Adjusting pension systems for financial shortfalls is politically difficult. A key first step is good-quality, professional, nonpolitical projections of the financial future of the existing system and of any proposed reforms. For countries that choose not to perform this task, or that lack the resources to do so, provision by an international body would be useful. To assist the political process in decisions about pension reform, such projections need to be not only of good quality, but organized and presented so that they are accepted as such by the public. A second element supporting long-run sustainability is to incorporate some degree of automatic adjustments, additional to inflation protection, to address anticipated growth in life expectancy at retirement age; as discussed in section 5.4.1, this can be done in a number of ways. Uncertainty about the speed of increase in life expectancy makes automatic adjustment particularly useful. Fully defined-contribution systems, which have no sustainability issues by design, still need careful projections to evaluate how well the system is fulfilling its social goals.

What tools are available to restore sustainability? Sustainability can be restored through a combination of higher revenue and lower expenditure. Raising contribution rates (without increasing benefits in step) increases revenue, assuming the rate is not already so high that any increase per worker is more than fully offset by decreased employment. Expanding coverage and increasing the maximum level of earnings subject to contributions also increase revenue in the short run, but they may not strengthen sustainability in the long run because of the induced increase in future expenditure. Expenditure can be lowered by decreasing the average benefit or by decreasing the number of pensioners eligible at a given average benefit level. Benefits typically increase if they start later, a relationship that is important for labor market efficiency. A reduction in the monthly benefit at all starting ages helps sustainability. If the increase in benefit for a delayed start is roughly actuarial, an increase in the earliest eligibility age, by itself, does not help long-run finances; however, such an increase, by limiting very low replacement rates, may ease the social cost of a reduction in benefits. Which package is most suitable depends on the country's circumstances: for example, if contributions are already high, a further increase may be undesirable; if the average retirement age is low, there is scope to increase it. Sustainability requires both respect for fiscal constraints and preserving the ability of the pension to fulfill its social goals. Increased funding—from higher contributions, lower benefits, or transfers from outside the system—can help sustainability if it entails higher national saving and so greater total consumption in the future.

How much funding should the mandatory system have? Some countries have no funding: Italy, for example, relies on general revenue to cover shortfalls. Others, like Chile, have full funding of contributory pensions, but not of the old minimum guarantee or the new noncontributory basic pension. Some countries fall in between: the United States has a partially funded defined-benefit system, and Sweden combines a partially funded NDC system with a separate, mandatory, fully funded defined-contribution system. Different levels of funding are appropriate under different circumstances. As discussed in Chapters 6 and 7, a move from PAYG toward funding in a mandatory system may or may not be good policy, depending on a range of country specifics. Similarly, when starting a new system, either PAYG or funding may be good policy, again depending on country specifics. Whatever the level of funding, long-term financial sustainability is a critical element in good design.

What balance between public and private management in a mandatory pension system? The country descriptions in section 11.4 illustrate that management of mandatory systems covers a wide spectrum from fully public (United States) to fully private (but regulated) (the post-1981 system in Chile). The theoretical analysis in the earlier chapters argues that diversity across countries is appropriate where it reflects different situations in different countries. However, in at least some aspects of account administration, costs decline with the scale of the operation; for example, it is cheaper to collect pension contributions along with other payroll deductions such as for income tax. Thus well-designed systems generally include some role for government to provide or organize the performance of certain specific administrative tasks.

Alongside questions about account administration are questions about fund management and the types of assets it makes sense for a pension fund to hold. Some countries with defined-benefit systems hold only government debt. Others hold diversified portfolios, both across assets and across countries. As discussed in Chapter 9, these portfolios can be managed by government agencies or by private firms hired to handle investment transactions or even to make investment decisions. Countries with defined-contribution systems range from publicly organized investment management (Singapore) to fully private, but heavily regulated, financial intermediaries (Chile). The political and administrative capacities of government and the quality of politically available private options are important for comparing alternative methods. With adequate political and technical ability, some portfolio diversification is good policy.

When do funded individual accounts make sense? As discussed in Chapter 6, a move to funding may or may not be welfare improving, depending on the country's circumstances. A more specific question to ask is when funded individual accounts make sense, either with increased funding or as a substitute for centralized funding. Chile, for example, increased funding through its development of individual accounts, whereas Sweden viewed individual accounts largely as a substitute for centralized funding. The deviations from first-best (Box 4.2) and the resulting problems with consumer choice (Box 9.6) argue that uncritical reliance on consumer choice and market competition is based on mistaken analysis. The issue of administrative cost also interacts with the implementation capacity necessary for a system to be feasible. The problem of cost is compounded by the fact that the administration of funded individual accounts is largely a fixed cost and thus bears most heavily on small accounts, particularly in poorer countries. Depending on how costs are allocated to accounts, they may bear more heavily on the smaller accounts of lower earners.

For such reasons, increased funding through individual funded accounts makes sense only in countries where the increase is likely to raise the economic growth rate and improve intergenerational distributional outcomes *and* where the necessary institutional capacity is in place. Where those conditions hold, there are good grounds for simplifying the choices facing individual workers and for organizing accounts in a way that keeps administrative costs very low. The Thrift Savings Plan for federal civil servants in the United States (Box 11.5) is an example. The proposed system of simple personal accounts in the United Kingdom (U.K. Department for Work and Pensions 2006*a*) may be another.

16.1.3   Other questions

The previous questions far from exhaust the list.

How are pensions adjusted after retirement? A major question is how to protect pensions against inflation. Pensions based on a nominal annuity are vulnerable to inflation and should be avoided. Some countries index benefits to prices, others to wages, and others to a proper weighted average of the two (section 5.3.4). Any of these approaches may be appropriate. In contrast, weighting that does not add to one should be avoided.

Should receipt of a pension be conditioned on stopping work? Well-designed systems can include a retirement test (a requirement to stop work as a condition for receiving a pension), or not, or have different rules at different ages. If there is a retirement test, the answer to the next question is especially important.

How much should benefits increase with a delayed start? The international evidence is clear that retirement decisions are strongly affected by the implicit tax on continued work that arises if benefits do not adequately reflect both a delayed start to receiving benefits and possibly also an extra year of contributions. High implicit taxes should be avoided. There are two straightforward ways of doing so: either benefits should start at a given age whether or not the person continues to work, or benefits should increase after a delayed start by an amount that does not vary greatly from what is actuarially fair.

How should the families of workers be protected? Pension systems often include a life insurance element to cover young children if a worker dies. Similarly, disability systems are an important part of supporting families when earnings in the family drop sharply. Among the elderly, living standards may drop sharply with the death of one member of a couple, especially if it is the higher earner. As discussed in section 8.3.4, it is important that protection of a surviving spouse, through joint-life annuities, pooled contributions, or both, be sufficient to avoid too steep a fall in living standards. Similar considerations apply to a divorced spouse.

16.2 KEY MESSAGES

16.2.1 Analytical conclusions

Pensions have multiple purposes. As discussed in Chapter 2, the main objectives of pensions include consumption smoothing, insurance, poverty relief, and redistribution. These will be given different weights in different countries and at different times, but policy needs to bear them all in mind.

Analysis should be framed in a second-best context. Formulating pensions policy within a first-best framework is analytically simple, but a bad guide to policy design in a world with limited policy tools and major market imperfections, of which the most important are information and decision-making problems (Box 4.2 and Box 9.6). A key part of second-best analysis is consideration of the pension system as a whole—one cannot judge components in isolation.

There is no single best pension system design for all countries. Sound principles of pension design take account of the multiple objectives and market imperfections just noted and of incentives for work and saving. Proper application of those principles can and does lead to widely different systems; that is entirely as it should be. Designs that do not conform with sensible principles, or with the capacity of the country to implement the design, will not work well.

This conclusion—that there is no single best pension system—has several roots, all of them continuing themes throughout the book:

- Different objectives: policymakers in different countries may give different relative weights to the different objectives;
- Different behavioral parameters: the strength of interactions between pension design and effects on labor supply and saving will generally differ across countries.

For example, the effect of a pension on saving, and its evaluation, will depend, among other things, on whether the country has high saving (China) or not (the United States);

- Different fiscal positions: countries have different revenues at their disposal and different expenditure needs.
- Different institutional capacity constraints.

The first two bullets speak to what is optimal, the last to what is feasible. The third, differences in fiscal position, reflects both what is optimal (policymakers' choices about the trade-off between pension spending and other spending) and what is feasible. All four sets of influences are important in shaping policy.

A move from PAYG toward funding in a mandatory system may or may not be welfare improving. Whether it is depends on the design details and the country specifics, but all countries should bear in mind the following conclusions (Chapters 6 and 7):

- Explicit public debt is not equivalent to implicit pension debt.
- Funding may increase national saving, or it may increase explicit public debt, or some of each.
- Funding may improve the operation of capital markets and may increase economic growth. Either is possible; neither is inevitable.
- Funding that increases national saving generally has major fiscal effects. Thus the analysis needs to take account of the costs of moving from one steady state to another; it is faulty analysis simply to compare steady states before and after. The analysis also needs to take account of differences in risk and of differences in the administrative costs of different pension arrangements.
- Funding can be organized in a variety of ways, both without and without funded individual accounts.
- Any decision that a system should be funded rather than PAYG is necessarily a decision about the intergenerational distribution of income and of risks. In a PAYG system the early cohorts receive a larger pension than they would in a fully funded system, resulting in later cohorts receiving smaller pensions than they would in a fully funded system. This may or may not be good policy, depending, among other things, on how benefits are distributed across retirees with different needs. Inescapably, any decision makes some people better off and some worse off. Hence, even if funding does increase output, the change cannot be presented as a Pareto improvement, since it comes at the expense of an earlier generation. It is not possible to airbrush out history.

16.2.2 Policy conclusions

The main cause of the pensions "crisis" is a failure to adapt to long-run trends. Pension systems in many countries face the overarching long-term trends discussed in Chapter 1: increasing life expectancy, declining fertility, and earlier retirement.[4] The first two,

---

4. The long-term trend to earlier retirement has attenuated or reversed in a number of countries (Scherer 2001; OECD 2002, Table V.1; Sigg 2005, Figure 3). But we have not seen a trend in the other direction proportional to continuing increase in life expectancy.

at least, are ongoing (with some sad exceptions in parts of the world on the mortality side). Superimposed on these are two more recent phenomena: the baby boom (widespread, though not universal) and the general increase in the scale of pension systems since World War II, in terms of both coverage and benefit levels.

Pension systems with contribution rates, monthly benefits, and retirement ages set for an earlier era are not consistent with the longer retirements implied by increasing life expectancy and earlier average retirement; this is all the more true given the future shrinkage in the workforce implied by declining fertility. Some adjustment is necessary. The scale of that adjustment is amplified by the fact of the baby boom and the increasing scale of pension systems, although, as the age pyramids in Figure 1.5 show, the problem would exist even in their absence. The main source of financing problems is that, with the exception of adjustment to price and wage growth, defined-benefit systems have had a static design with no automatic adjustment to long-term trends.

The main solutions to problems of paying for pensions. In responding to these trends, as discussed in section 11.2.2, any improvement to the finances of a pension system must involve one or more of

- Higher contribution rates,
- Lower benefits,
- Later retirement at the same benefit, and
- Policies, such as increased saving, designed to increase national output.

That statement remains true whatever the degree of funding; funded systems also have to respond to changes in wages and interest rates that are affected by demographic trends (section 6.3.3). If a public pension is regarded as unsustainable, the problem needs to be addressed directly by one of the methods just listed.

Some people think that later retirement will aggravate unemployment. That is a fallacy because it ignores the reaction of the supply of jobs to the supply of workers (section 5.3.1).

Reforming pensions. Unsustainable pension systems should be put on a sustainable footing. Many pension systems are poorly designed: many have poor coverage; some excessively discourage the labor supply of some prime-age workers; some unduly discourage participation in the pension system; some encourage too-early retirement (see Chapter 5). Such designs should be changed:

- Pensions should provide poverty relief. Labor-market experiences and life courses are varied, so that even in developed countries not all workers have a full contributions record, and in developing countries informal activity remains widespread. Thus the design of pensions to address poverty should recognize that gaps in contributions will occur. As discussed in section 11.2.1, gaps in contributions can be addressed in contributory systems through a variety of mechanisms, including minimum guarantees and credits for caring activities; an alternative is a noncontributory universal pension. These mechanisms can work well along with guaranteed minimum incomes for the elderly.

- Pensions should assist consumption smoothing. The design of this element should be consistent with economic and social conditions in the country and with the way the system provides poverty relief. In particular, design should take account of deviations from first-best (Box 4.2) and of problems with choice and competition (Box 9.6). Thus if there are choices, they should be limited, and a good default option is part of good design.

- The rules of pension systems should be gender neutral and chosen with sensitivity as to how they affect men and women differently (Chapter 8).

16.2.3 Implementation matters: Policy choices and economic development

As discussed in Chapter 9, any pension system must respect the constraints of limited budgets and limited implementation capacity. The discussion in this section is about these constraints; it is not about optimal design but about what limits on policy choices make sense for countries at different levels of development.[5]

We illustrate implementation in terms of three stylized types of country: a low-income developing country, a middle-income developing country, and a developed country. Actual countries may occupy intermediate positions and mixed positions for different parts of the economy. The discussion here uses the conventional terms of first-tier pensions (aimed primarily at poverty relief), second-tier pensions (mandatory, intended to strengthen consumption smoothing), and third-tier pensions (voluntary at the level of the firm or the individual, subject to regulation and perhaps tax favored, to accommodate differences in individual preferences). Although illustrated here in terms of these three separate tools, some countries use only two; in the United States and Mexico, for example, a single system addresses supplemental poverty relief and consumption smoothing. We refer to pension systems in specific countries without intending to imply that those countries are typical of the category.

The examples below are intended only as illustrations; they should *not* be taken as a template. A country's administrative capacity may, for example, have some parts that are typical of middle-income countries and others at a level more commonly found in low-income countries. Similarly, fiscal constraints may call for different systems for different sectors or forms of employment within a single country: for example, a middle-income country may have a formal system for urban areas and a much simpler one (or none) for rural areas. Similarly, a system designed for civil servants will differ sharply from one designed for an entire country. Once there is a national system, civil servants should be part of it, typically with a supplemental pension; large private firms may have a similar arrangement.

All the examples are based on the following assumptions:

- that the parameters of the system (such as benefit levels and the age at which a pension is first awarded) are consistent with fiscal sustainability, and
- that, alongside pensions, all countries with the necessary administrative capacity provide some degree of means-tested support for the elderly.

---

5. For useful institutional description see OECD (2007) and U.S. Social Security Administration (2007*a*). For links to descriptions provided by agencies and organizations see "Social Security in Other Countries" at the U.S. Social Security website (www.ssa.gov/international/links.html). See also the resources in AARP's Global Aging Program at www.aarp.org/research/international/map/.

Illustrative pension systems for a low-income country

First tier. The choice is highly constrained:

- A very poor country may be unable to finance or organize a national system of poverty relief, instead relying on family, charitable organizations, and local government.
- As capacity allows, it becomes possible to use general revenue to offer limited poverty relief, through transfers to local governments or through a national system that targets by age.

A country at a low level of development—typically with a large informal sector and substantial household production—will generally not have the capacity to administer an income test. A system of local discretion may be able to do so in an approximate way, based more on local knowledge than on formal assessment of a household's income.

Second tier. A country at this level of development will generally not have the capacity to manage a mandatory earnings-related system, which requires, among other things, enforcing contributions and measuring and recording a person's income over forty years or more. Such countries should leave such a system as an agendum for the future.

Third tier. Any voluntary saving plans operating in the country should not be tax favored, since fiscal resources are highly constrained, and tax advantages are typically regressive. Nevertheless, provision of a simple, reliable opportunity for voluntary savings is important.

Illustrative pension systems for a middle-income country

First tier. Countries in this category have a choice of

- A noncontributory, tax-financed pension with or without an affluence test (as in Australia, the Netherlands, New Zealand, South Africa, and, beginning in 2008, Chile); or
- A simple contributory PAYG pension, for example a flat-rate pension based on years of contributions (such as the basic state pension in the United Kingdom).

Second tier. The choice is between

- A publicly organized, earnings-related, defined-benefit pension, or possibly an NDC pension; or
- A defined-contribution pension as part of a provident fund (as in Malaysia and Singapore).

If there is a contributory first-tier pension, either of these can be separate from it or integrated. Tax treatment of contributions and benefits should consider the extent to which tax favoring is regressive.

Third tier. Voluntary, defined-contribution pensions at the level of the firm or the individual are possible; regulation is important, and any tax favoring should be designed to avoid excessive regressivity. Defined-benefit plans are difficult to regulate, and new ones should be avoided.

Options for pension systems in a developed country

First tier. Countries should consider either

- A contributory pension aimed at poverty relief (used in many countries, including the United Kingdom), with any of an array of different designs; or
- A noncontributory, tax-financed pension, either with an affluence test (as in Australia, Chile, and South Africa) or without (as in the Netherlands and New Zealand).

Second tier. The menu includes (separately or in combination)

- A publicly organized, defined-benefit pension, which may be integrated as a single system with the first-tier contributory pension (as in the United States) or not (as in France, Germany, and Sweden);
- An NDC system (as in Sweden);
- An administratively cheap savings plan with access to annuities (like the Thrift Savings Plan for federal employees in the United States);
- Mandatory, funded, defined-benefit pensions sponsored by industry (the de facto system in the Netherlands); or
- Funded, defined-contribution pensions (as in Chile and Sweden), possibly including an antipoverty element (as in Mexico).

Third tier. Voluntary, defined-contribution pensions can be organized at the level of the firm or the individual; regulation is important, and any tax favoring should seek to avoid excessive regressivity. Defined-benefit plans are difficult to regulate; a country without them should not tax-favor them, and a country with them should not mind their voluntary replacement by defined-contribution plans as long as the conversions suitably protect workers.

In sum. Clearly the range of choices widens as fiscal and administrative capacities grow. The less developed a country, the more narrowly feasibility concerns constrain choices. Specifically, a country

- Should not set up a system beyond its financial and administrative capability;
- Should not introduce a mandatory, earnings-related pension system until it has a robust capacity to keep records accurately over forty or more years; and
- Should not introduce individual funded accounts (whether mandatory or as an option in a mandatory system) until it can regulate investment, accumulation, and annuitization.

It is clear that a developed country has a full range of choices. Thus it is not surprising that the richer countries have very different systems one from another, from the United States with its progressive, earnings-related, partially funded pensions supplemented by voluntary employer and individual pension plans; to Sweden with its NDC pension system plus mandatory, individual funded accounts; to the Netherlands with its system of noncontributory, flat-rate pensions augmented by near-mandatory participation in a funded occupational pension plan. But the fact that the range of options is not greatly constrained by issues of feasibility should not be misinterpreted: that a country is capable of implementing an administratively demanding plan does not mean that such a plan is a good idea or that it is necessarily superior to a less administratively demanding system. New Zealand has a simple pension system through choice, not constraint.

The pensions "crisis" is an outcome of adapting too little or too slowly to long-term trends. Pensions are complex and not easy to understand, and pension reform is politically difficult when it disrupts long- and widely held economic expectations. Yet good pension reform is important for people's lives—as workers and as current or future pensioners—and for the economy as a whole. And, despite the many challenges, pension reform can be done well. The principles in this book suggest how.

$\triangleright$

Glossary

Actuarial benefits. A stream of benefits whose expected **discounted present value** equals the annuitant's accumulation at the time the benefits start. For a given accumulation, the size of the periodic benefit (for example, monthly) therefore depends on the person's remaining life expectancy and the rate of return on assets available to the pension provider over the period during which benefits will be paid. A pension system that follows this approach in broad outline, but without precise use of projected life expectancy and market interest rates, is referred to as quasi-actuarial.

Actuarial insurance. Insurance based on the **risk** of an event occurring and the size of the resulting loss. See Box 2.2.

Adverse selection. The tendency for **insurance** to be bought by people who are more likely to collect on the policy. This can occur when the purchasers are better informed than the insurer of their own degree of riskiness. For example, individuals with above-average life expectancy are more likely to buy **annuities**. This type of buyers' self-selection is adverse to the insurer.

Affluence test. A measure of eligibility for benefits that is designed to screen out only the best off. It thus differs from an **income test,** which screens out all except the poor.

AFPs. *Administradoras de fondos de pensiones,* competitive private pension providers in Chile.

Age dependency ratio. See **Dependency ratio**.

Age for full benefits (also called normal retirement age). The youngest age at which a person is entitled to a full pension. See also **Earliest eligibility age**.

Allocative efficiency. See **Pareto efficiency.**

Annual management fee. The annual administrative charge imposed by a pension fund manager, expressed as a percentage of the account balance being managed. See also **Charge ratio; Reduction in yield**.

Annuity. An arrangement whereby an individual exchanges his or her pension accumulation (or other lump sum) at retirement for periodic (for example, annual or monthly) payments for the rest of his or her life, thus allowing the individual to insure against the risk of outliving his or her pension savings. With an immediate annuity, payments begin immediately; with a deferred annuity, payments are delayed until some point after the purchase date. Different forms of annuities adjust payments on different bases.

Assets test. See **Means test**.

Backloading. The practice, in a **defined-benefit pension plan**, of increasing the benefit to which a worker is entitled by a larger fraction of the worker's wage in the later years of his or her career than in the earlier years. Backloading is intended to encourage workers to stay with the firm, since the increase in the value of the pension makes earnings in later years more valuable.

Bonds. Financial securities that constitute a loan from the purchaser (the bondholder) to the seller. Bonds normally specify a date on which the bondholder will be repaid (the redemption or maturity date) and a periodic interest payment stated in dollars (or other currency unit). Contrast with **Stocks**.

Broad funding. An increase in the assets of a public pension system that increases national savings. This can come from increased contributions or decreased benefits that are not offset by a decline in voluntary or other government saving. Contrast with **Narrow funding**.

Cash balance plan. An employer pension plan in which the employer credits a worker's cash balance account with a fixed fraction of the worker's earnings each year, plus an amount based on a fixed rate of interest on accumulated earnings. On reaching retirement, or leaving the firm, the worker may take the balance as a lump sum or use it to buy an **annuity**, with pricing organized by the employer. The plan is supposed to be fully funded.

Charge ratio. The percentage decrease in a person's pension accumulation at retirement due to administrative charges. Under plausible assumptions, over a full career, an **annual management fee** of 1 percent generates a charge ratio of about 20 percent; that is, the accumulation at retirement, and hence the value of any **annuity** for which it is exchanged, is 20 percent lower than it would be if the annual management fee were zero. See also **Reduction in yield**.

Citizen's pension. See **Noncontributory universal pension**.

Compliance. Adherence of a worker or employer to the laws and regulations governing a pension system. A covered worker who is not making contributions that are legally required is noncompliant (that is, is evading contributions); but a person who is not making contributions because he or she is currently not working in a covered job is not noncompliant.

Consumption smoothing. Behavior that allows a household to maintain its desired level of consumption over time despite variations in income. Pensions assist consumption smoothing by allowing individuals to redistribute their resources over their lifetime, by saving in their productive years so as to consume more in retirement. See Box 2.1. See also **Redistribution**.

Contributory basic pension. A pension paid, often at a flat rate, to a person with a full record of contributions, or pro rata to a person with an incomplete contributions record. See also **Earnings-related pension; Noncontributory universal pension**.

Cost-of-living adjustment. An increase in benefits in payment, usually adjusted annually, intended to have benefits keep pace with inflation. In the U.S. Social Security system, the adjustment has been automatic since 1975 and is determined by the change in the consumer price index for urban wage earners and clerical workers.

Coverage. As most commonly measured, the proportion of the employed population contributing to the pension system at a given time. This is distinct from the set of people with covered earnings records or individual accounts in that it omits workers who have contributed in the past and acquired at least some rights. See also **Compliance**.

Defined-benefit (DB) pension. A pension in which the benefit is determined as a function of the worker's history of pensionable earnings. The formula may be based on the worker's final wage and length of service, or on wages over a longer period, for example the worker's full career. Full matching of funds and obligations is in principle preserved by adjusting funds to meet anticipated obligations. See section 3.2.

Defined-contribution (DC) pension. A pension in which the benefit is determined by the value of assets accumulated in the worker's name over his or her career. The benefit may take the form of a lump sum, or a series of payments, or an **annuity**, but in all cases is determined by the size of the worker's lifetime pension accumulation. Full matching of funds and obligations is in principle preserved by adjusting obligations to available funds. See section 3.2.

Dependency ratio. The term is used in two different ways. The age dependency ratio is the ratio of people beyond some specified age (for example, 65) to people of working age (for example, 16 to 64). The system dependency ratio is the ratio of people receiving pensions to the number of active contributors.

Earliest eligibility age. The youngest age at which the rules of a pension system allow a person to receive a retirement pension. See also **Age for full benefits**.

Earnings-related pension. A pension whose benefits are positively related to the worker's earnings; the relationship may be strictly proportional, as with a **notional defined-contribution pension**, or less than strictly proportional, as in the U.S. Social Security system.

Economic efficiency. See **Pareto efficiency**.

Efficiency. See **Pareto efficiency**.

Engineering efficiency. See **Productive efficiency**.

Equities. See **Stocks**.

Equity. The principle that resources should be distributed or shared among individuals according to some notion of fairness. Equity *may* imply equality, but does not have to. See also **Horizontal equity; Vertical equity**.

Extensive margin. The margin of action or inaction, that is, whether or not a person participates at all in paid work. One measure of the extensive margin comes from responses to the survey question, "Did you work last week?" The change in the number of people working after a change in government policy is the response on the extensive margin. Contrast with **Intensive margin**.

Final-salary pension. A **defined-benefit pension** that is based on years of service and salary in a worker's final year or final few years.

First-best analysis. Analysis based on the assumptions, common in simple economic models, that economic agents are well informed, that there are no **incomplete markets**, and that the government uses interventions in the economy that do not cause economic distortions. That is, the government can intervene without having to rely on taxes that vary with earnings or savings. Contrast with **Second-best analysis**.

Formal sector.   All those types of employment that offer regular wages and hours, which carry with them employment rights, and on which income tax is paid. Contrast with **Informal sector**.

Funded pension.   A pension paid from an accumulated fund built up over a period of years out of contributions and the returns on the assets purchased with those contributions.

Funded individual account.   See **Defined-contribution pension**.

Horizontal equity.   Distribution in accordance with equal treatment of equals; for example, the same taxes for families of the same size with the same taxable income. When taxing families of different sizes, taxes must be suitably adjusted for the greater cost of reaching a given living standard with a larger family. What adjustments are suitable is not obvious, and economists differ. See also **Equity; Vertical equity**.

Implicit debt.   A measure of the unfunded obligations of a pension scheme.

Implicit tax rate.   The rate at which a family receiving a benefit subject to an **income test** loses the benefit as a consequence of extra income. If the benefit is lost dollar for dollar as earnings rise, the implicit tax rate is 100 percent.

Income test.   A way of determining benefit eligibility that awards benefits only to individuals or families with low incomes, that is, benefit is withdrawn as income rises. See also **Affluence test; Means test**.

Incomplete markets.   A market system in which not all goods and services that a person might wish to buy are available at some price. An example is the impossibility of buying **insurance** against future price inflation in a standardized market.

Index fund (in the United Kingdom sometimes called a tracker fund).   An investment fund that holds a portfolio whose return is designed to match the return on some category of assets, as measured by a standard price index for those assets. The assets may either be **bonds** or **stocks**, for example the stocks in the Dow Jones index in the United States or the FTSE-100 in the United Kingdom. When the index is based on a very large number of bonds or stocks, the fund may hold a subset chosen to have a high statistical probability of matching the index.

Indicator targeting (also called proxy targeting).   A mechanism for targeting benefits to poor people that identifies them not by their income but by some other indicator, ideally one that is highly correlated with poverty, that the individual cannot control, and that is easily observable. See Box 7.2.

Individual account.   See **Defined-contribution pension**.

Informal sector.   Employment that is not formally recognized; workers in the informal economy generally have no contacts, no fixed hours, and no employment benefits such as sick pay or maternity leave. Contrast with **Formal sector**.

Insurance.   The term is used in two different ways. Insurance can be an arrangement (such as a government program) that offers individuals protection against **risk**; or a contract to make payments under certain defined future circumstances, normally organized in the private sector. The former defines insurance in terms of its objective, the latter as a mechanism that provides payments under the circumstances insured against. An idealized market has **actuarial insurance**.

Intensive margin.   The margin between two positive amounts of work—that is, the number of hours a person works, conditional on working. For example, responses to the survey question, "How many hours did you work last week?" provide a measure of the intensive margin for hours worked. The change in the number of hours people work after a change in government policy is the response on the intensive margin. Contrast with **Extensive margin**.

Intertemporal marginal rate of substitution. The rate at which a person values consumption today relative to consumption in the future.

Joint-life annuity (also called joint-and-survivor annuity). An annuity that pays a regular monthly income to two people until both have died. The size of the monthly payment depends on whether one or both are still alive and may depend on which of the two is still alive. Contrast with **Single-life annuity**.

Legacy costs (also called legacy debt). The obligation of an unfunded pension system to pay the future benefits of **retirees** and the entitlements earned to date by workers who have not yet retired. In a partially funded system, the legacy cost is the obligation less the value of assets in the fund. In either case it is a future cost resulting from the previous working of the pension system.

Life-cycle fund. An investment fund in which, as the account holder grows older, the assets in the account are gradually and automatically shifted from mainly stocks to mainly bonds.

Means test. A measure of benefit eligibility that includes individuals whose income and wealth from all sources are both (or in combination) below a given amount. The term thus embraces both an **income test** and a wealth test (the latter also called an assets test). See also **Affluence test**.

Moral hazard. A situation in which a person with **insurance** can affect the insurer's liability without its knowledge, for example by taking less care to avoid an accident covered by the insurance than the person would without insurance.

Multipillar pension system. A pension system with several components designed to serve multiple objectives. As originally defined by the World Bank the system comprises three pillars: a publicly managed, **PAYG** system; a system of mandatory, privately managed plans, usually **defined-contribution** plans; and a system of voluntary, privately managed plans. The meaning of the term has evolved to include systems with multiple parts more generally. The categorization in this book talks about "parts" or "tiers" rather than "pillars" to make it clear that there are many ways of organizing the system as a whole.

Narrow funding. An increase in the assets of a national pension system which may or may not result in **broad funding**. Increasing contributions will increase narrow funding and usually increase broad funding as well. Transferring assets—newly created government **bonds** or shares in state enterprises—into the system (typically, into individual accounts) creates funded accounts and affects the distribution of **legacy costs** but has little effect on national saving and thus on **broad funding**.

NDC. See **Notional defined-contribution pension**.

Noncompliance. See **Compliance**.

Noncontributory universal pension. A public pension paid at a flat rate, usually on the basis of a record of residence rather than on the basis of contributions, and sometimes restricted to citizens (hence sometimes referred to as a citizens pension). Such a pension may or may not be subject to an **affluence test**. Contrast with **Contributory basic pension**.

Normal retirement age. See **Age for full benefits**.

Notional defined-contribution (NDC) pension. A pension financed through **social insurance** contributions, where benefits bear a quasi-actuarial relationship to lifetime pension contributions. See section 3.4.

Old-age dependency ratio. See **Dependency ratio**.

Pareto efficiency (also called allocative efficiency). A situation in which resources are allocated in such a way that no reallocation can make any individual better off without making at least one other individual worse off. A policy that makes someone better off and nobody worse off is referred to as Pareto improving.

Pay-as-you-go (PAYG) pension. A pension paid (usually by the government) out of current tax revenue rather than out of an accumulated fund.

PDV. See **Present discounted value**.

Pensioner. A person receiving pension benefits, whether or not he or she has stopped working. Contrast with **Retiree**.

Present discounted value. The capital value today of a stream of income received over some future period, calculated on the basis of a specified discount rate.

Productive efficiency (also called administrative efficiency or engineering efficiency). The allocation of resources so as to produce the maximum output from given inputs. A component of **Pareto efficiency**.

Provident fund. A publicly organized, mandatory, **defined-contribution pension** plan where workers have no choice of portfolio, but rather hold shares in a single, centrally held portfolio.

Proxy targeting. See **Indicator targeting**.

Real annuity (also called an inflation-indexed life annuity). A life **annuity** that is automatically adjusted to keep pace with inflation, typically as measured by a consumer price index.

Redistribution. The transfer of resources from one person or group to another. Pensions can bring about redistribution either within a generation (for example, from richer to poorer pensioners) or across generations (for example, from current workers to pensioners). Redistribution makes it possible to subsidize the **consumption smoothing** of lower-earning workers.

Reduction in yield. A measure of all charges that reduce the net return an individual realizes on his or her pension accumulation. For example, if the rate of return before charges is 5 percent, but the individual receives a return of 3 percent after charges, the reduction in yield is 2 percent. See also **Annual management fee; Charge ratio**.

Replacement rate. The ratio of pension benefits (for example, monthly) to monthly earnings (after taxes and transfers) during work. The term can be defined in different ways. Defined as the average pension benefit as a percent of the average wage, the replacement rate is a measure of the living standards of the elderly relative to those of the working population. Defined as an individual pensioner's benefit as a percent of his or her previous wage, the replacement rate is a measure of the effectiveness of **consumption smoothing**. In this book the term is used with the latter meaning unless otherwise stated. Sometimes replacement rates are reported gross of taxes and transfers rather than net.

Retiree. A person who has stopped work, whether or not he or she is receiving pension benefits. Contrast with **Pensioner**.

Retirement. The term is used in two different ways. It sometimes refers to the end of work and sometimes to the start of pension benefits. These are two separate events, which can happen at two separate times.

Risk. A situation in which the probability of a specified event (such as breaking a leg or becoming unemployed) is reasonably well known. Risk is to be distinguished from uncertainty, which pertains to events whose probability is much harder to predict, for example future improvements in life expectancy.

Second-best analysis. Analysis that seeks the optimal policy when government must rely on distorting taxes to alter the income distribution or to respond to economic distortions and other departures from the simple theoretical model, such as imperfect information, **incomplete markets**, and existing taxation. Contrast with **First-best analysis**.

Shares. See **Stocks**.

Single-life annuity. An **annuity** that pays an income (for example per year or per month) for the life of one person. Contrast with **Joint-life annuity**.

Social insurance. A set of arrangements, modeled on private insurance, under which individuals receive public benefits in respect of (for example) unemployment or **retirement**, often without any test of means or need, on the basis of previous (usually compulsory) contributions.

Social pension. See **Noncontributory universal pension**.

Social security. This term is ambiguous because it is used with different meanings in different countries. In the United States it refers to public retirement and disability benefits, in the United Kingdom to all publicly provided cash benefits, and in the European Union to all publicly provided cash benefits plus health care benefits. Where the term is used in this book, it refers to retirement pensions only.

Stocks (also called equities or shares). Financial securities that represent ownership of a fraction of a corporation. A corporation sells stock as a means of financing its investment and may pay a dividend, usually annually, to stockholders. If the corporation flourishes, the value of its stock rises, resulting in a capital gain to stockholders. If it goes bankrupt, the value of its stock is based on whatever value remains in the corporation after its creditors have been paid. Thus stocks represent a title to ownership, in contrast with **bonds**, which are a form of loan.

System dependency ratio. See **Dependency ratio**.

Taper of benefit. See **Implicit tax rate**.

Thrift Savings Plan (TSP). A retirement savings plan for U.S. federal employees, established in 1986 as part of the Federal Employees' Retirement System Act and administered by the Federal Retirement Thrift Investment Board. The TSP is a tax-deferred **defined-contribution pension** plan with three main characteristics: choice by participants restricted to a small number of clearly differentiated investment funds; centralized administration; and fund management on a wholesale basis. See Box 11.5.

Tracker fund. See **Index fund**.

Trust fund. An accumulation of financial assets intended to cover at least part of a pension plan's future liabilities. In a system that is mainly **PAYG**, the trust fund will hold only a few months' outflows as a buffer against temporary shortfalls, but trust funds may have a much greater degree of funding and may even be fully funded, containing resources sufficient to pay all liabilities generated to date.

Unfunded pension. See **Pay-as-you-go (PAYG) pension**.

Vertical equity. Distribution in accordance with the principle that the better off in a society are able to bear a disproportionate share of the burden of providing for government expenditures and for transfers to the needy, and thus a basis for redistribution of income, consumption, or wealth from richer to poorer people. See also **Equity; Horizontal equity**.

Voluntary pension. The term is used in two different ways. A voluntary pension may be that which an individual worker chooses to provide for himself or herself, such as (in the United States) an Individual Retirement Account. Alternatively, it can be a plan that an employer chooses to introduce for its employees (without a government mandate), whose participation may be either voluntary or compulsory on the part of the workers.

Withdrawal rate. See **Implicit tax rate.**

References

Aaron, Henry J. 1966. The social insurance paradox. *Canadian Journal of Economics and Political Science* 32 (Aug.): 371–74. Reprinted in Barr (2001*b*), vol. II: 79–82.

Akerlof, George A. 1978. The economics of "tagging" as applied to the optimal income tax, welfare programs and manpower planning. *American Economic Review* 68: 8–19. Reprinted in Barr (2001*b*), vol. II: 298–309.

Apps, Patricia, and Ray Rees. 2004. Fertility, taxation and family policy. *Scandinavian Journal of Economics* 106 (Dec.): 745–63.

———. 2007. The taxation of couples. IZA Discussion Paper 2910. Bonn Forschungsinstitut zur Zukunft der Arbeit (Jul.).

Arenas de Mesa, Alberto, and Carmelo Mesa-Lago. 2006. The structural pension reform in Chile: Effects, comparisons with other Latin American reforms, and lessons. *Oxford Review of Economic Policy* 22 (Spring): 149–67.

Arenas de Mesa, Alberto, and Veronica Montecinos. 1999. The privatization of social security and women's welfare: Gender effects of the Chilean reform. *Latin American Research Review* 34 (3): 7–37.

Arza, Camila. 2006. Distributional impacts on pension policy in Argentina: Winners and losers within and across generations. *International Social Security Review* 59 (Jul.-Sep.): 79–102.

Asher, Mukul G., and N. Amarendu. 2006. Mandatory savings for asset enhancement: The case of Singapore. *Social Development Issues* 28 (2): 57–70.

Asher, Mukul, Nicholas Barr, Peter Diamond, Edwin Lim, and James Mirrlees. 2005. *Social security reform in China: Issues and options.* Policy Study of the China Economic Research and Advisory Programme (Jan.). http://www.oup.com/us/pdf/social_security_study_2005 (in Chinese http://www.oup.com/us/pdf/china_social_security_study).

Atkinson, A. B. 1999. *The economic consequences of rolling back the welfare state.* Cambridge, Mass.: MIT Press.

Augusztinovics, M., R. I. Gál, Á. Matits, L. Máté, A. Simonovits, and J. Stahl. 2002. The Hungarian pension system before and after the 1998 reform. In *Pension reform in Central and Eastern Europe*, vols. 1–2, ed. Elaine Fultz. Geneva: International Labour Organization.

Baker, Michael, Emily Hanna, and Jasmin Kantarevic. 2003. The married widow: Marriage penalties matter! NBER Working Paper, no. 9782. Cambridge, Mass.: National Bureau of Economic Research. www.nber.org/papers/w9782.

Banks, James, and Sarah Smith. 2006. Retirement in the UK. *Oxford Review of Economic Policy* 22 (Spring): 44–56.

Barr, Nicholas. 1979. Myths my grandpa taught me. *Three Banks Review* no. 124 (Dec.): 27–55. Reprinted in Barr (2001*b*), vol. II: 83–111.

———. 1981. Empirical definitions of the poverty line. *Policy and Politics* 9 (Jan.): 1–21.

———. 1998. Towards a "third way": Rebalancing the role of the state. *New Economy* 4 (2): 71–76.

———. 2000. Reforming pensions: Myths, truths, and policy choices. Working Paper, no. WP/00/139. Washington: International Monetary Fund. www.imf.org/external/pubs/ft/wp/2000/wp00139.pdf.

———. 2001*a*. *The welfare state as piggy bank: Information, risk, uncertainty, and the role of the state*. London and New York: Oxford University Press. www.oxfordscholarship.com/oso/public/content/economicsfinance/0199246599/toc.html.

———, ed. 2001*b*. *Economic theory and the welfare state*, vol. I: *Theory*, vol. II: *Income transfers*, and vol. III: *Benefits in kind*. Edward Elgar Library in Critical Writings in Economics. Cheltenham, U.K., and Northampton, Mass.: Edward Elgar.

———. 2003. *The economics of the welfare state*, 3rd ed. Chinese translation including a new preface. Beijing: China Labour and Social Security Publishing House.

———. 2004*a*. *The economics of the welfare state*, 4th ed. Oxford: Oxford University Press, and Stanford, Calif.: Stanford University Press.

———. 2004*b*. Higher education funding. *Oxford Review of Economic Policy* 20 (Summer): 264–83. oxrep.oupjournals.org/cgi/content/abstract/20/2/264?ijkey=20GIFCugfcjFz& keytype=ref. Reprinted in *European Economy, Quality and efficiency in education*, Special Report No. 3/2004, 61–85.

Barr, Nicholas, and Iain Crawford. 2005. *Financing higher education: Answers from the UK*. London and New York: Routledge.

Barr, Nicholas, and Michal Rutkowski. 2005. Pensions. In *Labor markets and social policy: The accession and beyond*, ed. Nicholas Barr, 135–70. Washington, D.C.: World Bank.

Beck, Thorsten, Ross Levine, and Norman Loayza. 2000. Finance and the sources of growth. *Journal of Financial Economics* 58 (1–2): 261–300.

Belan, Pascal, and Pierre Pestieau. 1999. Privatizing social security: A critical assessment. *Geneva Papers on Risk and Insurance–Issues and Practice* 24: 114–30.

Berstein, Solange, Guillermo Larraín, and Francisco Pino. 2006. Chilean pension reform: Coverage facts and policy alternatives. *Economia* 6 (Spring): 227–79.

Bertranou, Fabio M., Rafael Rofman, and Carlos O. Grushka. 2003. From reform to crisis: Argentina's pension system. *International Social Security Review* 56 (2): 103–14.

Beshears, John, James Choi, David Laibson, and Brigitte Madrian. 2008. The importance of default options for retirement saving outcomes: Evidence from the United States. In *Lessons from pension reform in the Americas*, eds. Stephen J. Kay and Tapen Sinha, 59–87. Oxford: Oxford University Press.

Blake, David. 2006. Overregulating your pension out of existence: The long term consequences of British pension policy over the last 30 years. Discussion Paper, no. PI–0616. London: City University, Cass Business School, Pensions Institute. www.pensions-institute.org/workingpapers/wp0616.pdf.

Blau, Francine D., and Lawrence M. Kahn. 2007. The gender pay gap. *The Economists' Voice* 4 (4, article 5). www.bepress.com/ev/vol4/iss4/art5.

Bodie, Zvi. 2003. An analysis of investment advice to retirement plan participants. In *The pension challenge: Risk transfers and retirement income security*, eds. Olivia S. Mitchell and Kent Smetters, 19–32. New York: Oxford University Press.

Borowski, Allan. 2005. The revolution that faltered: Two decades of reform of Australia's retirement income system. *International Social Security Review* 58 (Oct.-Dec.): 45–65.

Börsch-Supan, Axel. 2005. The 2005 pension reform in Finland. Working Paper, no. 2005:1. Helsinki: Finnish Centre for Pensions.

Börsch-Supan, Axel, and Christina B. Wilke. 2006. The German public pension system: How it will become an NDC system look-alike. In *Pension reform: Issues and prospects for non-financial defined contribution (NDC) schemes*, eds. Robert Holzmann and Edward Palmer, 573–610. Washington, D.C.: World Bank.

Börsch-Supan, Axel, and Joachim Winter. 2001. Population aging, savings behavior and capital markets. NBER Working Paper, no. W8561. Cambridge, Mass.: National Bureau of Economic Research. www.nber.org/papers/w8561.

Boskin, Michael J., and Eytan Sheshinski. 1983. Optimal tax treatment of the family: Married couples. *Journal of Public Economics* 20 (Aug.): 281–97.

Bradshaw, Jonathan, and Naomi Finch. 2002. A comparison of child benefit packages in 22 countries. DWP Research Report, no. 174. Leeds, U.K.: Department for Work and Pensions.Breyer, Friedrich. 1989. On the intergenerational Pareto efficiency of pay-as-you-go financed pension systems. *Journal of Institutional and Theoretical Economics* 145 (Dec.): 643–58.

Brien, Michael J., Stacy Dickert-Conlin, and David A. Weaver. 2004. Widows waiting to wed? (Re)marriage and economic incentives in social security widow benefits. *Journal of Human Resources* 39 (Summer): 585–623.

Brown, Jeffrey R. 2001. Redistribution and insurance: Mandatory annuitization with mortality heterogeneity. Working Paper, no. CER WP 2001-02. Boston: Boston College, Center for Retirement Research. www.bc.edu/centers/crr/papers/wp_2001-02.pdf.

Budig, M., and P. England. 2001. The wage penalty for motherhood. *American Sociological Review* 66 (2): 204–25.

Burns, Justine, Malcolm Keswell, and Murray Leibbrandt. 2005. Social assistance, gender and the aged in South Africa. *Feminist Economics* 11 (Jul.): 103–15.

Burtless, Gary. 2002. Social security privatization and financial market risk. In *Social security reform in advanced countries*, eds. T. Ihori and T. Tachibanaki. London and New York: Routledge.

Buvinic, Mayra, and Elizabeth M. King. 2007. Smart economics. *Finance and Development* 44 (Jun.). www.imf.org/external/pubs/ft/fandd/2007/06/king.htm.

Carey, David. 1999. Coping with population ageing in Australia. Economics Department Working Paper, no. 217. Paris: Organization for Economic Cooperation and Development. www.oecd.org/dataoecd/0/19/1879131.pdf.

Case, Anne, and Angus Deaton. 1998. Large cash transfers to the elderly in South Africa. *Economic Journal* 108 (Sep.): 1330–61.

Chile Presidential Advisory Council. 2006a. *El derecho a una vida digna en la vejez: Hacia un contrato social con la previsión en Chile: Resumen ejecutivo* (The right to a dignified old age: Toward a welfare social contract in Chile: Executive summary). Santiago. www.consejoreformaprevisional.cl/view/informe.asp.

————. 2006*b*. *El derecho a una vida digna en la vejez: Hacia un contrato social con la previsión en Chile:* vol. 1, *Diagnostico y propuesta de reforma;* vol. 2, *Consulta cuidadana.* Santiago. www.consejoreformaprevisional.cl/view/informe.asp.

Chlon-Dominczak, Agnieszka. 2002. The Polish pension reform of 1999. In *Pension reform in Central and Eastern Europe,* vol. 1: *Restructuring with privatisation: Case studies of Hungary and Poland,* ed. Elaine Fultz. Budapest: International Labour Organization, Central and Eastern European Team.

Chlon-Dominczak, Agnieszka, and Marek Góra. 2006. The NDC system in Poland: Assessment after five years. In *Pension reform: Issues and prospects for non-financial defined contribution (NDC) schemes,* eds. Robert Holzmann and Edward Palmer, 425–49. Washington: World Bank.

Choi, J., D. Laibson, B. Madrian, and A. Metrick. 2001. Defined contribution pensions: Plan rules, participant decisions, and the path of least resistance. NBER Working Paper, no. W8655. Cambridge, Mass.: National Bureau of Economic Research. www.nber. org/papers/w8655.

Coady, David, Margaret Grosh, and John Hoddinot. 2004. *Targeting of transfers in developing countries: Review of lessons and experience.* Washington: World Bank.

Costa, Dora L. 1998. *The evolution of retirement: An American economic history, 1880 to 1990.* Chicago: University of Chicago Press.

Cremer, Helmuth, and Pierre Pestieau. 2003. Wealth transfer taxation: A survey. CESifo Working Paper, no. 1061. Munich: CESifo.

Dahlquist, Magnus, Stefan Engström, and Paul Söderlind. 2000. Performance and characteristics of Swedish mutual funds. *Journal of Financial and Quantitative Analysis* 35 (Sep.): 409–23.

Davies, R., and G. Pierre. 2005. The family gap in pay in Europe: A cross-country study. *Labour Economics* 12: 469–86.

Davis, E. Philip. 2002. Prudent person rules or quantitative restrictions? The regulation of long-term institutional investors' portfolios. *Journal of Pension Economics and Finance* 1 (July): 157–91.

Devesa-Carpio, José E., and Carlos Vidal-Meliá. 2002. Reformed pension systems in Latin America. Social Protection Discussion Paper Series, no. 0209. Washington D.C.: World Bank (May).

Diamond, Peter A. 1965. National debt in a neoclassical growth model. *American Economic Review* 55 (5, part 1, Dec.): 1126–50.

————. 2000. Administrative costs and equilibrium charges with individual accounts. In *Administrative costs and social security privatization,* ed. John Shoven. Chicago: University of Chicago Press.

————. 2002. *Social security reform.* Oxford and New York: Oxford University Press.

————. 2003. *Taxation, incomplete markets and social security.* Cambridge, Mass.: MIT Press.

————. 2004. Social security. *American Economic Review* 94 (Mar.): 1–24.

————. 2006*a*. Système de retraite et vieillissement de la population. *Revue Française d'Economie* 20 (Apr.): 21–49.

————. 2006*b*. Reforming public pensions in the U.S. and the U.K. *Economic Journal* 116, no. 509 (Feb.): F94–F118.

————. 2006*c*. Social Security, the government budget and national savings. In *Samuelsonian Economics in the 21st Century,* eds. M. Szenberg, L. Ramrattan, and A. A. Gottesman, 54–65. New York and Oxford: Oxford University Press.

Diamond, Peter A., and James A. Mirrlees 1971*a*. Optimal taxation and public production I: Production efficiency. *American Economic Review* 61 (Mar.): 8–27.

———. 1971*b*. Optimal taxation and public production II: Tax rules. *American Economic Review* 61 (Jun.): 261–78.

Diamond, Peter A., and Peter R. Orszag. 2002. An assessment of the proposals of the President's Commission to Strengthen Social Security. *Contributions to Economic Analysis & Policy* 1 (1, article 10). Berkeley Electronic Press. www.bepress.com/bejeap/contributions/vol1/iss1/art10/.

———. 2005*a*. *Saving Social Security: A balanced approach*, rev. ed. Washington, D.C.: Brookings Institution.

———. 2005*b*. Saving Social Security. *Journal of Economic Perspectives* 19 (Spring): 11–32.

Diamond, Peter A., and Salvador Valdes-Prieto. 1994. Social security reforms. In *The Chilean economy: Policy lessons and challenges*, eds. Barry Bosworth, Rudiger Dornbusch, and Raúl Labán, 257–328. Washington, D.C.: Brookings Institution.

Drouin, Anne, and Lawrence H. Thompson, with Aidi Hu, Mike Whitelaw, and Hiroshi Yamabana. 2006. Perspectives on the social security system of China. ESS Paper, no. 25. Geneva: International Labour Organization.

Dublin, Louis I., Alfred J. Lotka, and Mortimer Spiegelman. [1936] 1949. *Length of life—A study of the life table*. New York: Ronald Press.

Economic Policy Committee of the European Union. 2001. Budgetary challenges posed by ageing populations: The impact of public spending on pensions, health and long-term care for the elderly and possible indicators of the long-term sustainability of public finances. Economic Policy Committee/ECFIN/655/01-EN final. Brussels.

———. 2006. The impact of ageing on public expenditure: Projections for the EU25 Member States on pensions, health care, long-term care, education and unemployment transfers (2004-2050). Special Report, no. 1/2006. Brussels: European Commission Directorate-General for Economic and Financial Affairs.

Edwards, Sebastian, and Alejandra Cox Edwards. 2002. Social security privatization reform and labor markets: The case of Chile. NBER Working Paper, no. 8924. Cambridge, Mass.: National Bureau of Economic Research. www.nber.org/papers/w8924.

Ellwood, David T. 2000. The impact of the earned income tax credit and social policy reforms on work, marriage, and living arrangements. *National Tax Journal* 53 (Dec.): 1063–1105.

Ermisch, J., and M. Francesconi. 2000. The increasing complexity of family relationships: Lifetime experience of lone motherhood and stepfamilies in Great Britain. *European Journal of Population* 16: 235–50.

Escobar, Federico, and Osvaldo Nina. 2004. Pension reform in Bolivia: A review of approach and experience. Development Research Working Paper, no. 04/2004. La Paz: Institute for Advanced Development Studies.

Favreault, Melissa M., and C. Eugene Steuerle. 2007. Social Security spouse and survivor benefits for the modern family. Discussion Paper, no. 07-01. Washington: Urban Institute. www.urban.org/UploadedPDF/311436_Social_Security.pdf.

Feinstein, Leon. 2003. Inequality in the early cognitive development of British children in the 1970 cohort. *Economica* 70 (277): 73–98.

Feldstein, Martin S. 1996. The missing piece in policy analysis: Social Security reform. *American Economic Review* 86 (May): 1–14.

———. 2005. Structural reform of social security. *Journal of Economic Perspectives* 19 (Spring): 33–55.

Garibaldi, Pietro, Claudia Olivetti, Barbara Petrongolo, Christopher Pissarides, and Etienne Wasmer. 2005. Women in the labour force: How well is Europe doing? In *Women at work: An economic perspective*, eds. Tito Boeri, Daniela Del Boca, and Christopher Pissarides. Report for the Fondazione Rodolfo DeBenedetti. Oxford: Oxford University Press.

Geanakoplos, John, Olivia S. Mitchell, and Stephen P. Zeldes. 1999. Social Security money's worth. In *Prospects for social security reform*, eds. Olivia S. Mitchell, Robert J. Myers, and Howard Young. Philadelphia: University of Pennsylvania Press.

Gill, Indermit, Truman Packard, and Juan Yermo. 2005. *Keeping the promise of social security in Latin America*. Stanford, Calif.: Stanford University Press for the World Bank.

Ginn, J. 2003. *Gender, pensions and the lifecourse: How pensions need to adapt to changing family forms*. Bristol: The Policy Press.

Golinowska, Stanislawa, Katarzyna Pietka, and Maciej Zukowski. 2003. *Study on the social protection systems of the 13 applicant countries: Poland country study*. Brussels: European Commission.

Gollier, Christian. 2007. Intergenerational risk-sharing and risk-taking of a pension fund. IDEI Working Paper, no. 42. Toulouse, France: Institut d'Economie Industrielle (Jan.).

Góra, Marek, and Michal Rutkowski. 1998. The quest for pension reform: Poland's security through diversity. Social Protection Discussion Paper, no. 9815. Washington, D.C.: World Bank.

Grant, Jonathan, Stijn Hoorens, Suja Sivadasan, Mirjam van het Loo, Julie DaVanzo, Lauren Hale, Shawna Gibson, and William Butz. 2004. *Low fertility and population ageing: Causes, consequences and policy options*. Cambridge, U.K.: RAND Europe, prepared for the European Commission. www.rand.org/pubs/monographs/2004/RAND_MG206.pdf.

Grønvik, Gunnvald. 2006. The pension reform in Norway—A useful step, but more funding could be beneficial. Staff Memo, no. 2006/5. Oslo: Norway Central Bank. www.norges-bank.no/upload/import/publikasjoner/staff_memo/memo-2006-05.pdf.

Gruber, Jonathan, and David A. Wise, eds. 1999. *Social security and retirement around the world*. Chicago: University of Chicago Press.

———. 2004. *Social security programs and retirement around the world: Micro-estimation*, Chicago: University of Chicago Press.

Hakim, Catherine. 2004. *Key issues in women's work*, 2nd ed. London: Glasshouse Press.

Helpman, Elhanan. 2004. *The mystery of economic growth*. Cambridge, Mass.: Harvard University Press.

Hendy, Jane, Barnaby C. Reeves, Naomi Fulop, Andrew Hutchings, and Cristina Masseria. 2005. Challenges to implementing the national programme for information technology (NPfIT): A qualitative study. *British Medical Journal* (Aug. 6): 331–36.

Herchenroder, M. F. P. 1938. The capacity of married women in French law. *Journal of Comparative Legislation and International Law*, 3rd ser. 20 (4): 196–203.

Hills, John. 2006. A new pension settlement for the twenty-first century? The UK Pensions Commission's analysis and proposals. *Oxford Review of Economic Policy* 22 (Spring): 113–32.

Holden, Karen C., and Cathleen Zick. 1998. Insuring against the consequences of widowhood in a reformed Social Security system. In *Framing the Social Security debate, values, politics, and economics*, eds. R. Douglas Arnold, Michael J. Graetz, and Alicia H. Munnell, 157–178. Washington, D.C.: National Academy of Social Insurance.

Holzmann, Robert, and Richard Hinz. 2005. *Old age income support in the 21st century: An international perspective on pension systems and reform*. Washington, D.C.: World Bank.

Holzmann, Robert, and Edward Palmer, eds. 2006. *Pension reform: Issues and prospects for non-financial defined contribution (NDC) schemes*. Washington, D.C.: World Bank.

Horney, James, and Richard Kogan. 2005. Private accounts would substantially increase federal debt and interest payments. Washington, D.C.: Center on Budget and Policy Priorities (Jul. 27). www.cbpp.org/7-27-05socsec.pdf.

Hutton, Will. 2007. *The writing on the wall: China and the West in the 21st century*. London: Little Brown.

International Monetary Fund. 2001. *Government finance statistics manual 2001*. Washington, D.C. www.imf.org/external/pubs/ft/gfs/manual/index.htm. International Organisation of Pension Supervisors. 2008, *Good practices in risk management of alternative investments by pension funds*. www.iopsweb.org/dataoecd/47/20/40010212.pdf.

Investment Company Institute. 2007. Fees and expenses of mutual funds, 2006. *Research Fundamentals* 16 (2).

James, Estelle. 1998. New models for old-age security: Experiments, evidence, and unanswered questions. *World Bank Research Observer* 13 (Aug.): 271–301.

James, Estelle, Alejandra Cox Edwards, and Rebecca Wong. 2003. The gender impact of pension reform. *Journal of Pension Economics and Finance* 2 (2): 181–219.

James, Simon, and Christopher Nobes. 1988. *The economics of taxation*, 3rd ed. Oxford: Philip Allan.

Jaumotte, Florence, and Irina Tytell. 2007. Globalization of labor. *Finance and Development* 44 (Jun.). www.imf.org/external/pubs/ft/fandd/2007/06/picture.htm.

Jefferson, Therese, and Alison Prestion. 2005. Australia's "other" gender wage gap: Baby boomers and compulsory superannuation accounts. *Feminist Economics* 11 (Jul.): 79–101.

Jiang Shi Ming. 2004. The Chinese labor market: Wages, employment and retirement.

Joshi, Heather, Pierella Paci, and Jane Waldfogel. 1999. The wages of motherhood: Better or worse? *Cambridge Journal of Economics* 23: 543–64.

Kakwani, Nanak, and Kalanidhi Subbarao. 2007. Poverty among the elderly in Sub-Saharan Africa and the role of social pensions. *Journal of Development Studies* 43 (Aug.): 987-1008. www.informaworld.com/smpp/content?content=10.1080/00220380701466476.

Karamcheva, Nadia, and Alicia H. Munnell. 2007. Why are widows so poor? Issue in Brief, no. 7-9. Boston: Center for Retirement Research, Boston College.

Kleven, Henrik Jacobsen, and Claus Thustrup Kreiner. 2005. A note on the efficient taxation of couples. University of Copenhagen.

Kleven, Henrik Jacobsen, Claus Thustrup Kreiner, and Emmanuel Saez. 2007. The optimal income taxation of couples as a multi-dimensional screening problem. University of Copenhagen and University of California, Berkeley.

Kotlikoff, Laurence J., and Jeffrey Sachs. 1998. The Personal Security System: A framework for reforming Social Security. *Federal Reserve Bank of St. Louis Review* (Mar.-Apr.): 11–13.

Leach, Jennifer. 1998. Bolivia's bonosol. Presented at the Transfers & Social Assistance for the Poor in the LAC Regional Workshop, Washington, D.C., February 24–25. wbln0018. worldbank.org/network/prem/premdoclib.nsf/58292ab451257bb9852566b4006ea0c8/fb45d2fe76c4e27b852567130004bca2?OpenDocument.

Legros, Florence. 2006. NDCs: A comparison of the French and German points systems. In *Pension reform: Issues and prospects for non-financial defined contribution (NDC) schemes*, eds. Robert Holzmann and Edward Palmer, 203–24. Washington, D.C.: World Bank.

Leibfried, Stephan, and Steffen Mau. 2007. *Welfare states: Construction, deconstruction, reconstruction,* vol. I: *Analytical approaches,* vol. II: *Varieties and transformations,* vol. III: *Legitimation, achievement and integration.* Northampton, Mass., and Cheltenham, U.K.: Edward Elgar.

Leimer, Dean R. 1994. Cohort-specific measures of lifetime net Social Security transfers. Social Security Administration Office of Research and Statistics Working Paper, no. 59 (Feb.). Washington, D.C.

Leitner, S. 2001. Sex and gender discrimination within EU pension systems. *Journal of European Social Policy* 11: 99–115.

Lesthaeghe, Ron. 1983. A century of demographic and cultural change in Western Europe: An exploration of underlying dimensions. *Population and Development Review* 9 (Sep.): 411–35.

Lewis, Jane. 2001. *The end of marriage.* Cheltenham, U.K.: Edward Elgar.

———. 2002. Gender and welfare state change. *European Societies* 4 (4): 331–57. Reprinted in Leibfried and Mau (2007), vol. III.

Lewis, Maureen A., and Marlaine E. Lockheed. 2007. Getting all girls into school. *Finance and Development* 44 (2). www.imf.org/external/pubs/ft/fandd/2007/06/lewis.htm.

Light, Paul C. 1985. *Artful work: The politics of Social Security reform.* New York: Random House.

Lindbeck, Assar, and Mats Persson. 2003. The gains from pension reform. *Journal of Economic Literature* 41 (Mar.): 74–112.

Lund, Frances. 2002. "Crowding in" care, security and micro-enterprise formation: Revisiting the role of the state in poverty reduction and in development. *Journal of International Development* 14: 681–94.

Lundberg, Shelly J., and Robert A. Pollak. 2007. The American family and family economics. *Journal of Economic Perspectives* 21 (Spring): 3–26.

Lundberg, Shelly J., Robert A. Pollak, and Terence J. Wales. 1997. Do husbands and wives pool their resources? Evidence from the United Kingdom child benefit. *Journal of Human Resources* 32 (3): 463–80.

Madrian, B., and D. Shea. 2001. The power of suggestion: Inertia in 401(k) participation and savings behavior. *Quarterly Journal of Economics* 116 (4): 1149–87.

Martinez, Sebastian. 2004. Pensions, poverty and household investments in Bolivia. University of California, Berkeley. emlab.berkeley.edu/users/webfac/bardhan/e271_f04/martinez.pdf.

Matits, Agnes. 2004. Practical experience with the second pillar of the Hungarian mandatory pension system. Paper delivered at an International Labour Organization pension conference, Budapest, December 9–10.

Megginson, William L., and Jeffry M. Netter. 2001. From state to market: A survey of empirical studies on privatization. *Journal of Economic Literature* 39 (Jun.): 321–89.

Merton, Robert C. 1983. On the role of social security as a means for efficient risk sharing in an economy where human capital is not tradable. In *Financial aspects of the US pension system,* eds. Zvi Bodie and John Shoven, 325–58. Chicago: University of Chicago Press.

Mesa-Lago, Carmelo. 2005. Assessing the World Bank report *Keeping the promise. International Social Security Review* 58 (Apr.-Sep.): 97–117.

———. 2007. *Reassembling social security: A survey of pensions and health care reforms in Latin America.* New York and Oxford: Oxford University Press.

Mitchell, Brian R. 1998*a*. *International historical statistics: Africa, Asia and Oceania, 1750-1993*, 3rd ed. New York: Stockton Press.

———. 1998*b*. *International historical statistics: The Americas, 1750-1993*, 4th ed. New York: Stockton Press.

———. 1998*c*. *International historical statistics: Europe, 1750-1993*. New York: Stockton Press.

Mitchell, Deborah. 2002. Participation and opportunity: Redefining social security in Australia and New Zealand. *International Social Security Review* 55 (4): 127–41.

Müller, Katharina. 1999. *The political economy of pension reform in Central-Eastern Europe*. Cheltenham, U.K., and Northampton, Mass.: Edward Elgar.

Munnell, Alicia H., and Annika Sundén, with the assistance of Cynthia Perry and Ryan Kling. 1999. Investment practices of state and local pension funds: Implications for Social Security reform. Prepared for presentation at the First Annual Joint Conference for the Retirement Research Consortium, New Developments in Retirement Research, Washington, May 20-21, www.bc.edu/centers/crr/papers/cp_munnell.pdf.

Murthi, Mamta, Peter Orszag, and J. Michael Orszag. 2001. The charge ratio on individual accounts: Lessons from the UK experience. In *New ideas about old-age security: Toward sustainable pension systems in the 21st century*, eds. Robert Holzmann and Joseph E. Stiglitz, 308–35. Washington, D.C.: World Bank.

Muturi, Slawomir, Marcin Zdral, Marcin Zajkowski, and Agnieszka Chlon-Dominczak. 2000. Transformation of social security institution (ZUS) under the Polish pension system reform. Warsaw: ZUS.

New, Bill. 1999. Paternalism and public policy. *Economics and Philosophy* 15: 63–83.

New Zealand Ministry of Social Development. 2005. Social report indicators for low incomes and inequality: Update from the 2004 Household Economic Survey. Wellington. www.msd.govt.nz/work-areas/cross-sectoral-work/indicators-for-low-incomes-and-inequality.html.

Nordhaus, William. 2007. The *Stern Review* on the economics of climate change. *Journal of Economic Literature* 45 (Sep.): 686–702.

Norway Central Bank. 2005. Corporate governance in the Norwegian Government Petroleum Fund. Letter to the Ministry of Finance, December 8. Oslo.

———. 2006. *The Government Pension Fund—Global, Annual Report*. Oslo. www.norges-bank.no/nbim/pension_fund/reports/.

O'Keefe, Philip. 2006. Social assistance in China: An evolving system. Washington, D.C.: World Bank.

Okun, Arthur. 1981. *Prices and quantities*. Washington, D.C.: Brookings Institution.

Orbán, Gábor, and Dániel Palotai. 2005. The sustainability of the Hungarian pension system: A reassessment. Occasional Paper, no. 40. Budapest: Magyar Nemzeti Bank.

Organization for Economic Cooperation and Development (OECD). 2002. Increasing employment: The role of later retirement. *Economic Outlook*, no. 72. Paris (December).

———. 2004*a*. Financial education and saving for retirement. Paris. www.oecd.org/dataoecd/26/2/39197801.pdf.

———. 2004*b*. *Income disparities in China: An OECD perspective*. Paris.

———. 2004*c*. *Reforming public pensions: Sharing the experience of transition and OECD countries. Transition Economies*, 2004, no. 1. Paris. titania.sourceoecd.org/vl=6782642/cl=20/nw=1/rpsv/~6686/v2004n1/s1/p1l.

———. 2006*a*. Guidelines on pension fund asset management. *Financial Market Trends* 91 (November): 169–85.

———. 2006*b*. *Live longer, work longer*. Paris.

———. 2007. *Pensions at a glance: Public policies across OECD countries*. Paris.

Orloff, Ann. 1996. Gender in the welfare state. *Annual Review of Sociology* 22: 51–78. Reprinted in Leibfried and Mau (2007), vol. III.

Orszag, Peter. 1999. Individual accounts and Social Security: Does Social Security really provide a lower rate of return? Washington D.C.: Center on Budget and Policy Priorities. www.cbpp.org/3-11-99socsec.pdf.

Orszag, Peter R., and Joseph E. Stiglitz. 2001. Rethinking pension reform: 10 myths about social security systems. In *New ideas about old age security: Toward sustainable pension systems in the 21st century*, eds. Robert Holzmann and Joseph E. Stiglitz, with Louise Fox, Estelle James, and Peter R. Orszag, 17–62. Washington, D.C.: World Bank.

Palmer, Edward. 2005. What is NDC? In *Pension reform through NDCs: Issues and prospects for non-financial defined contribution schemes*, eds. Robert Holzmann and Edward Palmer. Washington, D.C.: World Bank.

Pappas, Gregory, Susan Queen, Wilbur Hadden, and Gail Fisher. 1993. The increasing disparity in mortality between socioeconomic groups in the United States, 1960 and 1986. *New England Journal of Medicine* 329 (Jul. 8): 103–09, with correction in the October 7, 1993, issue.

Paull, Gillian. 2006. The impact of children on women's paid work. *Fiscal Studies* 27 (4): 473–512.

Pestieau, Pierre. 2006. *The welfare state in the European Union*. Oxford: Oxford University Press.

Pestieau, Pierre, and Uri M. Possen. 2000. "Investing Social Security in the Equity Market: Does it Make a Difference?" *National Tax Journal* 53 (1): 41–57.

Piñera, Jose E. 1995. Empowering workers: The privatization of social security in Chile. *Cato Journal* 15: 155–66. www.cato.org/pubs/journal/cj15n2-3/cj15n2-3-1.pdf.

Pollak, Robert A. 2007. Family bargaining and taxes: A prolegomenon to the analysis of joint taxation. IZA Discussion Paper, no. 3109. Bonn, Germany: Forschungsinstitut zur Zukunft der Arbeit. (Also forthcoming in *Taxation and the Family*. CESifo Economic Studies. Cambridge, Mass.: MIT Press.)

Ponds, Eduard H. M., and Bart van Riel. 2007. The recent evolution of pension funds in the Netherlands: The trend to hybrid DB-DC plans and beyond. CRR Working Paper, no. 2007-9. Boston: Center for Retirement Research, Boston College. www.bc.edu/centers/crr/papers/wp_2007-9.pdf.

Queisser, Monika, and Edward Whitehouse. 2006. Comparing the pension promises of 30 OECD countries. *International Social Security Review* 59 (3): 49–77.

Rake, Katherine, Jane Falkingham, and Martin Evans. 2000. British pension policy in the twenty-first century: A partnership in pensions or a marriage to the means test? *Social Policy and Administration* 34: 123–34.

Ravallion, Martin, and Shaoshua Chen. 2007. China's (uneven) progress against poverty. *Journal of Development Economics* 82 (Jan.): 1–42.

Ravallion, Martin, and Youjuan Wang. 2006. *Di bao*: A guaranteed minimum income in China's cities? Policy Research Working Paper, no. 3805. Washington, D.C.: World Bank.

Rees, Ray. 2006. Where have all the babies gone? *Royal Economic Society Newsletter* no. 134 (Jul.): 3–4.

Reno, Virginia P., Michael J. Graetz, Kenneth S. Apfel, Joni Lavery, and Catherine Hill, eds. 2005. *Uncharted waters: Paying benefits from individual accounts in federal retirement policy*. Study Panel Final Report. Washington, D.C.: National Academy of Social Insurance.

Rodríguez, L. Jacobo. 1999. Chile's private pension system at 18: Its current state and future challenges. SSP, no. 17. Washington, D.C.: Cato Institute. www.cato.org/pubs/ssps/ssp-17es.html.

Rofman, Rafael. 2007. Pension reform and the development of pension systems: An evaluation of World Bank assistance. Background paper, Peru Country Study, Independent Evaluation Group. Washington, D.C.: World Bank.

Rofman, Rafael, and Leonardo Lucchetti. 2006. Pension systems in Latin America: Concepts and measurements of coverage. Social Protection Discussion Paper Series, no. 0616. Washington, D.C.: World Bank (Nov.).

Salditt, Felix, Peter Whiteford, and Willem Adema. 2007. Pension reform in China: Progress and prospects. OECD Social, Employment and Migration Working Paper, no. 53. Paris. www.olis.oecd.org/olis/2007doc.nsf/FREDATCORPLOOK/NT00002B36/$FILE/JT03228722.PDF.

Samuelson, Paul A. 1958. An exact consumption-loan model of interest with or without the social contrivance of money. *Journal of Political Economy* 66 (Dec.): 467–82. Reprinted in Barr (2001*b*), vol. II, 63–78.

Scherer, Peter. 2001, Age of withdrawal from the labour market in OECD countries. Occasional Paper, no. DEELSA/ELSA/WD(2001)2, Directorate for Education, Employment, Labour and Social Affairs. Paris: Organization for Economic Cooperation and Development.

Shanley, Mary Lyndon. 1986. Suffrage, protective labor legislation, and married women's property laws in England. *Signs* 12 (Autumn): 62–77.

Sheshinski, Eytan. 2003. Privatization and its benefits: Theory and evidence. In *Markets and Governments*, eds. K. Basu, P. Nayak, and R. Ray, 185–243. Oxford: Oxford University Press.

———. 2008. *Lectures on annuities.* Princeton, N.J.: Princeton University Press.

Sigg, Roland. 2005. Extending working life: Policy challenges and responses. In *Toward newfound confidence,* eds. Richard Levinsky and Roddy McKinnon, 25–140. Geneva: International Social Security Association.

Simonovits, András. 2006. Optimal design of old-age pension rule with flexible retirement: The two-type case. *Journal of Economics* 89: 197–222.

South Africa National Treasury. 2007. Social security and retirement reform. Second Discussion Paper. Pretoria: National Treasury (Feb.).

Spiezia, V. 2002. The greying population: A wasted human capital or just a social liability? *International Labor Review* 141: 71–113.

St John, Susan. 2005. Retirement incomes in New Zealand. *Economic and Labour Relations Review* 15 (2): 217–39.

———. 2007. Farewell to tax neutrality: The implications for an aging population. Presented at the 15th Australian Colloquium of Superannuation Researchers: Financial Consequences of Longevity, Sydney, July.

Stier, Haya, Noah Lewin-Epstein, and Michael Braun. 2001. Welfare regimes, family-supportive policies, and women's employment along the life-course. *American Journal of Sociology* 106 (6): 1731–60. [Reprinted in Leibfried and Mau (2007), vol. III.]

Stotsky, Janet G. 2007. Budgeting with women in mind. *Finance and Development* 44, no. 2. www.imf.org/external/pubs/ft/fandd/2007/06/stotsky.htm.

Sundén, Annika. 2006. The Swedish experience with pension reform. *Oxford Review of Economic Policy* 22 (Spring): 133–48.

Sweden Ministry of Finance. 2005. Difficult waters: Premium pension savings on course. Premium Pension Committee, SOU 2005:87. Stockholm. www.sweden.gov.se/sb/d/574/a/52265;jsessionid=alkgAkqIj71g.

Tapia, Waldo, and Juan Yermo. 2007. Implications of behavioural economics for mandatory individual account pension systems. OECD Working Paper on Insurance and Private Pensions, no. 11. Paris: OECD. www.oecd.org/dataoecd/5/22/39368306.pdf.

Thaler, R. H., and S. Benartzi. 2004. Save more tomorrow: Using behavioral economics to increase employee saving. *Journal of Political Economy* 112 (1, part 2): 164–87.

Thompson, Lawrence H. 2006. US retirement income system. *Oxford Review of Economic Policy* 22 (Spring): 95–112.

Trapido, Denis. 2007. Gendered transition: Post-Soviet trends in gender wage inequality among young full-time workers. *European Sociological Review* 23 (2): 223–37.

Turner, John. 2007. Social security pensionable ages in OECD countries: 1949–2035. *International Social Security Review* 60 (Jan.-Mar.): 81–99.

U.K. Department for Work and Pensions. 2005. *Women and pensions: The evidence.* London.

———. 2006a. *Security in retirement: Towards a new pensions system.* Cm 6841. London: The Stationery Office.

———. 2006b. *Inheritance of SERPS pension.* London. www.thepensionservice.gov.uk/pdf/serps/serpsl1jan08.pdf. U.K. Office of Fair Trading. 1997. *Report of the director general's inquiry into pensions*, vol. 1. London.

U.K. Pension Law Review Committee. 1993. *Pension law reform: Report of the Pension Law Review Committee*, vol. I, *Report*, and vol. II, *Research*. London: Her Majesty's Stationery Office.

U.K. Pensions Commission. 2004a. *Pensions: Challenges and choices: The first report of the Pensions Commission.* London: The Stationery Office. www.webarchive.org.uk/pan/16806/20070802/www.pensionscommission.org.uk/publications/2004/annrep/index.html.

———. 2004b. *Pensions: Challenges and choices: The first report of the Pensions Commission: Appendices.* London: The Stationery Office. www.webarchive.org.uk/pan/16806/20070802/www.pensionscommission.org.uk/publications/2004/annrep/appendices-all.pdf.

———. 2005. *A new pension settlement for the twenty-first century: Second report of the Pensions Commission.* London: The Stationery Office. www.webarchive.org.uk/pan/16806/20070802/www.pensionscommission.org.uk/publications/2005/annrep/annrep-index.html.

U.K. Pensions Policy Institute. 2005. Should state pensions be contributory or universal? London. www.pensionspolicyinstitute.org.uk/uploadeddocuments/PPI_Nuffield_Seminar_3_Paper_Jul05.pdf.

———. 2006. The new 'contributory' test: Principle or practicality? PPI Briefing Note, no. 32. London. www.pensionspolicyinstitute.org.uk/uploadeddocuments/Briefing%20Notes/PPI_Briefing_Note_32.pdf.

U.K. Treasury. 2005. Tax credits: Reforming financial support for families. The Modernisation of Britain's Tax and Benefit System, no. 11. London. www.hm-treasury.gov.uk./media/3/3/bud05_taxcredits_500.pdf.

———. 2006. *The economics of climate change (The Stern Review).* London. www.hm-treasury.gov.uk/independent_reviews/stern_review_economics_climate_change/sternreview_index.cfm.

U.S. President's Commission to Strengthen Social Security. 2001. *Strengthening Social Security and creating wealth for all Americans.* Washington, D.C. www.csss.gov/reports/Final_report.pdf.

U.S. Social Security Administration. 2007*a*. *The 2007 annual report of the Board of Trustees of the Federal Old-Age and Survivors Insurance and Federal Disability Insurance Trust Funds.* Washington, D.C.

———. 2007*b*. *Social security programs throughout the world.* Washington, D.C. www.ssa.gov/policy/docs/progdesc/ssptw/index.html.

Valdés-Prieto, Salvador. 2005*a*. Securitization of taxes implicit in PAYG pensions. *Economic Policy* 20, no. 42 (Apr.): 215–65.

———. 2005*b*. Para aumentar la competencia entre las AFP. Estudios Públicos, no. 98 (Autumn): 87–142. Santiago: Centro de Estudios Públicos.

———. 2007*a*. Pension reform and the development of pension systems: An evaluation of World Bank assistance. Background paper, Bolivia Country Study, Independent Evaluation Group. Washington, D.C.: World Bank.

———. 2007*b*. Pension reform and the development of pension systems: An evaluation of World Bank assistance. Background paper, Regional Summary: Latin America and the Caribbean, Independent Evaluation Group. Washington, D.C.: World Bank.

von Gersdorff, Hermann. 1997. The Bolivian pension reform: Innovative solutions to common problems. Policy Research Working Paper, no. 1832. Washington, D.C.: World Bank, Financial Sector Development Department.

Whiteford, Peter, and Gregory Angenent. 2001. The Australian system of social protection – an overview, 2nd ed. Occasional Paper, no. 6. Canberra: Department of Family and Community Services.

Whiteford, Peter, and Edward Whitehouse. 2006. Pension challenges and pension reform in OECD countries. *Oxford Review of Economic Policy* 22 (Spring): 78–94.

Williamson, John B. 2004. Assessing the pension reform potential of a notional defined contribution pillar. *International Social Security Review* 57 (1): 47–64.

Williamson, John B., and Bingwen Zheng. 2003. The applicability of the notional defined contribution model for China. *China and World Economy* 11 (3): 8–13.

Willmore, Larry. 2004. Universal pensions in low income countries. Discussion Paper, no. IPD-01-05. New York: Initiative for Policy Dialogue, Pensions and Social Insurance Section, Columbia University (Oct.).

———. 2006. *Non-contributory pensions: Bolivia and Antigua in an international context.* Santiago, Chile: CEPAL, Special Studies Unit.

Winkler, Anne E., Timothy D. McBride, and Courtney Andrews. 2005. Wives who outearn their husbands: A transitory or persistent phenomenon for couples? *Demography* 42 (3): 523–35.

World Bank. 1993. *Poland: Income support and the social safety net during the transition.* Washington, D.C.

———. 1994. *Averting the old age crisis.* New York: Oxford University Press.

———. 2004. *World development indicators.* Washington, D.C.

———. 2005. Hungary: Pension—Competition and performance in the Hungarian second pillar. Financial Sector Assessment Program Update. Washington, D.C.: World Bank and International Monetary Fund (Dec.).

———. 2006*a*. *Pension reform and the development of pension systems: An evaluation of World Bank assistance.* Washington, D.C.: Independent Evaluation Group, World Bank.

1nweb18.worldbank.org:80/oed/oeddoclib.nsf/DocUNIDViewForJavaSearch/ 43B436DFBB2723D085257108005F6309/$file/pensions_evaluation.pdf.

———. 2006*b*. Pension reform: How to strengthen World Bank assistance. *IEG Reach* (Feb. 2). lnweb18.worldbank.org:80/oed/oeddoclib.nsf/DocUNIDViewForJavaSearch/ 86FAFFBFBA032ED085257108005EDE9E/$file/pensions_evaluation_reach.pdf.

Zaidi, Asghar, Aaron Grech, and Michael Fuchs. 2006. Pension policy in EU25 and its possible impact on elderly poverty. CASE/116. London: London School of Economics, Centre for the Analysis of Social Exclusion (Dec.). sticerd.lse.ac.uk/dps/case/cp/ CASEpaper116.pdf.

Zheng, Bingwen. 2004*a*. Social security. Second draft. Beijing: Institute of European Studies, Chinese Academy of Social Sciences (Jul.).

———. 2004*b*. The NDC model: A way to resolve moral hazard in China's social security system. *China and World Economy* 12 (3): 91–101.

Index